you ... the WRONG WAY!!

IT'S TRUE: In keeping with the original Japanese comic format, this book reads from right to left—so action, sound effects and word balloons are completely reversed. This preserves the orientation of the original artwork—plus, it's fun! Check out the diagram shown here to get the hang of things, and then turn to the other side of the book to get started!

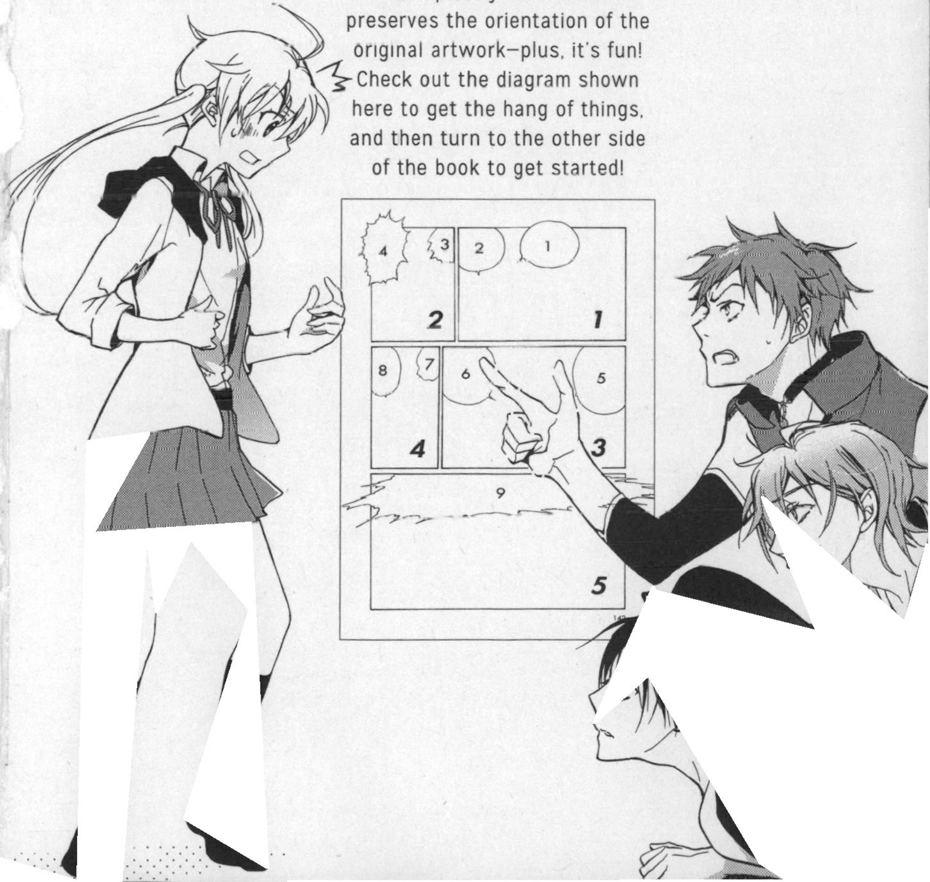
1
2
1
3
4
2
5
6
3
7
8
4
9
5

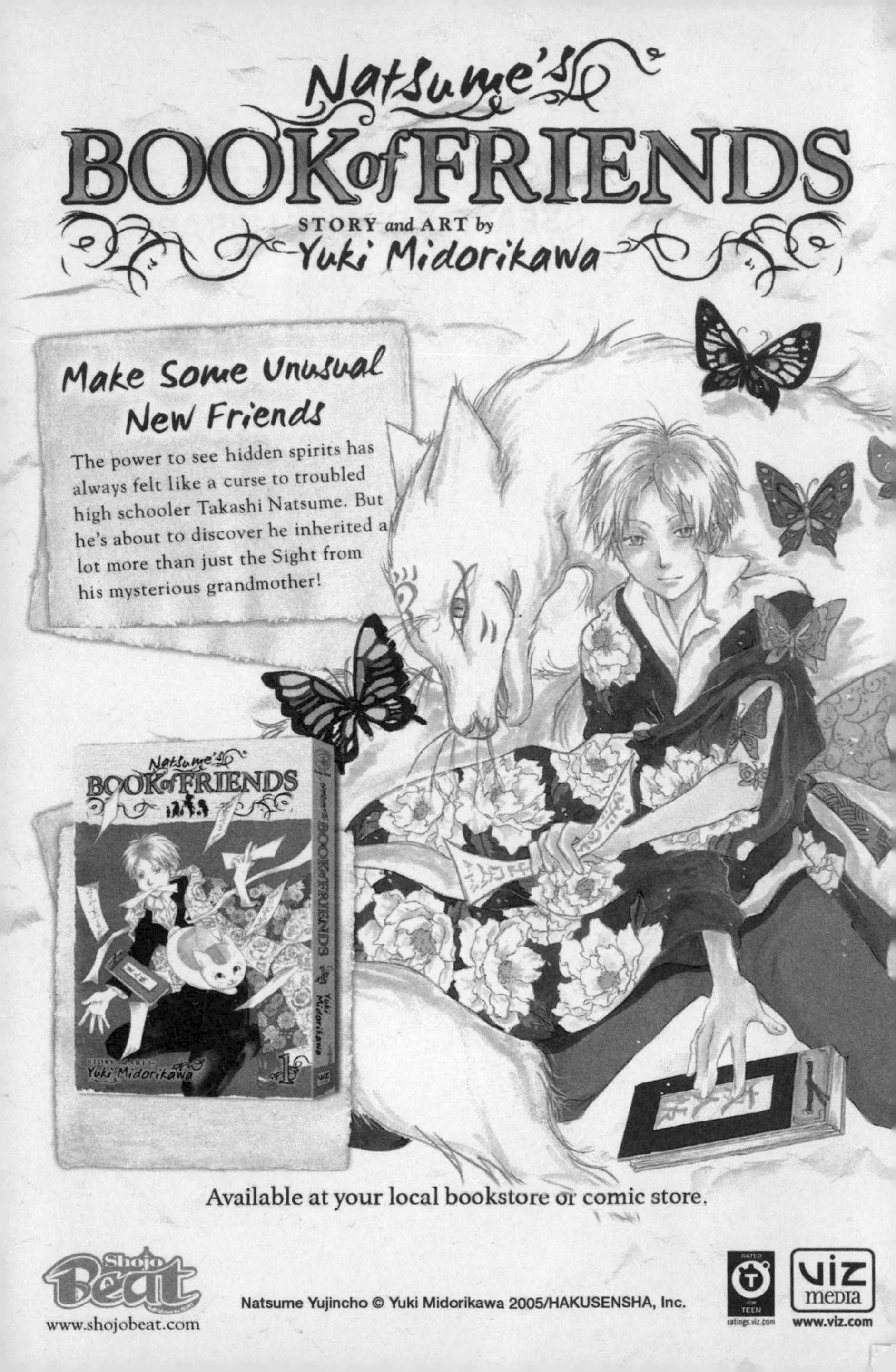
Natsume's BOOK of FRIENDS
STORY and ART by Yuki Midorikawa
Make Some Unusual New Friends
The power to see hidden spirits has always felt like a curse to troubled high schooler Takashi Natsume. But he's about to discover he inherited a lot more than just the Sight from his mysterious grandmother!
Natsume's BOOK of FRIENDS
STORY and ART by Yuki Midorikawa
1
Available at your local bookstore or comic store.
Shojo Beat
www.shojobeat.com
Natsume Yujincho © Yuki Midorikawa 2005/HAKUSENSHA, Inc.
RATED T FOR TEEN
ratings.viz.com
VIZ media
www.viz.com

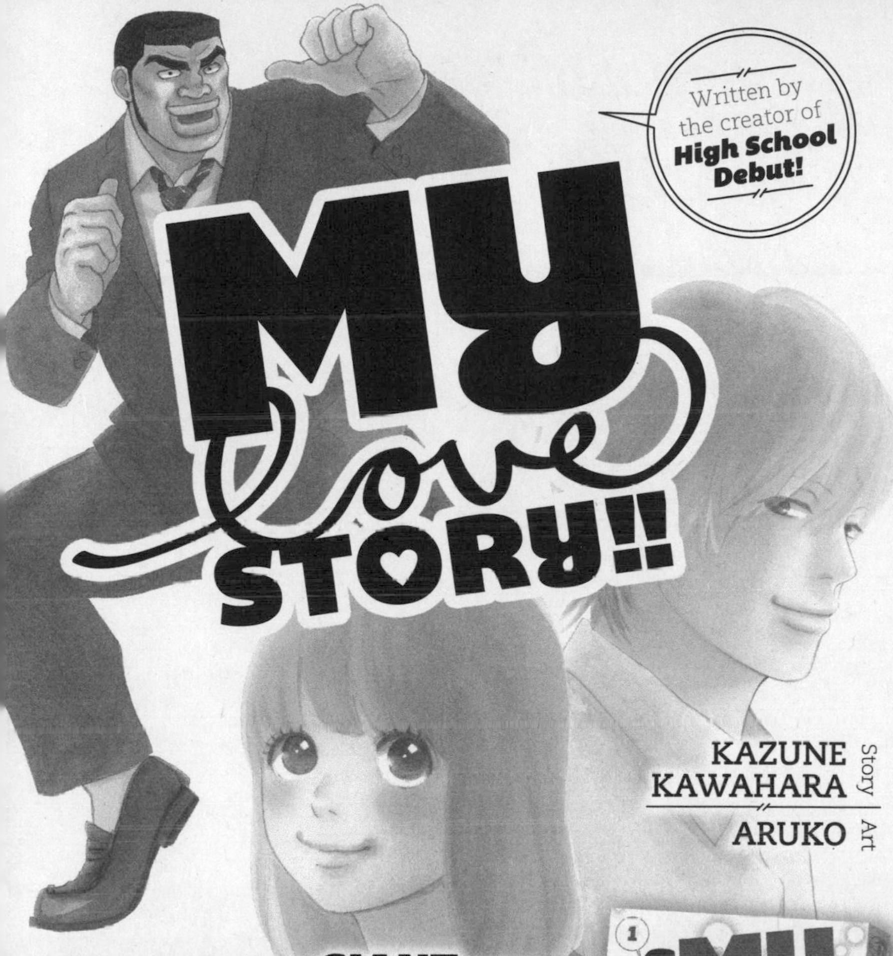

MY love STORY!!

KAZUNE KAWAHARA — Story

ARUKO — Art

Takeo Goda is a GIANT guy with a GIANT *heart*

Too bad the girls don't want him!
(They want his good-looking best friend, Sunakawa.)

Used to being on the sidelines, Takeo simply stands tall and accepts his fate. But one day when he saves a girl named Yamato from a harasser on the train, his (love!) life suddenly takes an incredible turn!

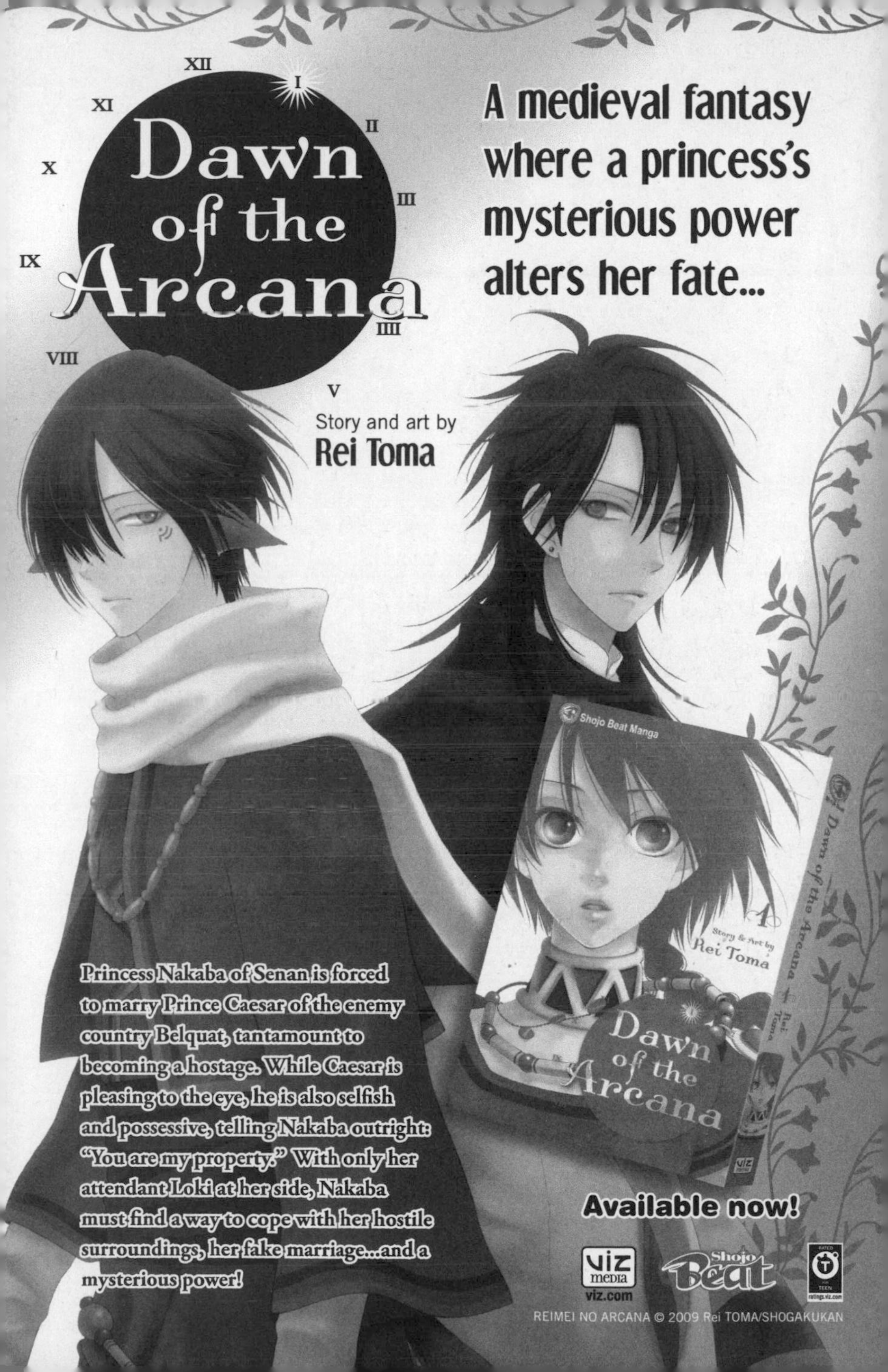

Dawn of the Arcana
A medieval fantasy where a princess's mysterious power alters her fate...
Story and art by
Rei Toma
Shojo Beat Manga
Dawn of the Arcana
1
Story & Art by Rei Toma
Princess Nakaba of Senan is forced to marry Prince Caesar of the enemy country Belquat, tantamount to becoming a hostage. While Caesar is pleasing to the eye, he is also selfish and possessive, telling Nakaba outright: "You are my property." With only her attendant Loki at her side, Nakaba must find a way to cope with her hostile surroundings, her fake marriage...and a mysterious power!
Available now!
viz media
viz.com
Shojo Beat
RATED T TEEN
ratings.viz.com
REIMEI NO ARCANA © 2009 Rei TOMA/SHOGAKUKAN

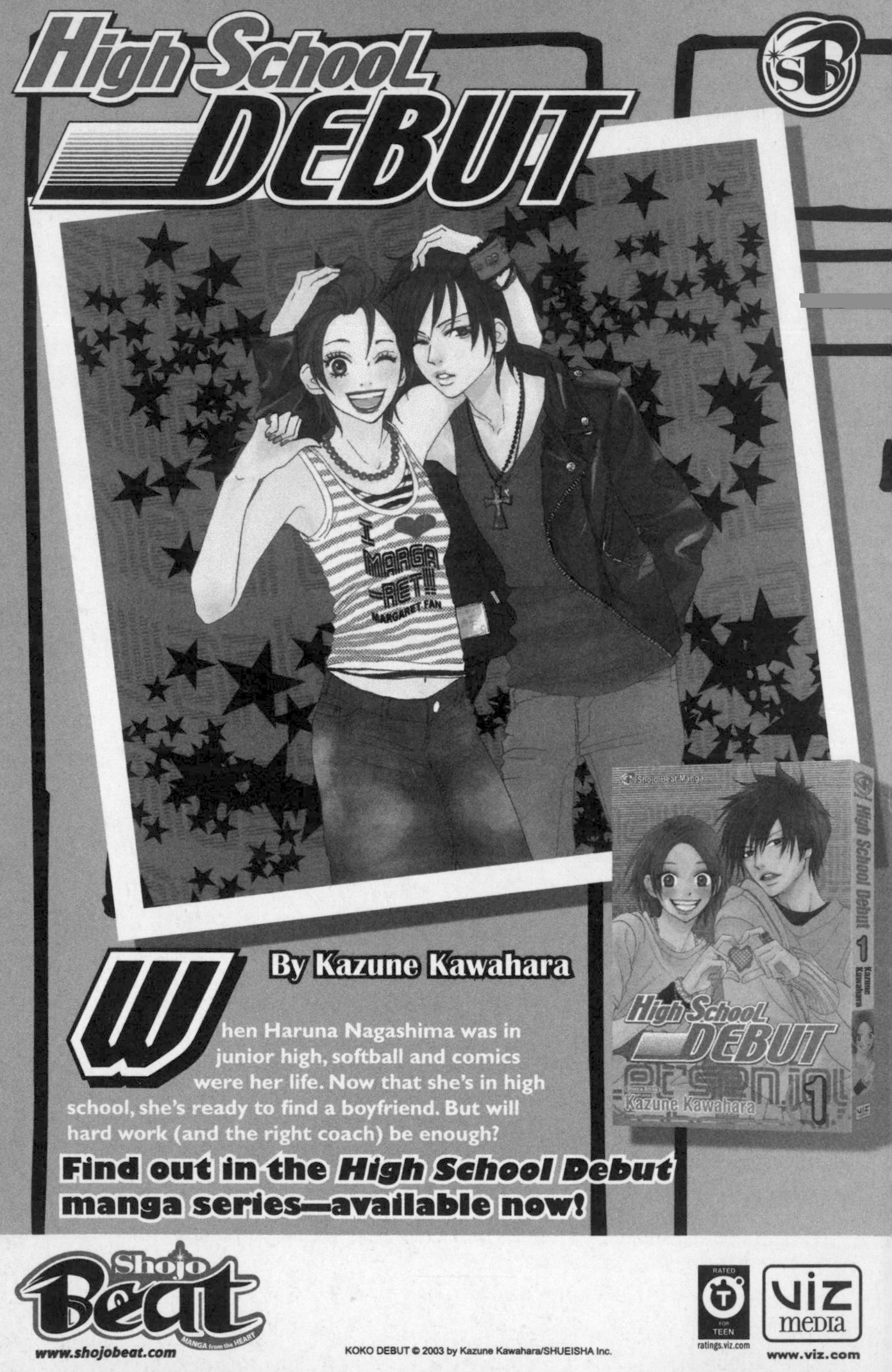
High School DEBUT
By Kazune Kawahara
When Haruna Nagashima was in junior high, softball and comics were her life. Now that she's in high school, she's ready to find a boyfriend. But will hard work (and the right coach) be enough?
Find out in the *High School Debut* manga series—available now!
Shojo Beat
MANGA from the HEART
www.shojobeat.com
KOKO DEBUT © 2003 by Kazune Kawahara/SHUEISHA Inc.
RATED T FOR TEEN
ratings.viz.com
VIZ media
www.viz.com

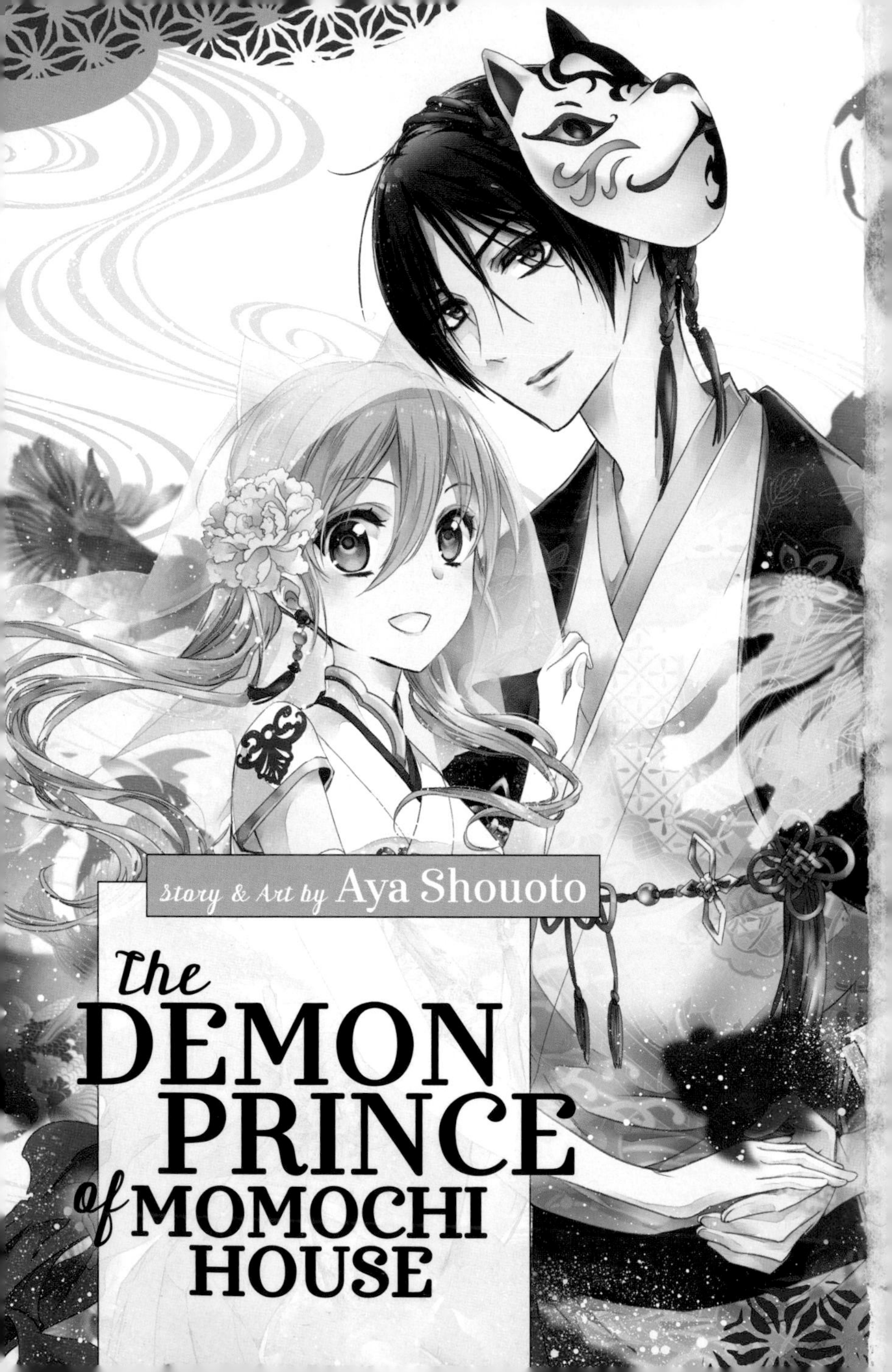
Story & Art by Aya Shouoto
The DEMON PRINCE of MOMOCHI HOUSE

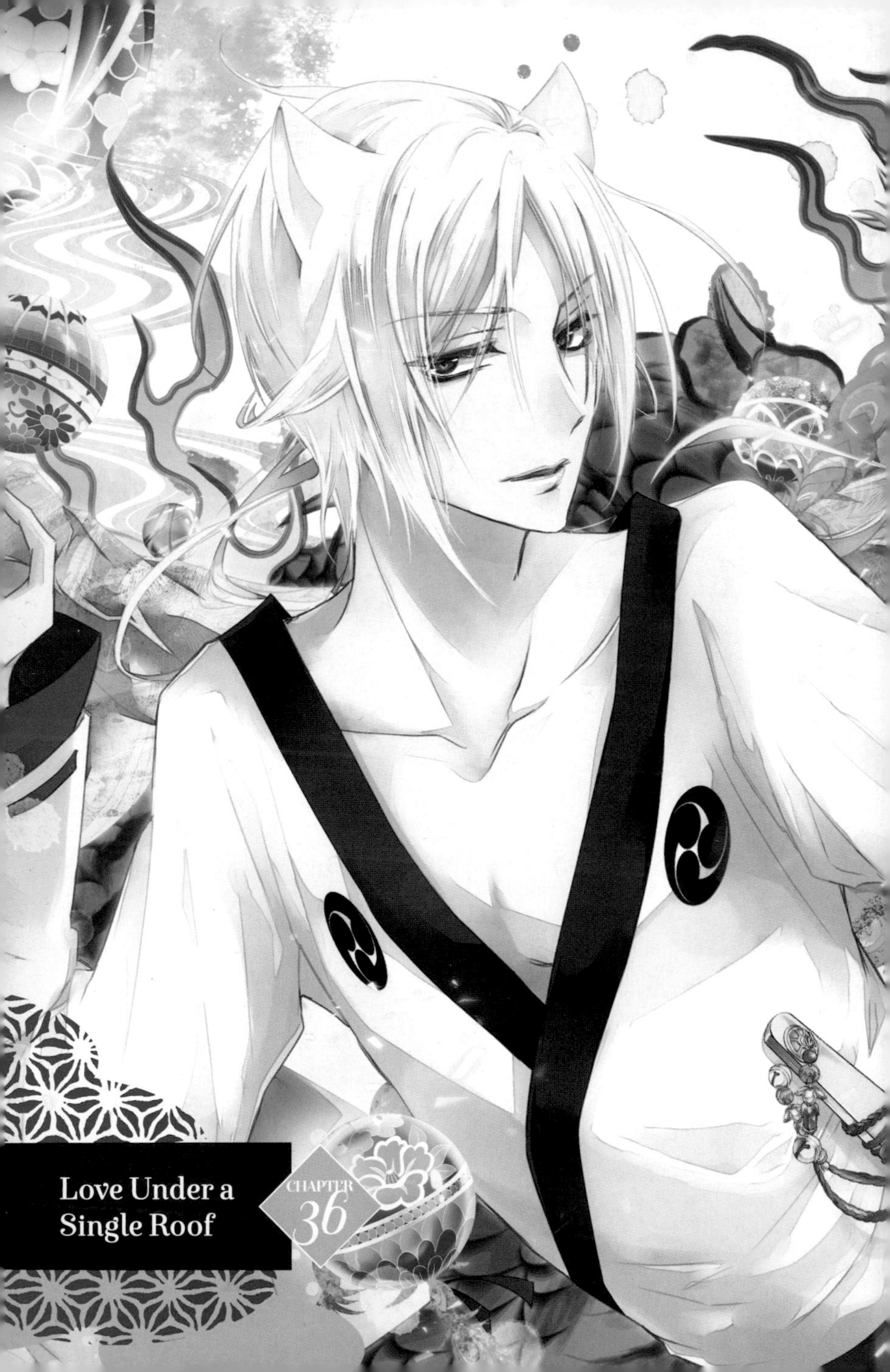
Love Under a Single Roof
CHAPTER 36

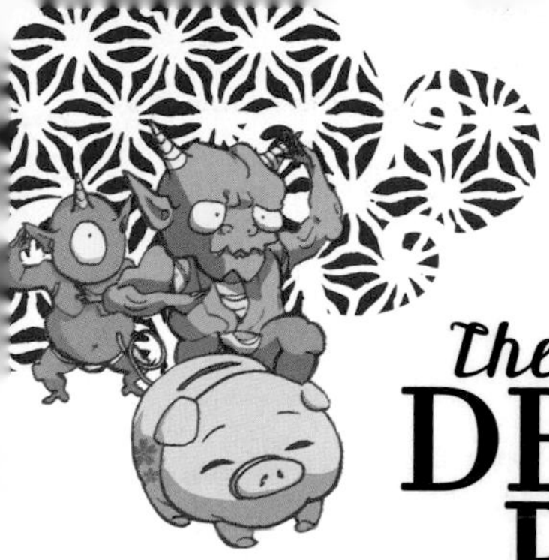

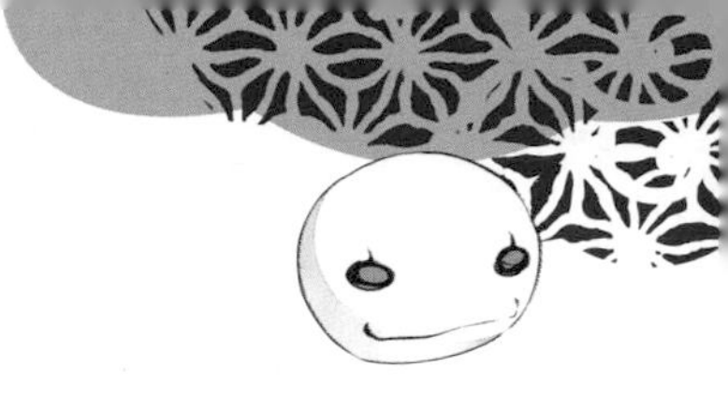

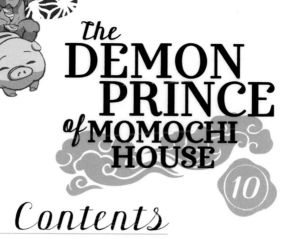

The DEMON PRINCE of MOMOCHI HOUSE

10

Contents

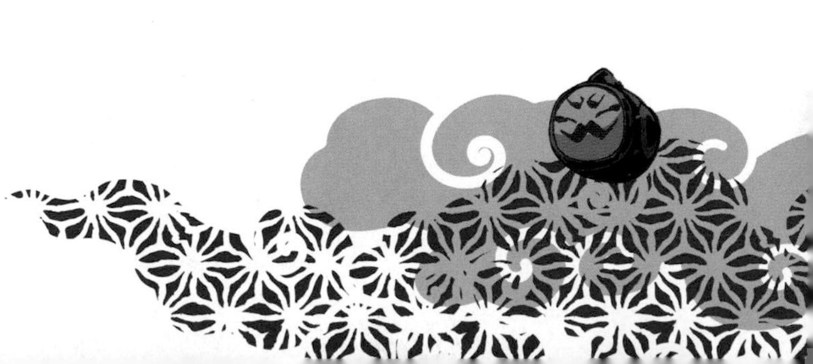

The Mysterious Residents of Momochi House

Aoi Nanamori

When he was 7 years old, he wandered into Momochi House and was chosen as the Omamori-sama. He transforms into a nue to perform his duties, but it seems this role was meant for Himari.

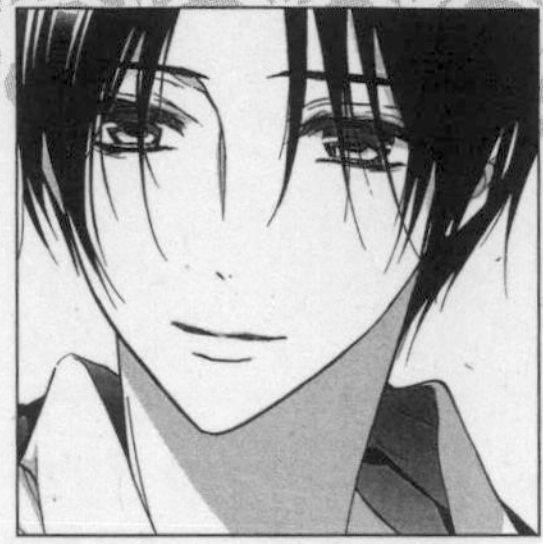

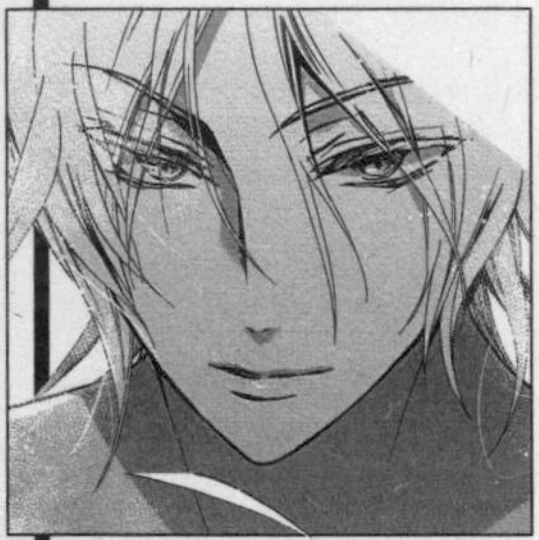

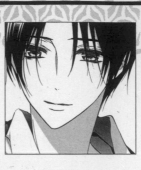

Omamori-sama (Nue)

An ayakashi, or demon, with the ears of a cat, the wings of a bird, and the tail of a fox. As the Omamori-sama, the nue protects Momochi House and eliminates demons who make their way in from the spiritual realm.

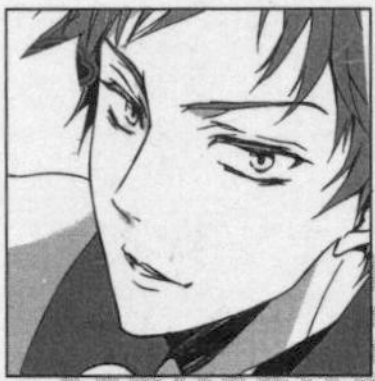

Ise

One of Omamori-sama's shikigami. He's an orangutan.

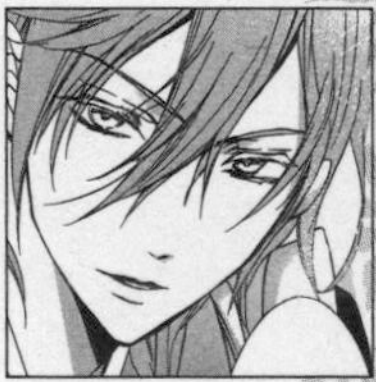

Yukari

One of Omamori-sama's shikigami. He's a water serpent.

Lesser Yokai

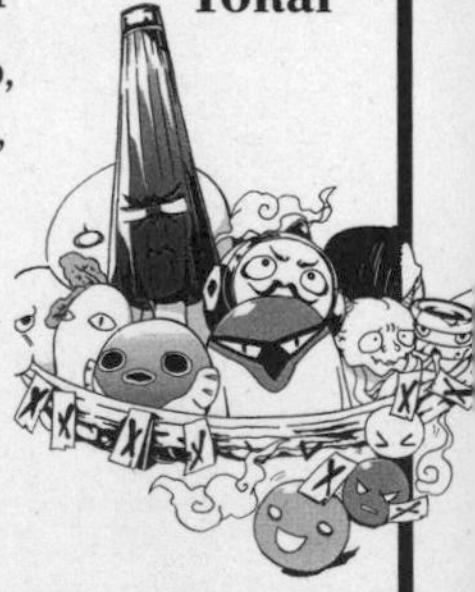

Himari Momochi

A 16-year-old orphan who, according to a certain will, has inherited Momochi House. As rightful owner, she has the ability to expel beings from the house.

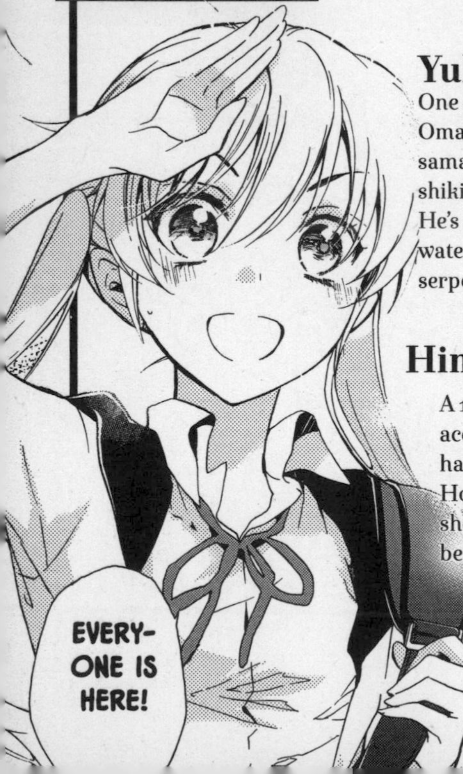
EVERY-ONE IS HERE!

Momochi House: Story Thus Far

Having accepted his past, Aoi is able to return to human form. While preparing for Aoi's welcome-back party, Himari searches the storeroom for items with Yukari. Yukari tells her the story of how Aoi found the diary belonging to her parents. The diary contained her mother's final loving words to her daughter. This experience rekindled the fire in Aoi's eyes that had been lost after he had been trapped in Momochi House. It gave him the drive to keep on living so that he could keep Himari safe when she arrived at Momochi House... Protecting Himari became Aoi's reason for living. As the party's final surprise, Himari prepares some yokai fireworks. She and Aoi ride on one into the night sky. Himari shows Aoi the lights of the town he protects, and upon seeing the lights, Aoi remembers the meaning of Himari's name written in the diary: "A light of great distance." Her parents wrote, "May your light extend over great distances." Himari is amazed by the bond she has with Aoi, and he says something unexpected and kisses her...

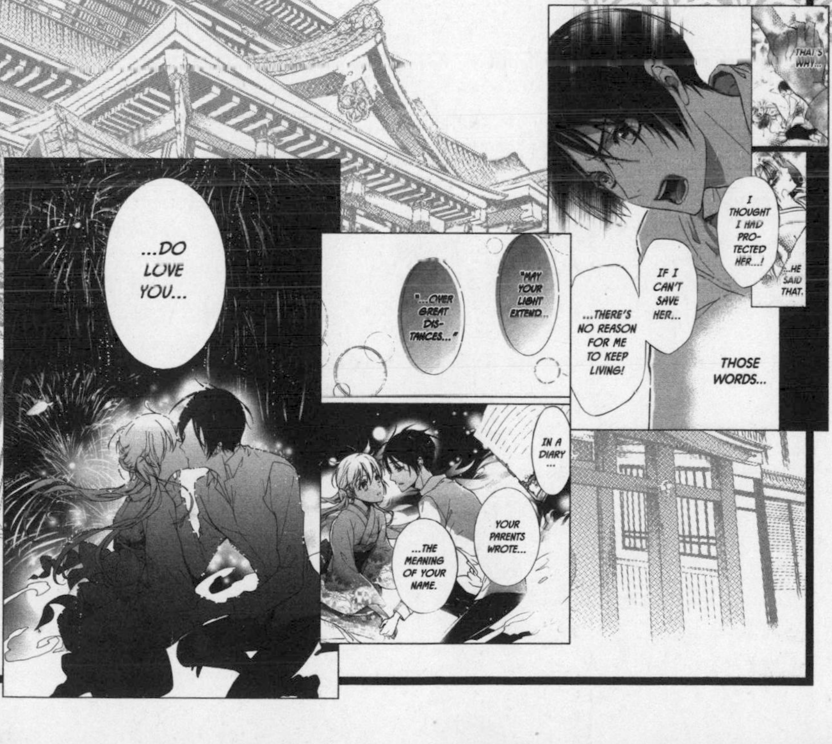
THAT'S WHY...
I THOUGHT I HAD PRO-TECTED HER...!
...HE SAID THAT.
IF I CAN'T SAVE HER...
...THERE'S NO REASON FOR ME TO KEEP LIVING!
THOSE WORDS...
"MAY YOUR LIGHT EXTEND...
"...OVER GREAT DIS-TANCES..."
IN A DIARY...
YOUR PARENTS WROTE...
...THE MEANING OF YOUR NAME.
...DO LOVE YOU...

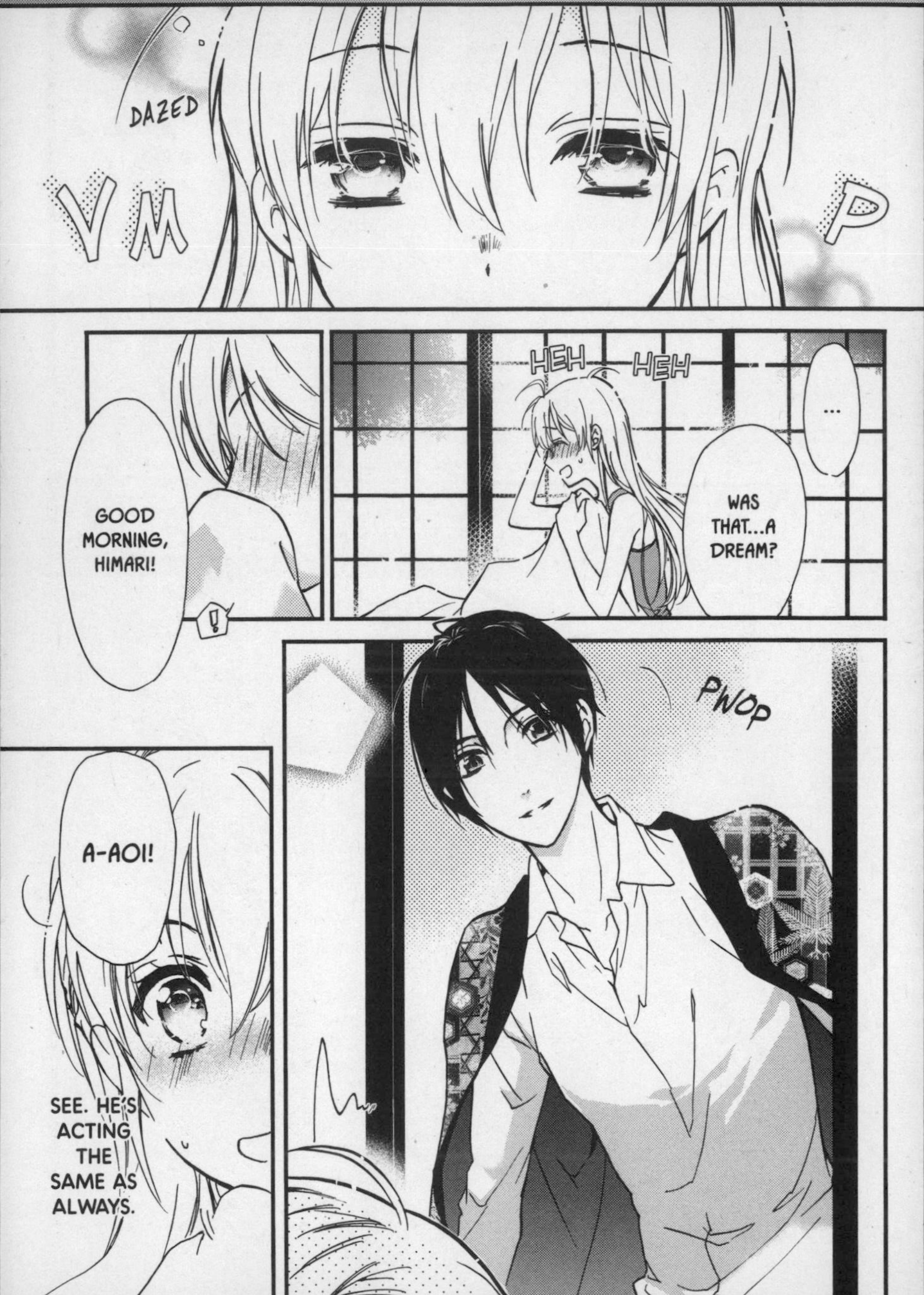
DAZED
VMP
HEH HEH
...
WAS THAT...A DREAM?
!
GOOD MORNING, HIMARI!
PWOP
A-AOI!
SEE. HE'S ACTING THE SAME AS ALWAYS.

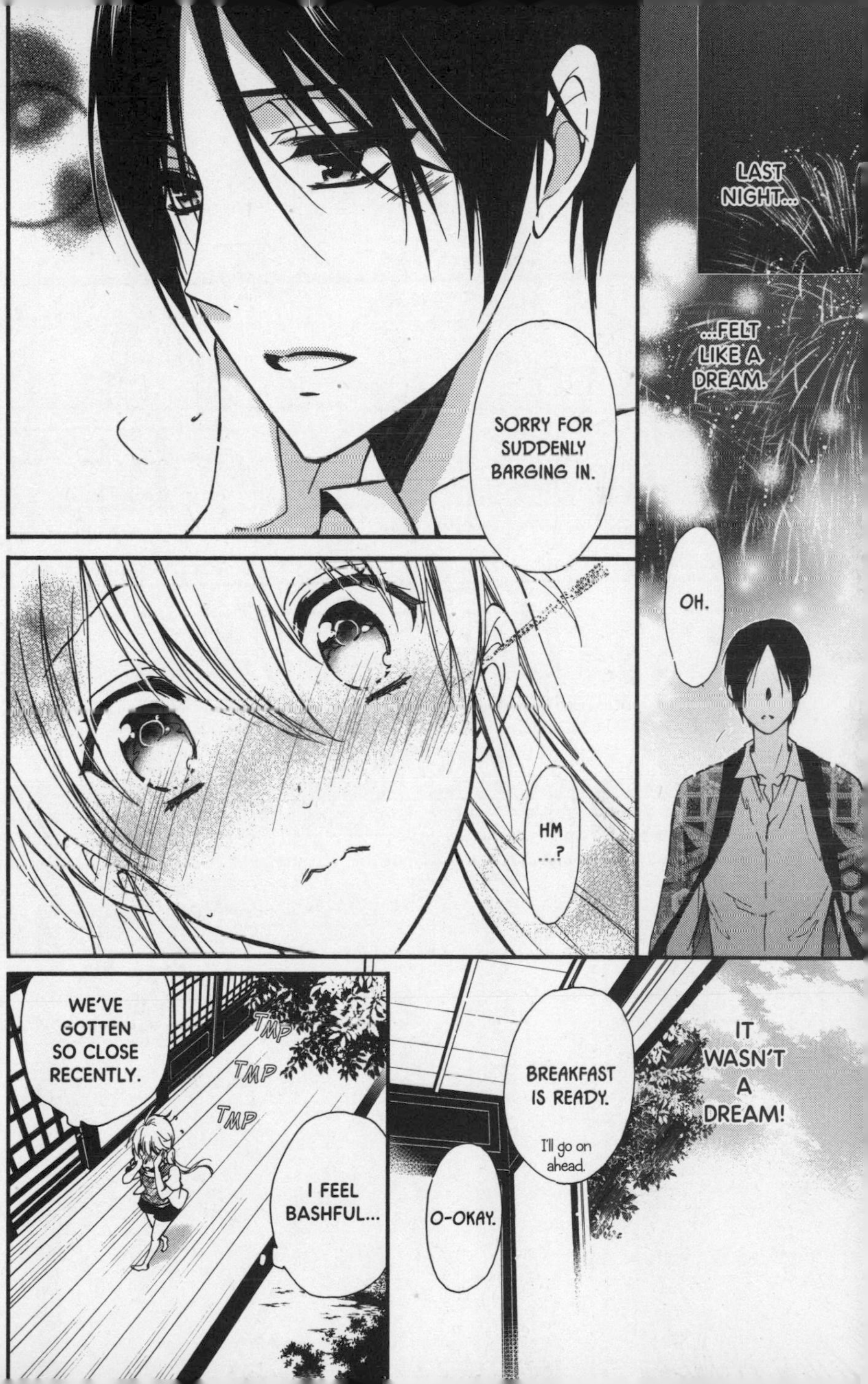
LAST NIGHT...
...FELT LIKE A DREAM.
OH.
SORRY FOR SUDDENLY BARGING IN.
HM ...?
IT WASN'T A DREAM!
BREAKFAST IS READY.
I'll go on ahead.
O-OKAY.
WE'VE GOTTEN SO CLOSE RECENTLY.
TMP
TMP
TMP
I FEEL BASHFUL...

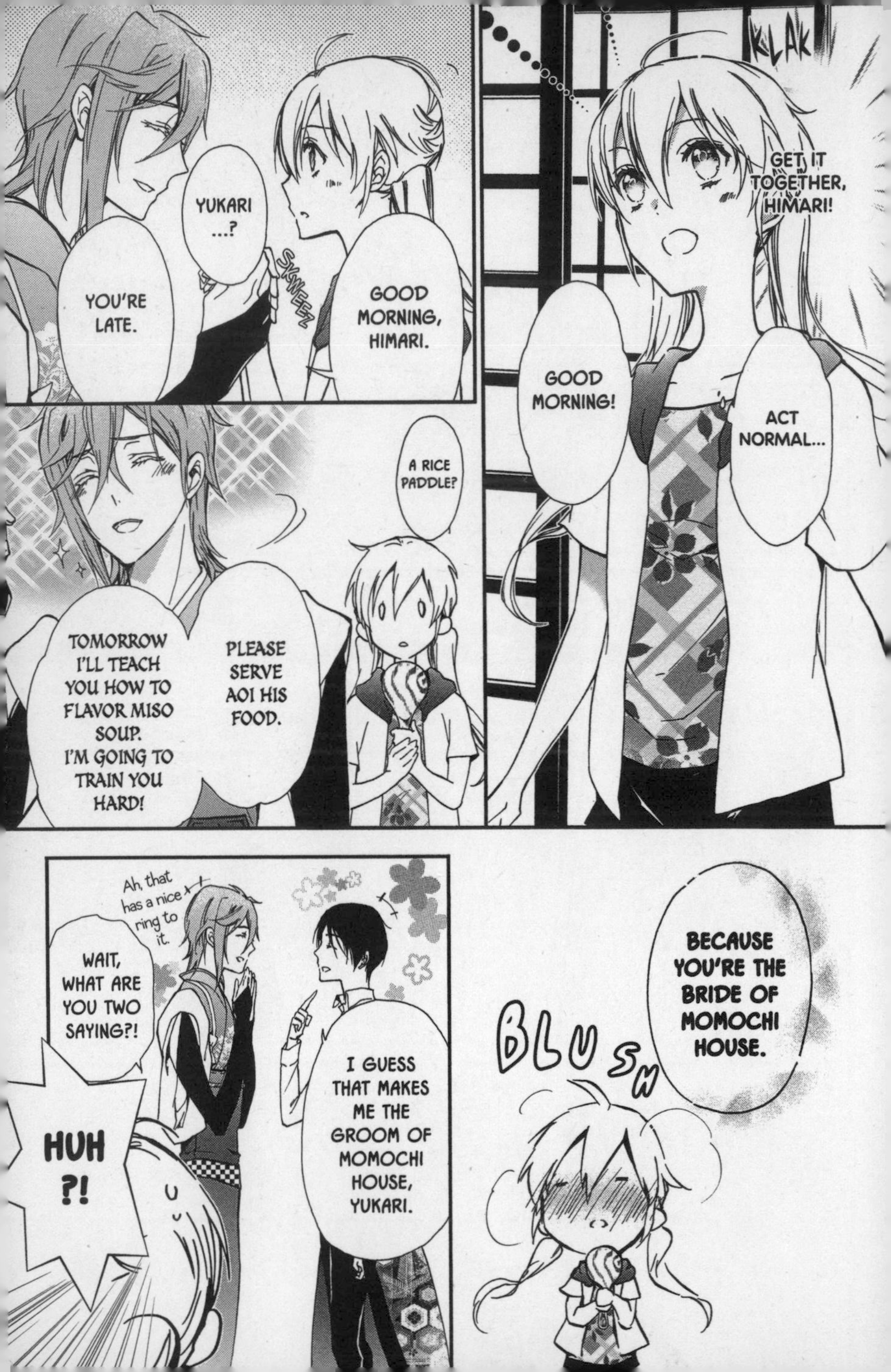
KLAK
GET IT TOGETHER, HIMARI!
ACT NORMAL...
GOOD MORNING!
GOOD MORNING, HIMARI.
YUKARI ...?
SKWEEZ
YOU'RE LATE.
A RICE PADDLE?
PLEASE SERVE AOI HIS FOOD.
TOMORROW I'LL TEACH YOU HOW TO FLAVOR MISO SOUP. I'M GOING TO TRAIN YOU HARD!
BECAUSE YOU'RE THE BRIDE OF MOMOCHI HOUSE.
BLUSH
I GUESS THAT MAKES ME THE GROOM OF MOMOCHI HOUSE, YUKARI.
Ah, that has a nice ring to it.
WAIT, WHAT ARE YOU TWO SAYING?!
HUH ?!

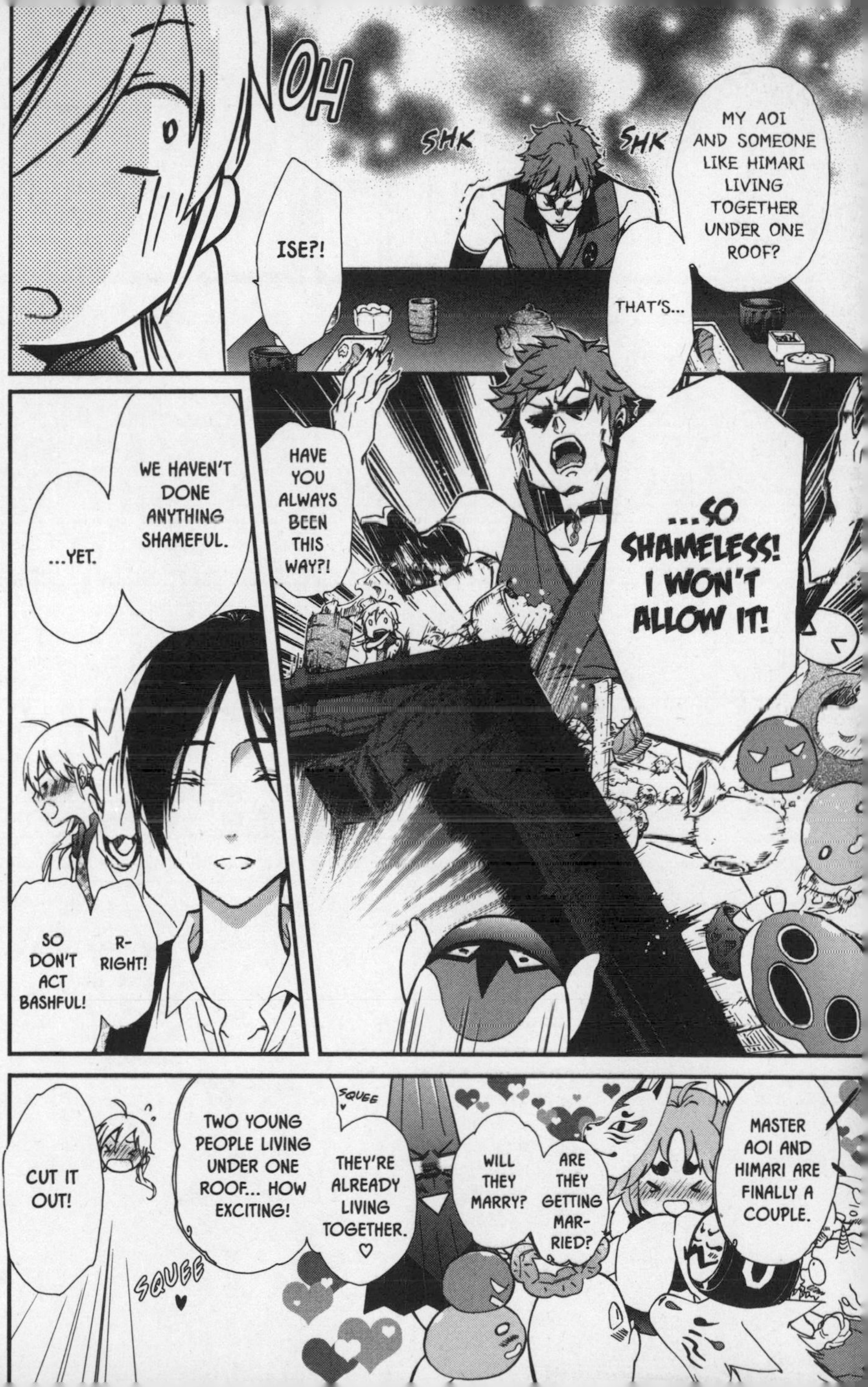
SHK
SHK
MY AOI AND SOMEONE LIKE HIMARI LIVING TOGETHER UNDER ONE ROOF?
THAT'S...
OH
ISE?!
...SO SHAMELESS! I WON'T ALLOW IT!
HAVE YOU ALWAYS BEEN THIS WAY?!
WE HAVEN'T DONE ANYTHING SHAMEFUL.
...YET.
R-RIGHT!
SO DON'T ACT BASHFUL!
MASTER AOI AND HIMARI ARE FINALLY A COUPLE.
ARE THEY GETTING MARRIED?
WILL THEY MARRY?
SQUEE ♥
THEY'RE ALREADY LIVING TOGETHER. ♡
TWO YOUNG PEOPLE LIVING UNDER ONE ROOF... HOW EXCITING!
SQUEE ♥
CUT IT OUT!

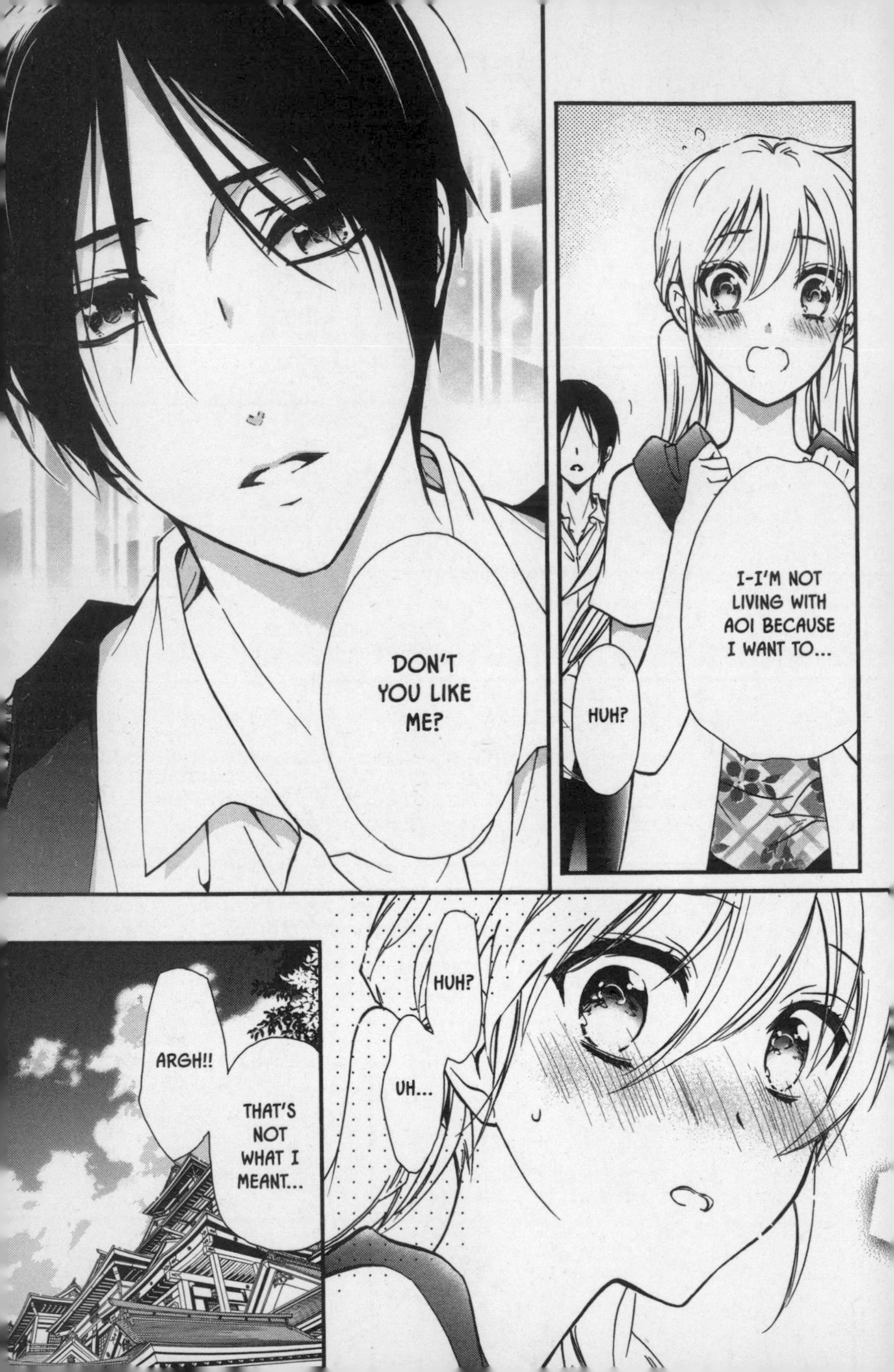
I-I'M NOT LIVING WITH AOI BECAUSE I WANT TO...
HUH?
DON'T YOU LIKE ME?
HUH?
UH...
ARGH!!
THAT'S NOT WHAT I MEANT...

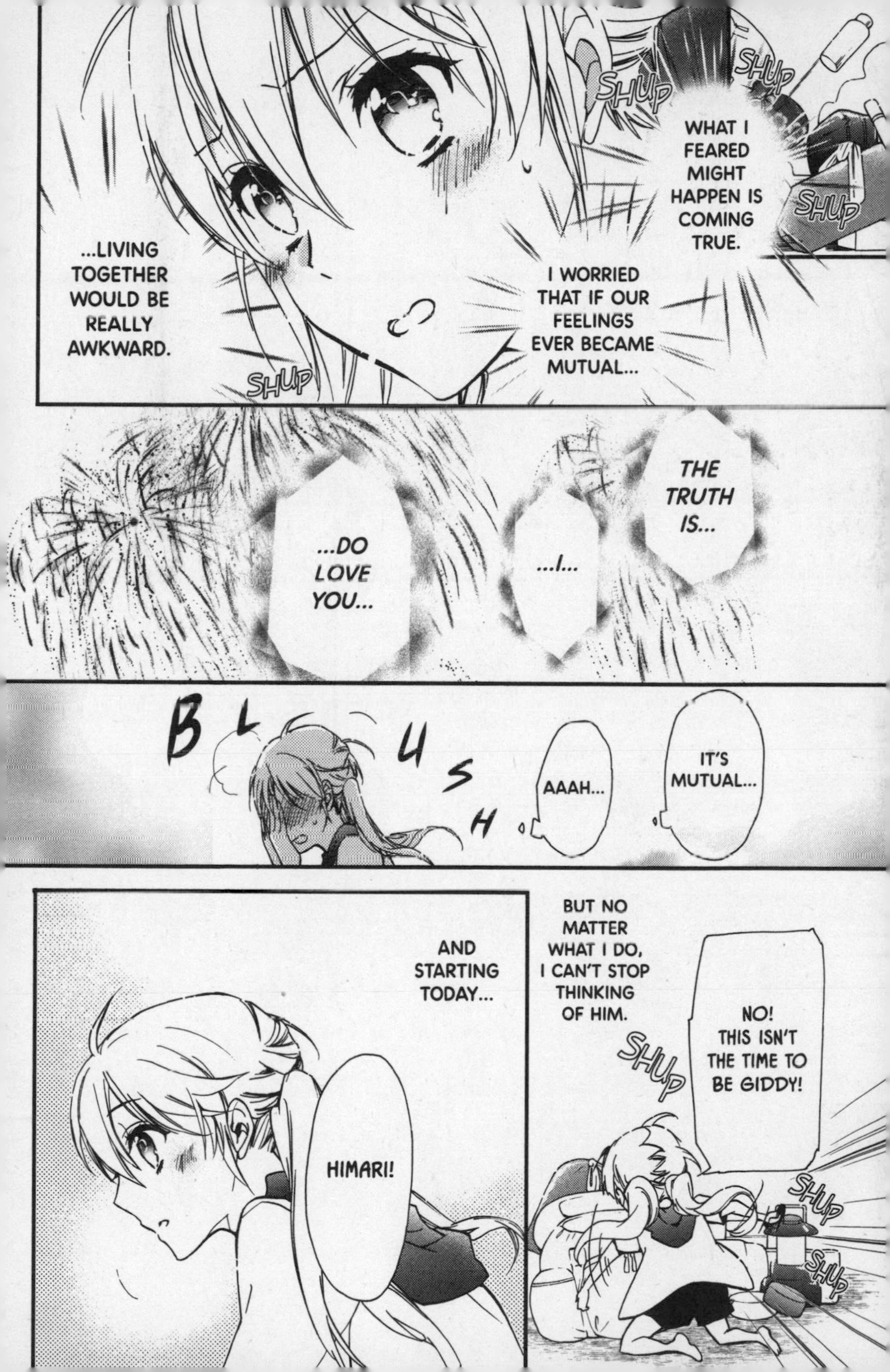
SHUP
SHUP
WHAT I FEARED MIGHT HAPPEN IS COMING TRUE.
SHUP
I WORRIED THAT IF OUR FEELINGS EVER BECAME MUTUAL...
...LIVING TOGETHER WOULD BE REALLY AWKWARD.
SHUP
THE TRUTH IS...
...I...
...DO LOVE YOU...
IT'S MUTUAL...
AAAH...
BLUSH
BUT NO MATTER WHAT I DO, I CAN'T STOP THINKING OF HIM.
NO! THIS ISN'T THE TIME TO BE GIDDY!
SHUP
SHUP
SHUP
AND STARTING TODAY...
HIMARI!

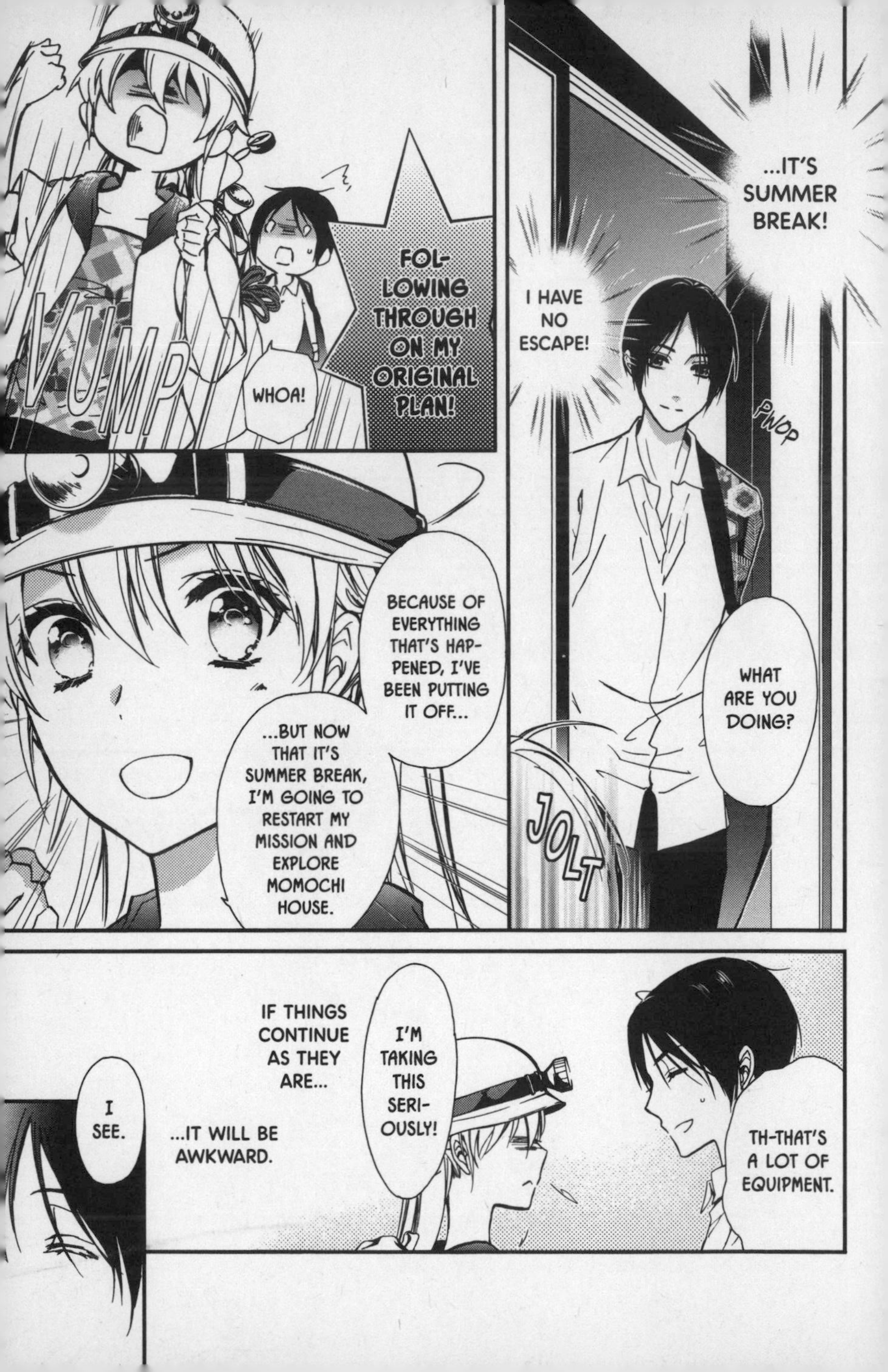
...IT'S SUMMER BREAK!
I HAVE NO ESCAPE!
PWOP
WHAT ARE YOU DOING?
JOLT
FOL-LOWING THROUGH ON MY ORIGINAL PLAN!
WHOA!
VUMP
BECAUSE OF EVERYTHING THAT'S HAP-PENED, I'VE BEEN PUTTING IT OFF...
...BUT NOW THAT IT'S SUMMER BREAK, I'M GOING TO RESTART MY MISSION AND EXPLORE MOMOCHI HOUSE.
TH-THAT'S A LOT OF EQUIPMENT.
I'M TAKING THIS SERI-OUSLY!
IF THINGS CONTINUE AS THEY ARE...
...IT WILL BE AWKWARD.
I SEE.

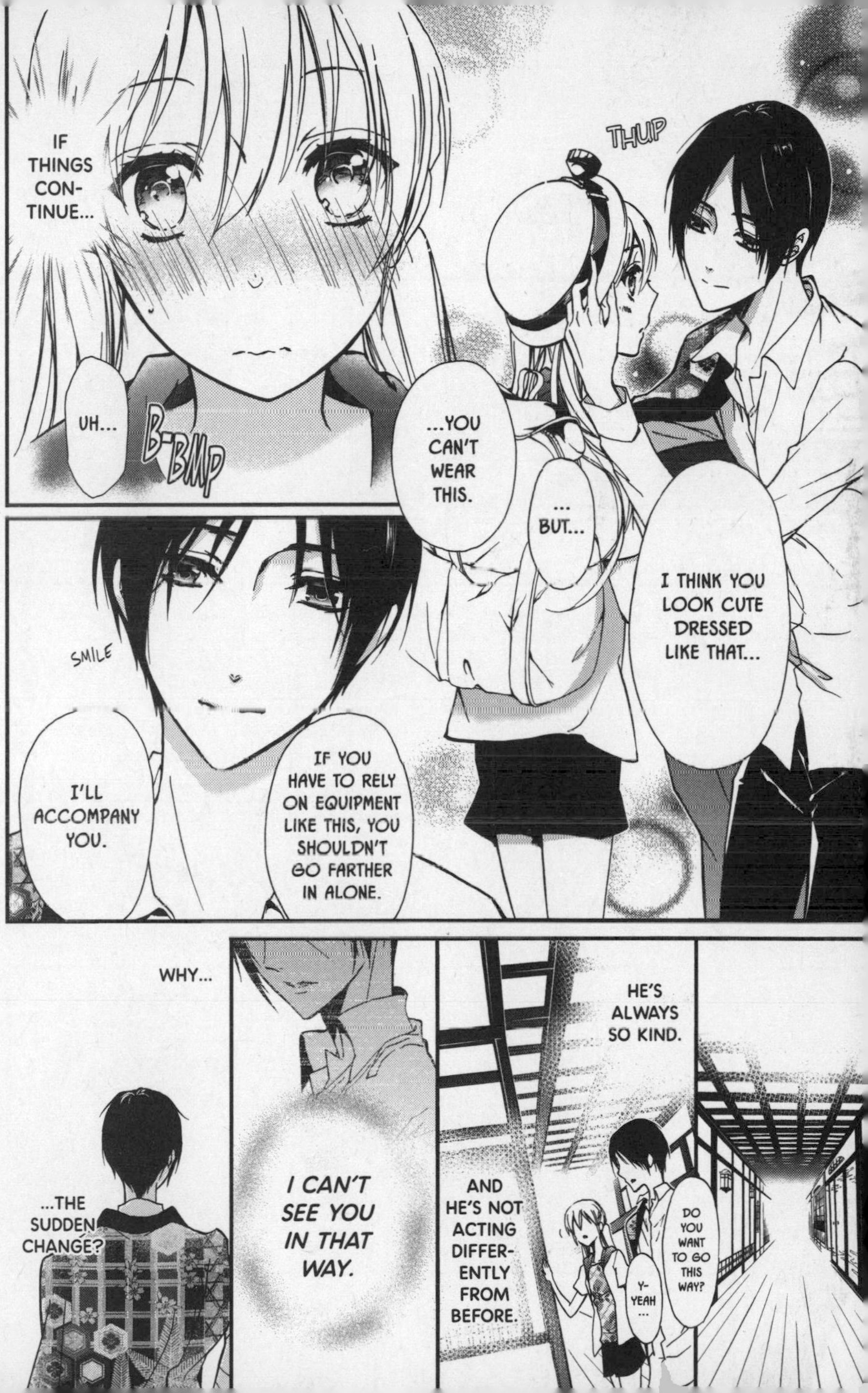
THUP
...YOU CAN'T WEAR THIS.
...BUT...
I THINK YOU LOOK CUTE DRESSED LIKE THAT...
IF THINGS CON-TINUE...
B-BMP
UH...
SMILE
IF YOU HAVE TO RELY ON EQUIPMENT LIKE THIS, YOU SHOULDN'T GO FARTHER IN ALONE.
I'LL ACCOMPANY YOU.
HE'S ALWAYS SO KIND.
DO YOU WANT TO GO THIS WAY?
Y-YEAH...
AND HE'S NOT ACTING DIFFER-ENTLY FROM BEFORE.
I CAN'T SEE YOU IN THAT WAY.
WHY...
...THE SUDDEN CHANGE?

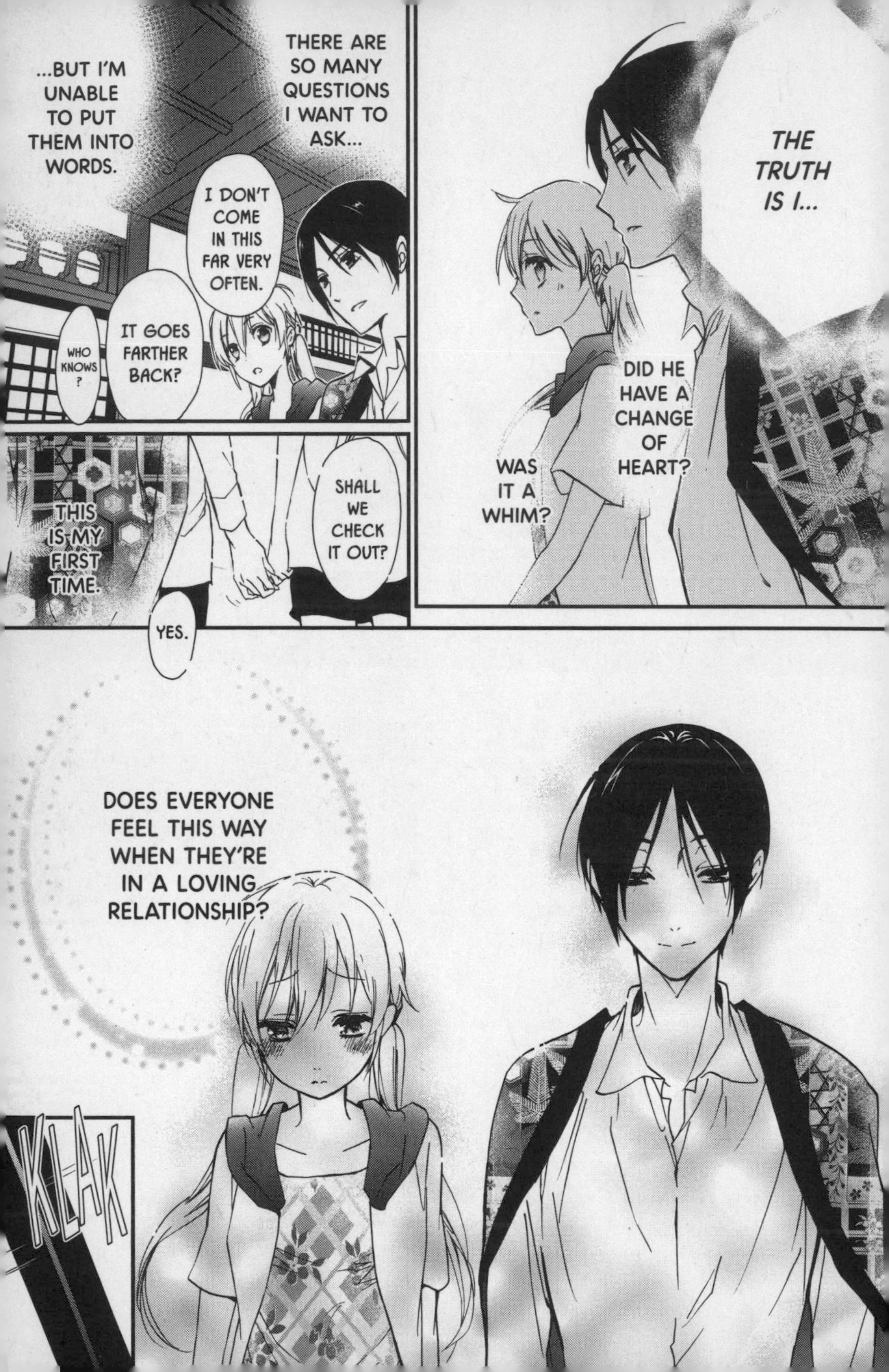
THE TRUTH IS I...
DID HE HAVE A CHANGE OF HEART?
WAS IT A WHIM?
THERE ARE SO MANY QUESTIONS I WANT TO ASK...
...BUT I'M UNABLE TO PUT THEM INTO WORDS.
I DON'T COME IN THIS FAR VERY OFTEN.
IT GOES FARTHER BACK?
WHO KNOWS?
SHALL WE CHECK IT OUT?
THIS IS MY FIRST TIME.
YES.
DOES EVERYONE FEEL THIS WAY WHEN THEY'RE IN A LOVING RELATIONSHIP?
KLAK

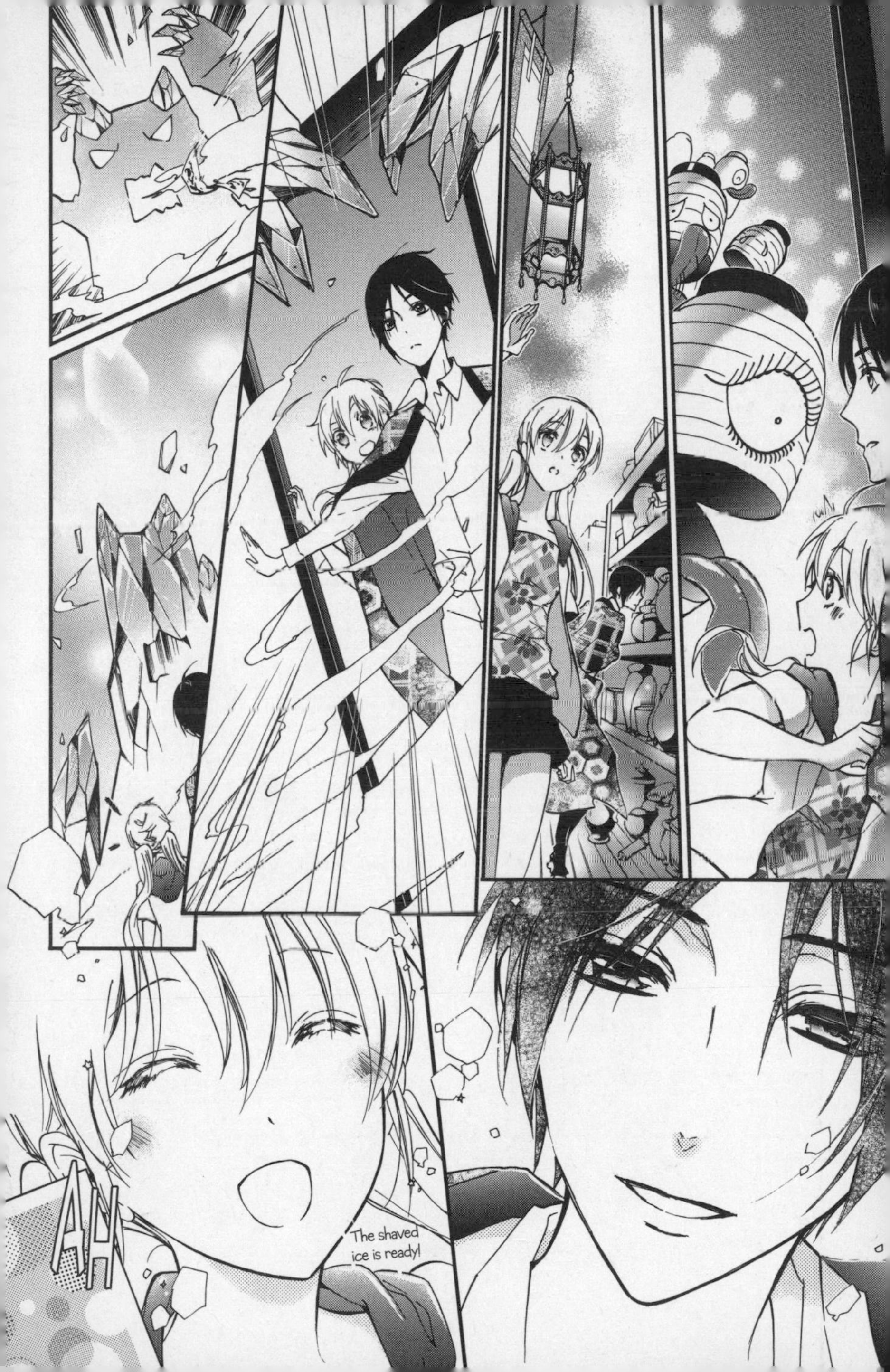
The shaved ice is ready!
AH

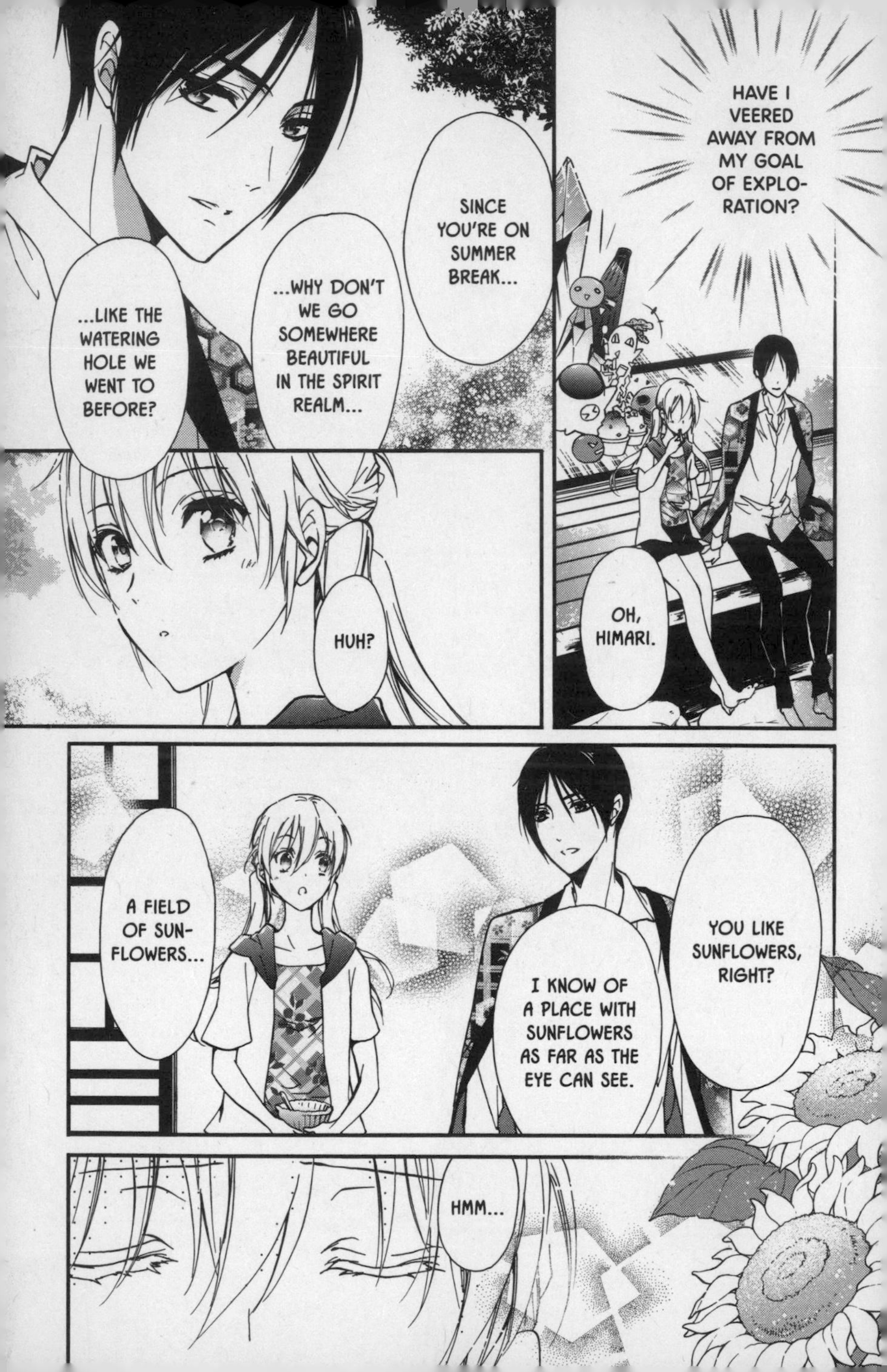
HAVE I VEERED AWAY FROM MY GOAL OF EXPLO-RATION?
OH, HIMARI.
SINCE YOU'RE ON SUMMER BREAK...
...WHY DON'T WE GO SOMEWHERE BEAUTIFUL IN THE SPIRIT REALM...
...LIKE THE WATERING HOLE WE WENT TO BEFORE?
HUH?
YOU LIKE SUNFLOWERS, RIGHT?
I KNOW OF A PLACE WITH SUNFLOWERS AS FAR AS THE EYE CAN SEE.
A FIELD OF SUN-FLOWERS...
HMM...

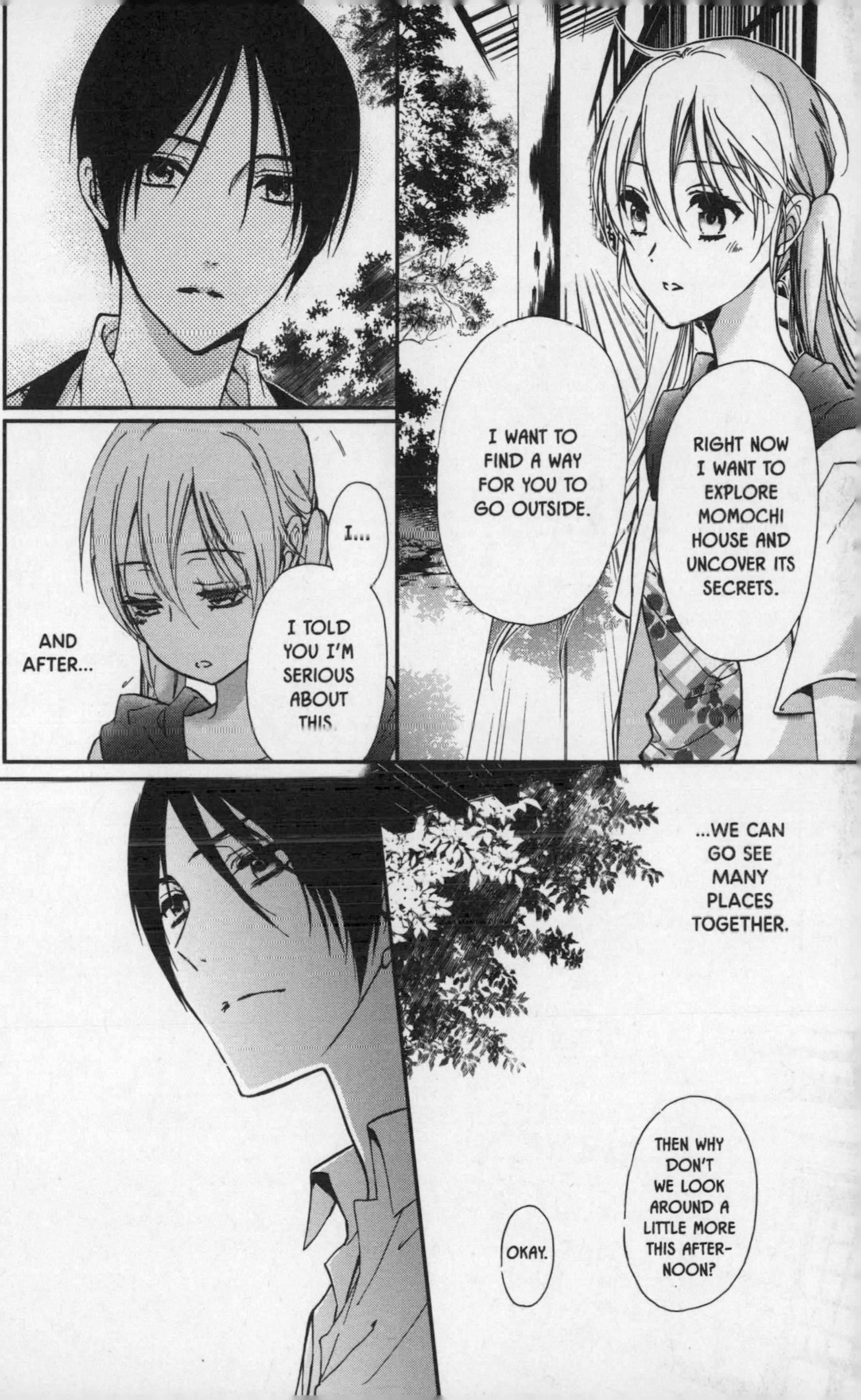
RIGHT NOW I WANT TO EXPLORE MOMOCHI HOUSE AND UNCOVER ITS SECRETS.
I WANT TO FIND A WAY FOR YOU TO GO OUTSIDE.
I...
I TOLD YOU I'M SERIOUS ABOUT THIS.
AND AFTER...
...WE CAN GO SEE MANY PLACES TOGETHER.
THEN WHY DON'T WE LOOK AROUND A LITTLE MORE THIS AFTERNOON?
OKAY.

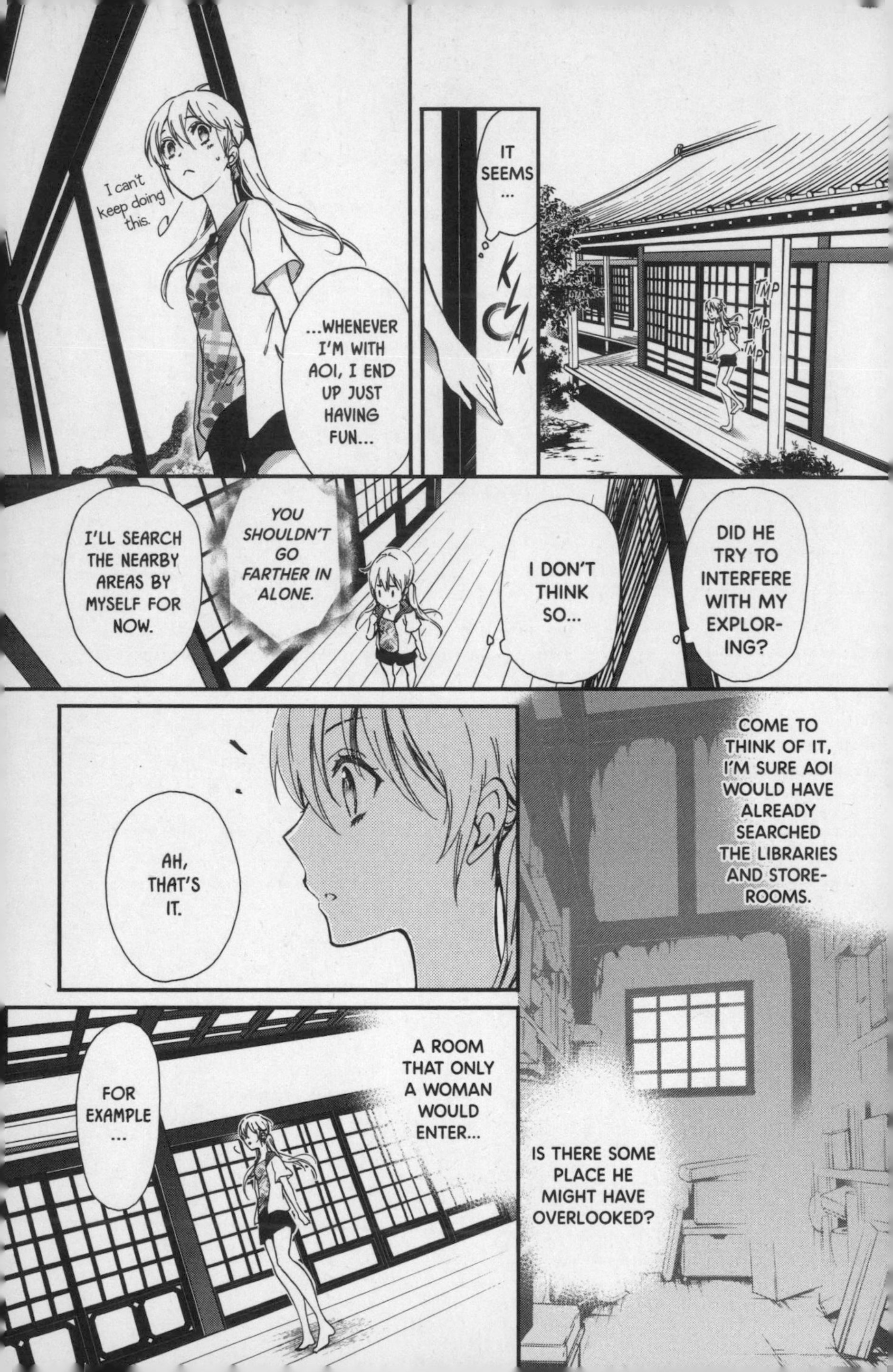
TMP
TMP
TMP
IT SEEMS...
KLAK
...WHENEVER I'M WITH AOI, I END UP JUST HAVING FUN...
I can't keep doing this.
DID HE TRY TO INTERFERE WITH MY EXPLOR-ING?
I DON'T THINK SO...
YOU SHOULDN'T GO FARTHER IN ALONE.
I'LL SEARCH THE NEARBY AREAS BY MYSELF FOR NOW.
COME TO THINK OF IT, I'M SURE AOI WOULD HAVE ALREADY SEARCHED THE LIBRARIES AND STORE-ROOMS.
IS THERE SOME PLACE HE MIGHT HAVE OVERLOOKED?
AH, THAT'S IT.
A ROOM THAT ONLY A WOMAN WOULD ENTER...
FOR EXAMPLE...

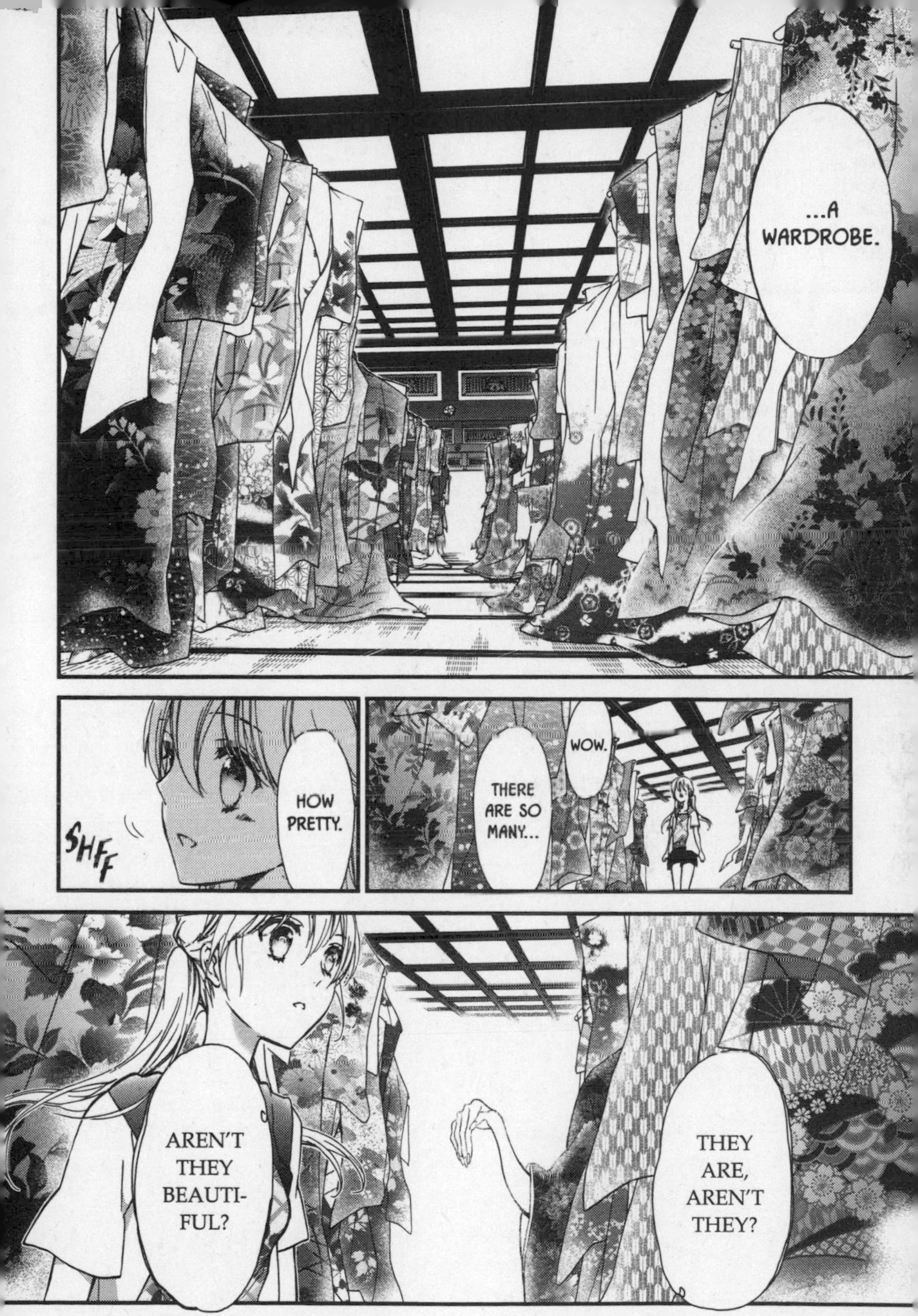
...A WARDROBE.
WOW.
THERE ARE SO MANY...
HOW PRETTY.
SHFF
THEY ARE, AREN'T THEY?
AREN'T THEY BEAUTI-FUL?

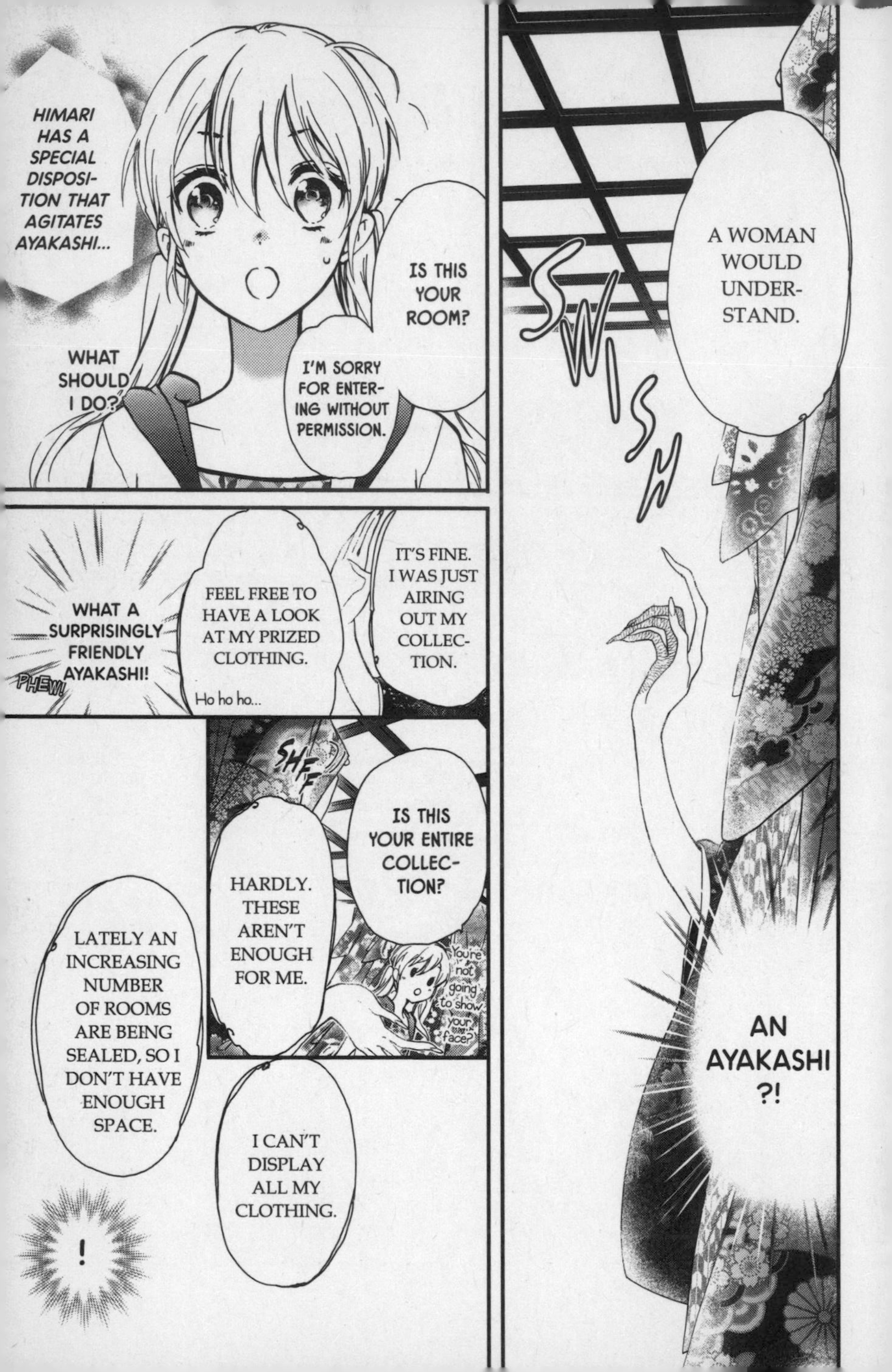
A WOMAN WOULD UNDERSTAND.
SWISH
AN AYAKASHI?!
IS THIS YOUR ROOM?
I'M SORRY FOR ENTERING WITHOUT PERMISSION.
HIMARI HAS A SPECIAL DISPOSITION THAT AGITATES AYAKASHI...
WHAT SHOULD I DO?
IT'S FINE. I WAS JUST AIRING OUT MY COLLECTION.
FEEL FREE TO HAVE A LOOK AT MY PRIZED CLOTHING.
Ho ho ho...
WHAT A SURPRISINGLY FRIENDLY AYAKASHI!
PHEW!
SHFF
IS THIS YOUR ENTIRE COLLECTION?
You're not going to show your face?
HARDLY. THESE AREN'T ENOUGH FOR ME.
LATELY AN INCREASING NUMBER OF ROOMS ARE BEING SEALED, SO I DON'T HAVE ENOUGH SPACE.
I CAN'T DISPLAY ALL MY CLOTHING.
!

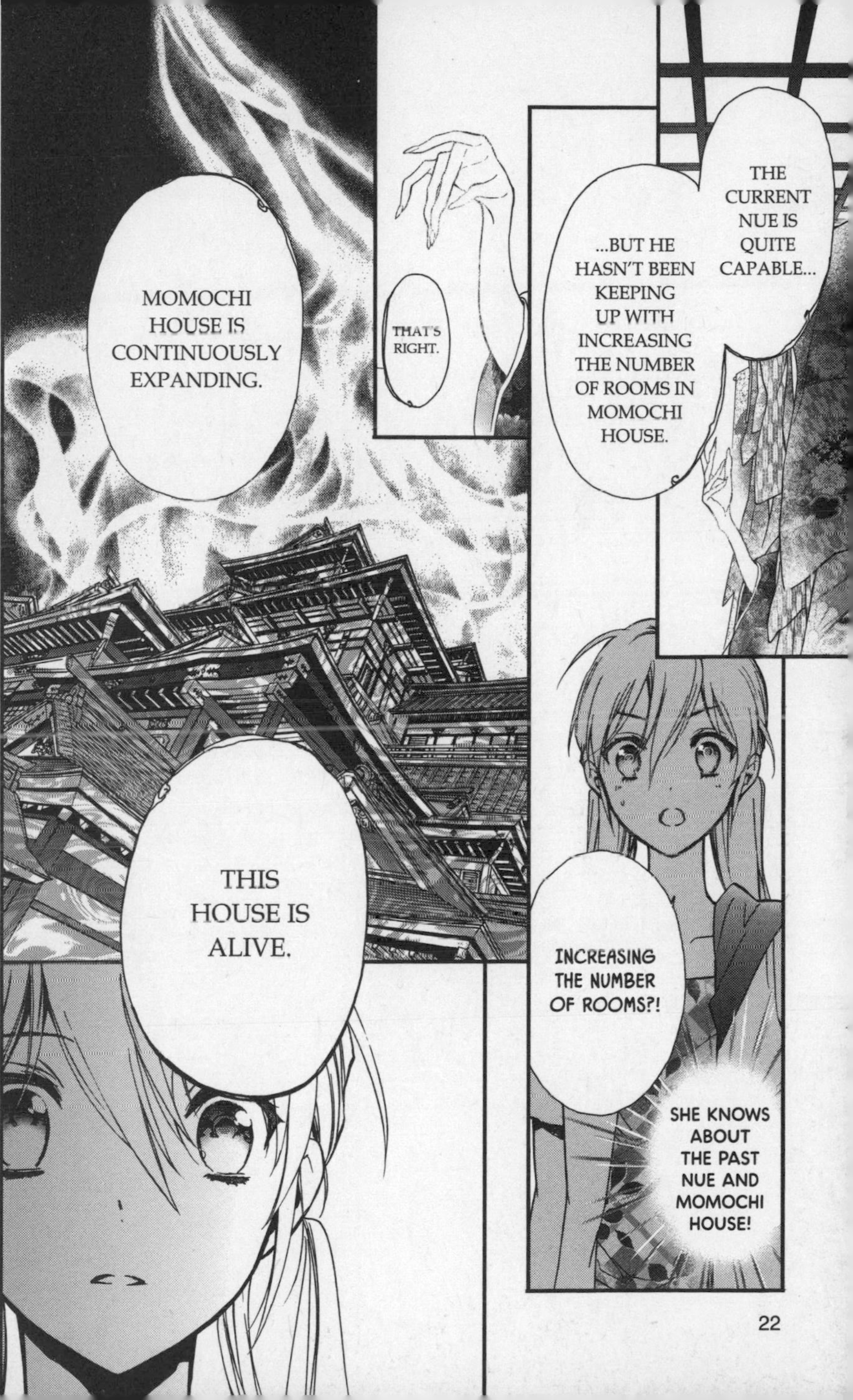
THE CURRENT NUE IS QUITE CAPABLE...
...BUT HE HASN'T BEEN KEEPING UP WITH INCREASING THE NUMBER OF ROOMS IN MOMOCHI HOUSE.
INCREASING THE NUMBER OF ROOMS?!
SHE KNOWS ABOUT THE PAST NUE AND MOMOCHI HOUSE!
THAT'S RIGHT.
MOMOCHI HOUSE IS CONTINUOUSLY EXPANDING.
THIS HOUSE IS ALIVE.

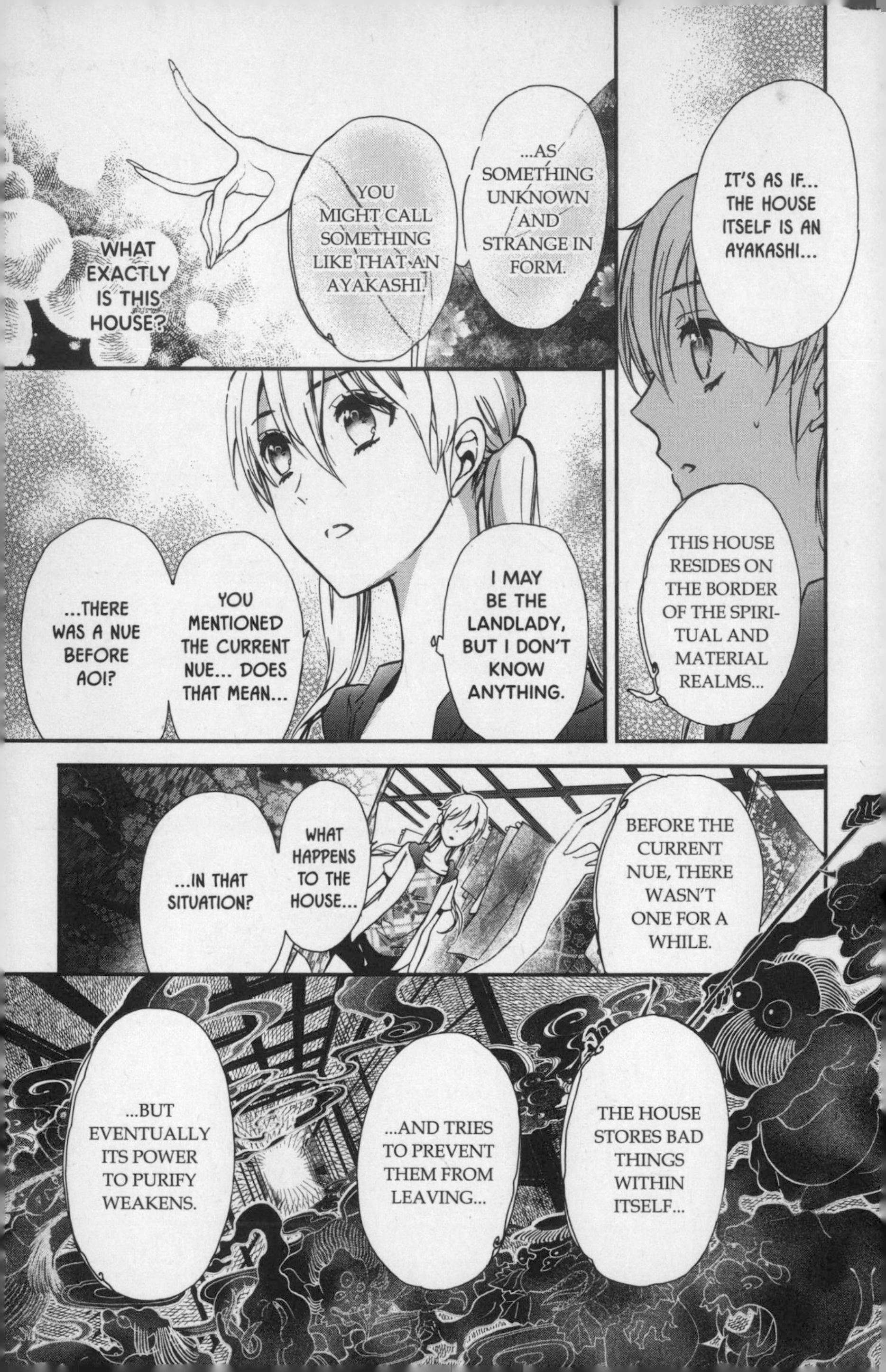
IT'S AS IF... THE HOUSE ITSELF IS AN AYAKASHI...
THIS HOUSE RESIDES ON THE BORDER OF THE SPIRI-TUAL AND MATERIAL REALMS...
...AS SOMETHING UNKNOWN AND STRANGE IN FORM.
YOU MIGHT CALL SOMETHING LIKE THAT AN AYAKASHI.
WHAT EXACTLY IS THIS HOUSE?
I MAY BE THE LANDLADY, BUT I DON'T KNOW ANYTHING.
YOU MENTIONED THE CURRENT NUE... DOES THAT MEAN...
...THERE WAS A NUE BEFORE AOI?
BEFORE THE CURRENT NUE, THERE WASN'T ONE FOR A WHILE.
WHAT HAPPENS TO THE HOUSE...
...IN THAT SITUATION?
THE HOUSE STORES BAD THINGS WITHIN ITSELF...
...AND TRIES TO PREVENT THEM FROM LEAVING...
...BUT EVENTUALLY ITS POWER TO PURIFY WEAKENS.

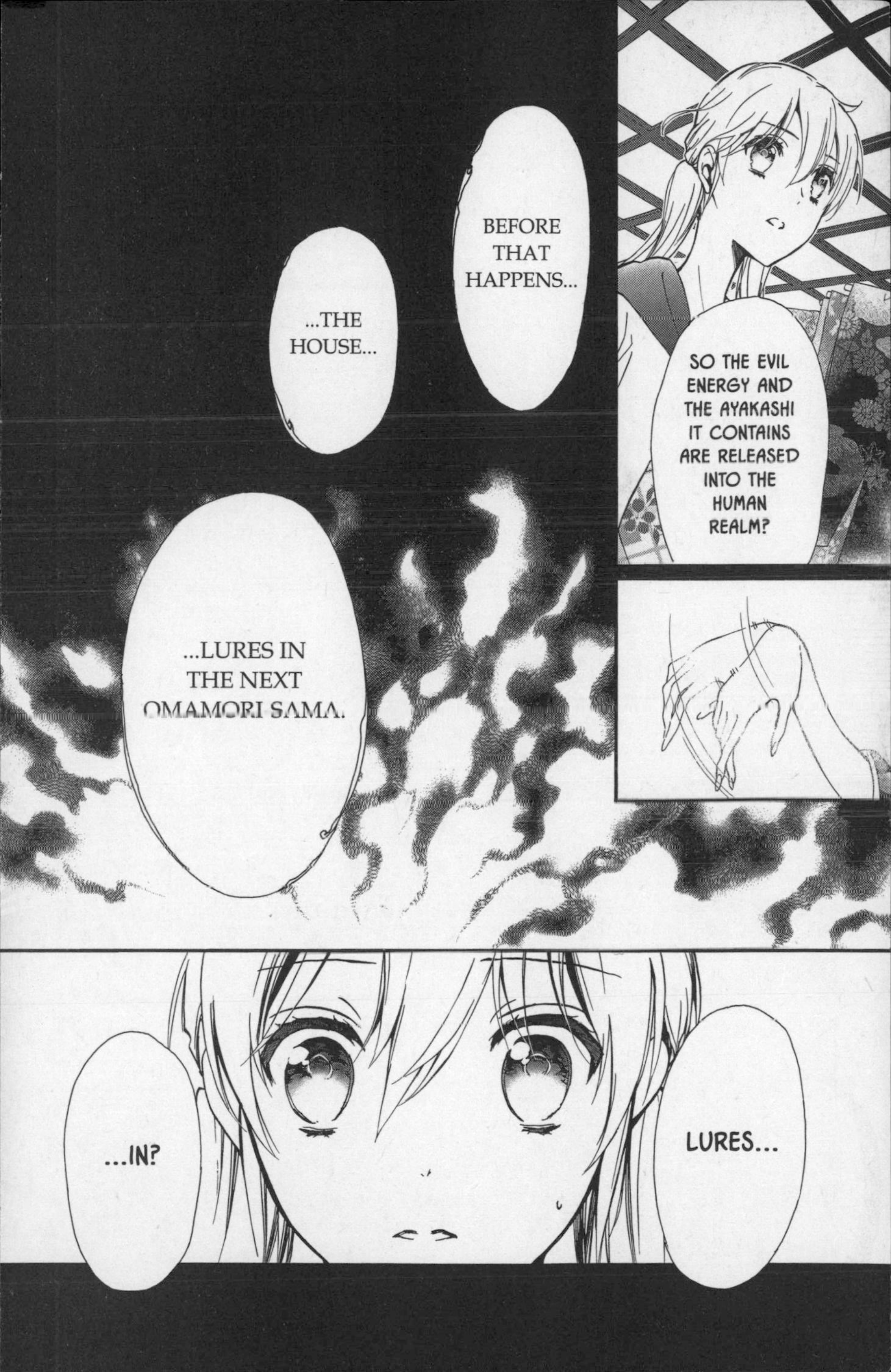
SO THE EVIL ENERGY AND THE AYAKASHI IT CONTAINS ARE RELEASED INTO THE HUMAN REALM?
BEFORE THAT HAPPENS...
...THE HOUSE...
...LURES IN THE NEXT OMAMORI SAMA.
LURES...
...IN?

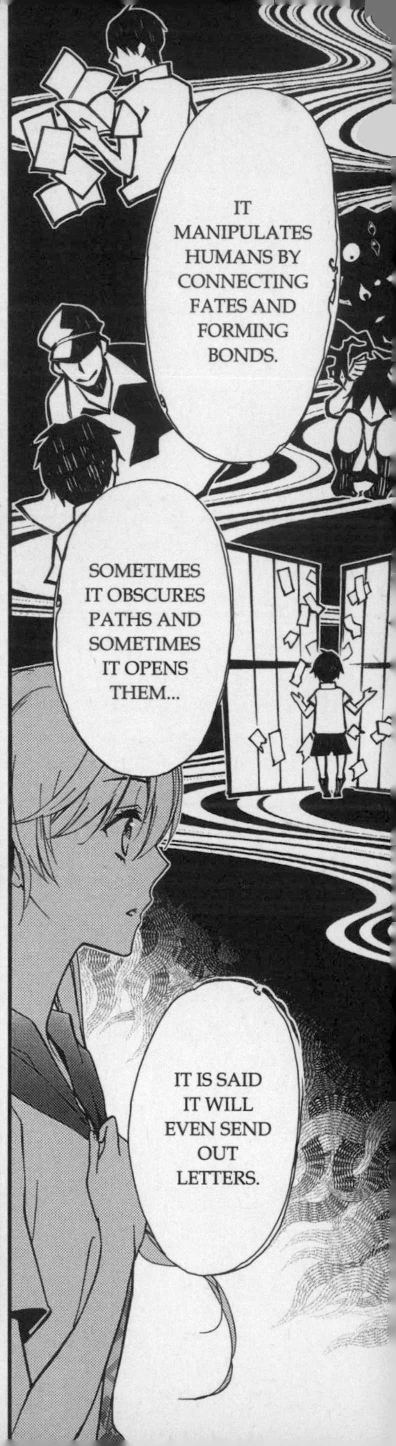
IT MANIPULATES HUMANS BY CONNECTING FATES AND FORMING BONDS.
SOMETIMES IT OBSCURES PATHS AND SOMETIMES IT OPENS THEM...
IT IS SAID IT WILL EVEN SEND OUT LETTERS.
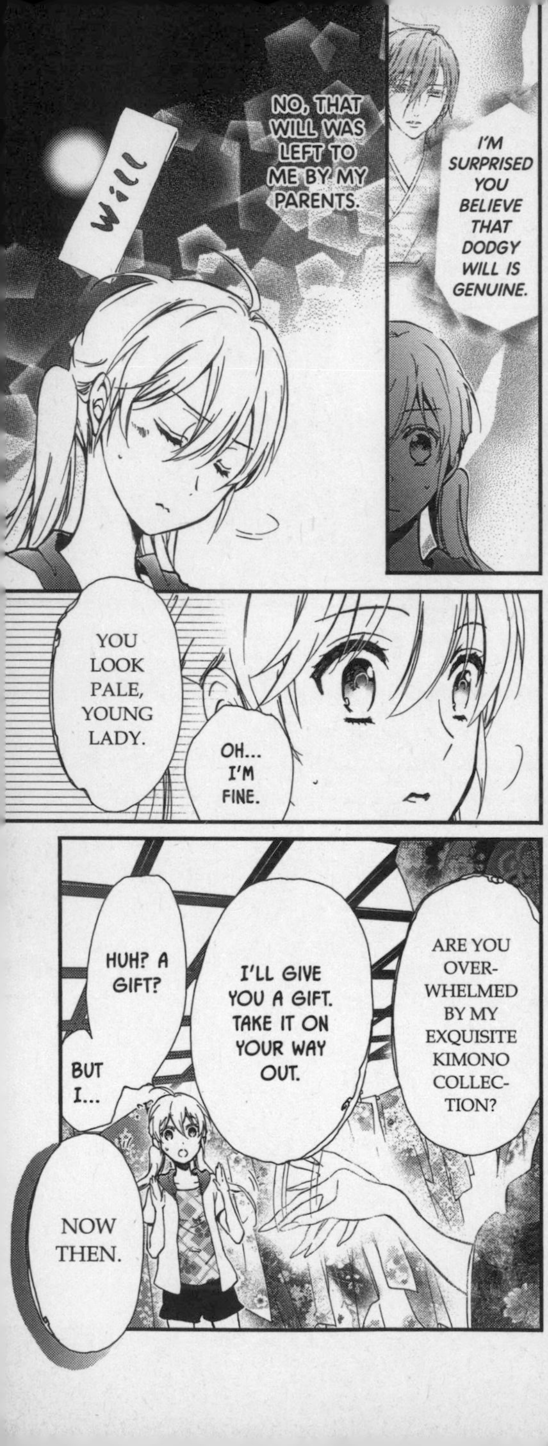
I'M SURPRISED YOU BELIEVE THAT DODGY WILL IS GENUINE.
NO, THAT WILL WAS LEFT TO ME BY MY PARENTS.
Will
YOU LOOK PALE, YOUNG LADY.
OH... I'M FINE.
ARE YOU OVER-WHELMED BY MY EXQUISITE KIMONO COLLEC-TION?
I'LL GIVE YOU A GIFT. TAKE IT ON YOUR WAY OUT.
HUH? A GIFT?
BUT I...
NOW THEN.

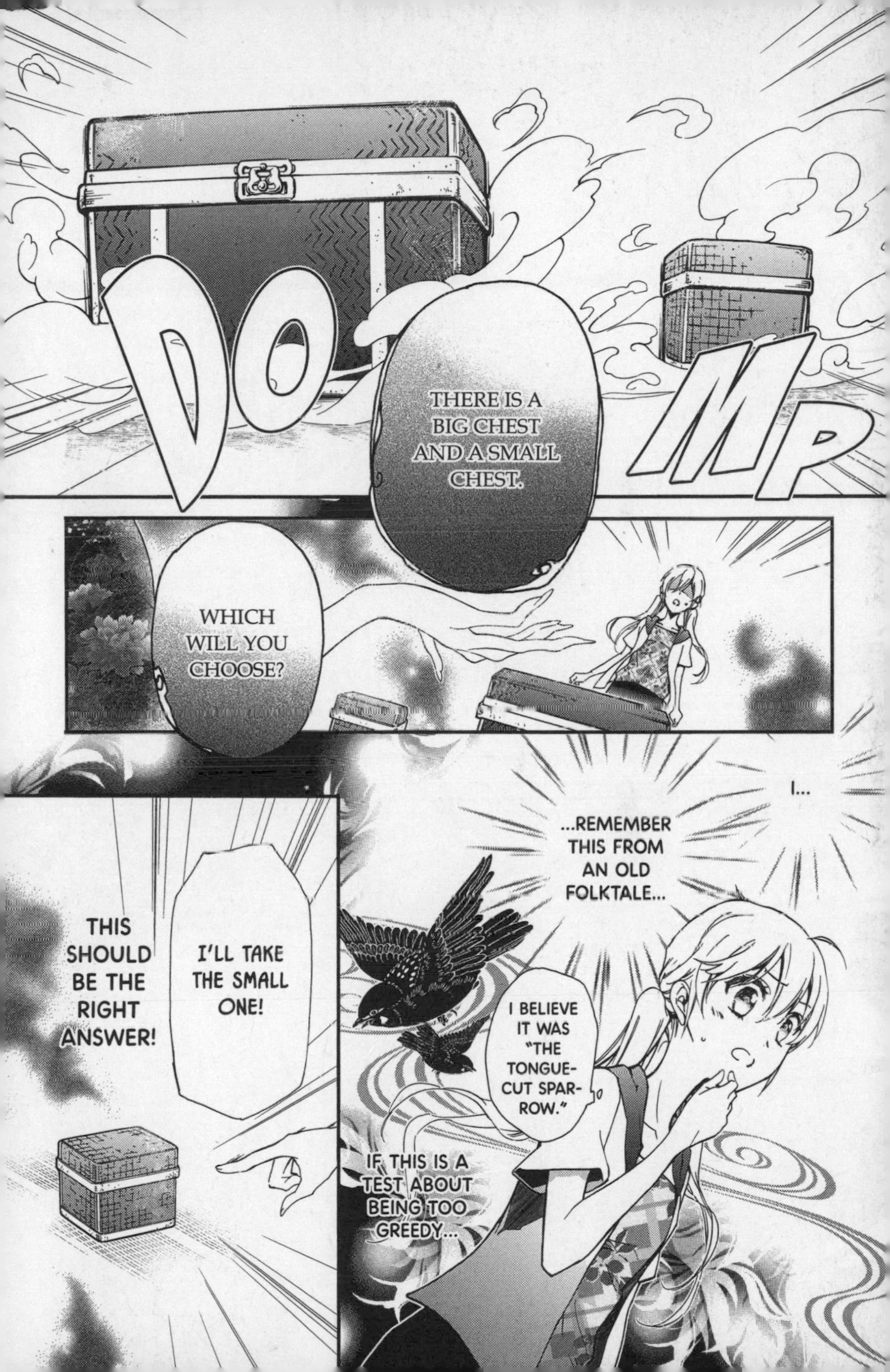
DOMP
THERE IS A BIG CHEST AND A SMALL CHEST.
WHICH WILL YOU CHOOSE?
I...
...REMEMBER THIS FROM AN OLD FOLKTALE...
I BELIEVE IT WAS "THE TONGUE-CUT SPARROW."
IF THIS IS A TEST ABOUT BEING TOO GREEDY...
I'LL TAKE THE SMALL ONE!
THIS SHOULD BE THE RIGHT ANSWER!

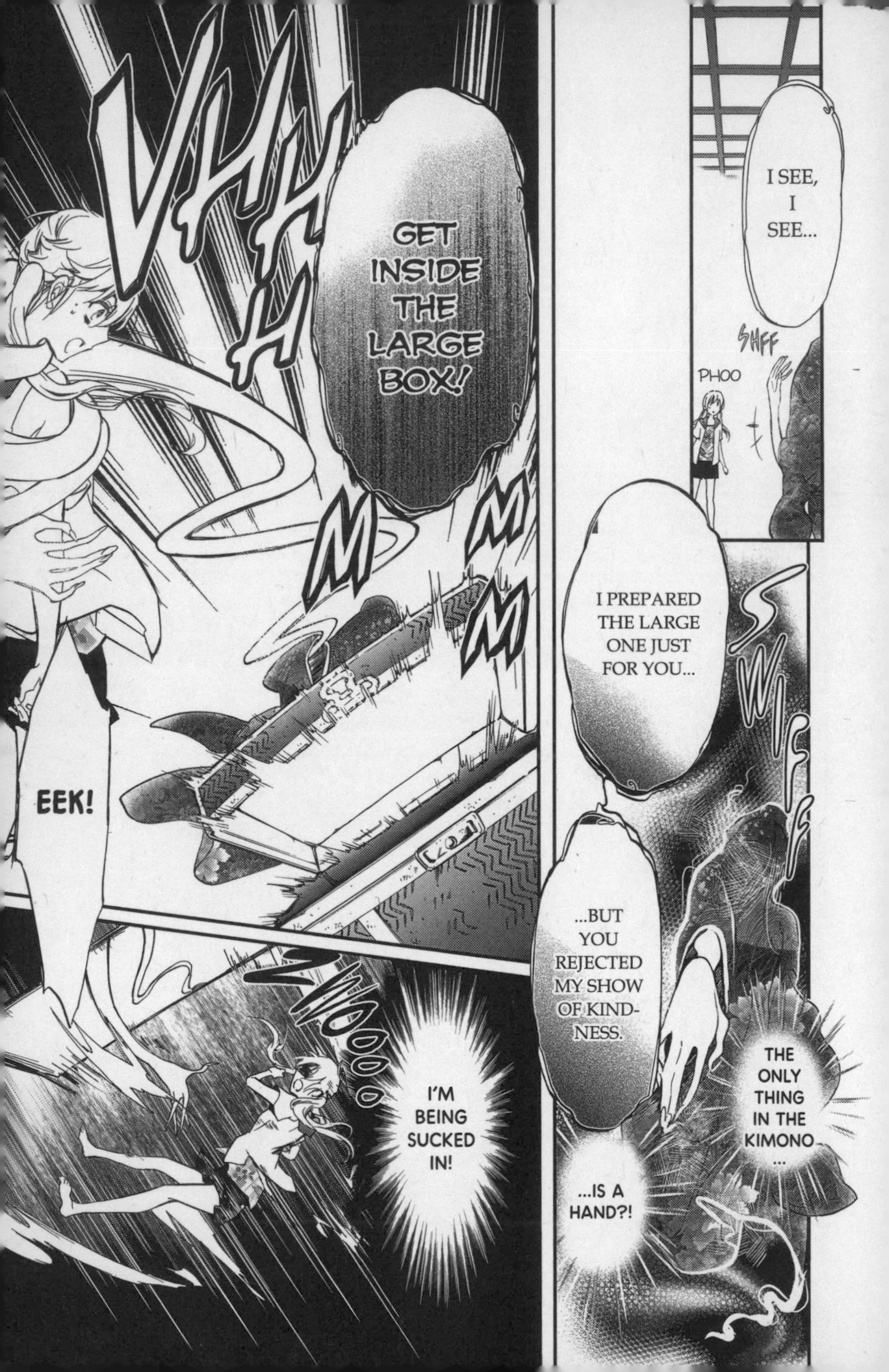
I SEE, I SEE...
SHFF
PHOO
I PREPARED THE LARGE ONE JUST FOR YOU...
...BUT YOU REJECTED MY SHOW OF KINDNESS.
THE ONLY THING IN THE KIMONO...
...IS A HAND?!
GET INSIDE THE LARGE BOX!
EEK!
I'M BEING SUCKED IN!

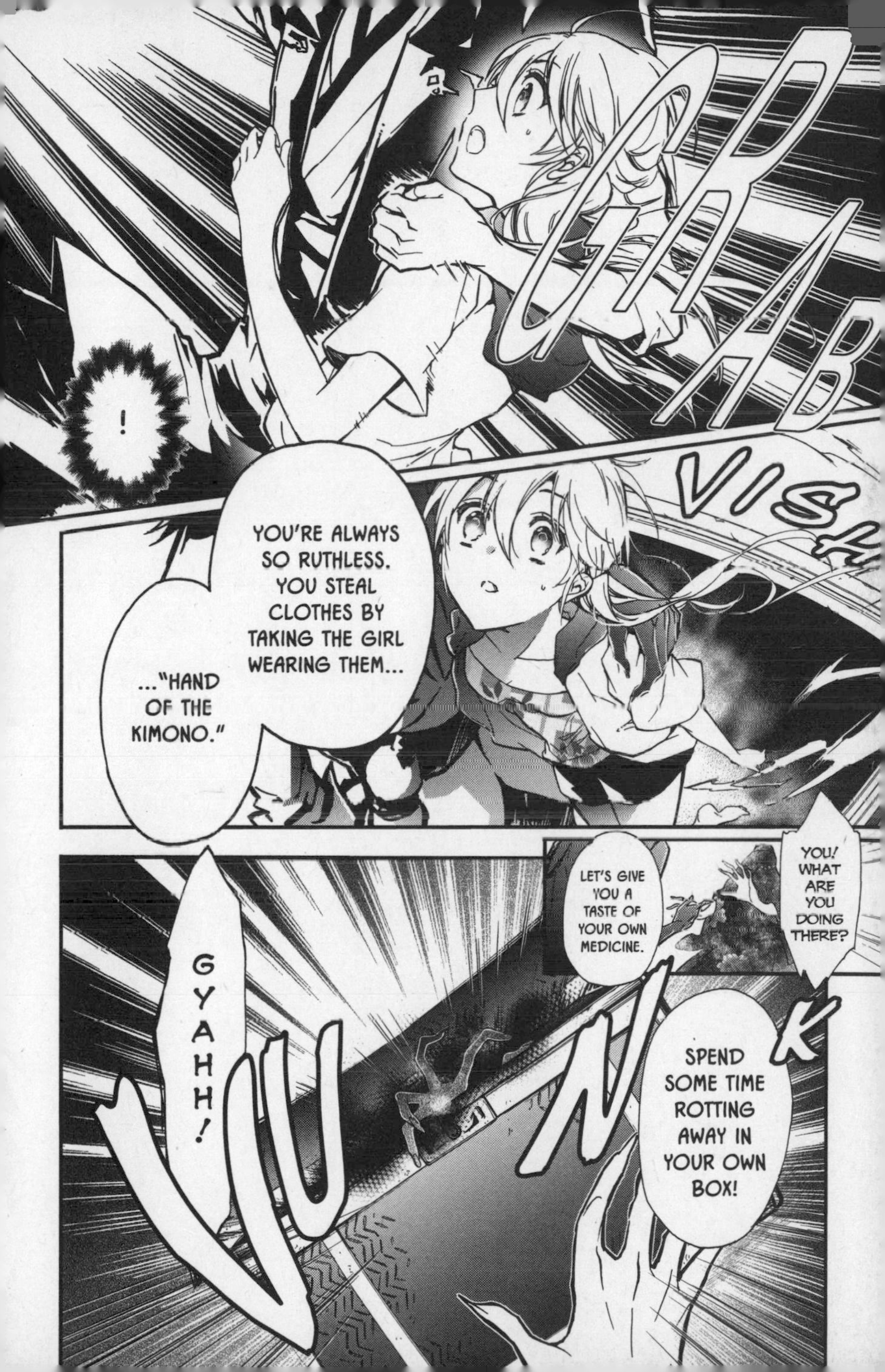
GRAAB
!
VISH
YOU'RE ALWAYS SO RUTHLESS. YOU STEAL CLOTHES BY TAKING THE GIRL WEARING THEM...
..."HAND OF THE KIMONO."
YOU! WHAT ARE YOU DOING THERE?
LET'S GIVE YOU A TASTE OF YOUR OWN MEDICINE.
SPEND SOME TIME ROTTING AWAY IN YOUR OWN BOX!
VUNK
GYAHH!

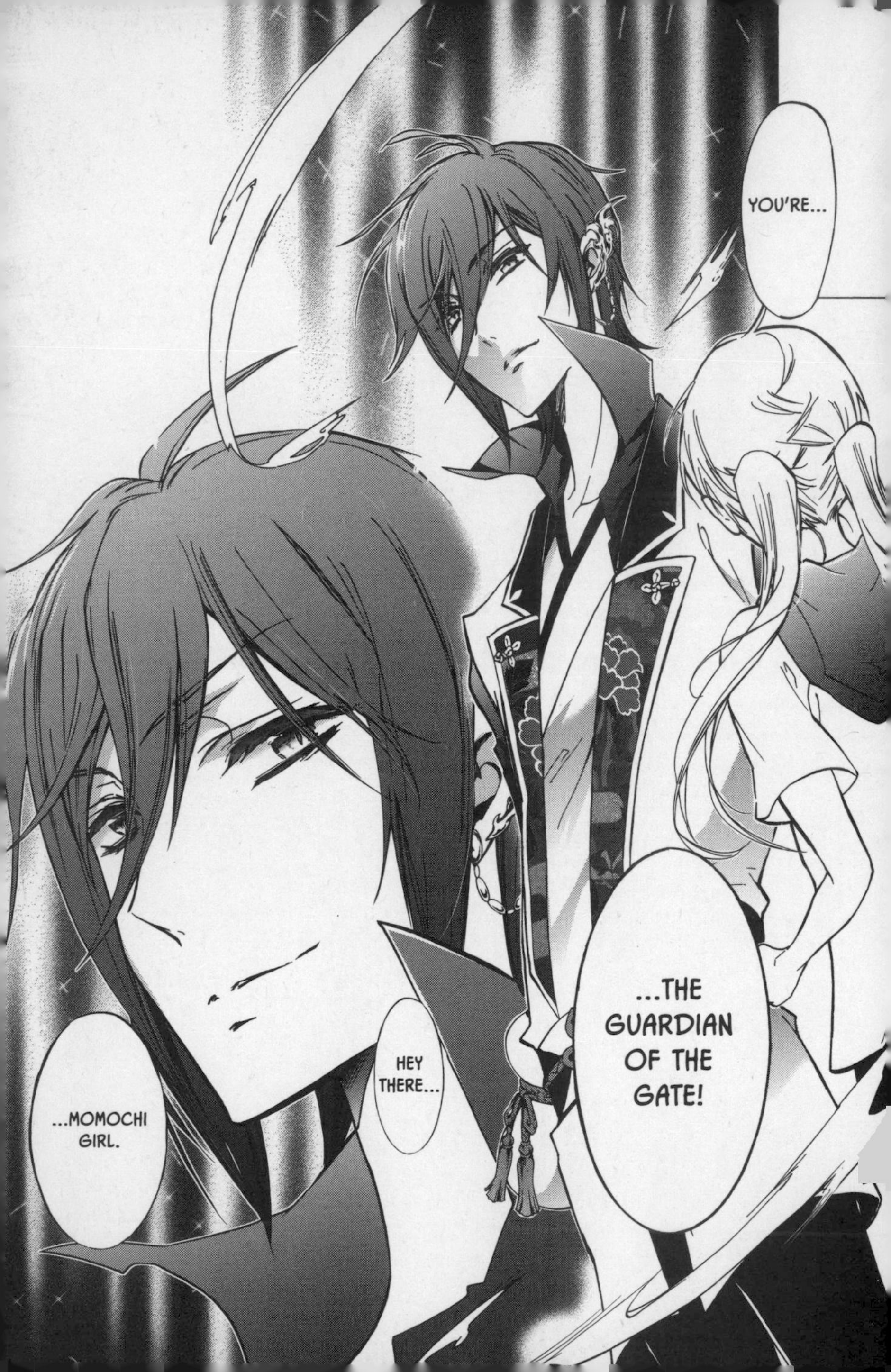
YOU'RE...
...THE GUARDIAN OF THE GATE!
HEY THERE...
...MOMOCHI GIRL.

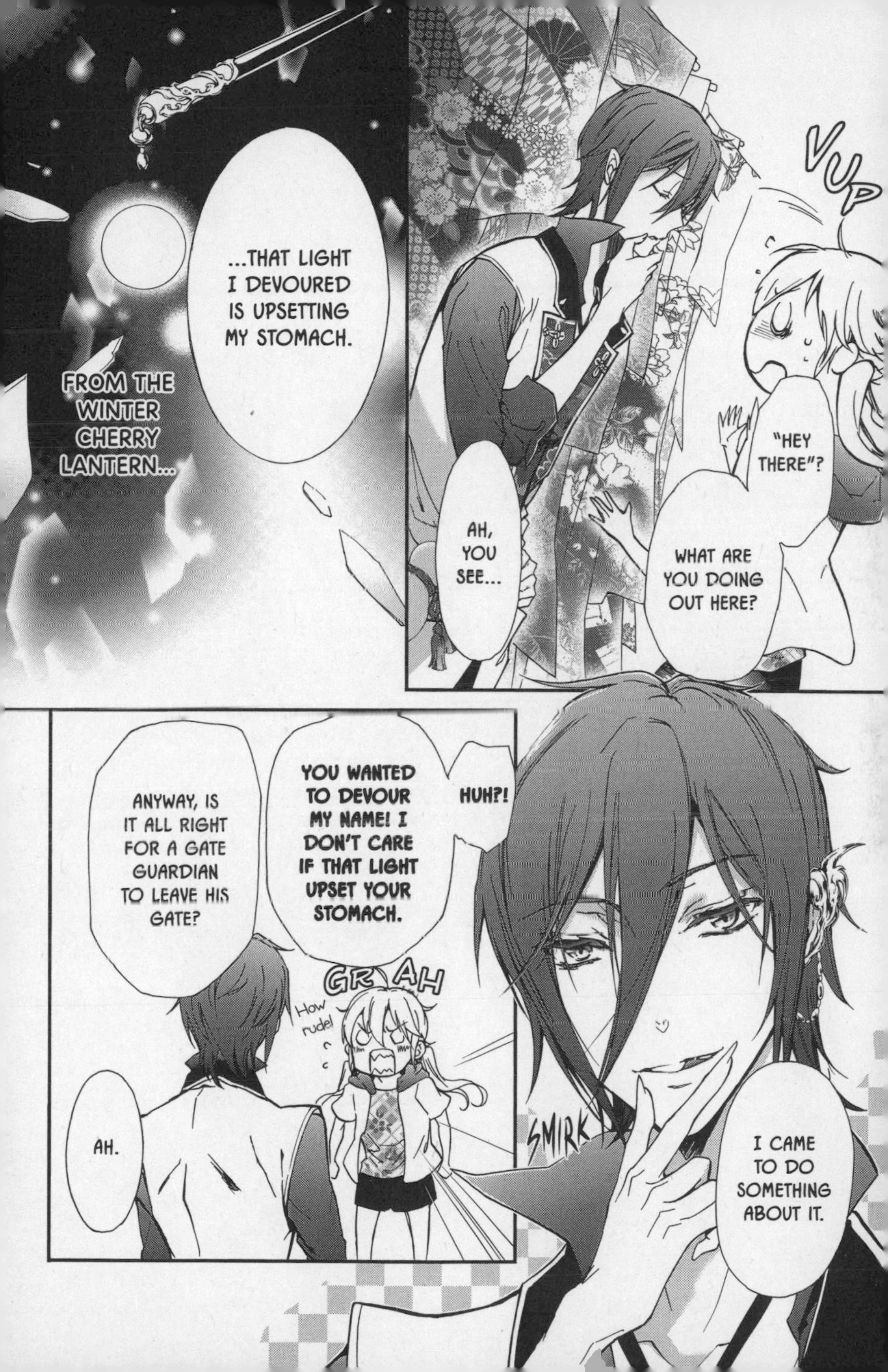
VUP
"HEY THERE"?
WHAT ARE YOU DOING OUT HERE?
AH, YOU SEE...
...THAT LIGHT I DEVOURED IS UPSETTING MY STOMACH.
FROM THE WINTER CHERRY LANTERN...
I CAME TO DO SOMETHING ABOUT IT.
SMIRK
HUH?!
YOU WANTED TO DEVOUR MY NAME! I DON'T CARE IF THAT LIGHT UPSET YOUR STOMACH.
GRAAH
How rude!
ANYWAY, IS IT ALL RIGHT FOR A GATE GUARDIAN TO LEAVE HIS GATE?
AH.

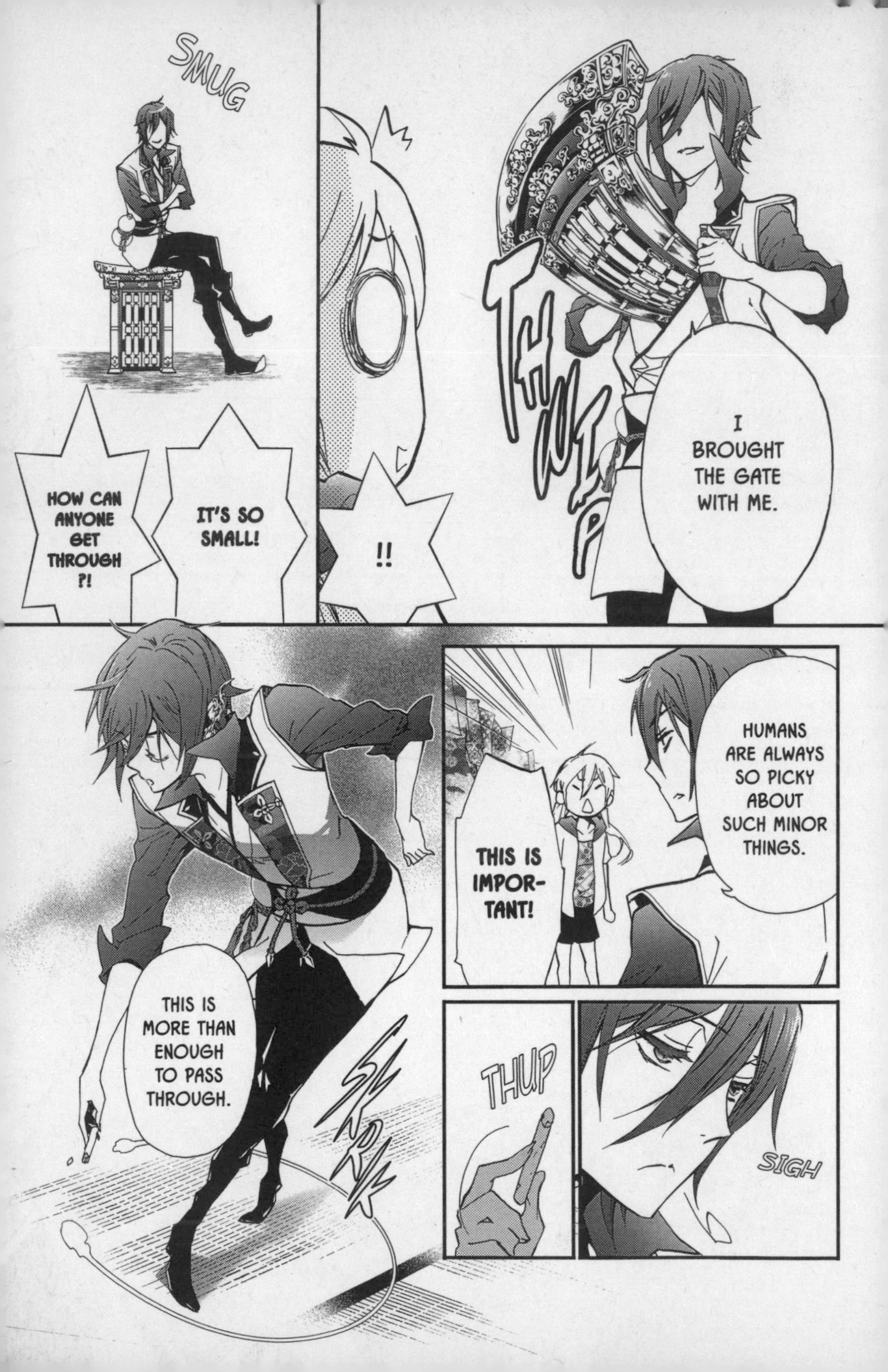
THWIP
I BROUGHT THE GATE WITH ME.
!!
SMUG
IT'S SO SMALL!
HOW CAN ANYONE GET THROUGH ?!
HUMANS ARE ALWAYS SO PICKY ABOUT SUCH MINOR THINGS.
THIS IS IMPOR-TANT!
SIGH
THUP
THIS IS MORE THAN ENOUGH TO PASS THROUGH.
SKRRK

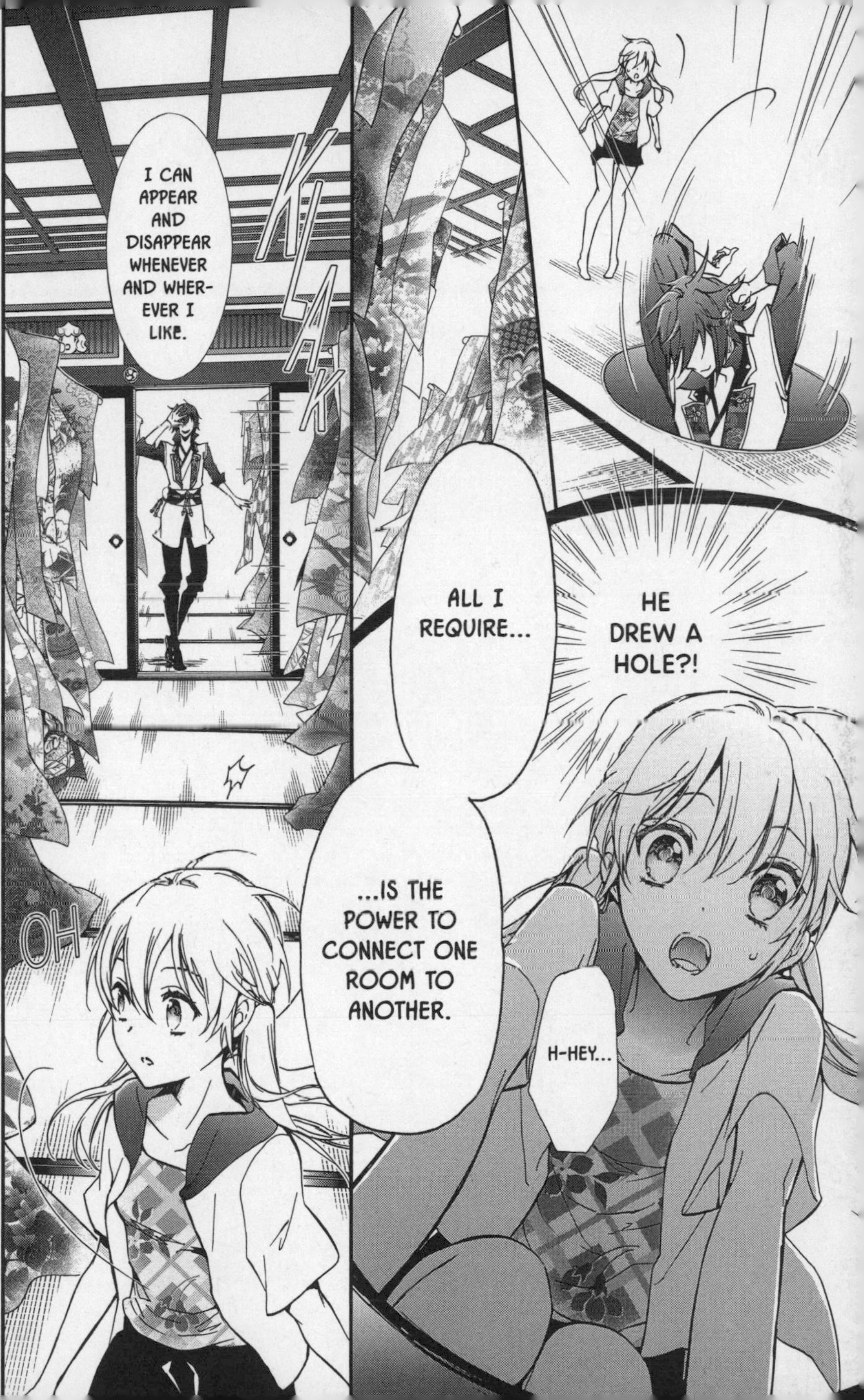
HE DREW A HOLE?!
H-HEY...
ALL I REQUIRE...
...IS THE POWER TO CONNECT ONE ROOM TO ANOTHER.
KLAK
I CAN APPEAR AND DISAPPEAR WHENEVER AND WHER-EVER I LIKE.
OH

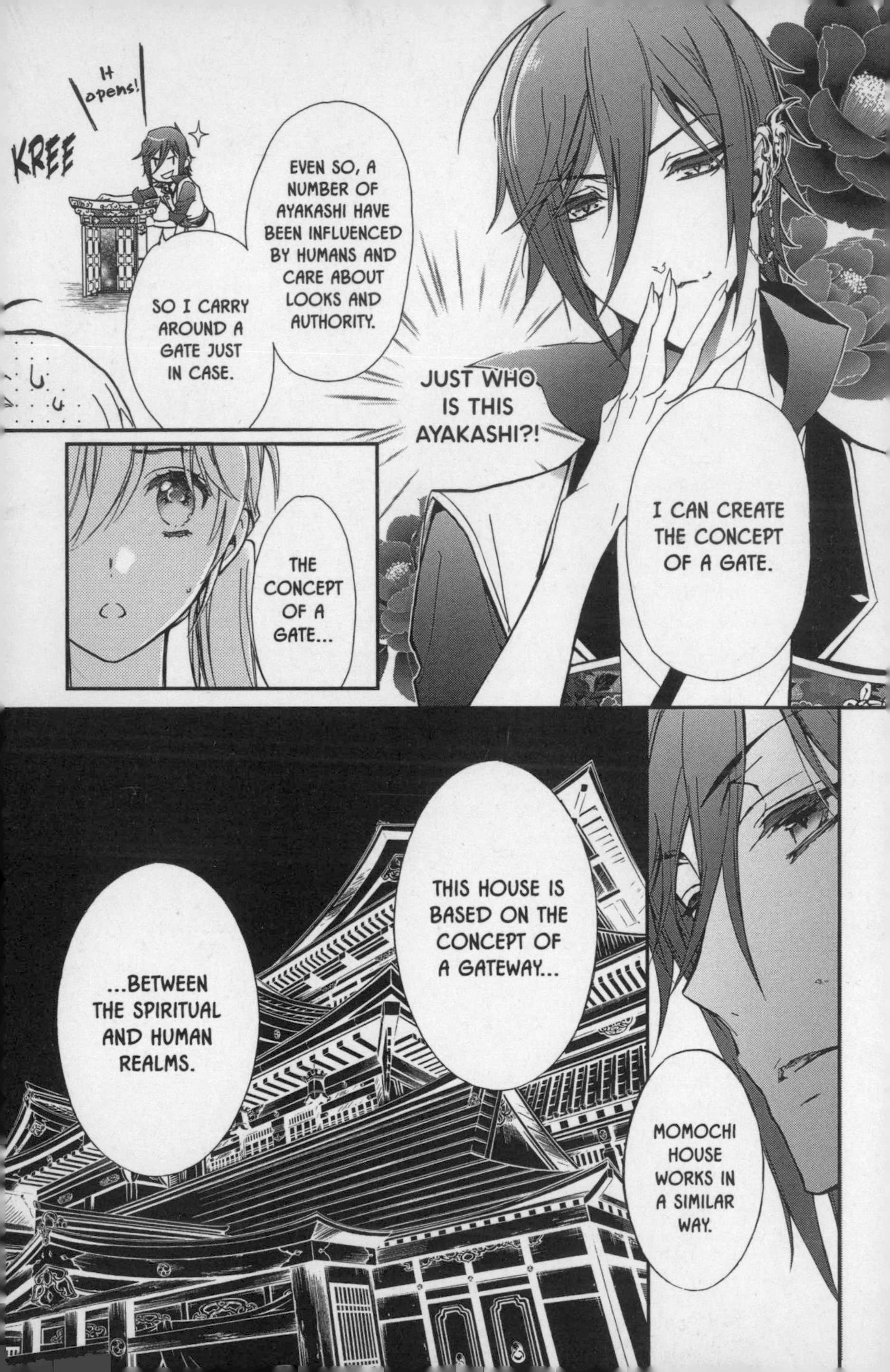
JUST WHO IS THIS AYAKASHI?!
I CAN CREATE THE CONCEPT OF A GATE.
It opens!
KREE
EVEN SO, A NUMBER OF AYAKASHI HAVE BEEN INFLUENCED BY HUMANS AND CARE ABOUT LOOKS AND AUTHORITY.
SO I CARRY AROUND A GATE JUST IN CASE.
THE CONCEPT OF A GATE...
MOMOCHI HOUSE WORKS IN A SIMILAR WAY.
THIS HOUSE IS BASED ON THE CONCEPT OF A GATEWAY...
...BETWEEN THE SPIRITUAL AND HUMAN REALMS.

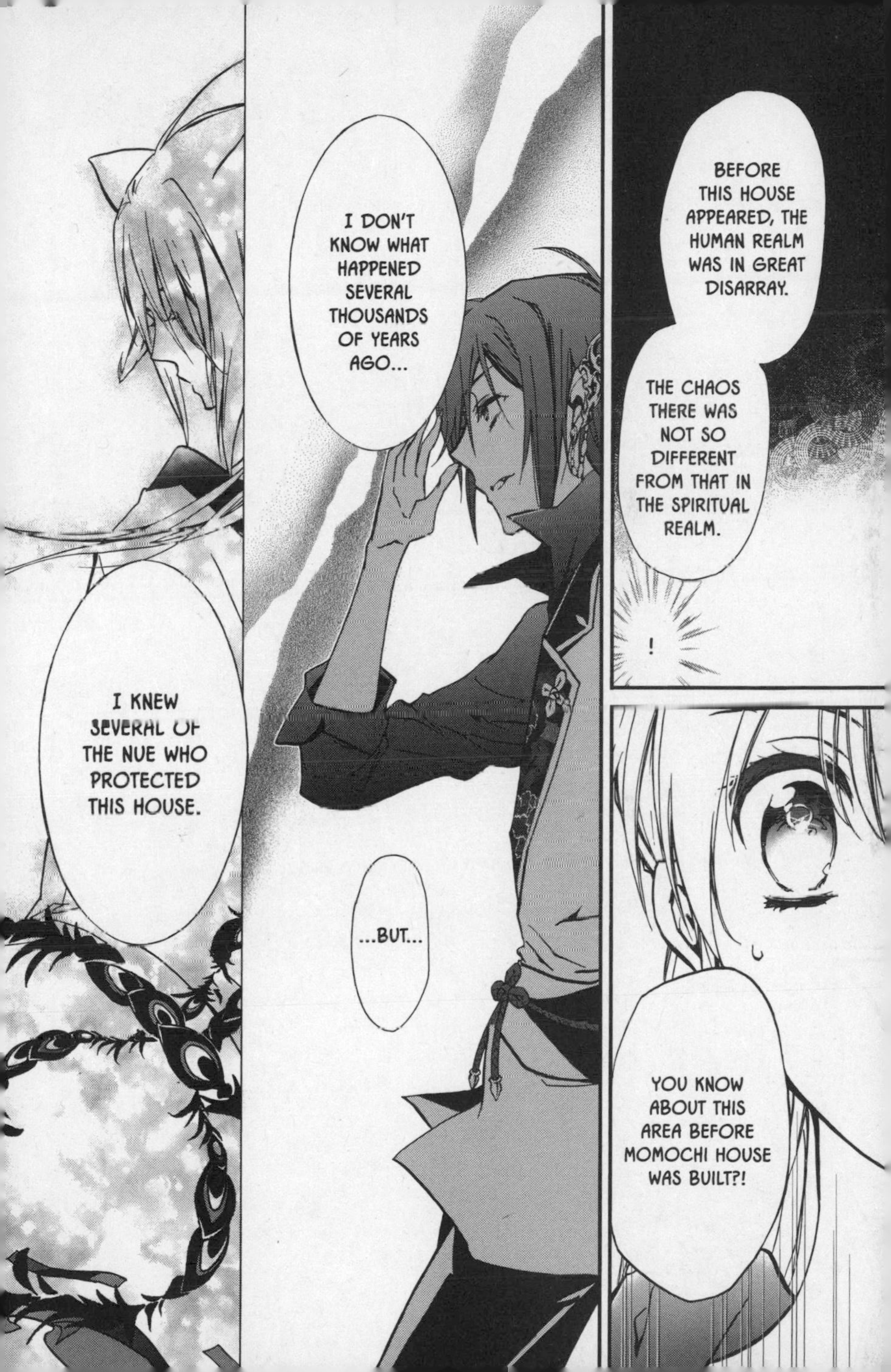
BEFORE THIS HOUSE APPEARED, THE HUMAN REALM WAS IN GREAT DISARRAY.
THE CHAOS THERE WAS NOT SO DIFFERENT FROM THAT IN THE SPIRITUAL REALM.
!
YOU KNOW ABOUT THIS AREA BEFORE MOMOCHI HOUSE WAS BUILT?!
I DON'T KNOW WHAT HAPPENED SEVERAL THOUSANDS OF YEARS AGO...
...BUT...
I KNEW SEVERAL OF THE NUE WHO PROTECTED THIS HOUSE.

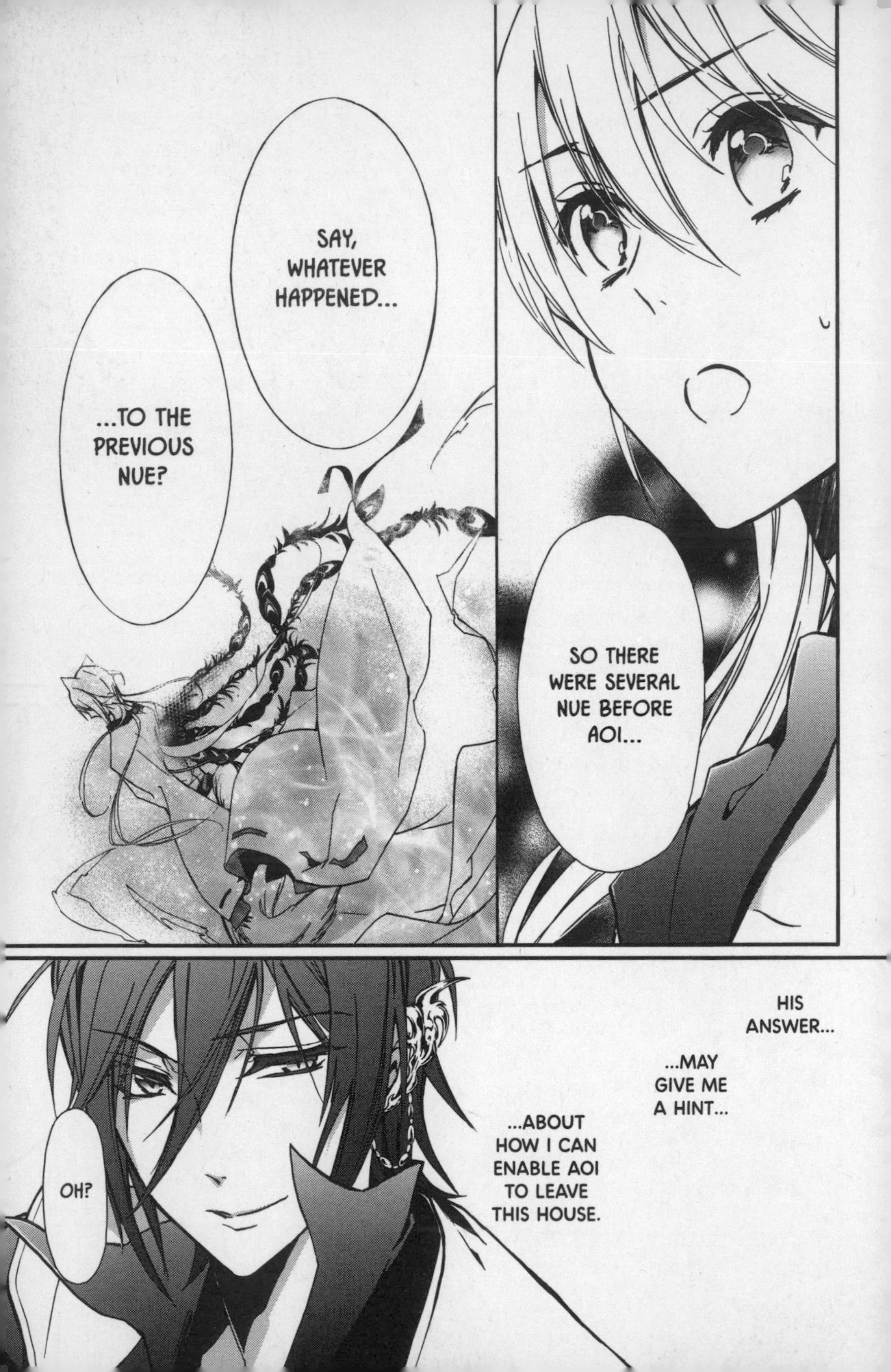
SO THERE WERE SEVERAL NUE BEFORE AOI...
SAY, WHATEVER HAPPENED...
...TO THE PREVIOUS NUE?
HIS ANSWER...
...MAY GIVE ME A HINT...
...ABOUT HOW I CAN ENABLE AOI TO LEAVE THIS HOUSE.
OH?

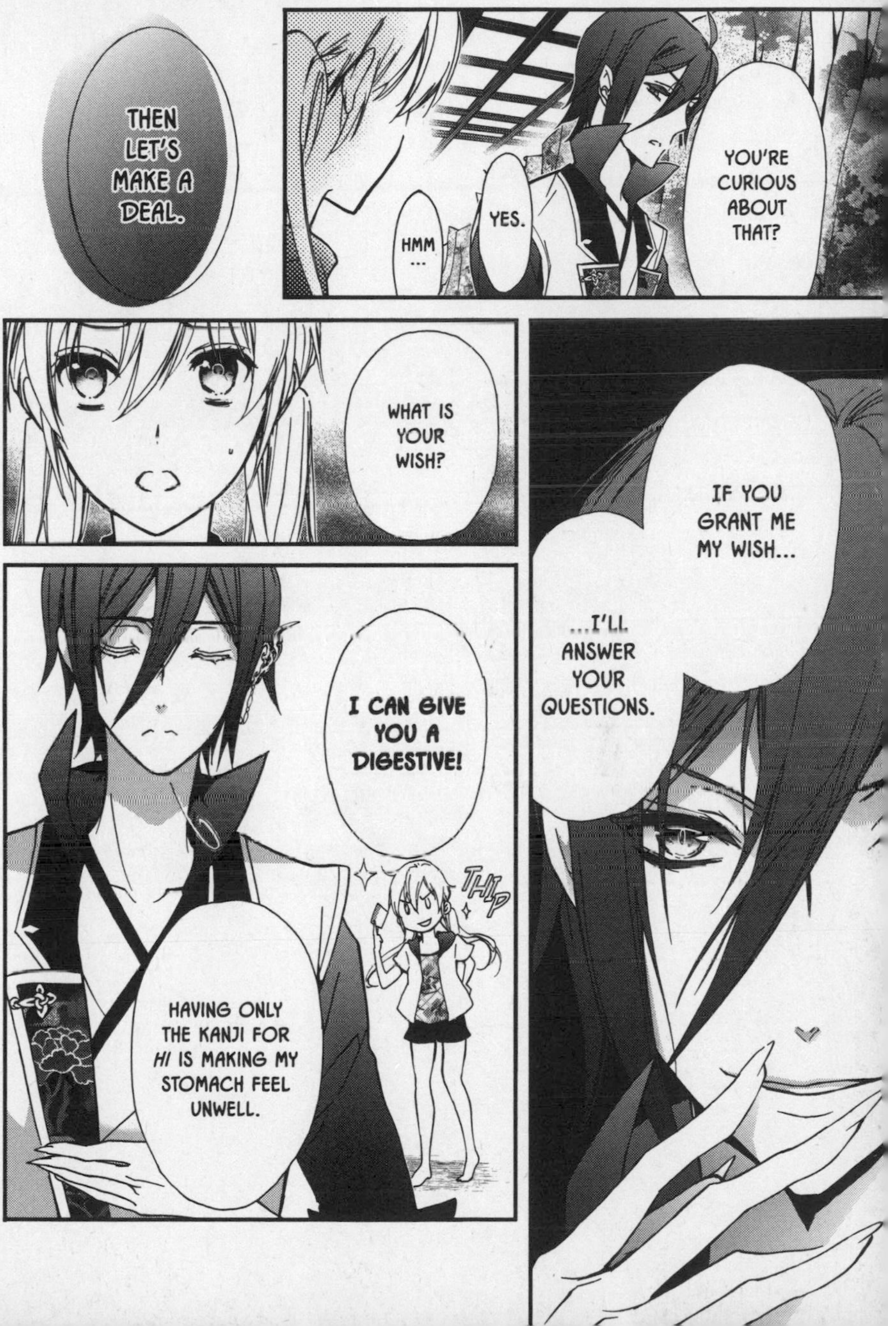
YOU'RE CURIOUS ABOUT THAT?
YES.
HMM...
THEN LET'S MAKE A DEAL.
IF YOU GRANT ME MY WISH...
...I'LL ANSWER YOUR QUESTIONS.
WHAT IS YOUR WISH?
I CAN GIVE YOU A DIGESTIVE!
THIP
HAVING ONLY THE KANJI FOR *HI* IS MAKING MY STOMACH FEEL UNWELL.

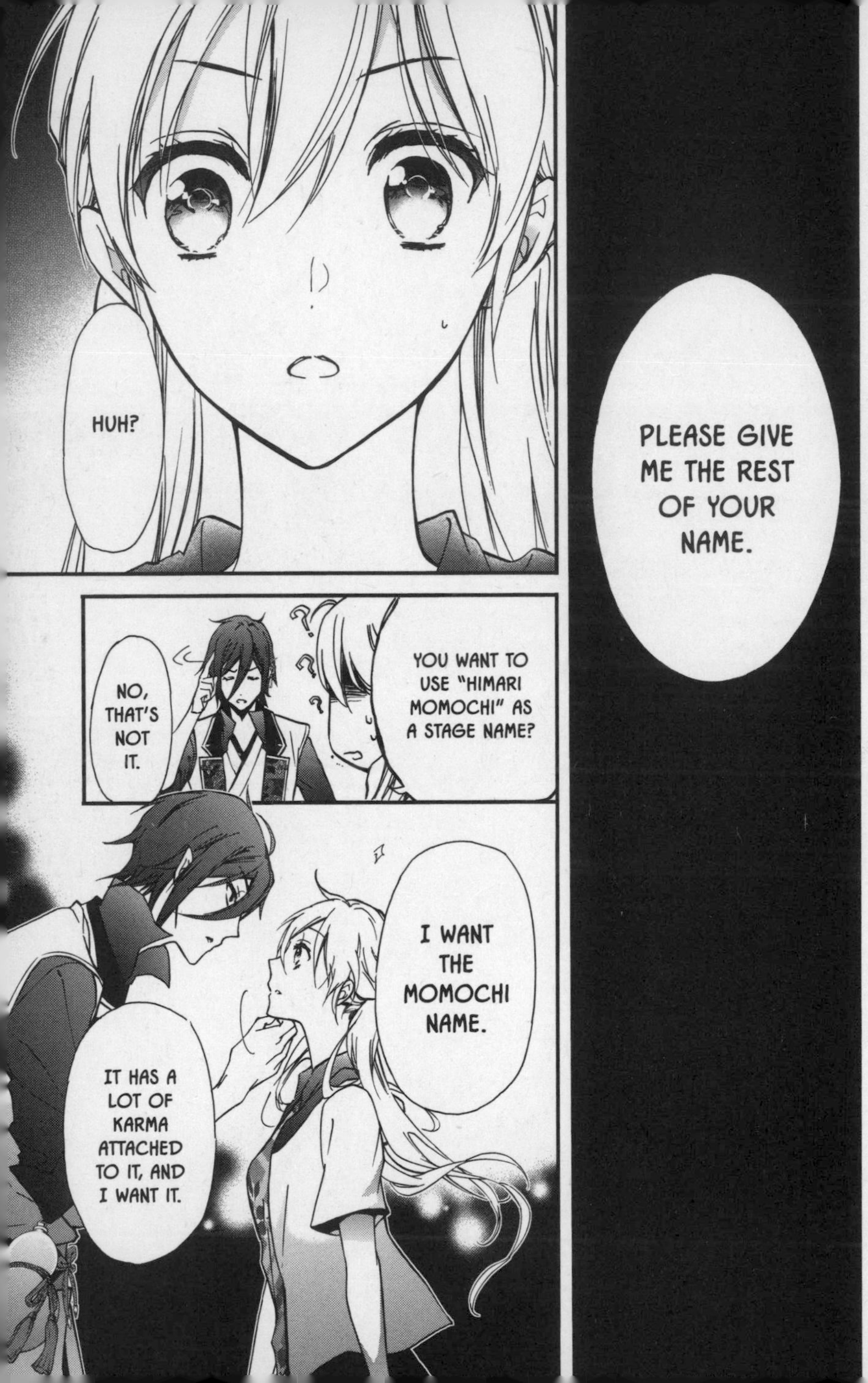
PLEASE GIVE ME THE REST OF YOUR NAME.
HUH?
YOU WANT TO USE "HIMARI MOMOCHI" AS A STAGE NAME?
NO, THAT'S NOT IT.
I WANT THE MOMOCHI NAME.
IT HAS A LOT OF KARMA ATTACHED TO IT, AND I WANT IT.

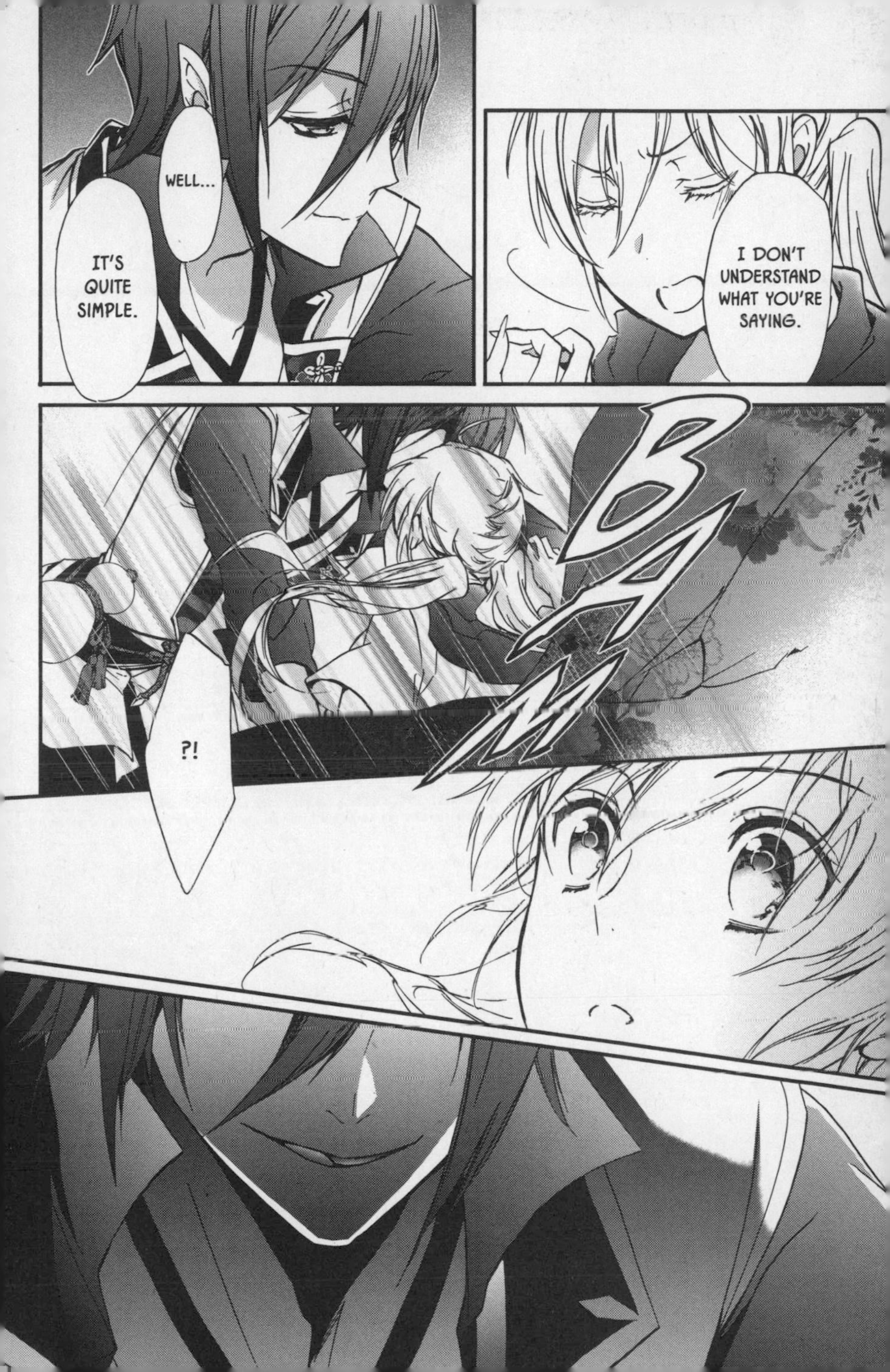
I DON'T UNDERSTAND WHAT YOU'RE SAYING.
WELL...
IT'S QUITE SIMPLE.
BAM
?!

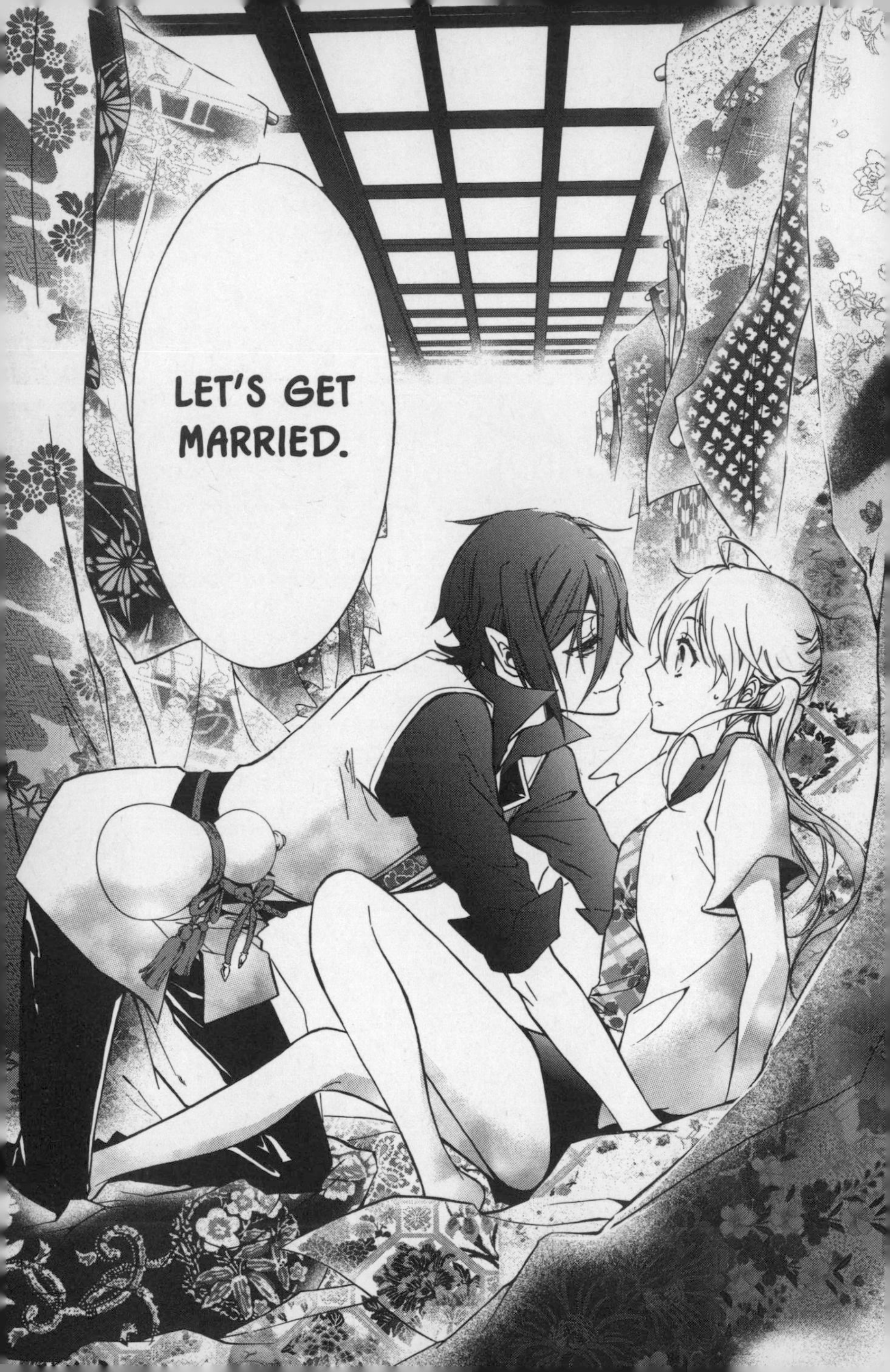
LET'S GET MARRIED.

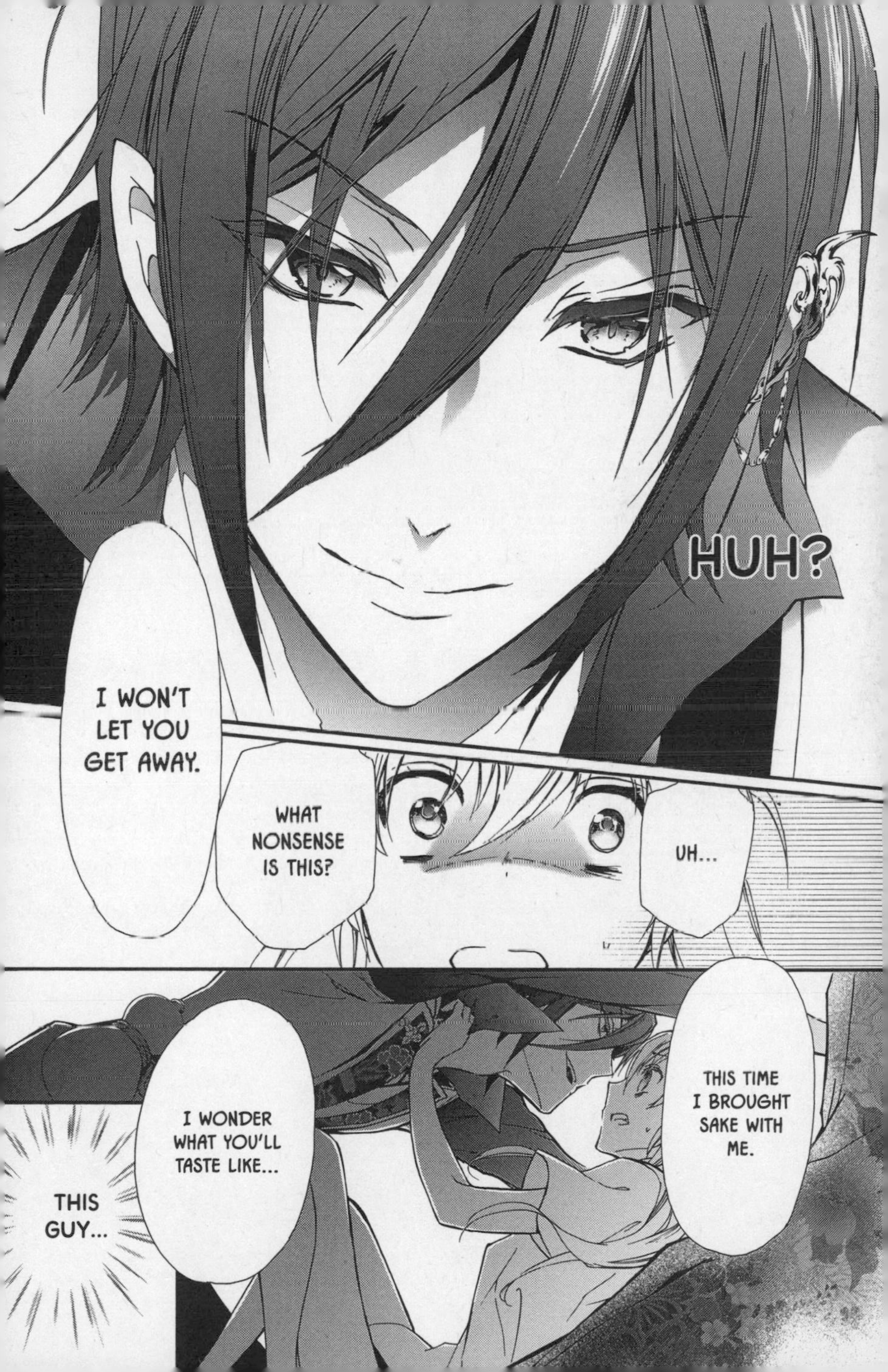
HUH?
I WON'T LET YOU GET AWAY.
UH...
WHAT NONSENSE IS THIS?
THIS TIME I BROUGHT SAKE WITH ME.
I WONDER WHAT YOU'LL TASTE LIKE...
THIS GUY...

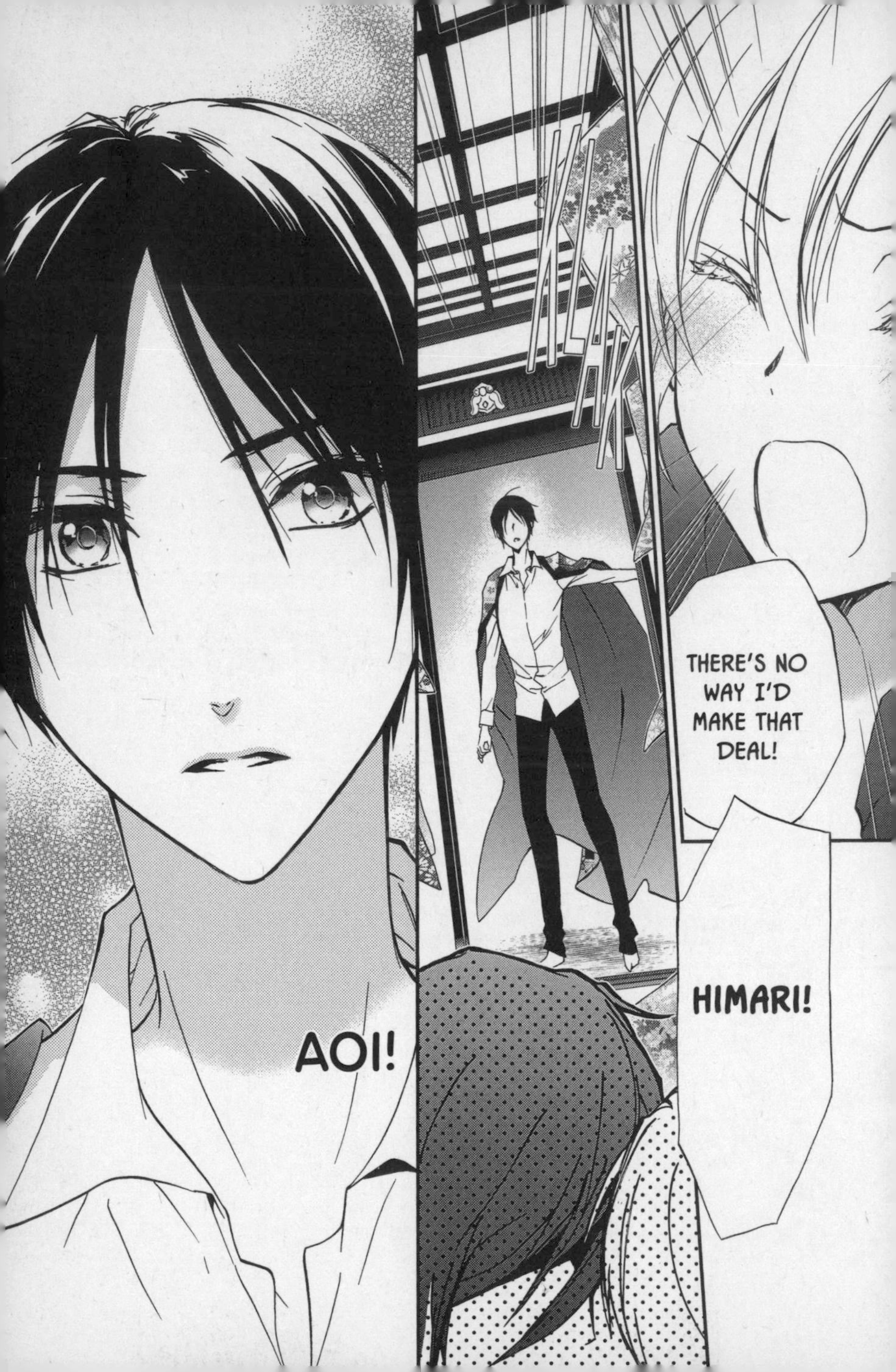
THERE'S NO WAY I'D MAKE THAT DEAL!
KLAK
HIMARI!
AOI!

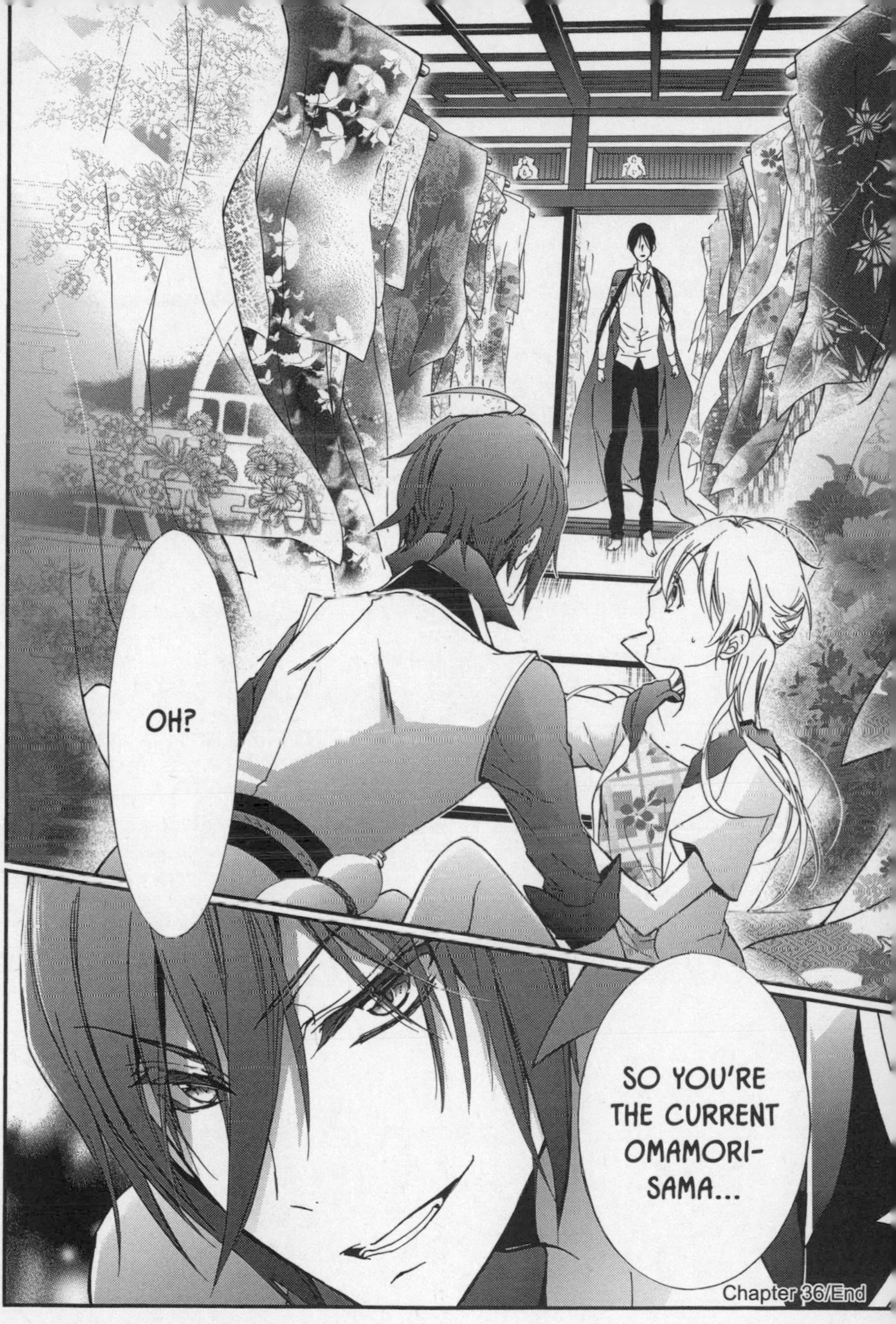
OH?
SO YOU'RE THE CURRENT OMAMORI-SAMA...
Chapter 36/End

The DEMON PRINCE *of* MOMOCHI HOUSE

The DEMON PRINCE of MOMOCHI HOUSE

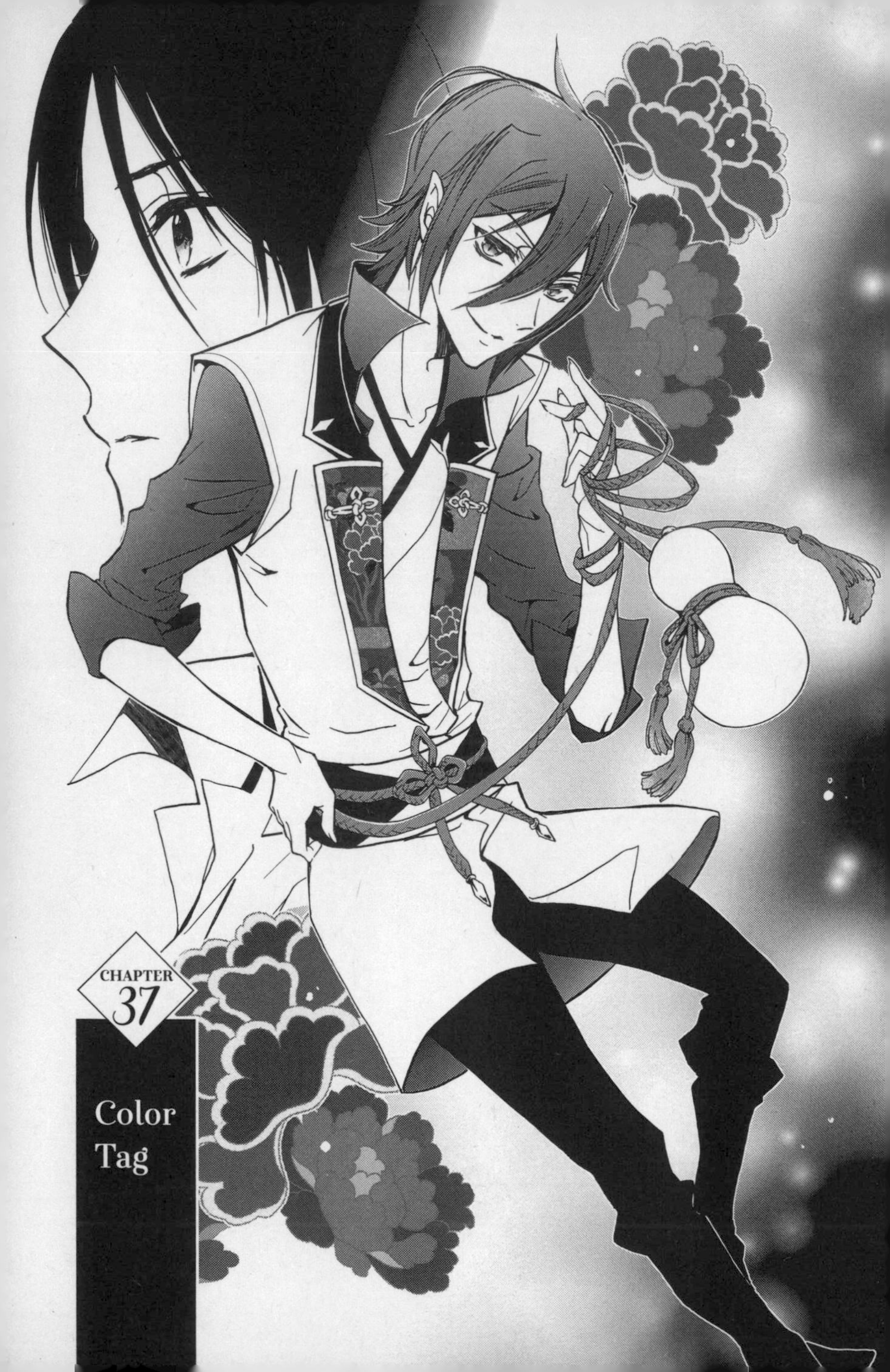
CHAPTER
37
Color
Tag

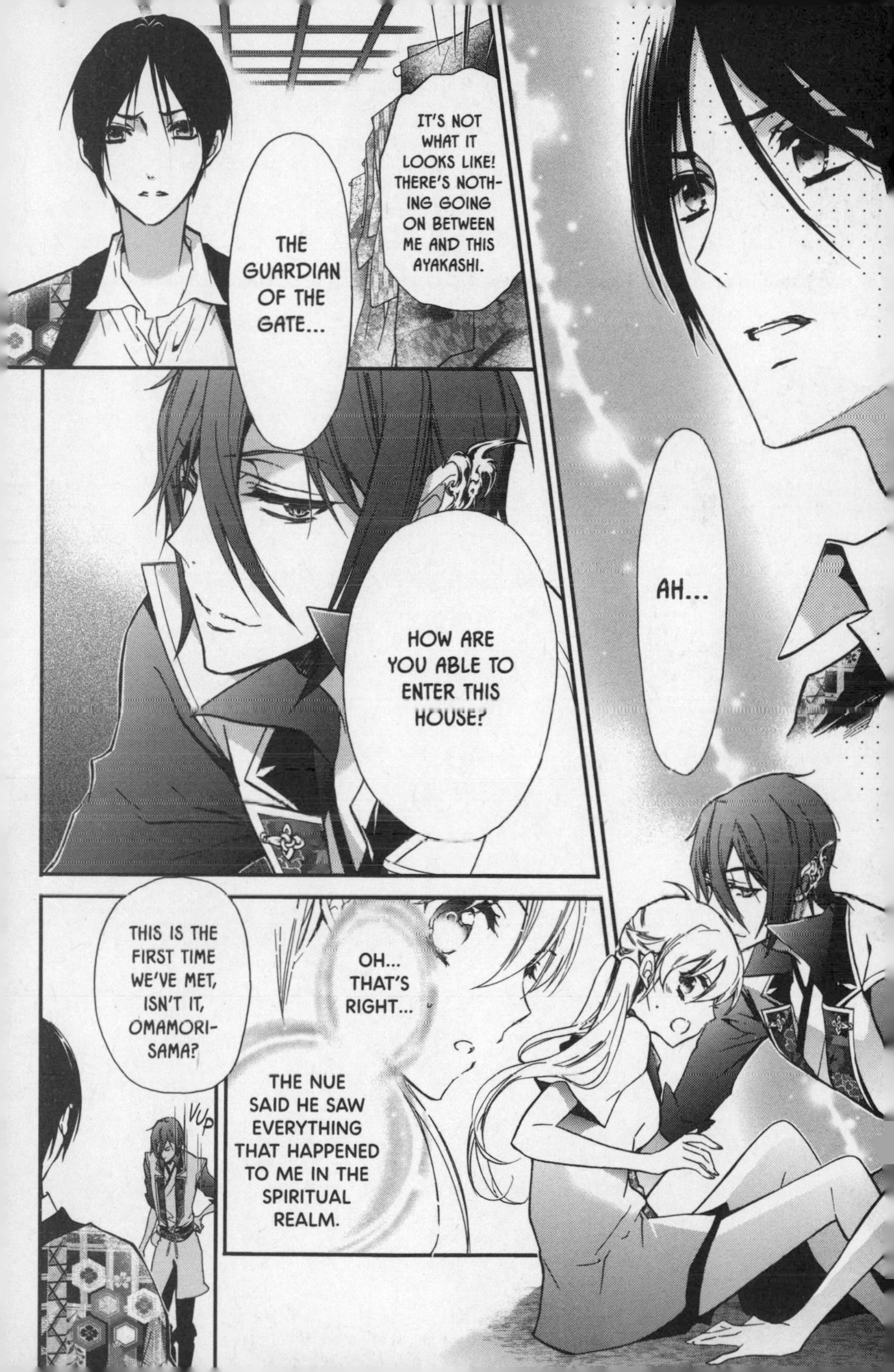
AH...
IT'S NOT WHAT IT LOOKS LIKE! THERE'S NOTHING GOING ON BETWEEN ME AND THIS AYAKASHI.
THE GUARDIAN OF THE GATE...
HOW ARE YOU ABLE TO ENTER THIS HOUSE?
OH... THAT'S RIGHT...
THE NUE SAID HE SAW EVERYTHING THAT HAPPENED TO ME IN THE SPIRITUAL REALM.
THIS IS THE FIRST TIME WE'VE MET, ISN'T IT, OMAMORI-SAMA?
VUP

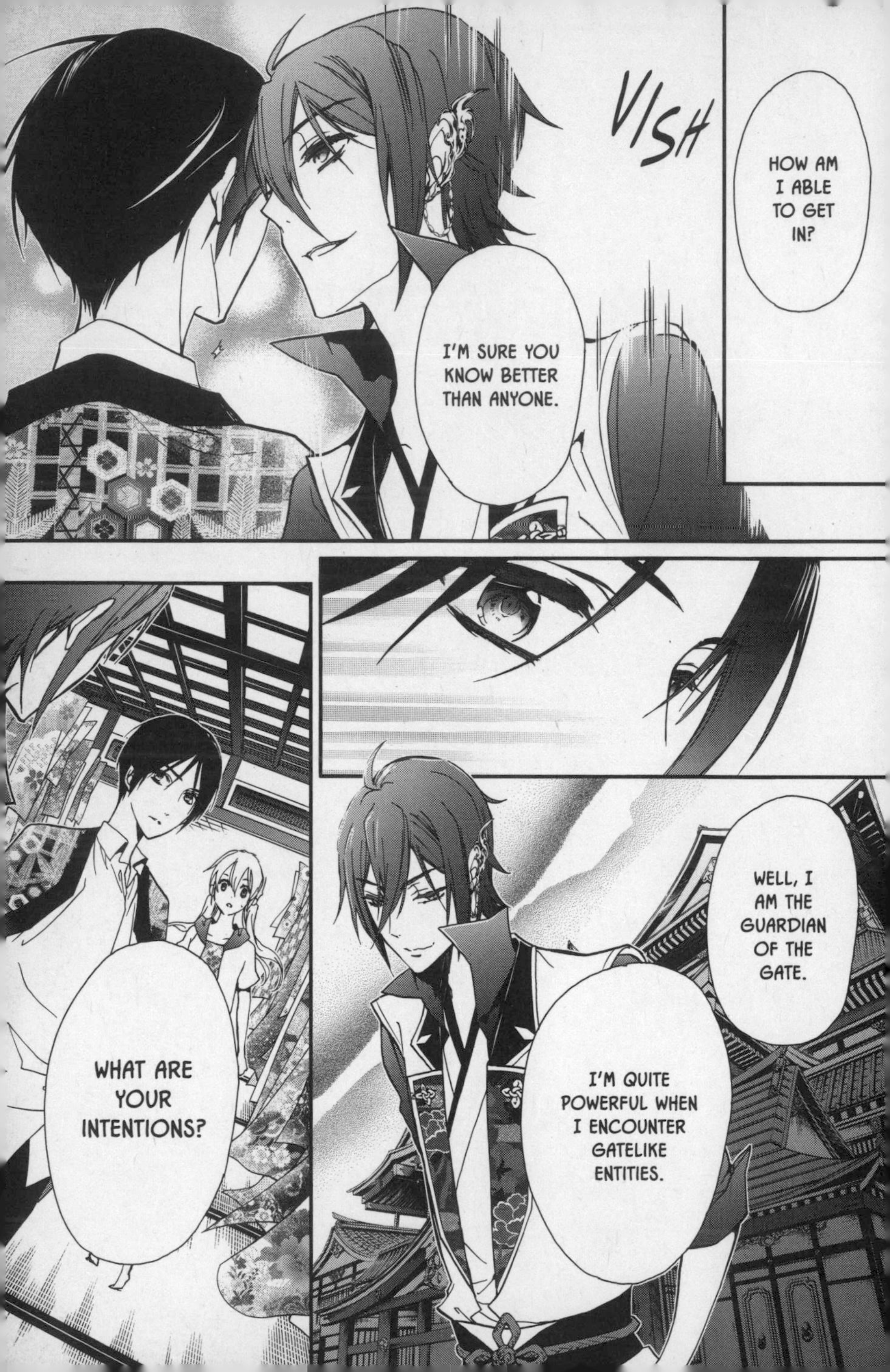
HOW AM I ABLE TO GET IN?
VISH
I'M SURE YOU KNOW BETTER THAN ANYONE.
WELL, I AM THE GUARDIAN OF THE GATE.
I'M QUITE POWERFUL WHEN I ENCOUNTER GATELIKE ENTITIES.
WHAT ARE YOUR INTENTIONS?

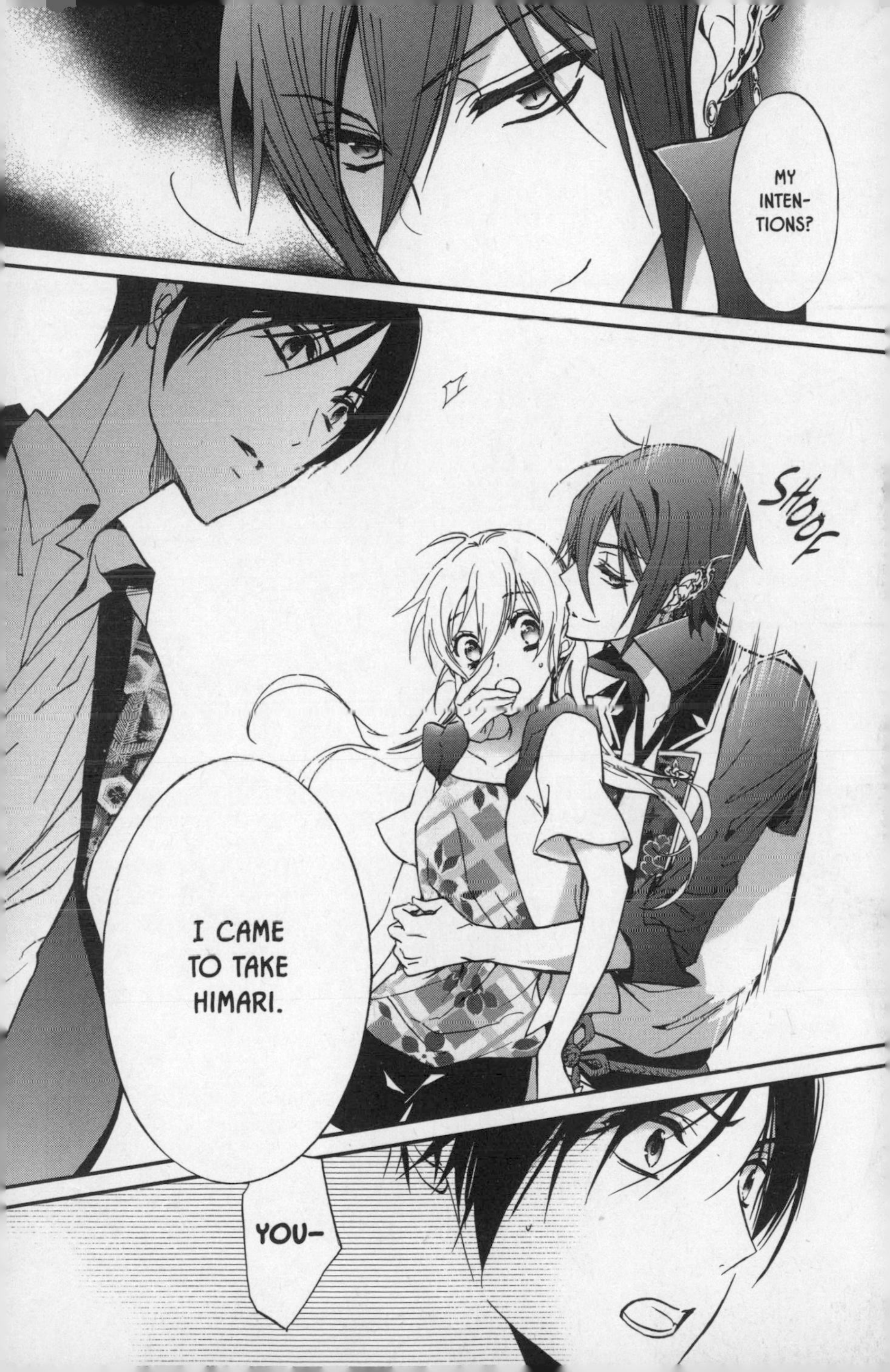
MY INTEN-TIONS?
SHOOP
I CAME TO TAKE HIMARI.
YOU-

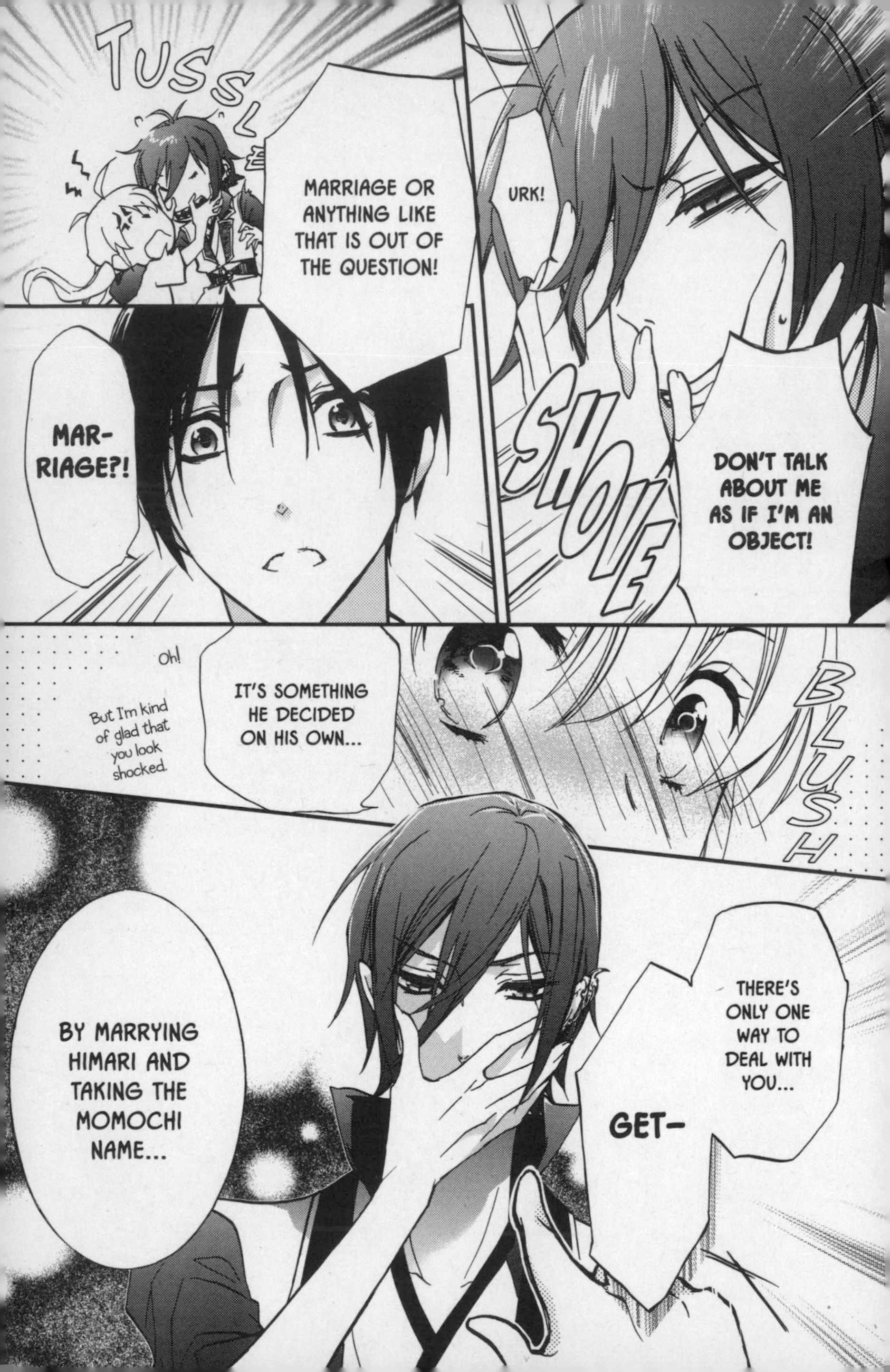
URK!
SHOVE
DON'T TALK ABOUT ME AS IF I'M AN OBJECT!
TUSSLE
MARRIAGE OR ANYTHING LIKE THAT IS OUT OF THE QUESTION!
MAR-RIAGE?!
BLUSH
IT'S SOMETHING HE DECIDED ON HIS OWN...
Oh!
But I'm kind of glad that you look shocked.
THERE'S ONLY ONE WAY TO DEAL WITH YOU...
GET-
BY MARRYING HIMARI AND TAKING THE MOMOCHI NAME...

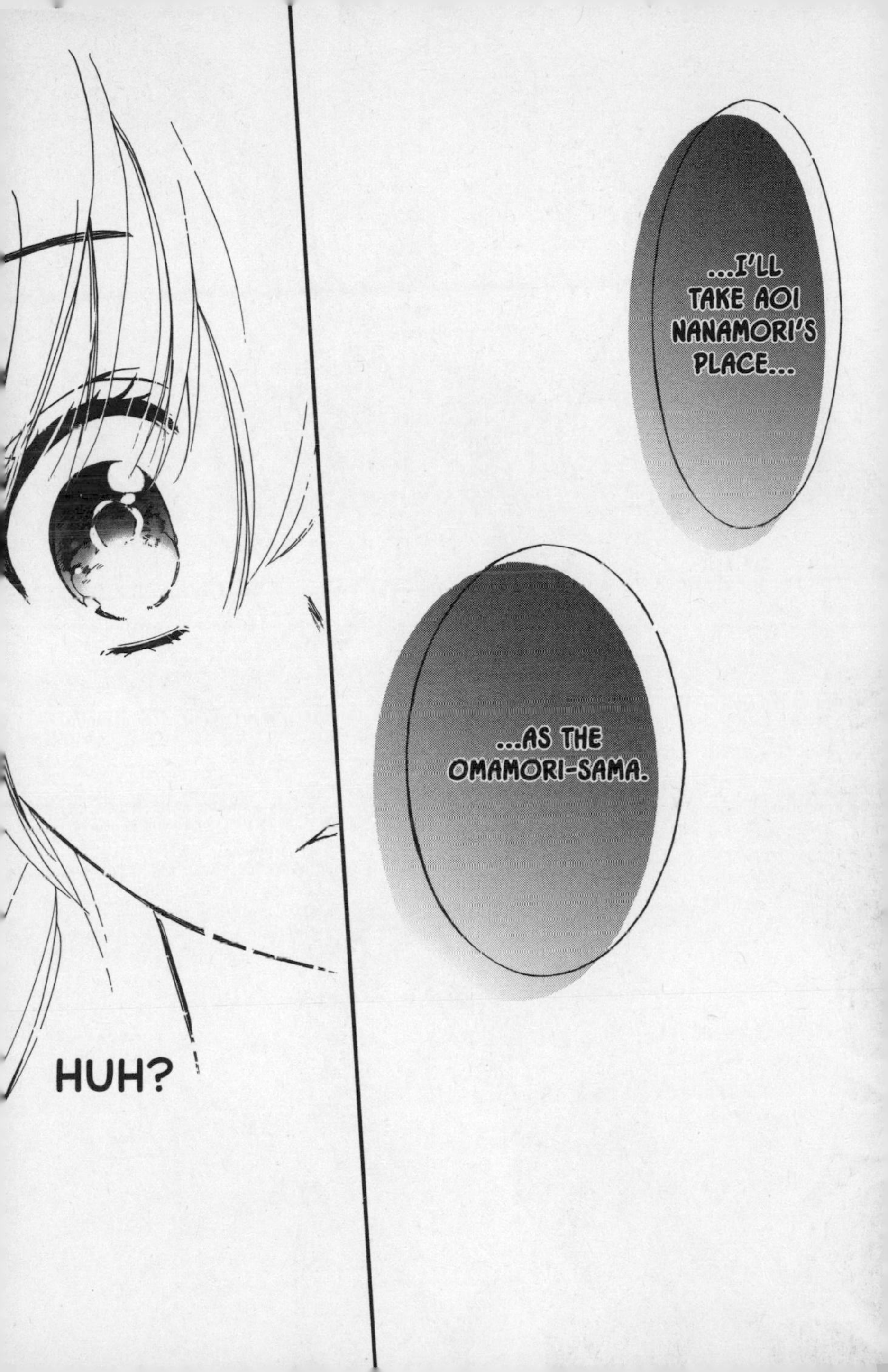
...I'LL TAKE AOI NANAMORI'S PLACE...
...AS THE OMAMORI-SAMA.
HUH?

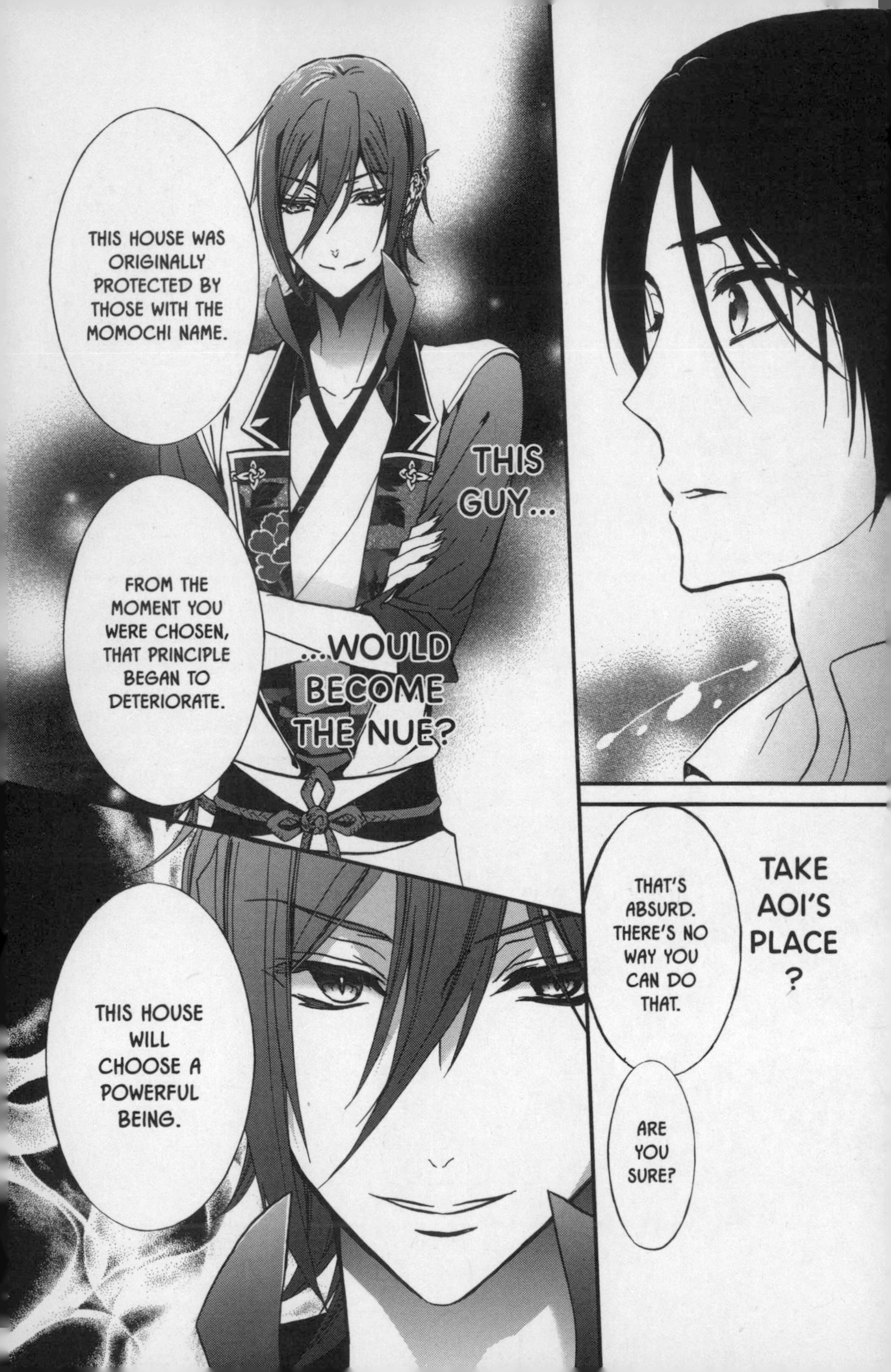
THIS HOUSE WAS ORIGINALLY PROTECTED BY THOSE WITH THE MOMOCHI NAME.
THIS GUY...
FROM THE MOMENT YOU WERE CHOSEN, THAT PRINCIPLE BEGAN TO DETERIORATE.
...WOULD BECOME THE NUE?
TAKE AOI'S PLACE?
THAT'S ABSURD. THERE'S NO WAY YOU CAN DO THAT.
ARE YOU SURE?
THIS HOUSE WILL CHOOSE A POWERFUL BEING.

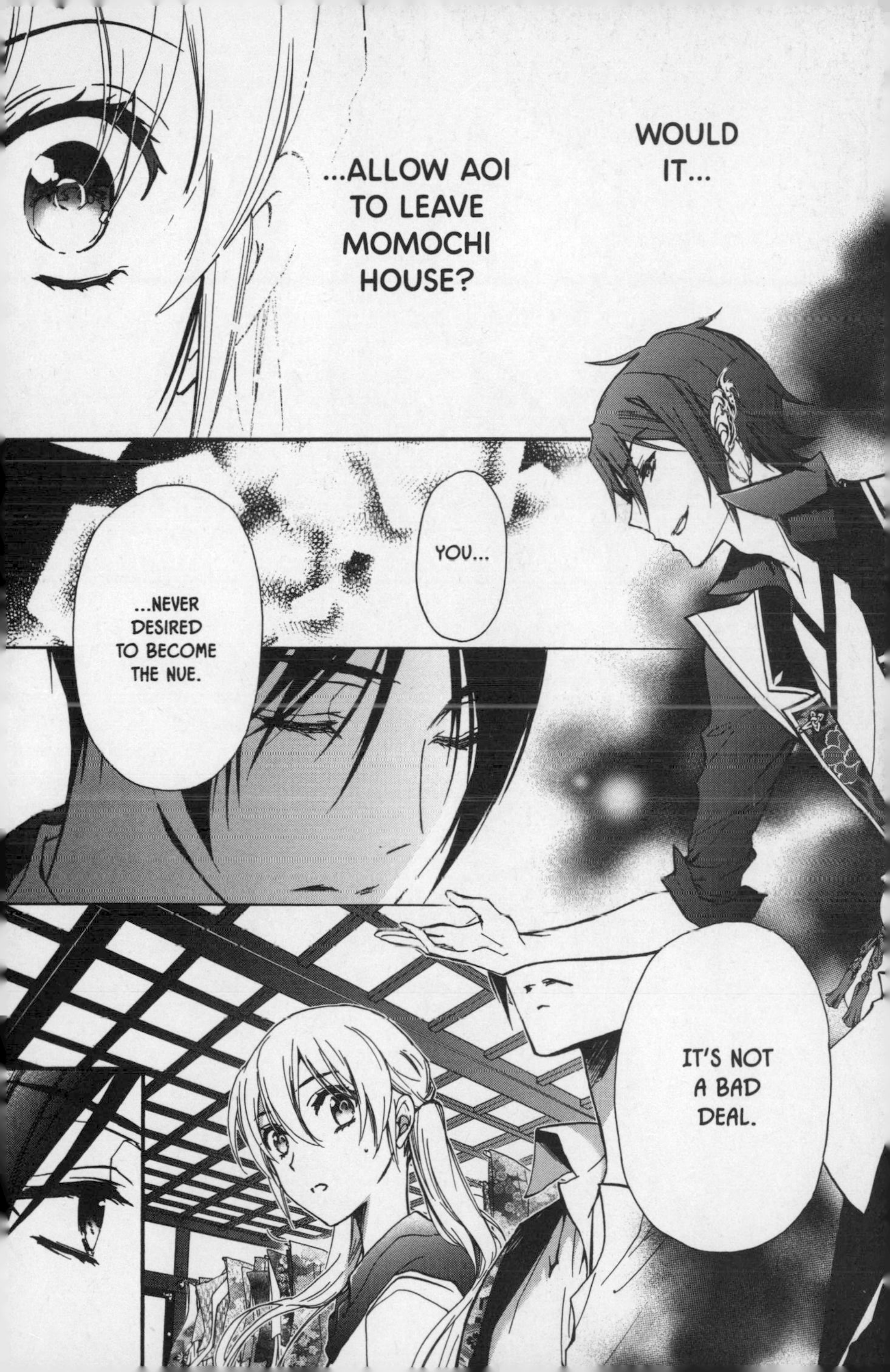
WOULD IT...
...ALLOW AOI TO LEAVE MOMOCHI HOUSE?
YOU...
...NEVER DESIRED TO BECOME THE NUE.
IT'S NOT A BAD DEAL.

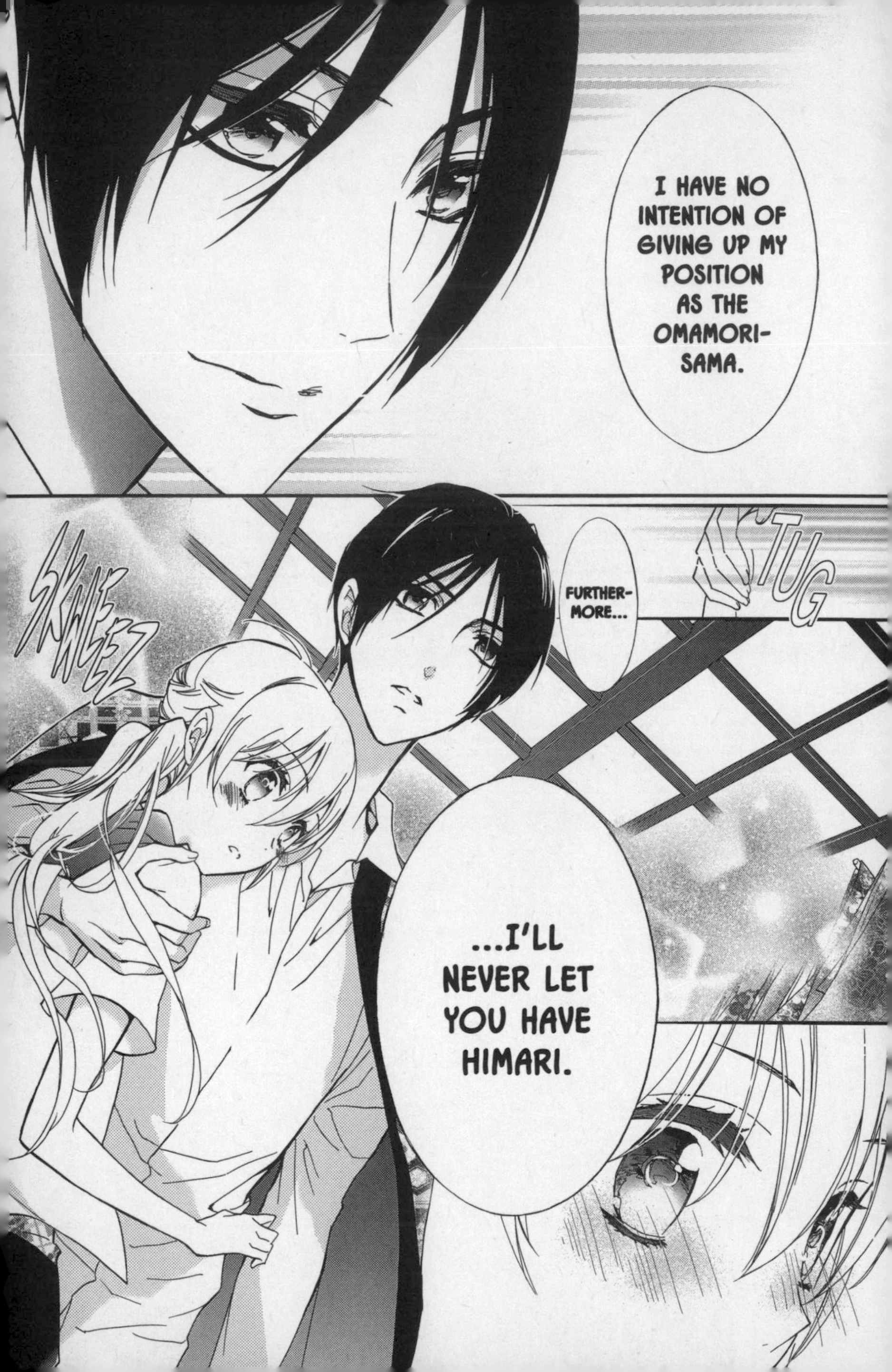
I HAVE NO INTENTION OF GIVING UP MY POSITION AS THE OMAMORI-SAMA.
TUG
FURTHER-MORE...
SKWEEZ
...I'LL NEVER LET YOU HAVE HIMARI.

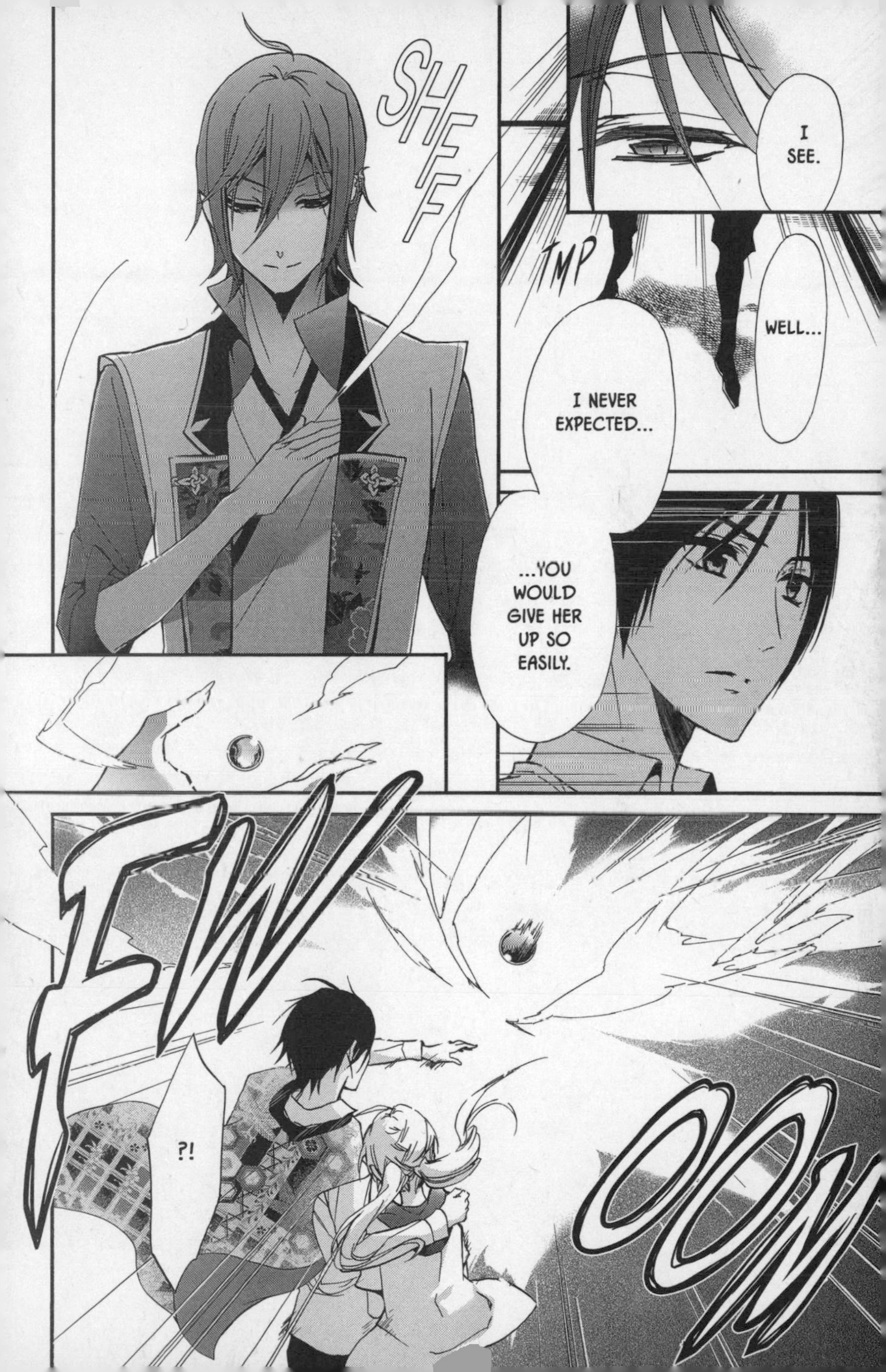
I SEE.
TMP
WELL...
I NEVER EXPECTED...
...YOU WOULD GIVE HER UP SO EASILY.
SHFF
FWOOM
?!

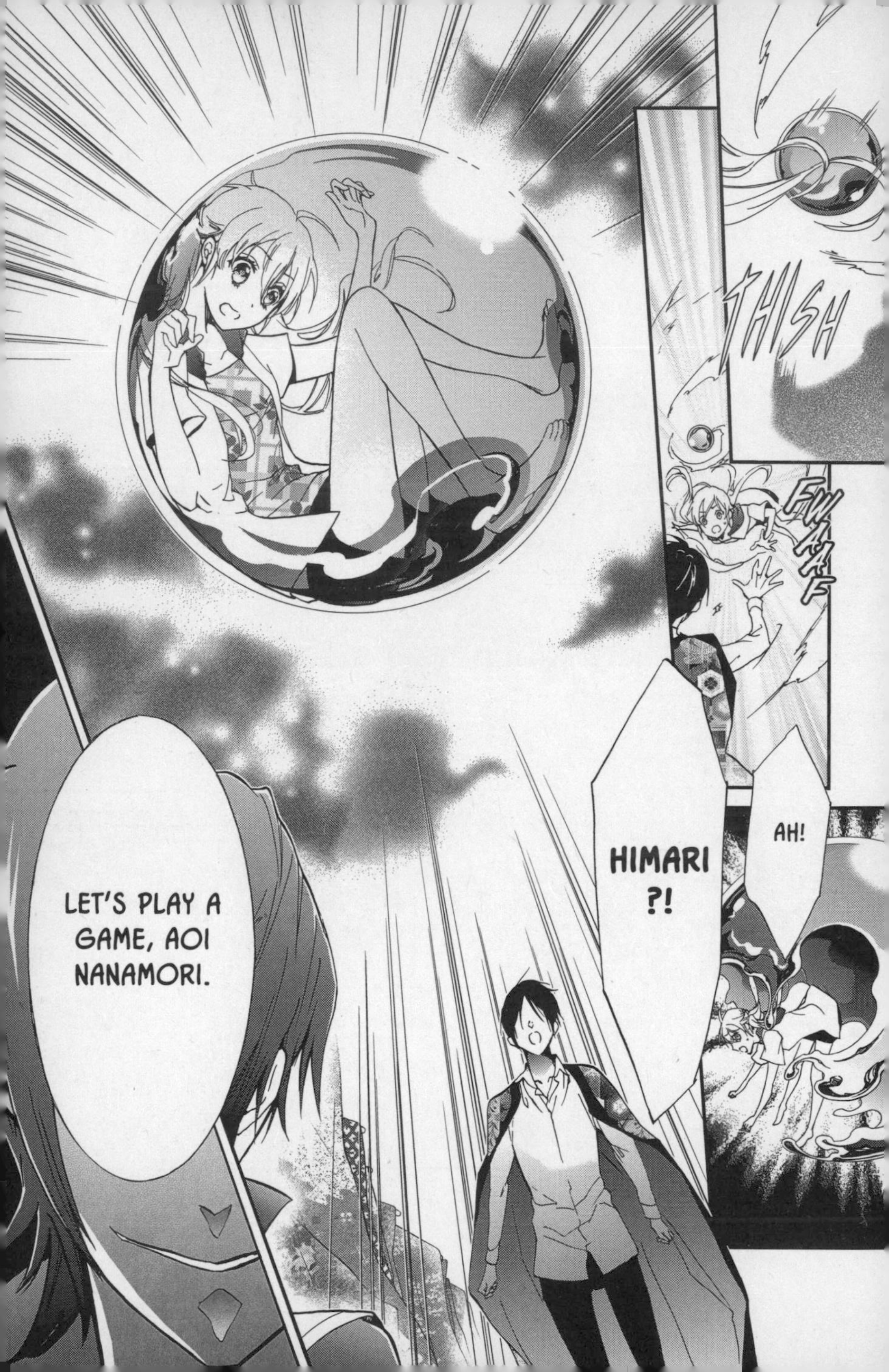
THISH
FWAAF
AH!
HIMARI?!
LET'S PLAY A GAME, AOI NANAMORI.

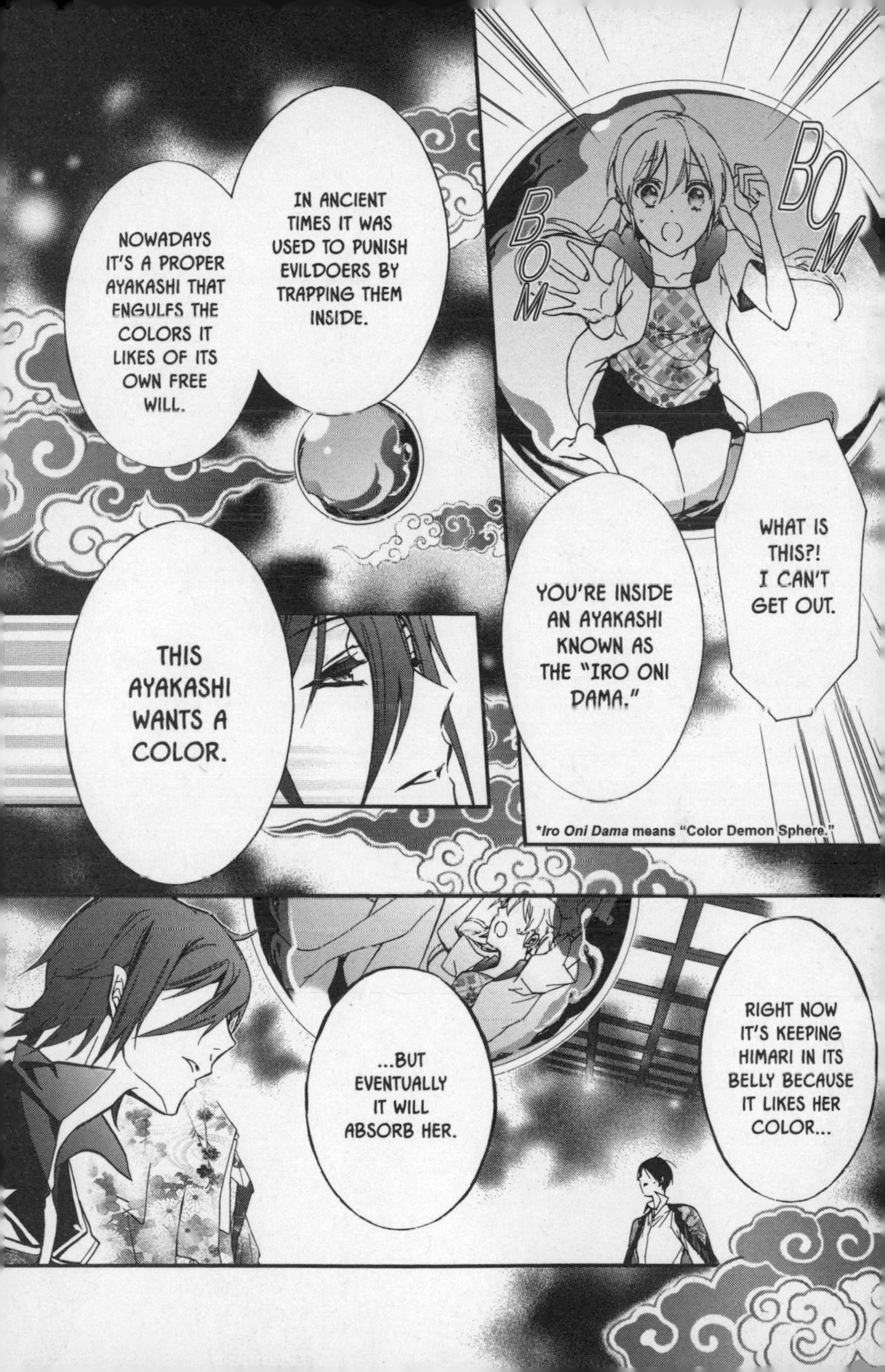
BOM
BOM
WHAT IS THIS?! I CAN'T GET OUT.
YOU'RE INSIDE AN AYAKASHI KNOWN AS THE "IRO ONI DAMA."
*Iro Oni Dama means "Color Demon Sphere."
IN ANCIENT TIMES IT WAS USED TO PUNISH EVILDOERS BY TRAPPING THEM INSIDE.
NOWADAYS IT'S A PROPER AYAKASHI THAT ENGULFS THE COLORS IT LIKES OF ITS OWN FREE WILL.
THIS AYAKASHI WANTS A COLOR.
RIGHT NOW IT'S KEEPING HIMARI IN ITS BELLY BECAUSE IT LIKES HER COLOR...
...BUT EVENTUALLY IT WILL ABSORB HER.

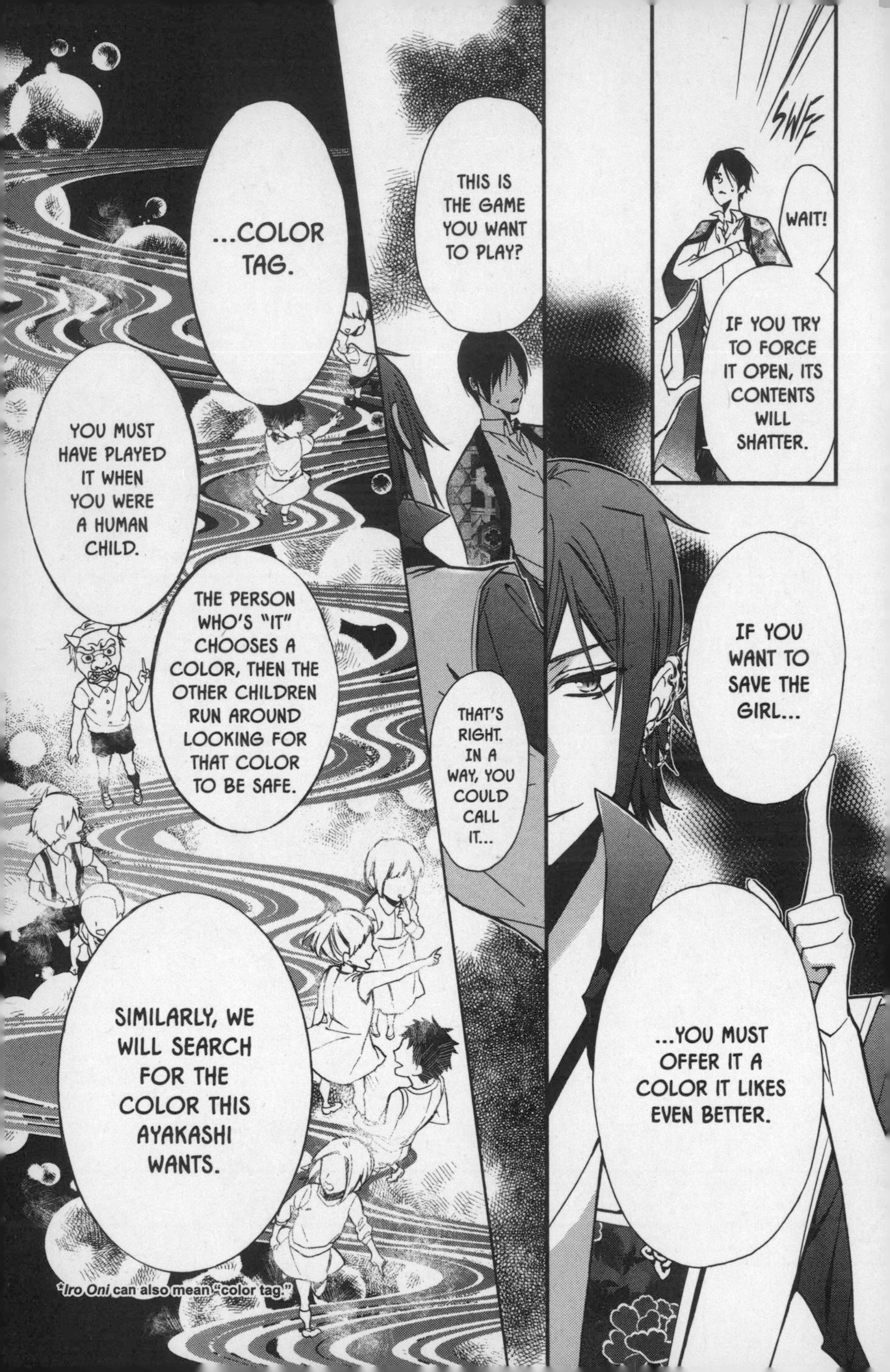
SWFF
WAIT!
IF YOU TRY TO FORCE IT OPEN, ITS CONTENTS WILL SHATTER.
IF YOU WANT TO SAVE THE GIRL...
...YOU MUST OFFER IT A COLOR IT LIKES EVEN BETTER.
THIS IS THE GAME YOU WANT TO PLAY?
THAT'S RIGHT. IN A WAY, YOU COULD CALL IT...
...COLOR TAG.
YOU MUST HAVE PLAYED IT WHEN YOU WERE A HUMAN CHILD.
THE PERSON WHO'S "IT" CHOOSES A COLOR, THEN THE OTHER CHILDREN RUN AROUND LOOKING FOR THAT COLOR TO BE SAFE.
SIMILARLY, WE WILL SEARCH FOR THE COLOR THIS AYAKASHI WANTS.
*Iro Oni can also mean "color tag."

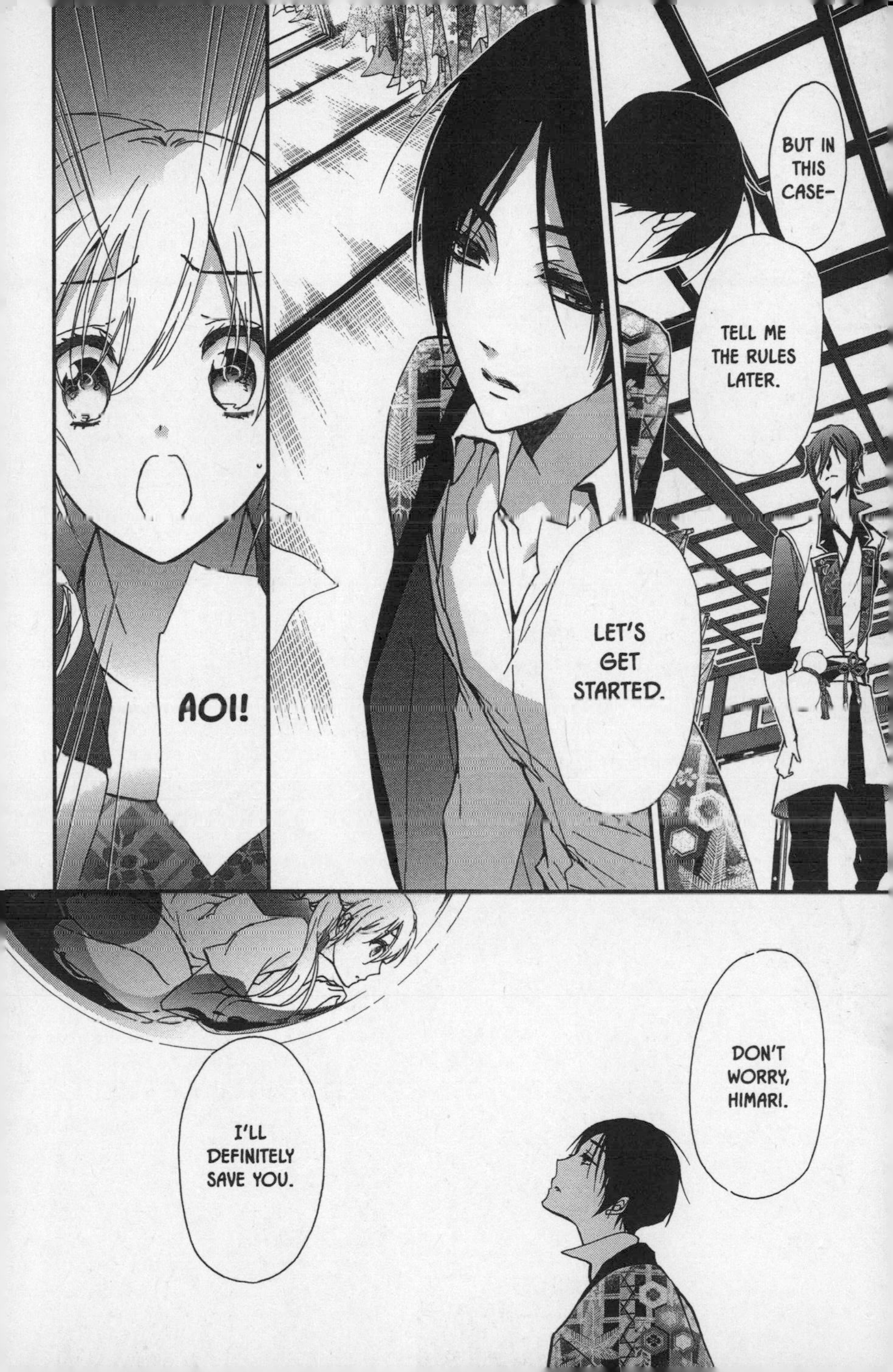
BUT IN THIS CASE–
TELL ME THE RULES LATER.
LET'S GET STARTED.
AOI!
DON'T WORRY, HIMARI.
I'LL DEFINITELY SAVE YOU.

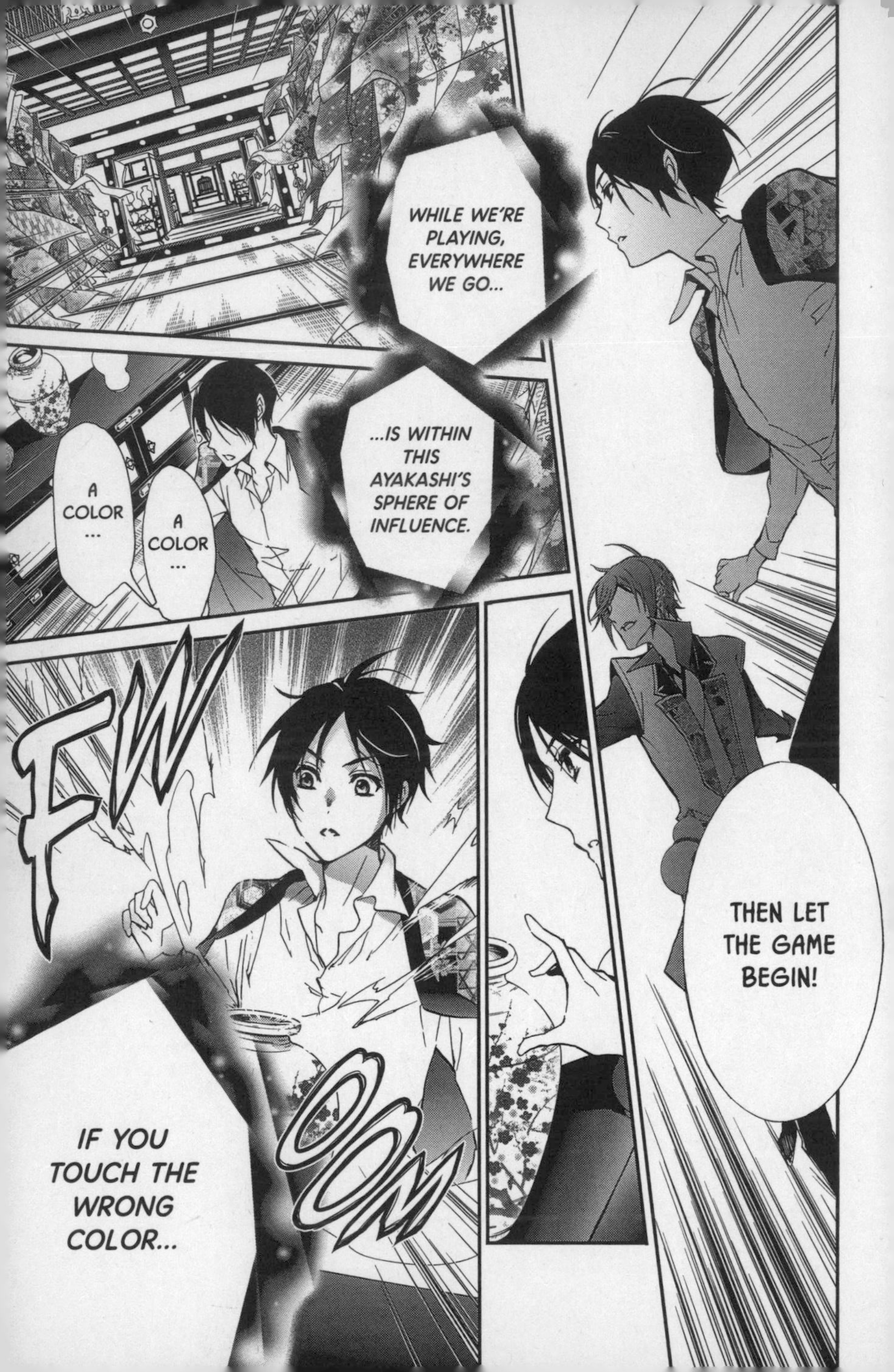
WHILE WE'RE PLAYING, EVERYWHERE WE GO...
...IS WITHIN THIS AYAKASHI'S SPHERE OF INFLUENCE.
A COLOR ...
A COLOR ...
THEN LET THE GAME BEGIN!
FWOOM
IF YOU TOUCH THE WRONG COLOR...

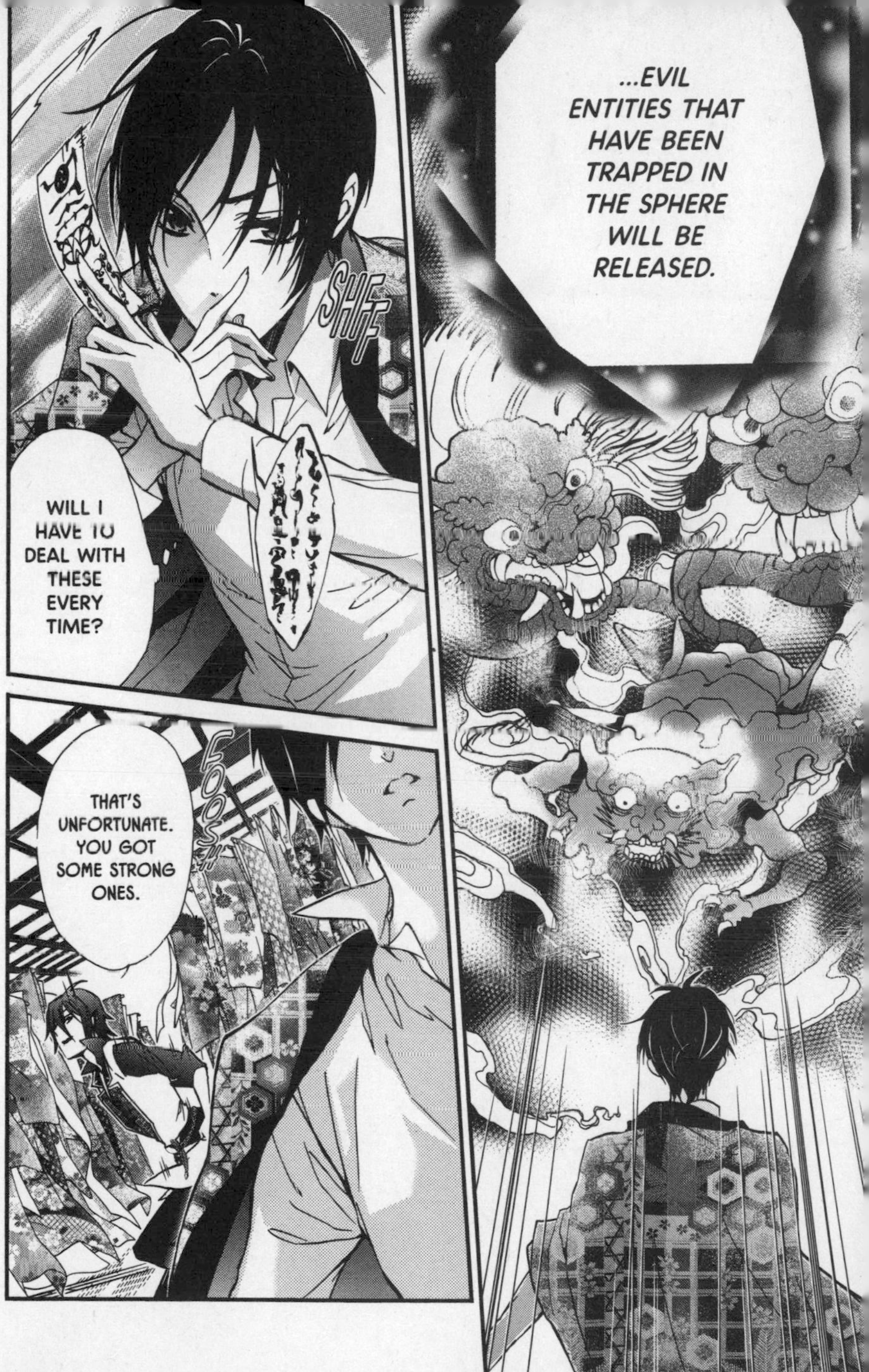
...EVIL ENTITIES THAT HAVE BEEN TRAPPED IN THE SPHERE WILL BE RELEASED.
SHFF
WILL I HAVE TO DEAL WITH THESE EVERY TIME?
FOOSH
THAT'S UNFORTUNATE. YOU GOT SOME STRONG ONES.

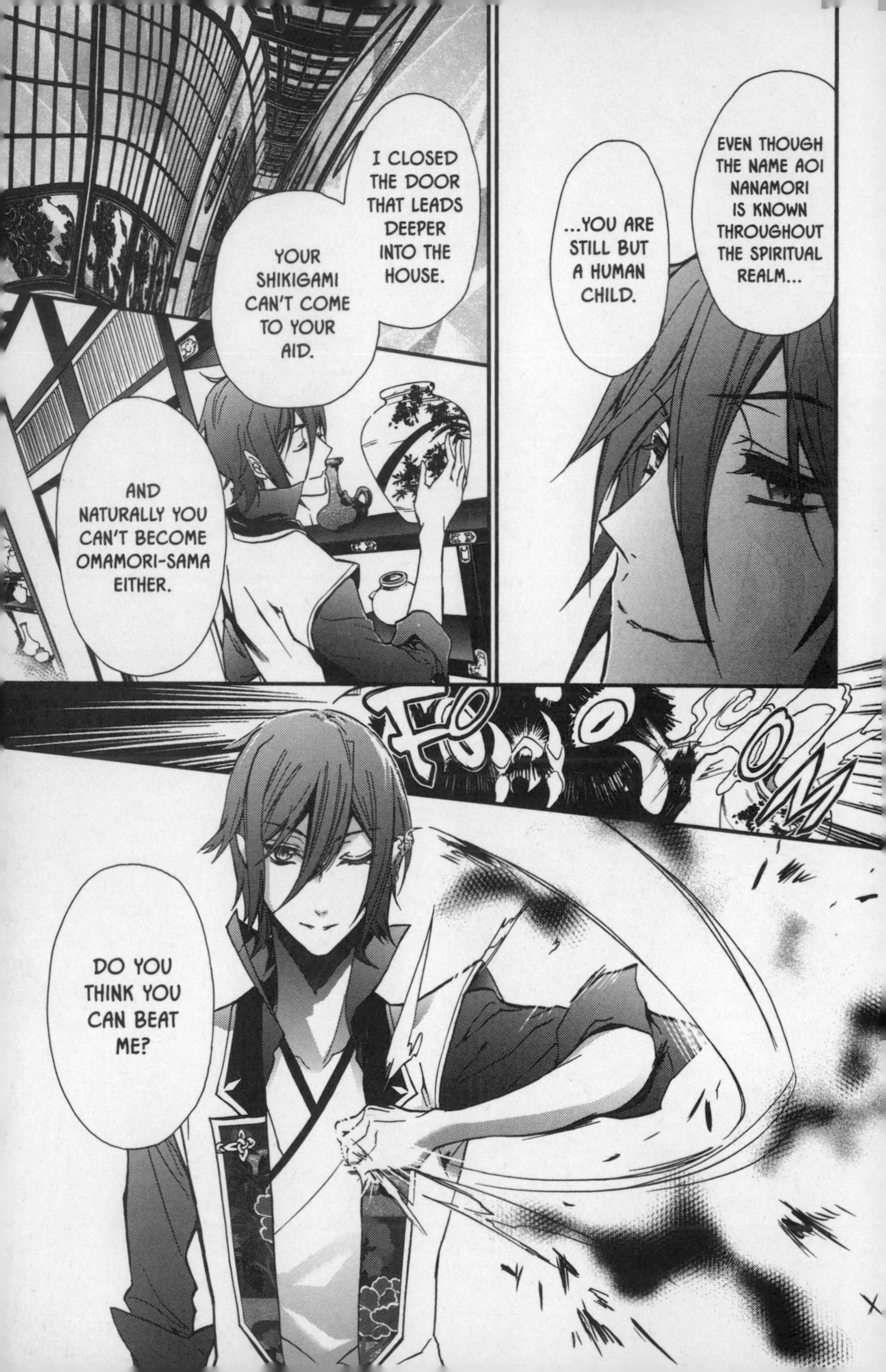
EVEN THOUGH THE NAME AOI NANAMORI IS KNOWN THROUGHOUT THE SPIRITUAL REALM...
...YOU ARE STILL BUT A HUMAN CHILD.
I CLOSED THE DOOR THAT LEADS DEEPER INTO THE HOUSE.
YOUR SHIKIGAMI CAN'T COME TO YOUR AID.
AND NATURALLY YOU CAN'T BECOME OMAMORI-SAMA EITHER.
FOOOOM
DO YOU THINK YOU CAN BEAT ME?

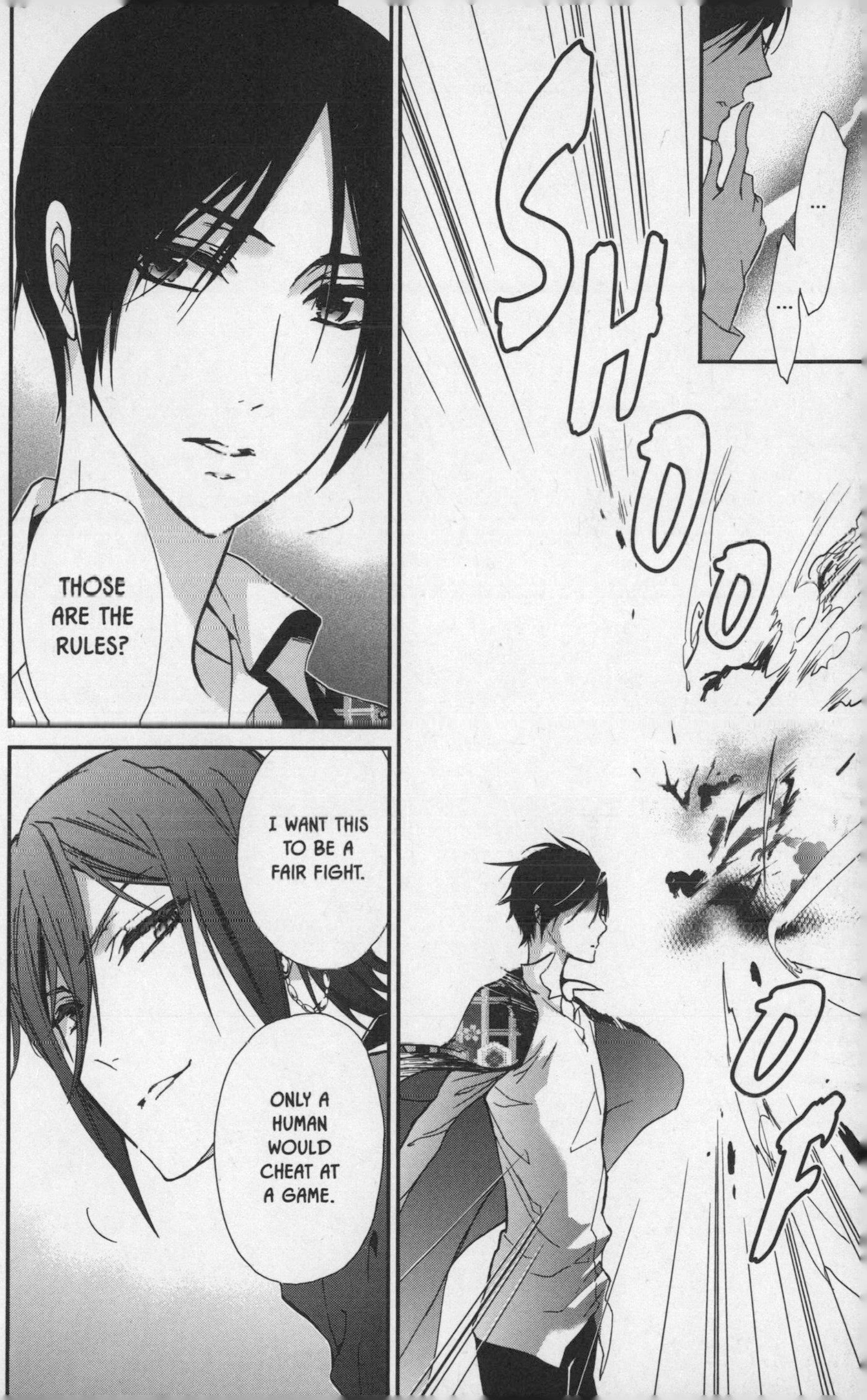
...
...
SHOOOF
THOSE ARE THE RULES?
I WANT THIS TO BE A FAIR FIGHT.
ONLY A HUMAN WOULD CHEAT AT A GAME.

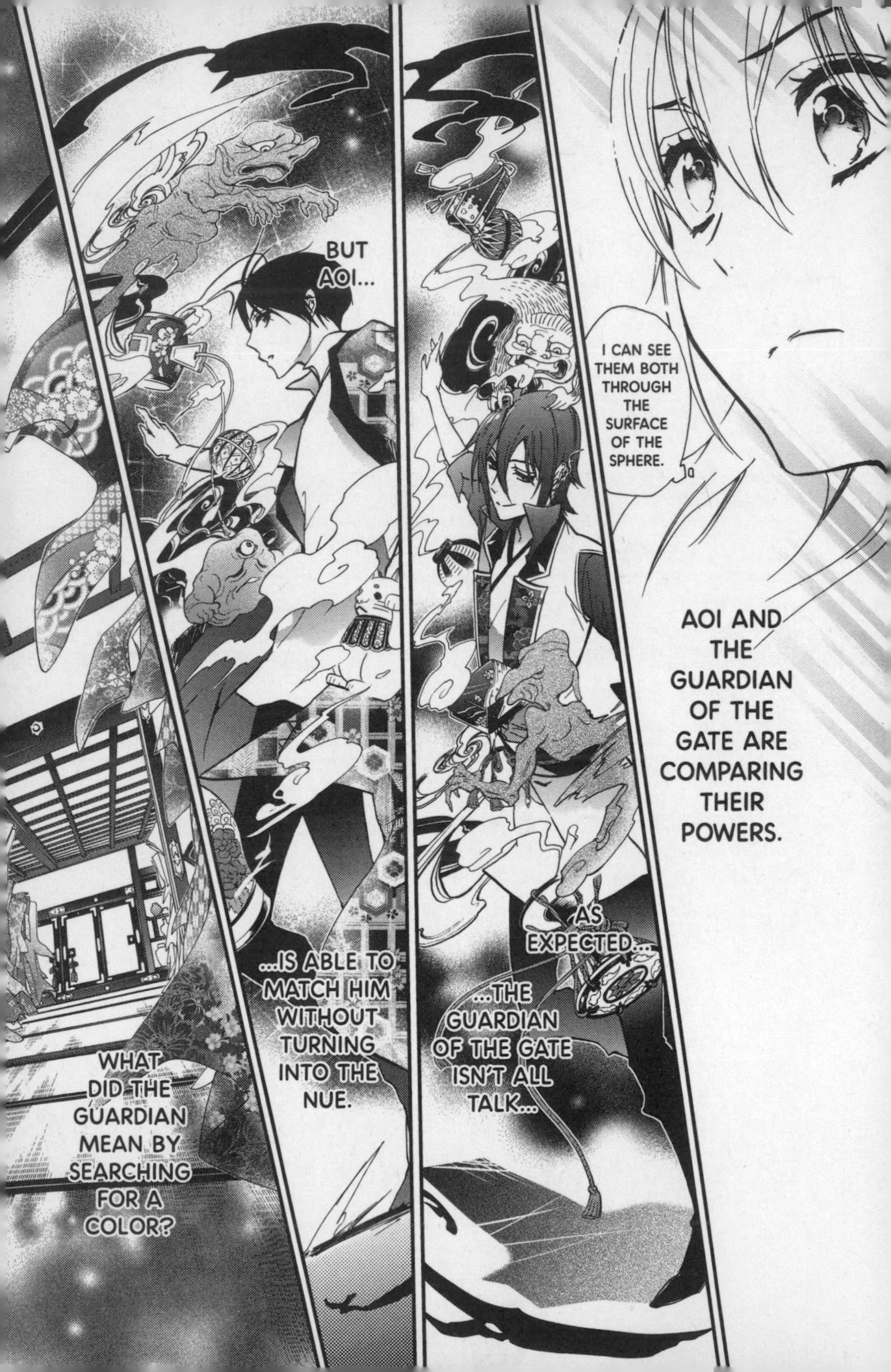
I CAN SEE THEM BOTH THROUGH THE SURFACE OF THE SPHERE.
AOI AND THE GUARDIAN OF THE GATE ARE COMPARING THEIR POWERS.
AS EXPECTED...
...THE GUARDIAN OF THE GATE ISN'T ALL TALK...
BUT AOI...
...IS ABLE TO MATCH HIM WITHOUT TURNING INTO THE NUE.
WHAT DID THE GUARDIAN MEAN BY SEARCHING FOR A COLOR?

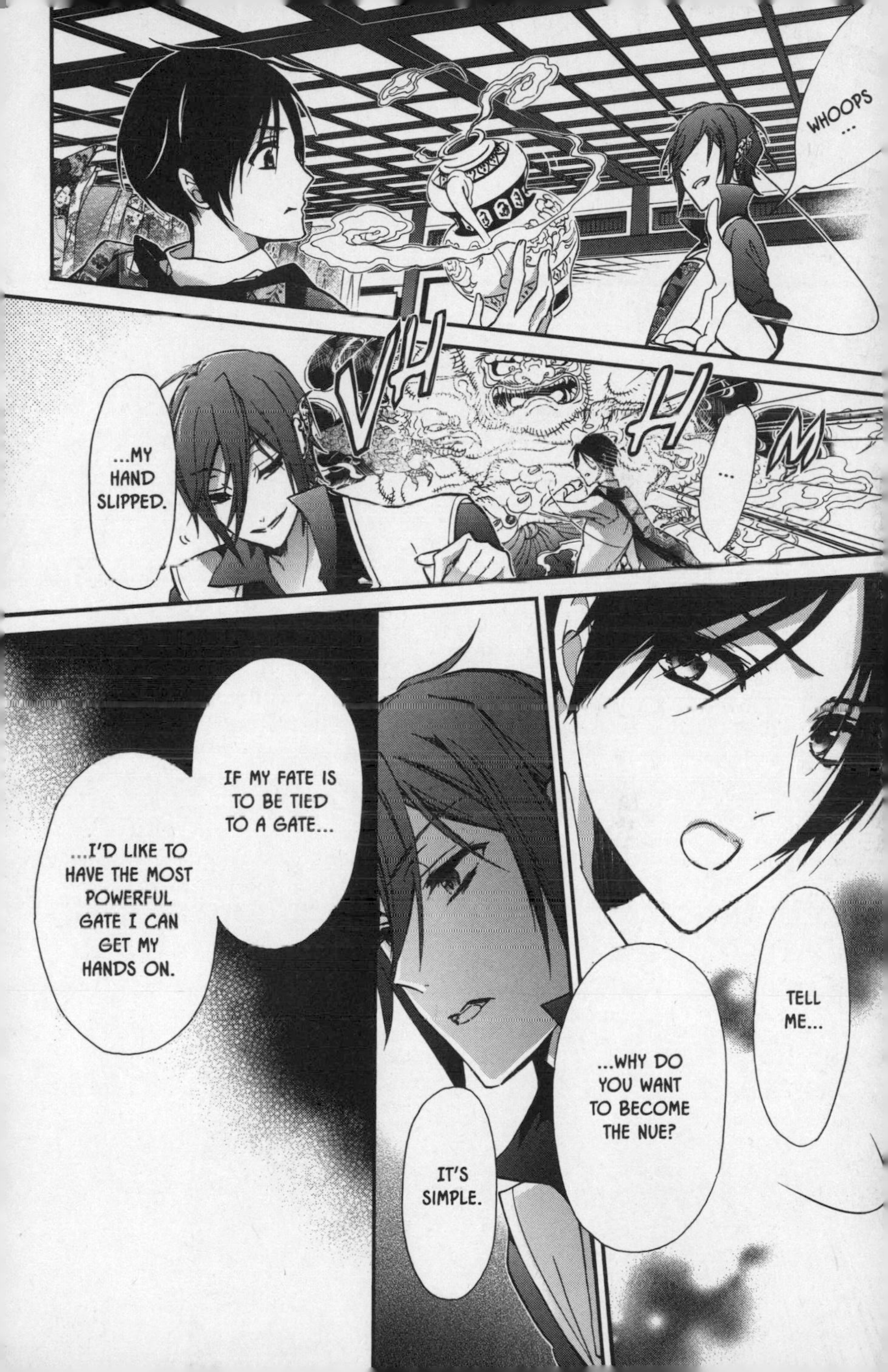
WHOOPS ...
VH H M
...
...MY HAND SLIPPED.
TELL ME...
...WHY DO YOU WANT TO BECOME THE NUE?
IT'S SIMPLE.
IF MY FATE IS TO BE TIED TO A GATE...
...I'D LIKE TO HAVE THE MOST POWERFUL GATE I CAN GET MY HANDS ON.

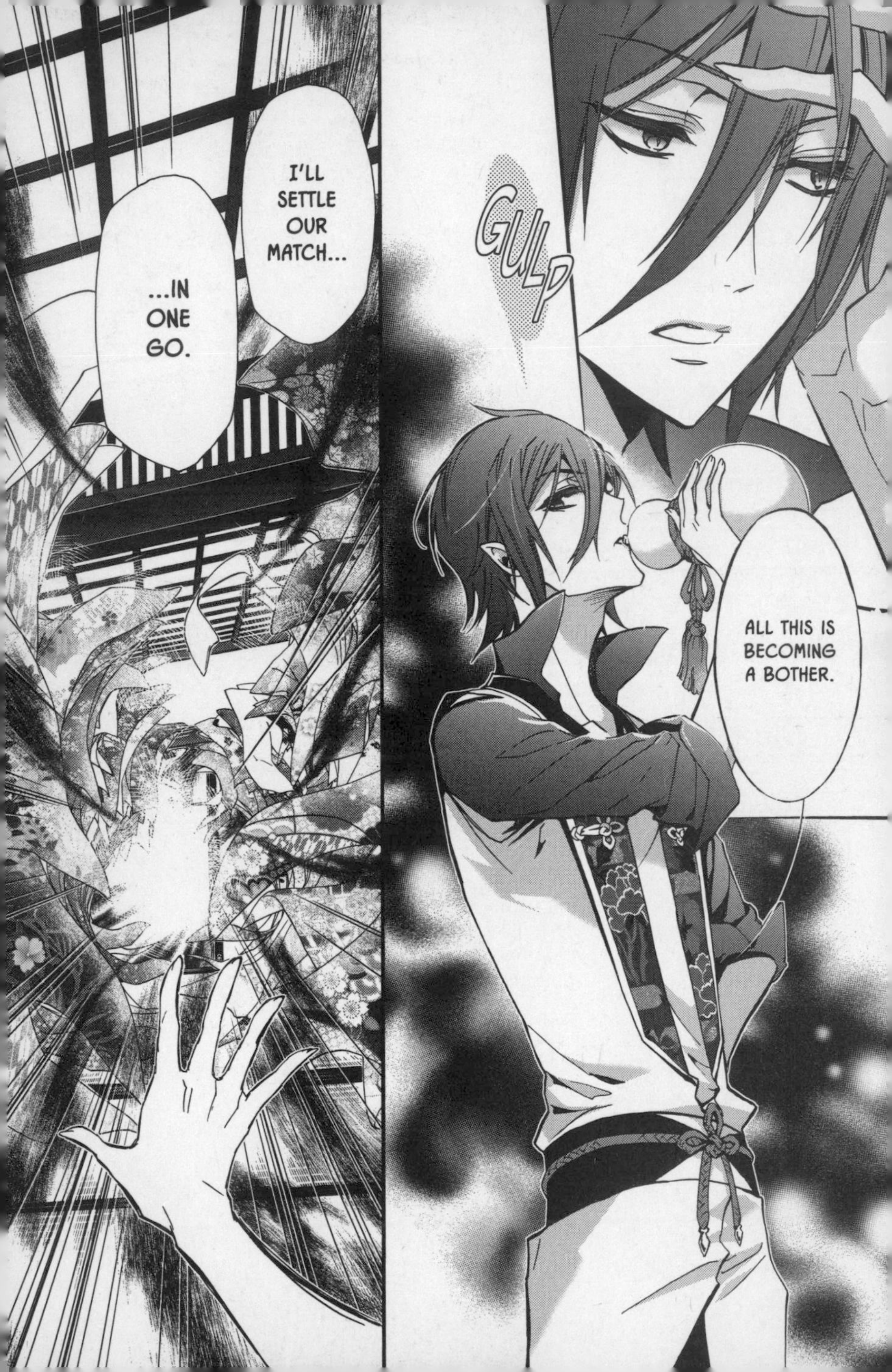
GULP
ALL THIS IS BECOMING A BOTHER.
I'LL SETTLE OUR MATCH...
...IN ONE GO.

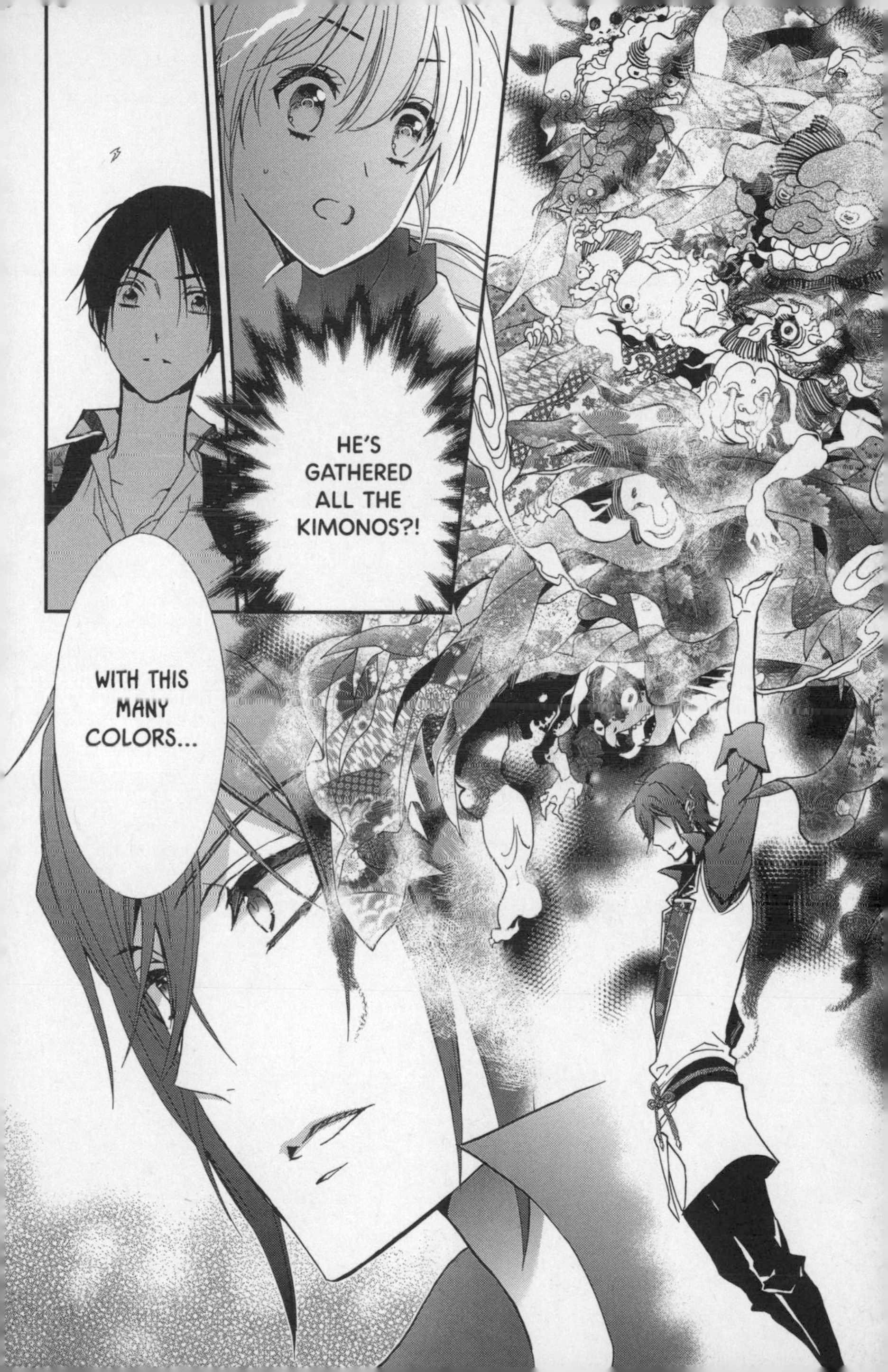
HE'S GATHERED ALL THE KIMONOS?!
WITH THIS MANY COLORS...

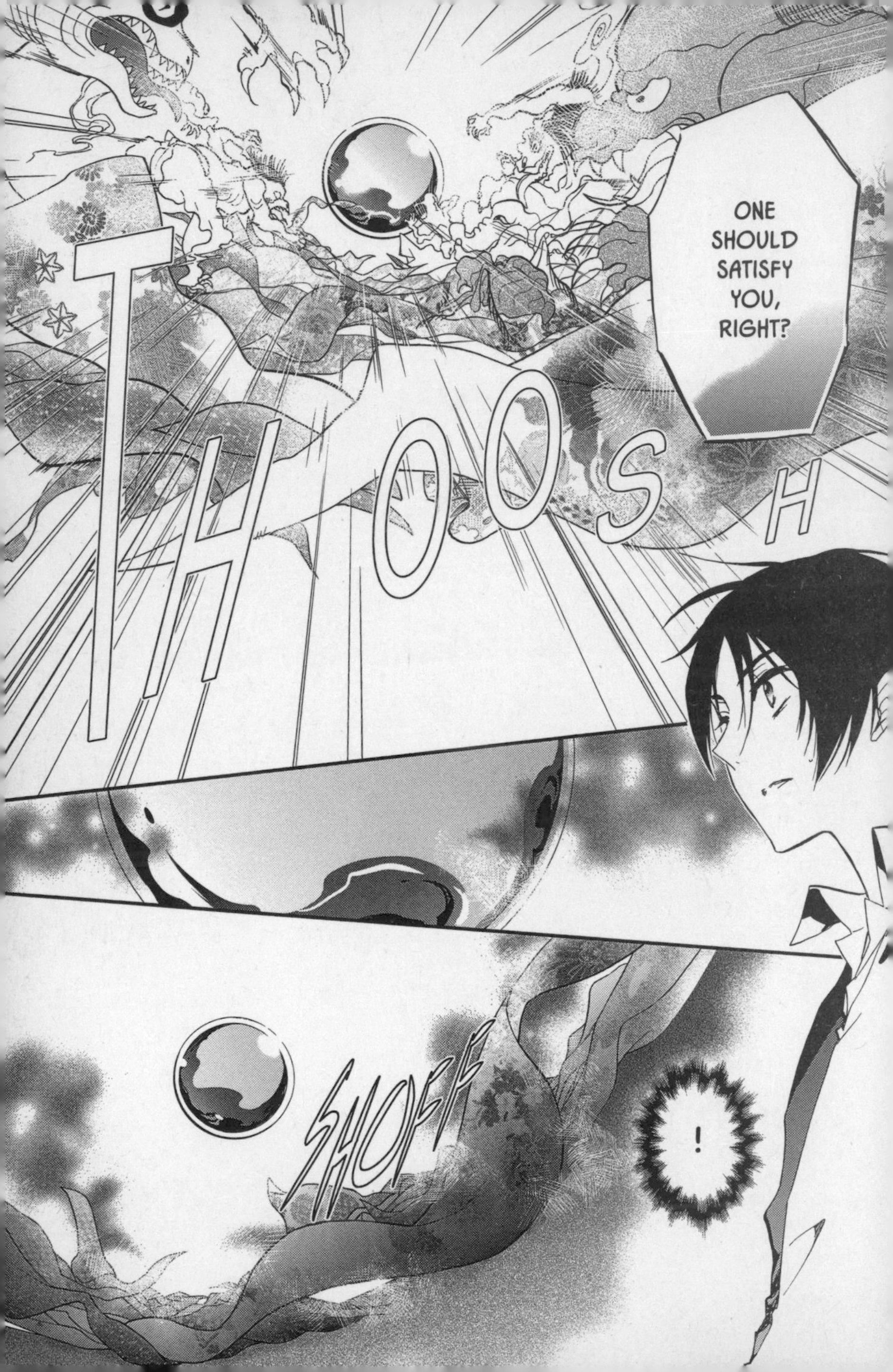
ONE SHOULD SATISFY YOU, RIGHT?
THOOSH
!
SHOFF

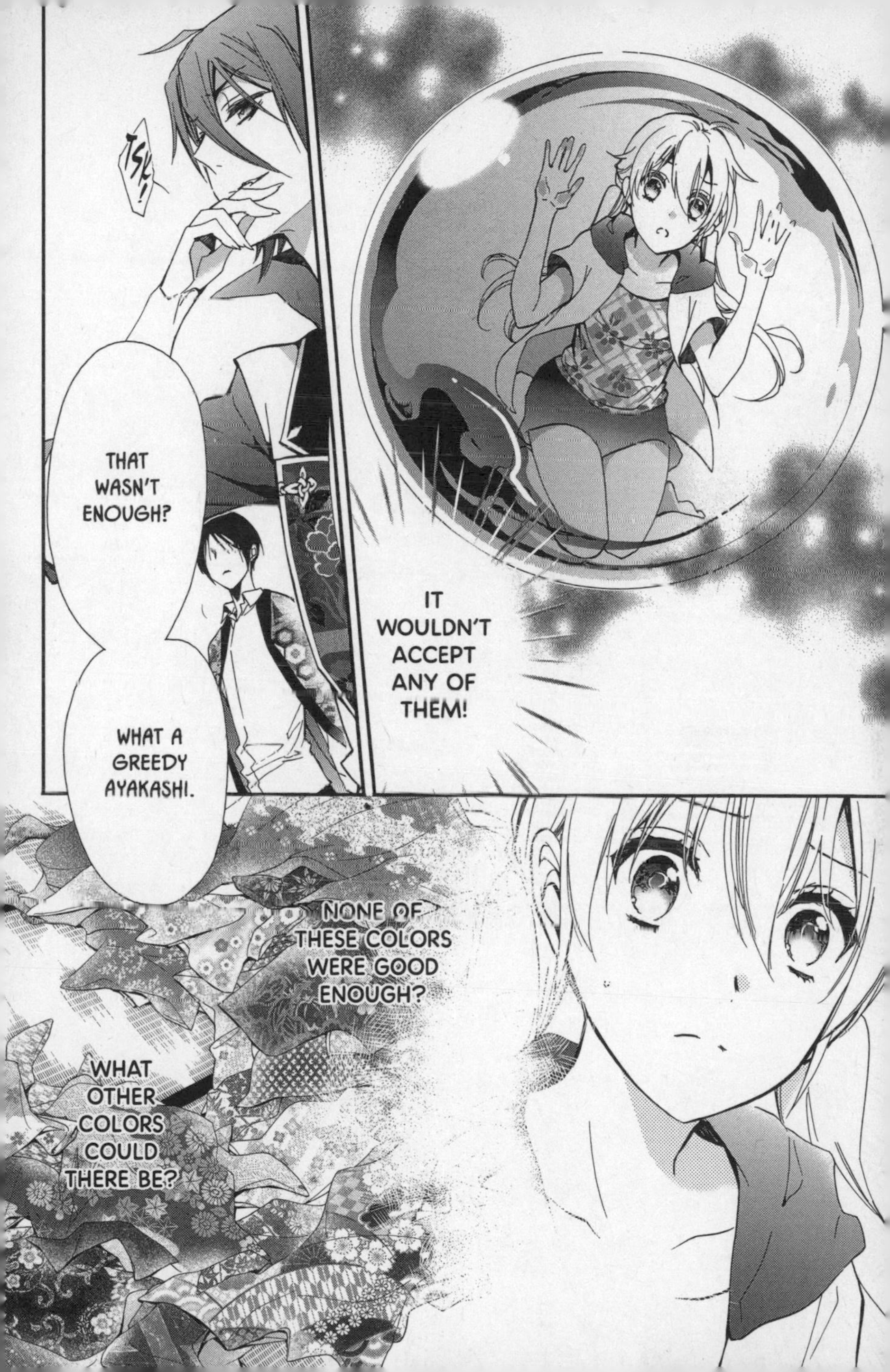
IT WOULDN'T ACCEPT ANY OF THEM!
TSK!
THAT WASN'T ENOUGH?
WHAT A GREEDY AYAKASHI.
NONE OF THESE COLORS WERE GOOD ENOUGH?
WHAT OTHER COLORS COULD THERE BE?

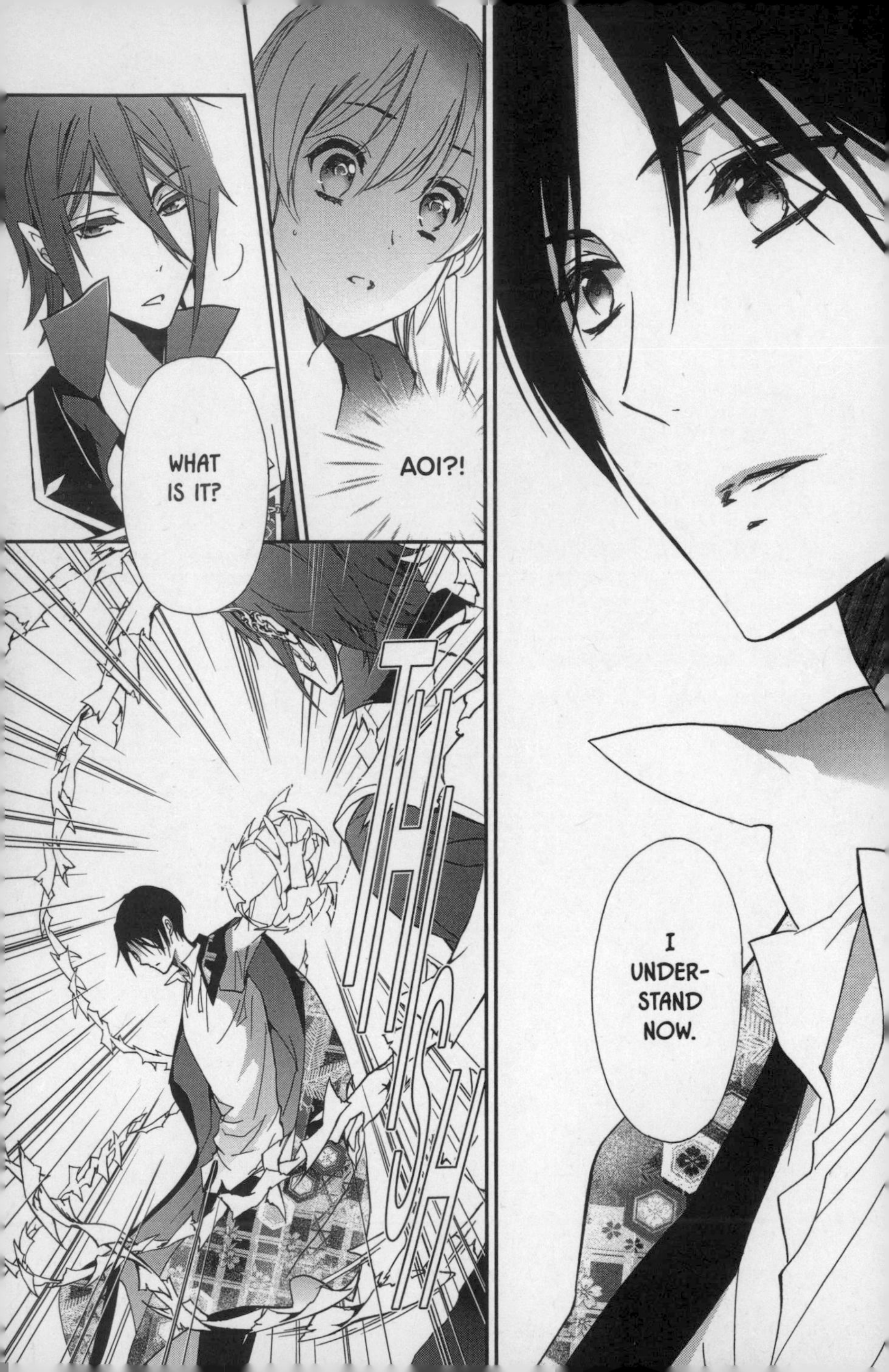
I UNDER-STAND NOW.
AOI?!
WHAT IS IT?
THSSH

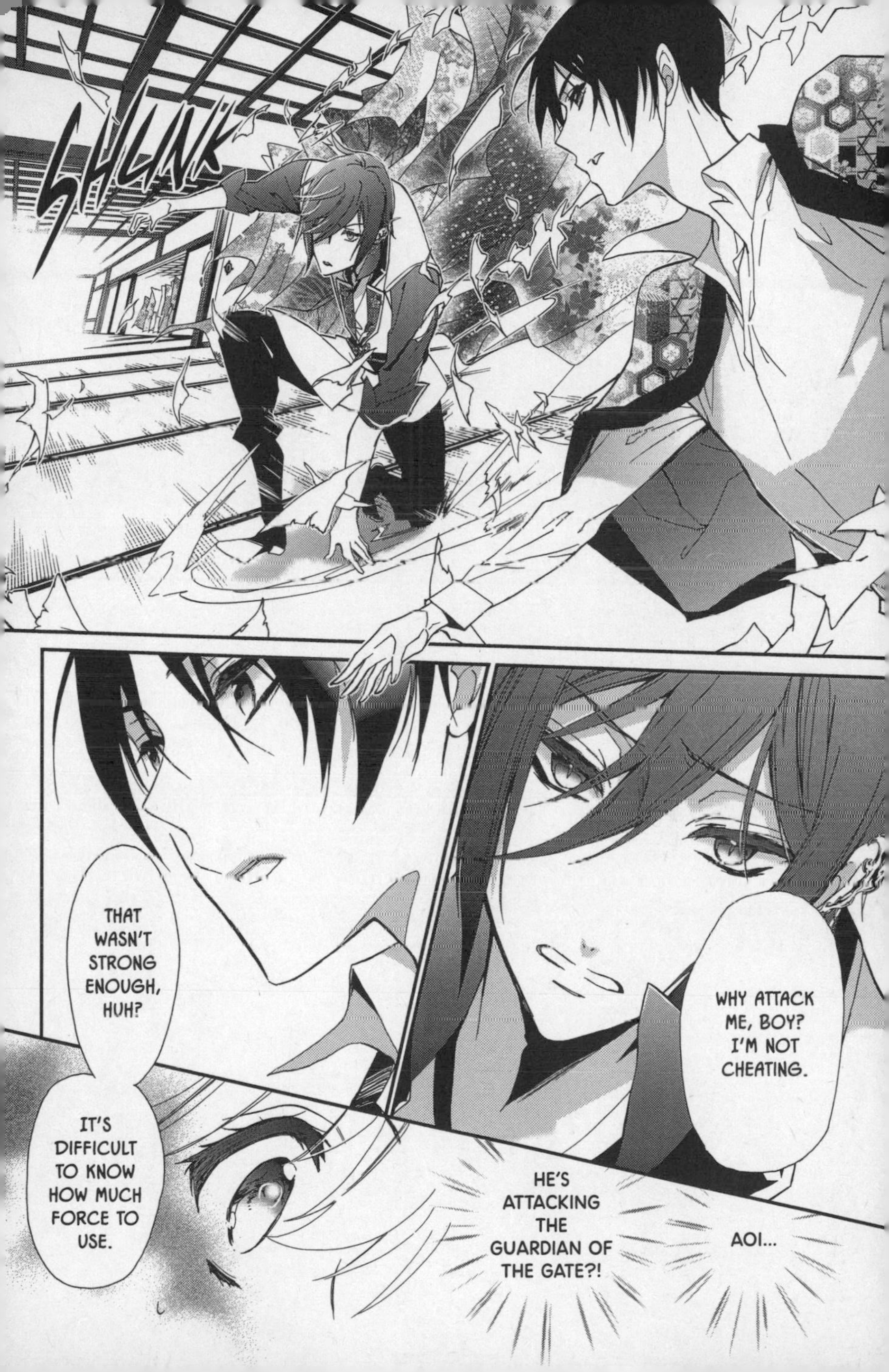
SHUNK
WHY ATTACK ME, BOY? I'M NOT CHEATING.
THAT WASN'T STRONG ENOUGH, HUH?
AOI...
HE'S ATTACKING THE GUARDIAN OF THE GATE?!
IT'S DIFFICULT TO KNOW HOW MUCH FORCE TO USE.

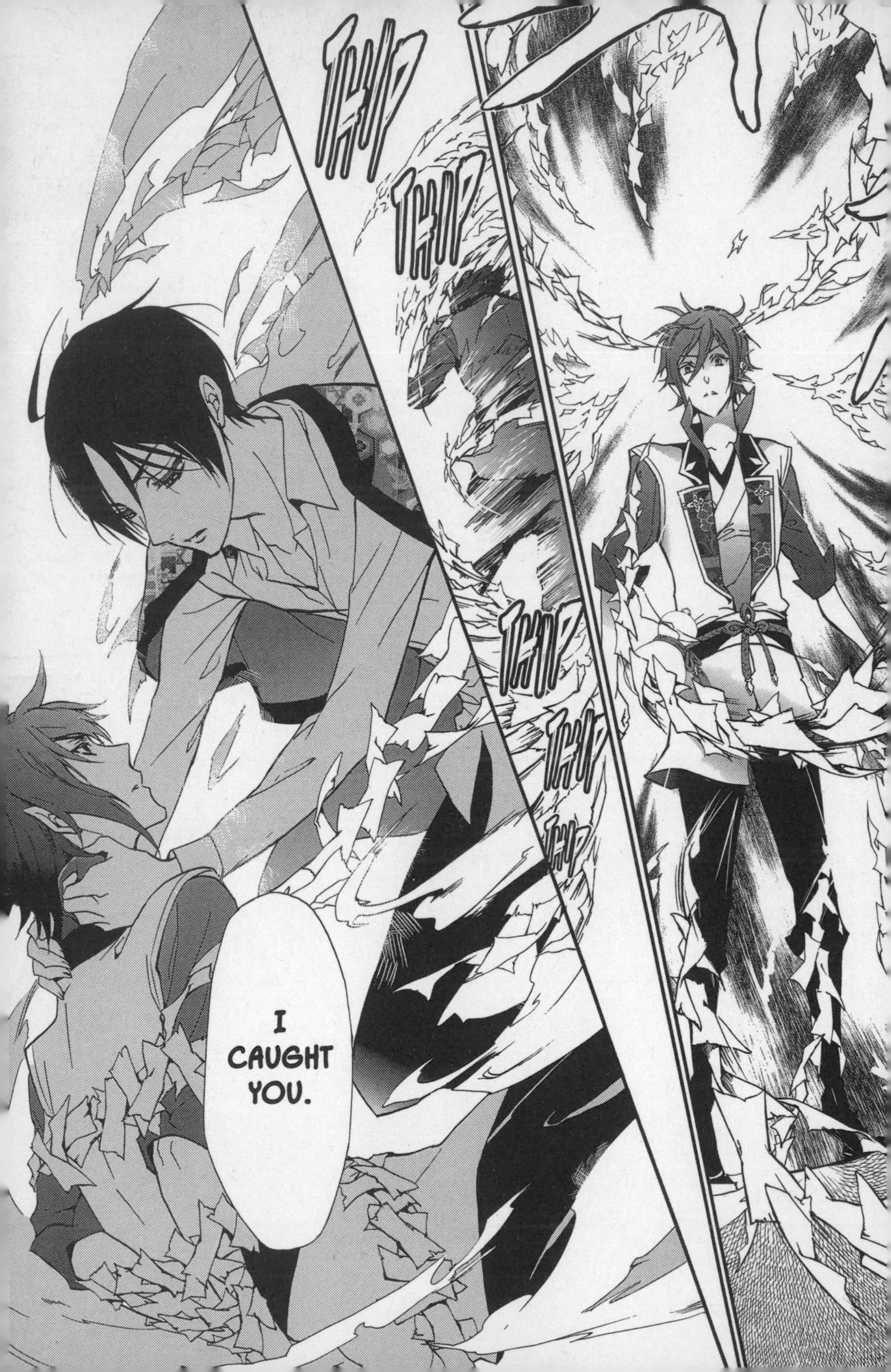
THIP
THIP
THIP
THIP
THIP
I CAUGHT YOU.

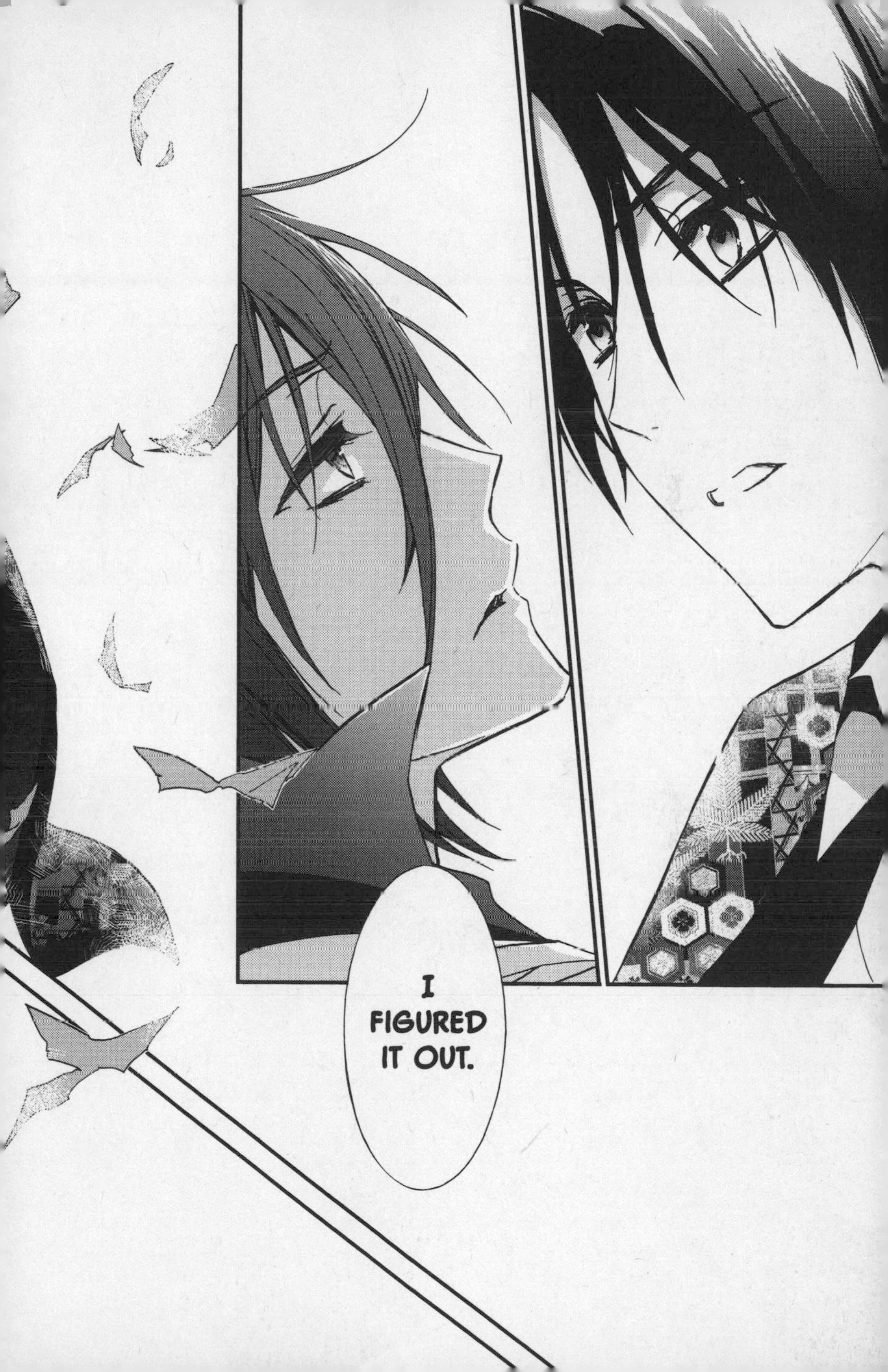
I FIGURED IT OUT.

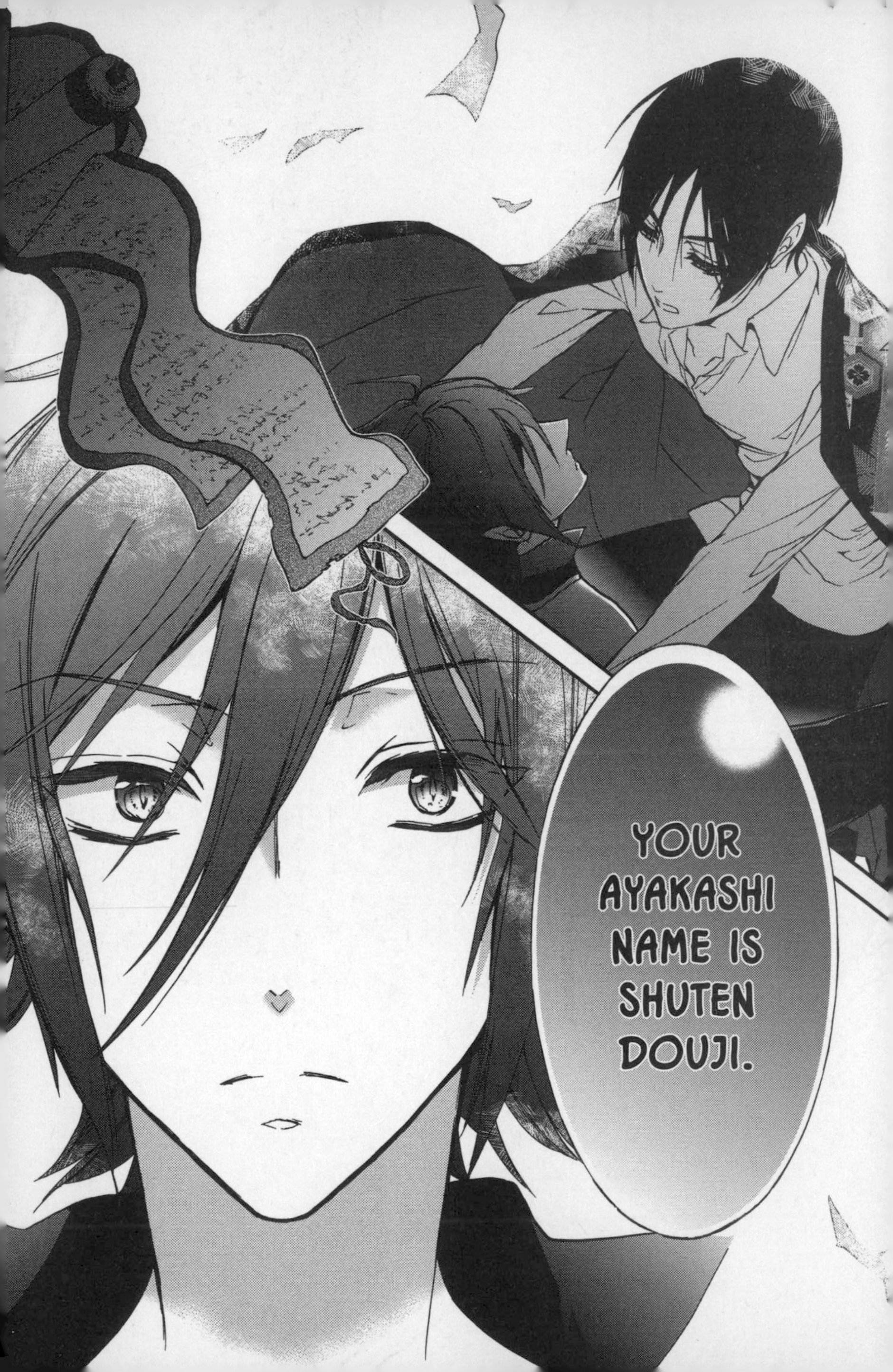
YOUR AYAKASHI NAME IS SHUTEN DOUJI.

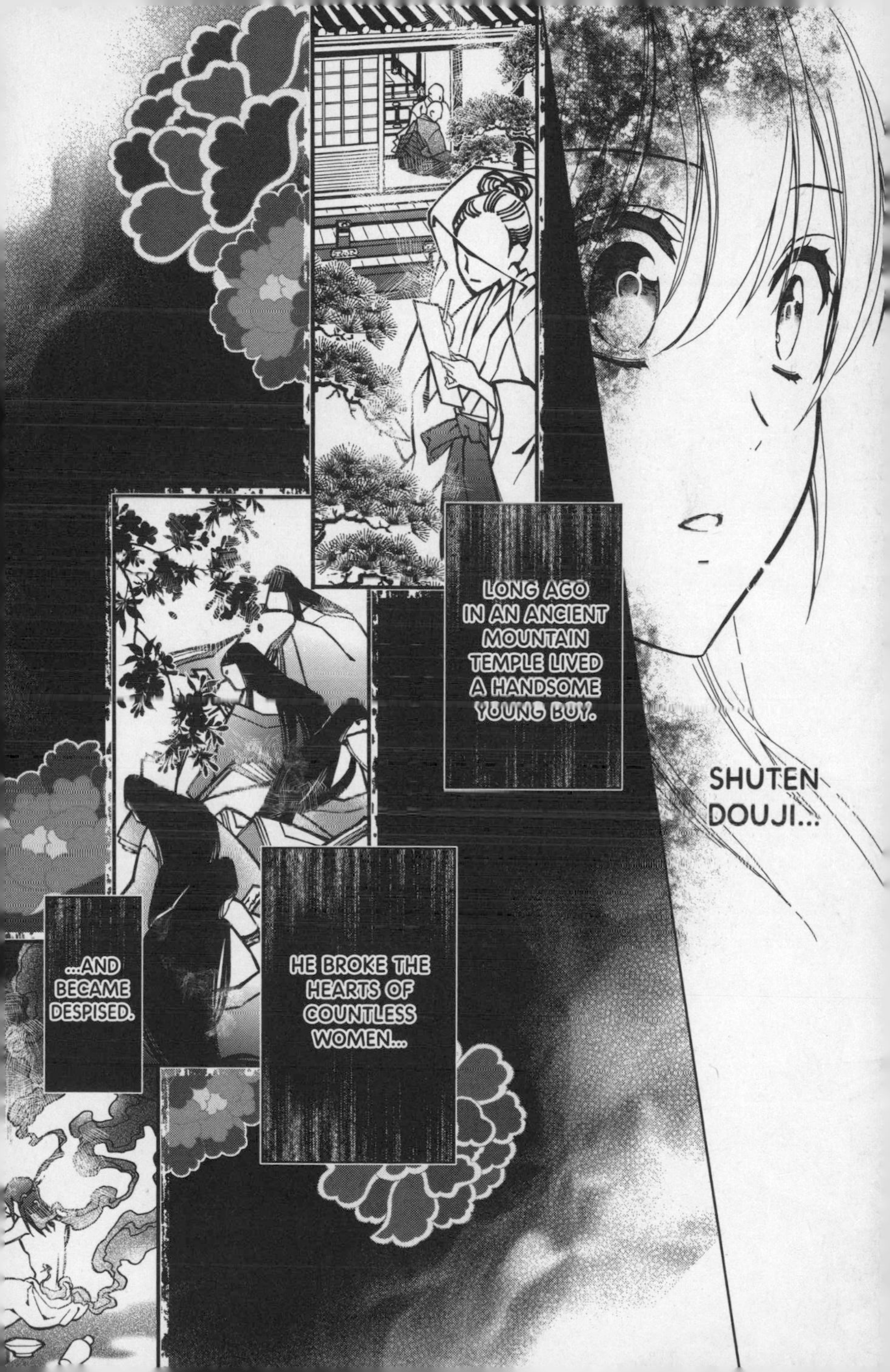
LONG AGO IN AN ANCIENT MOUNTAIN TEMPLE LIVED A HANDSOME YOUNG BOY.
SHUTEN DOUJI...
HE BROKE THE HEARTS OF COUNTLESS WOMEN...
...AND BECAME DESPISED.

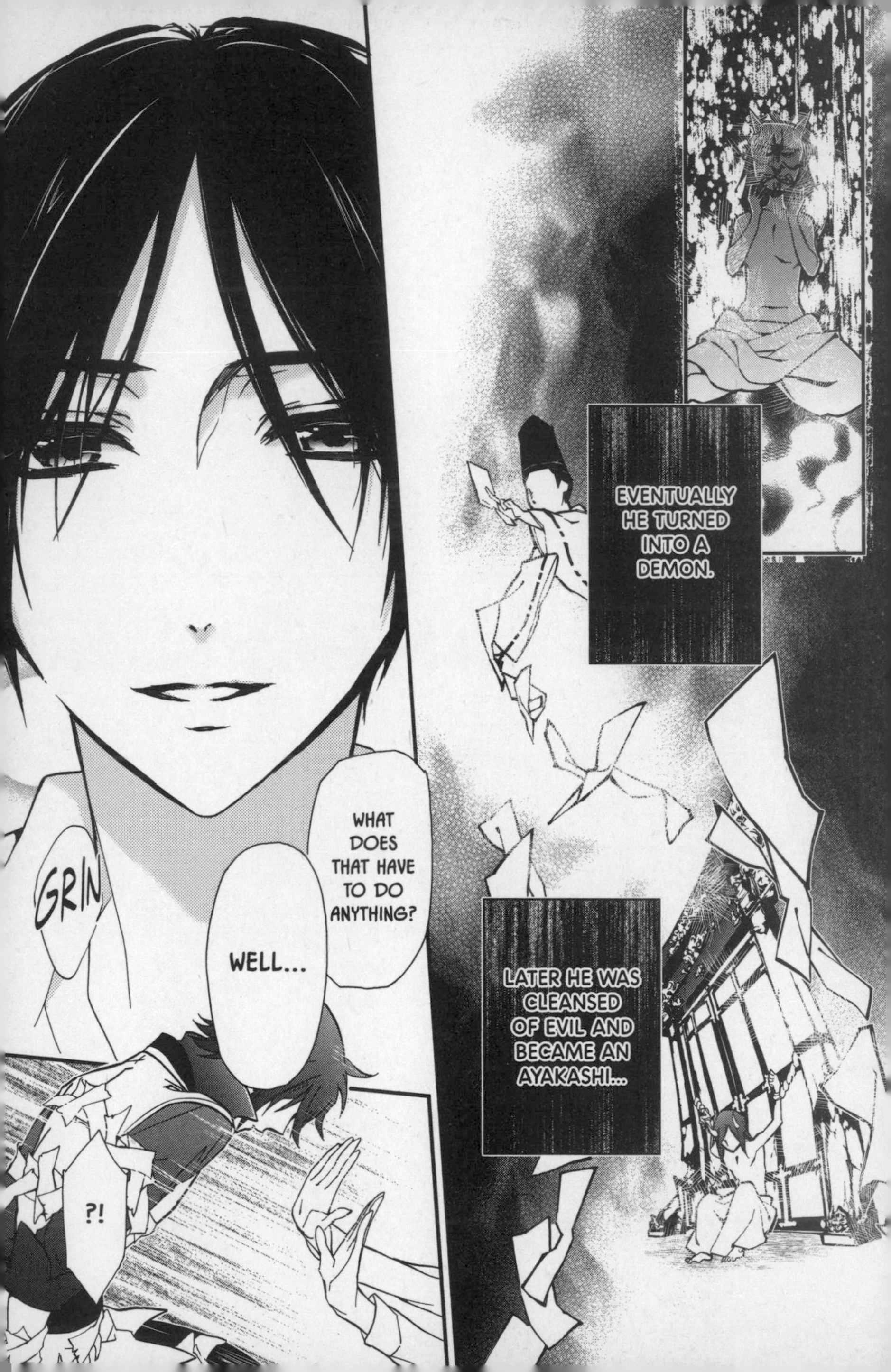
EVENTUALLY HE TURNED INTO A DEMON.
LATER HE WAS CLEANSED OF EVIL AND BECAME AN AYAKASHI...
WHAT DOES THAT HAVE TO DO ANYTHING?
WELL...
GRIN
?!

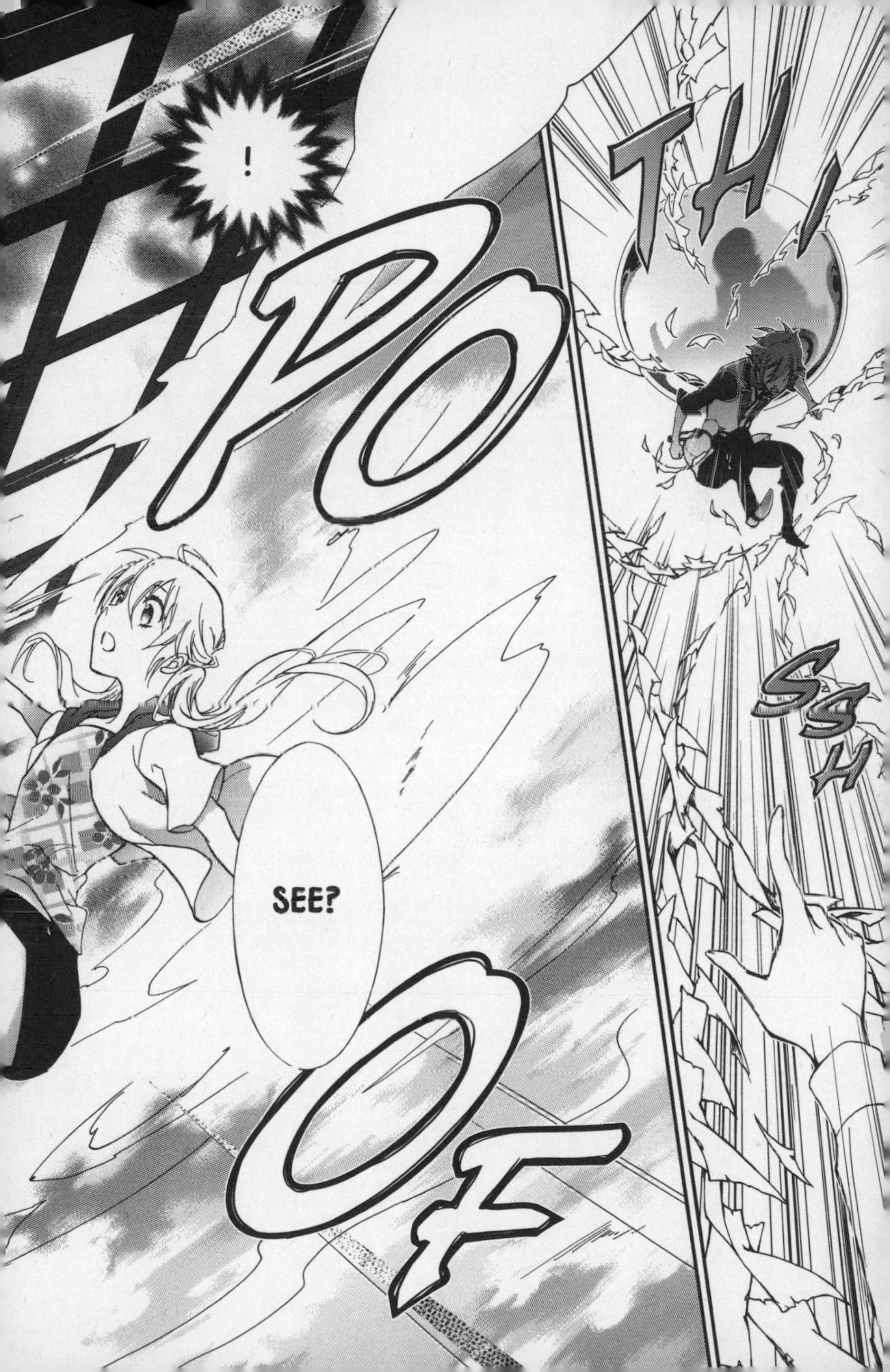
THI
SSH
!
DOOF
SEE?

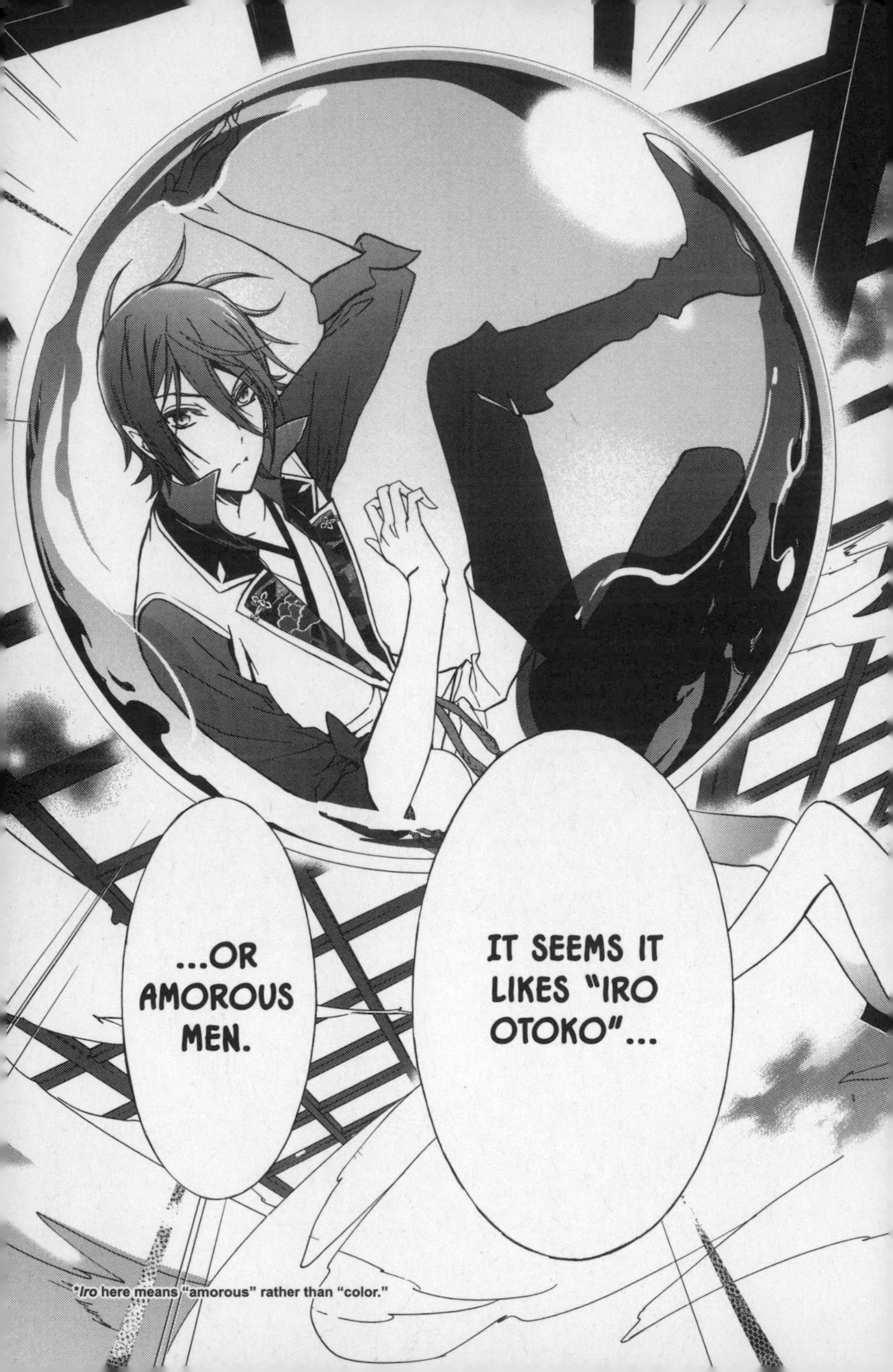
IT SEEMS IT LIKES "IRO OTOKO"...
...OR AMOROUS MEN.

*Iro here means "amorous" rather than "color."

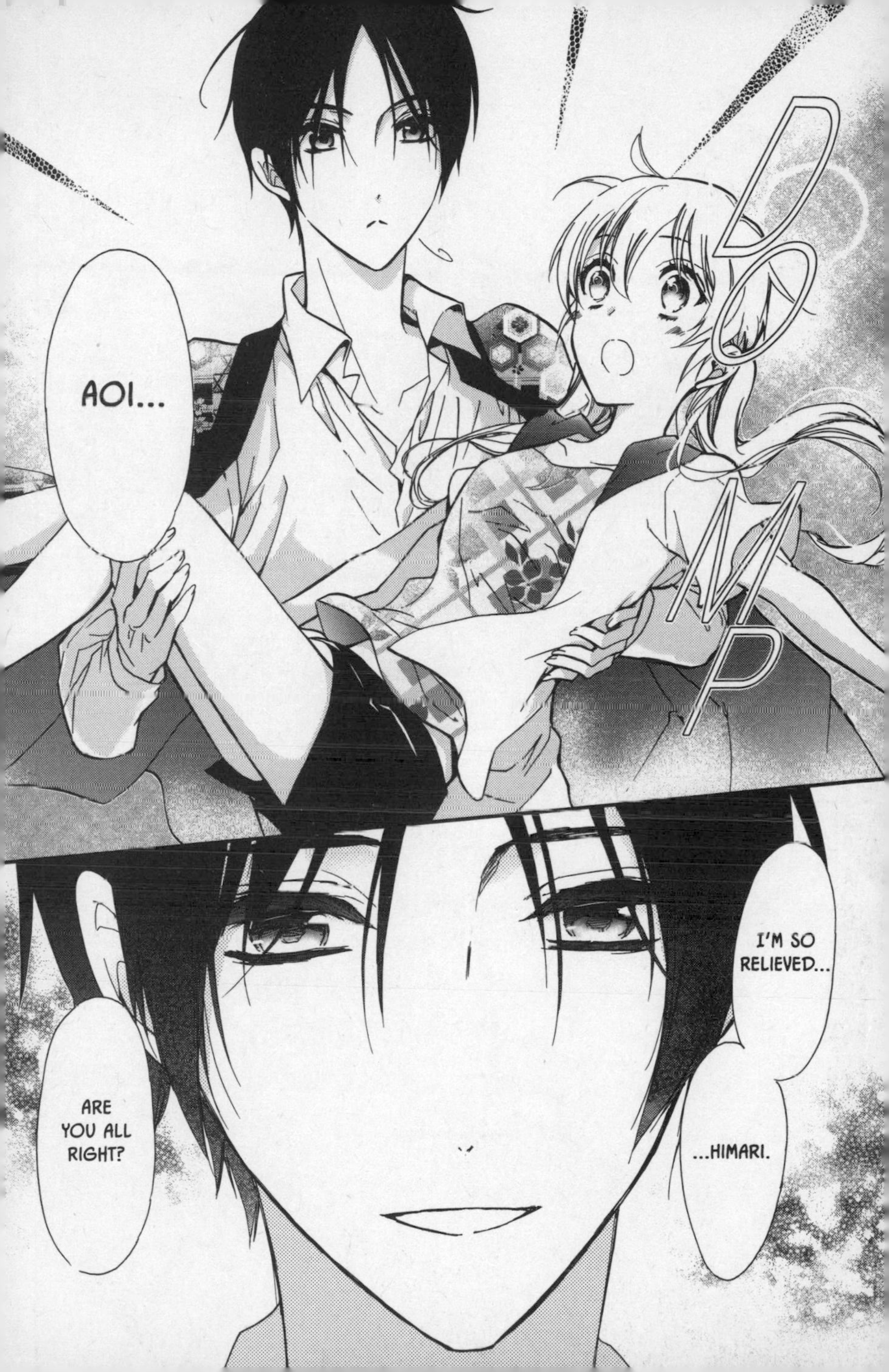
DOMP
AOI...
I'M SO RELIEVED...
ARE YOU ALL RIGHT?
...HIMARI.

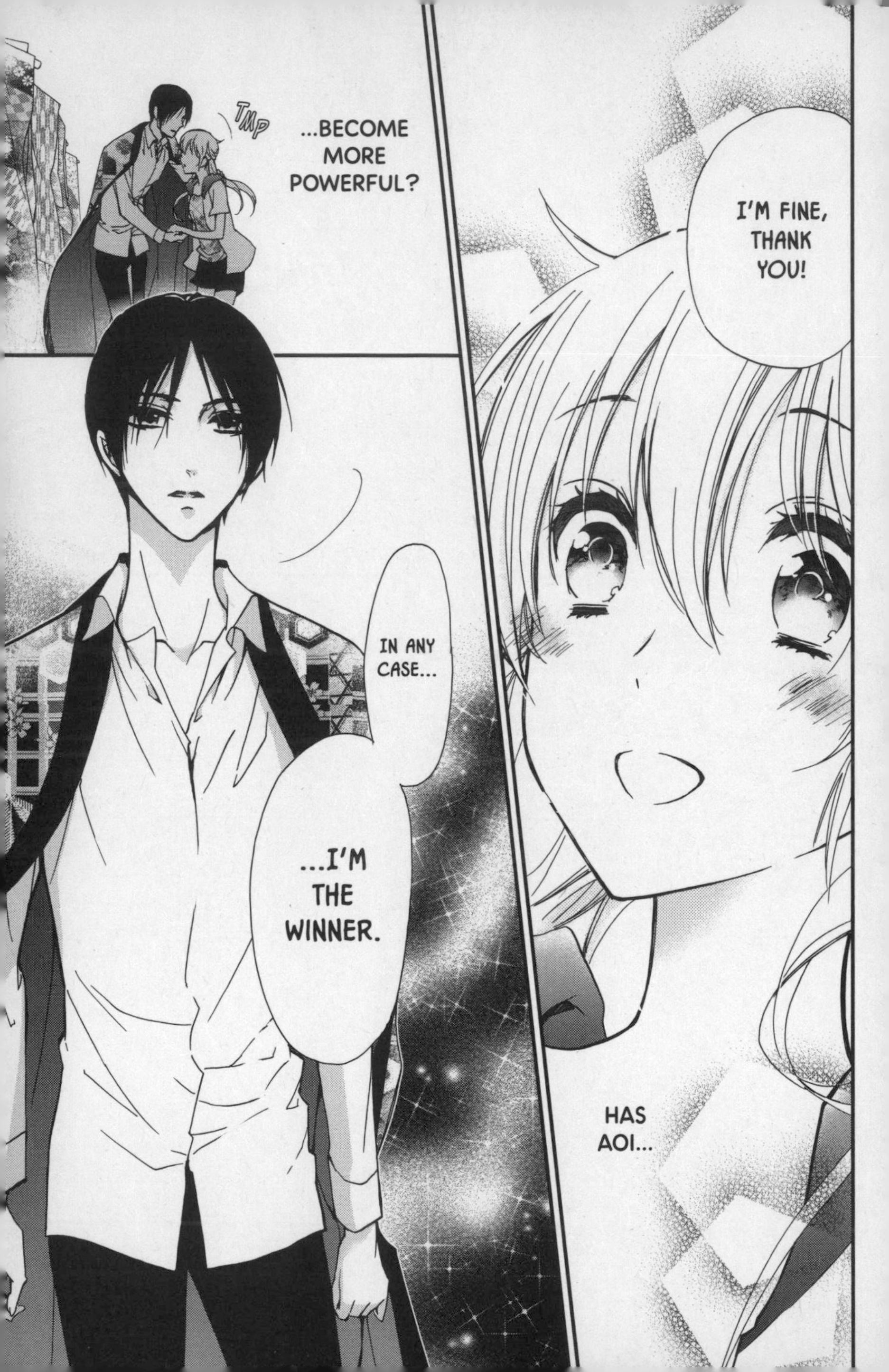
I'M FINE, THANK YOU!
HAS AOI...
TMP
...BECOME MORE POWERFUL?
IN ANY CASE...
...I'M THE WINNER.

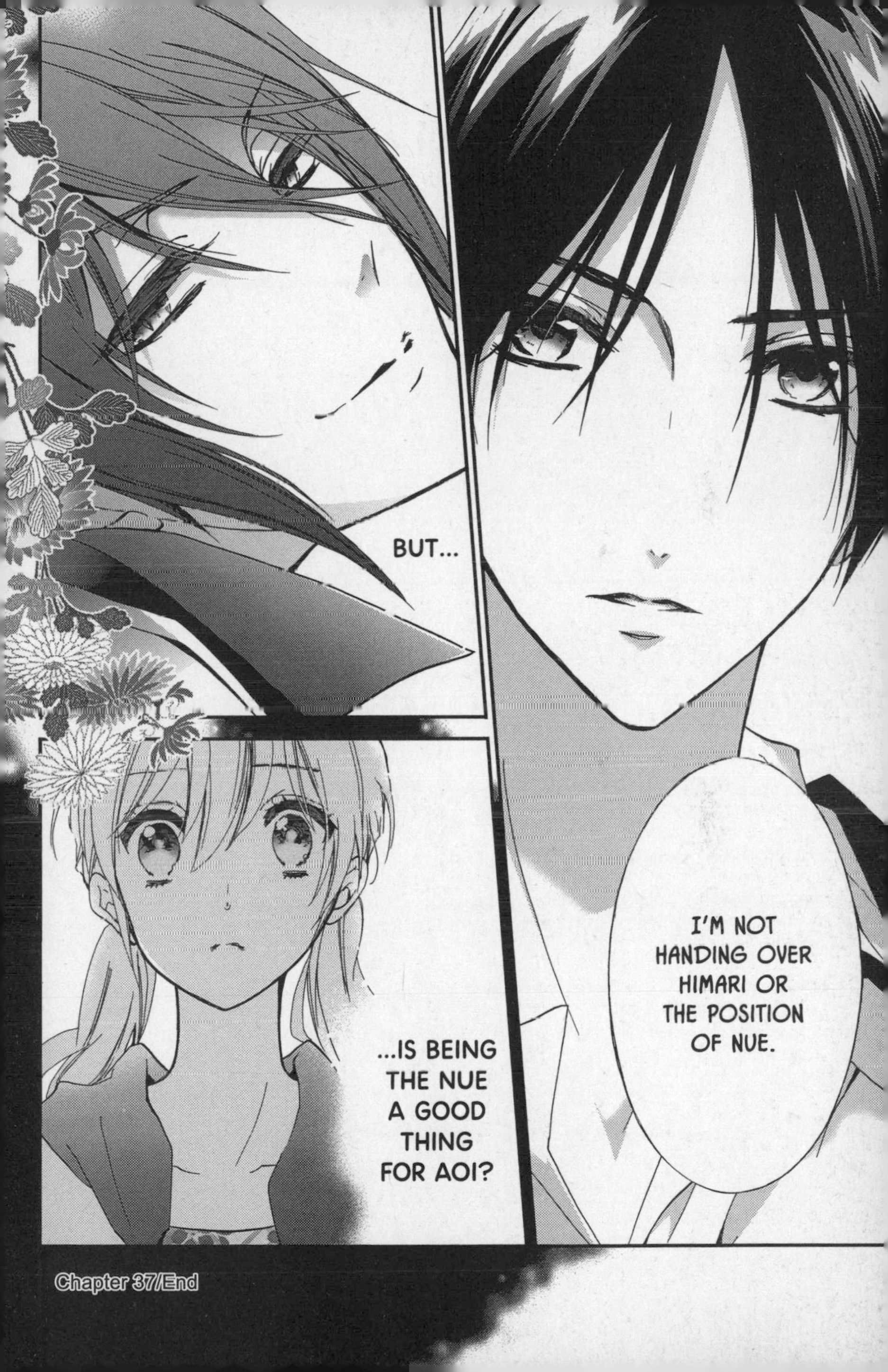
I'M NOT HANDING OVER HIMARI OR THE POSITION OF NUE.
BUT...
...IS BEING THE NUE A GOOD THING FOR AOI?

Chapter 37/End

the DEMON PRINCE *of* MOMOCHI HOUSE

The DEMON PRINCE of MOMOCHI HOUSE

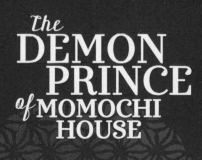

CHAPTER 38
There Are Limits to Being a Free-loader!

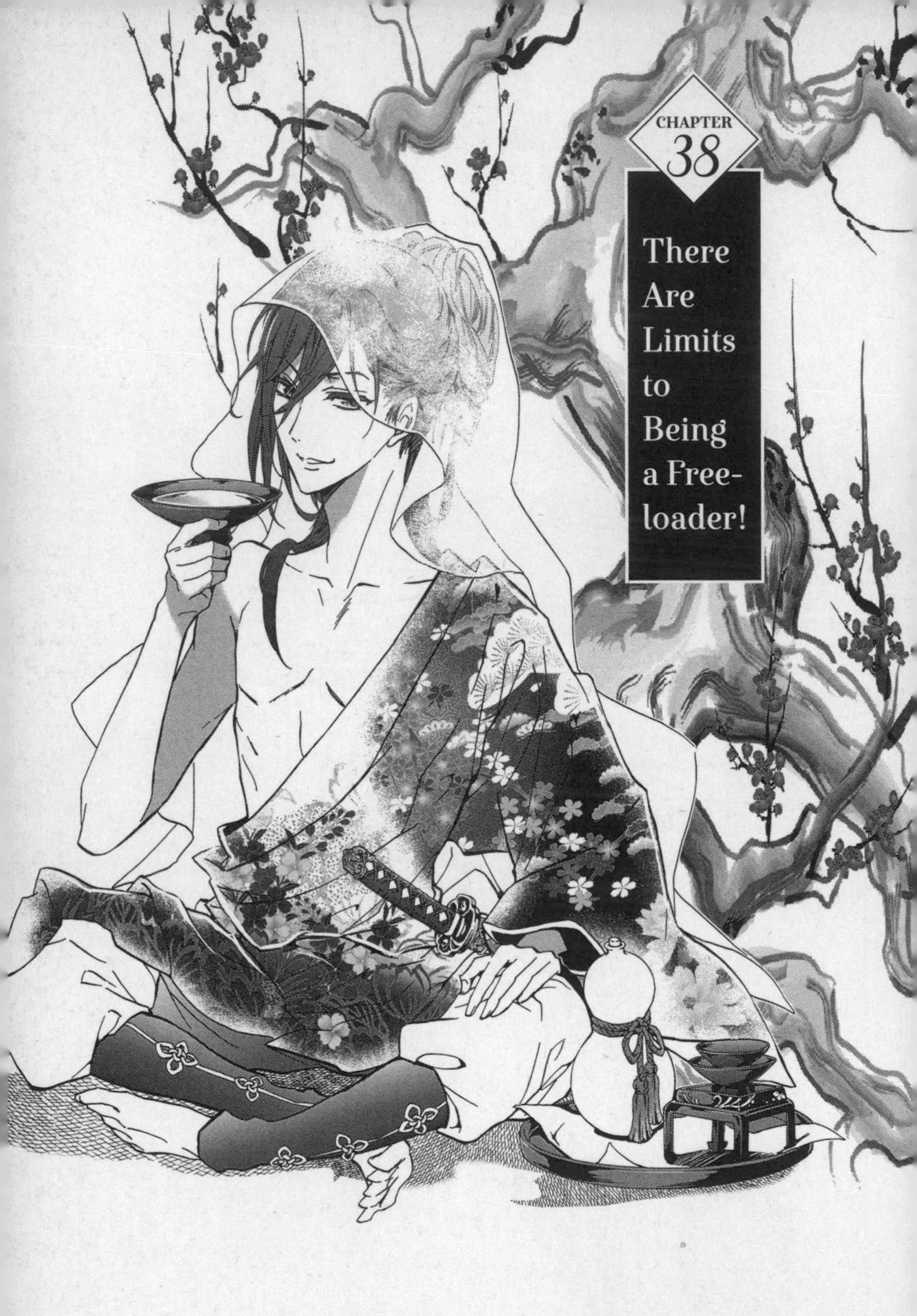

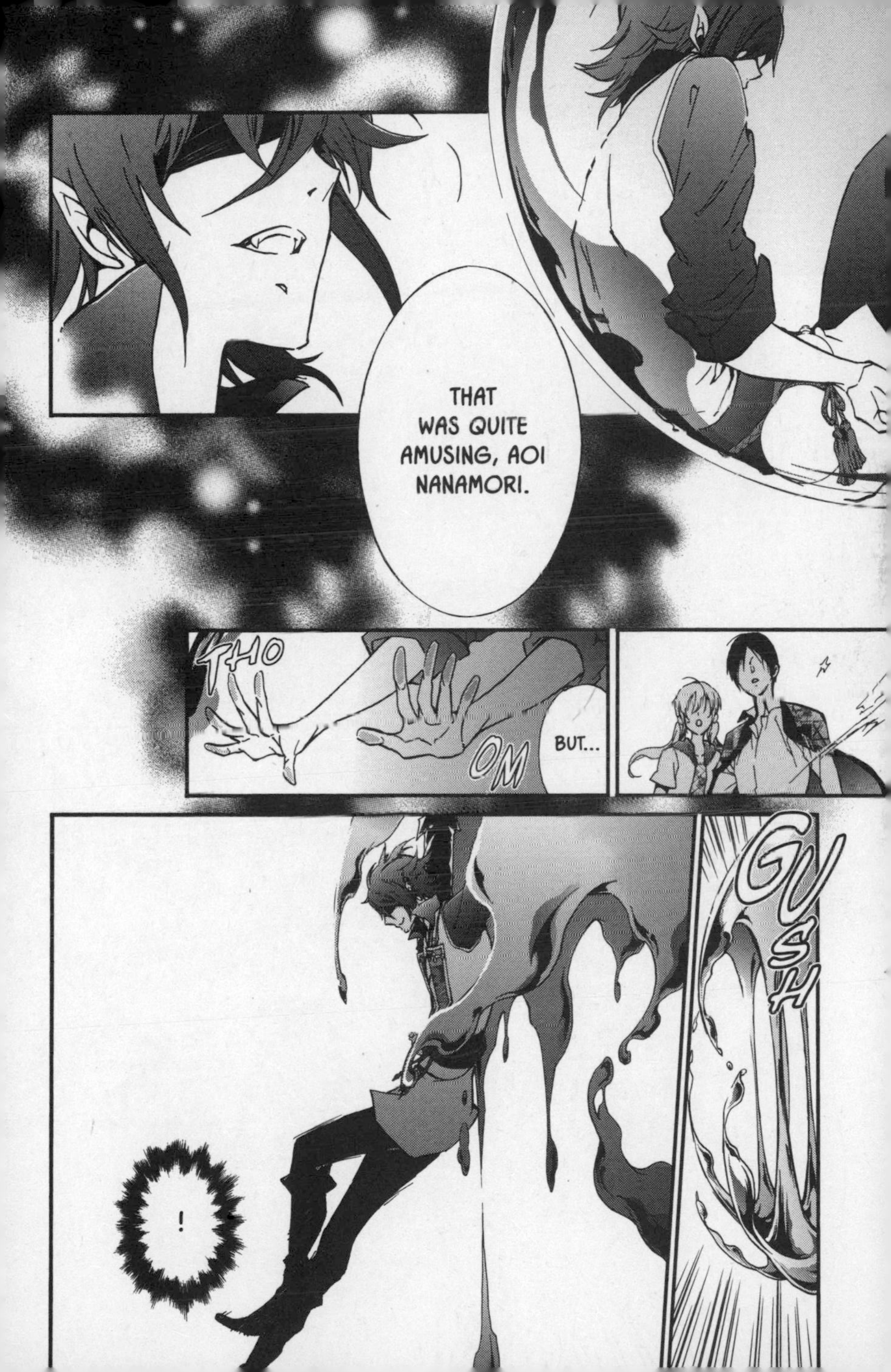
THAT WAS QUITE AMUSING, AOI NANAMORI.
BUT...
THOOM
GUSH
!

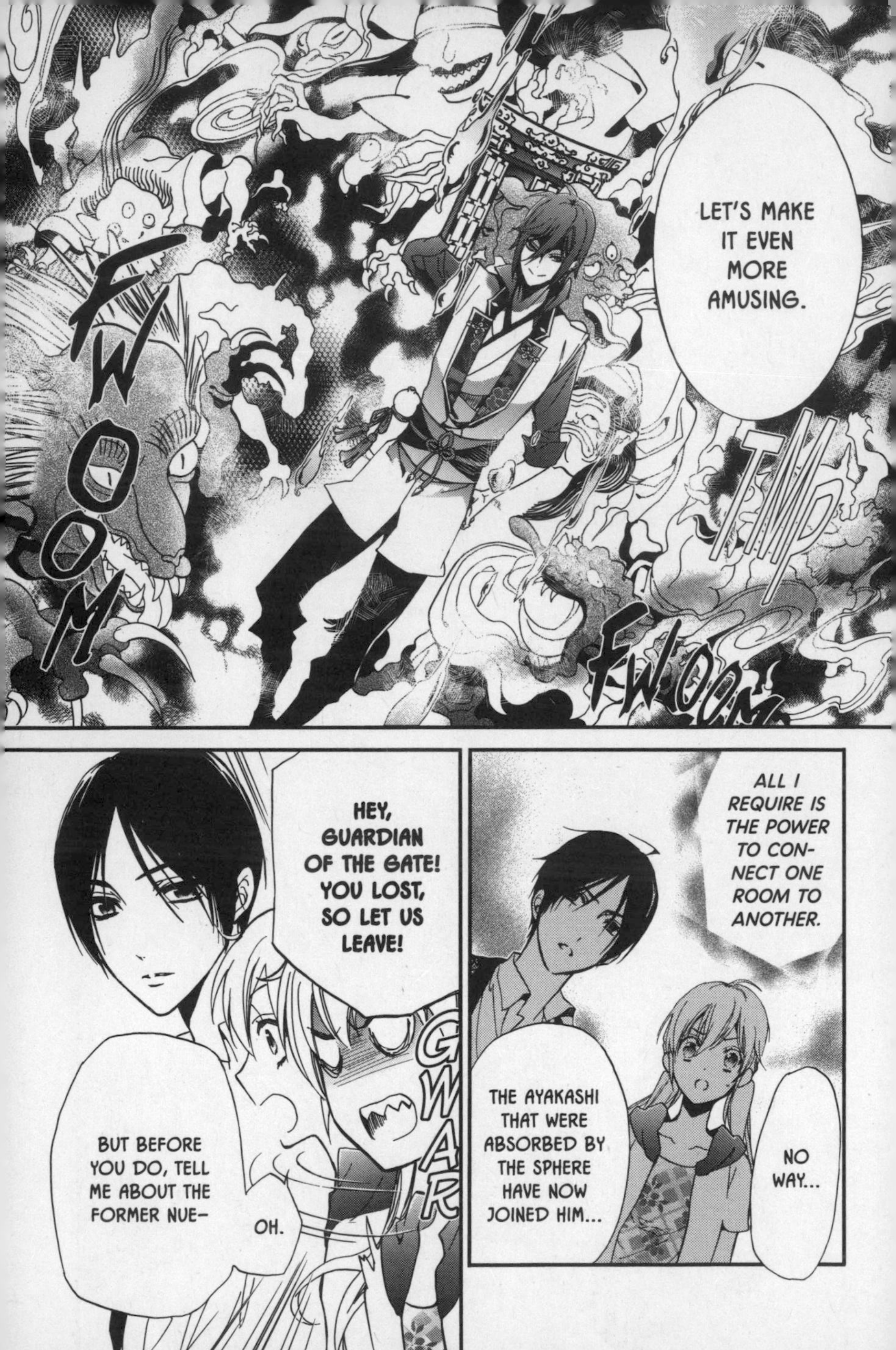
LET'S MAKE IT EVEN MORE AMUSING.
TMP
FWOOM
FWOOOM
ALL I REQUIRE IS THE POWER TO CON-NECT ONE ROOM TO ANOTHER.
THE AYAKASHI THAT WERE ABSORBED BY THE SPHERE HAVE NOW JOINED HIM...
NO WAY...
HEY, GUARDIAN OF THE GATE! YOU LOST, SO LET US LEAVE!
GWAR
BUT BEFORE YOU DO, TELL ME ABOUT THE FORMER NUE–
OH.

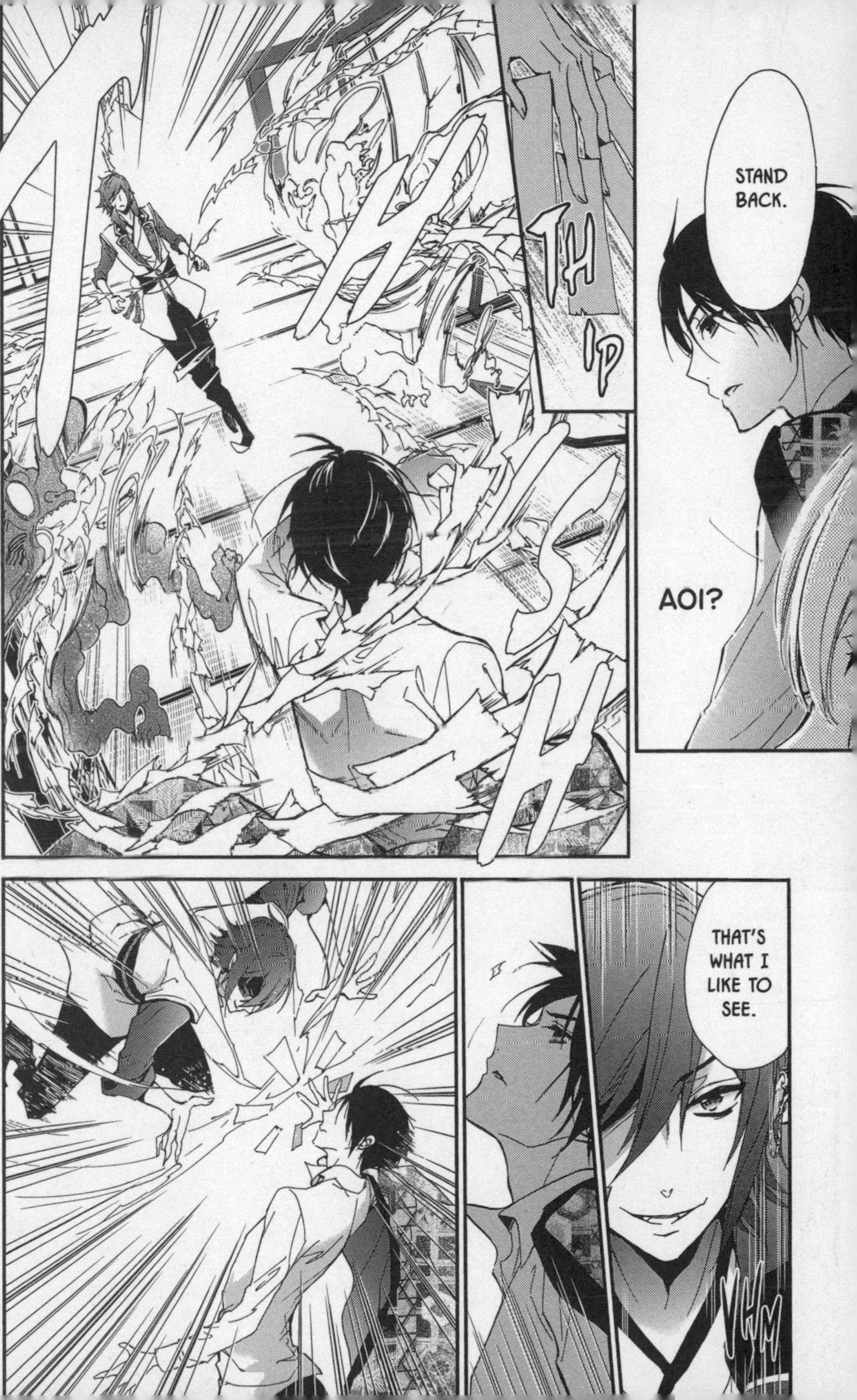
STAND BACK.
AOI?
THIP
THAT'S WHAT I LIKE TO SEE.

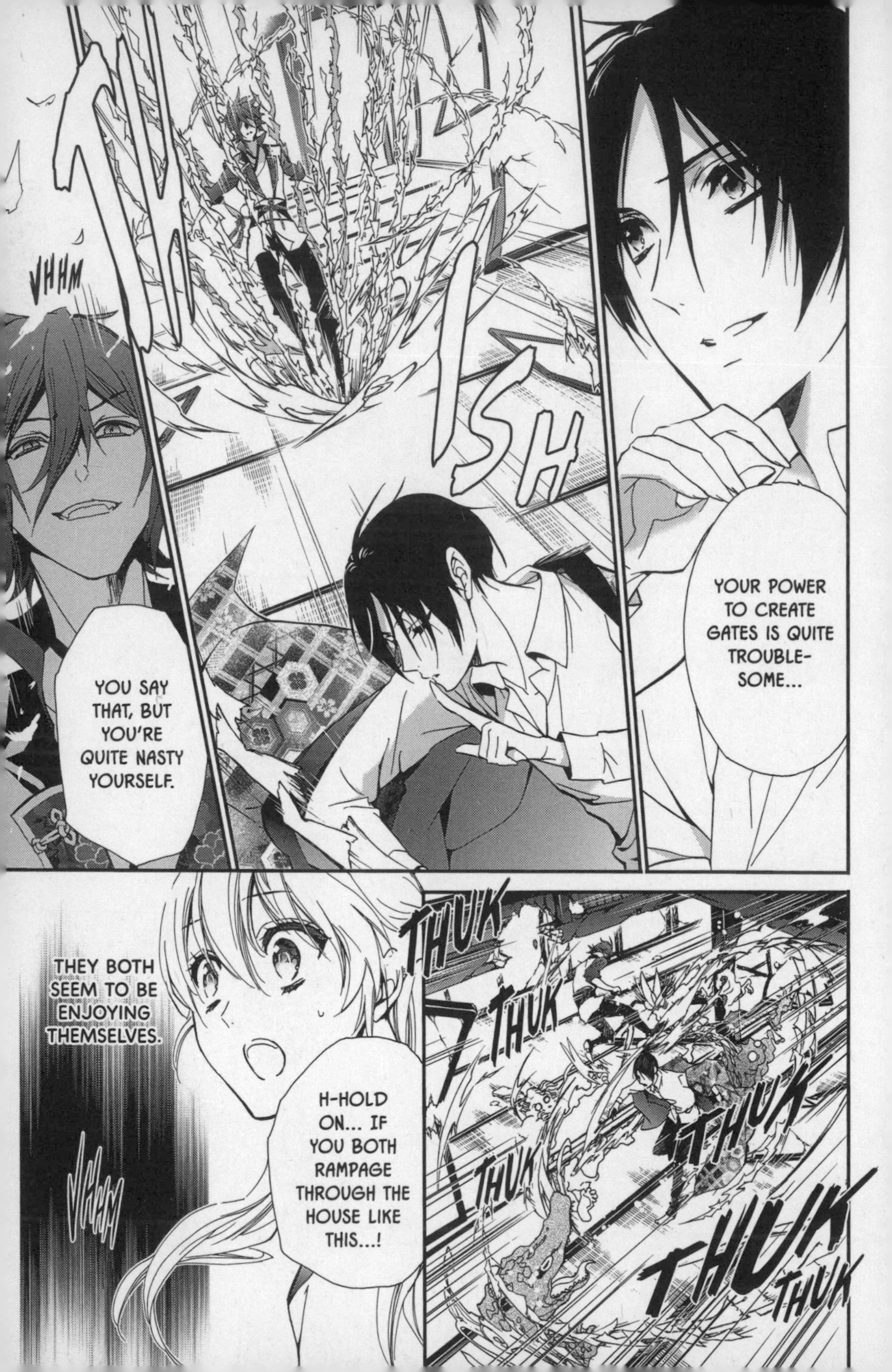
YOUR POWER TO CREATE GATES IS QUITE TROUBLE-SOME...
VHHM
YOU SAY THAT, BUT YOU'RE QUITE NASTY YOURSELF.
THUK
THUK
THUK
THUK
THUK
THUK
THUK
H-HOLD ON... IF YOU BOTH RAMPAGE THROUGH THE HOUSE LIKE THIS...!
THEY BOTH SEEM TO BE ENJOYING THEMSELVES.
VHHM

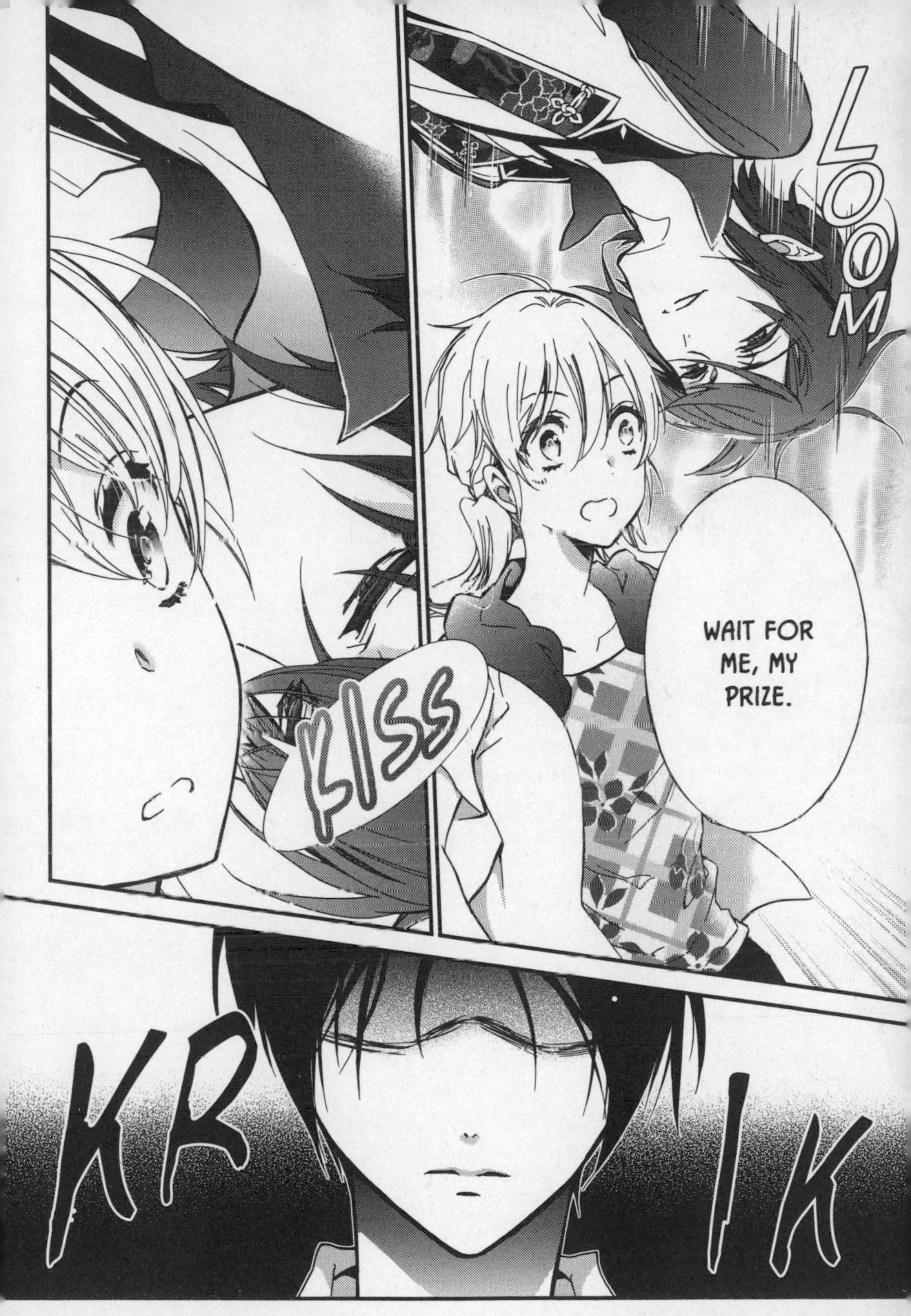
LOOM
WAIT FOR ME, MY PRIZE.
KISS
KR IK

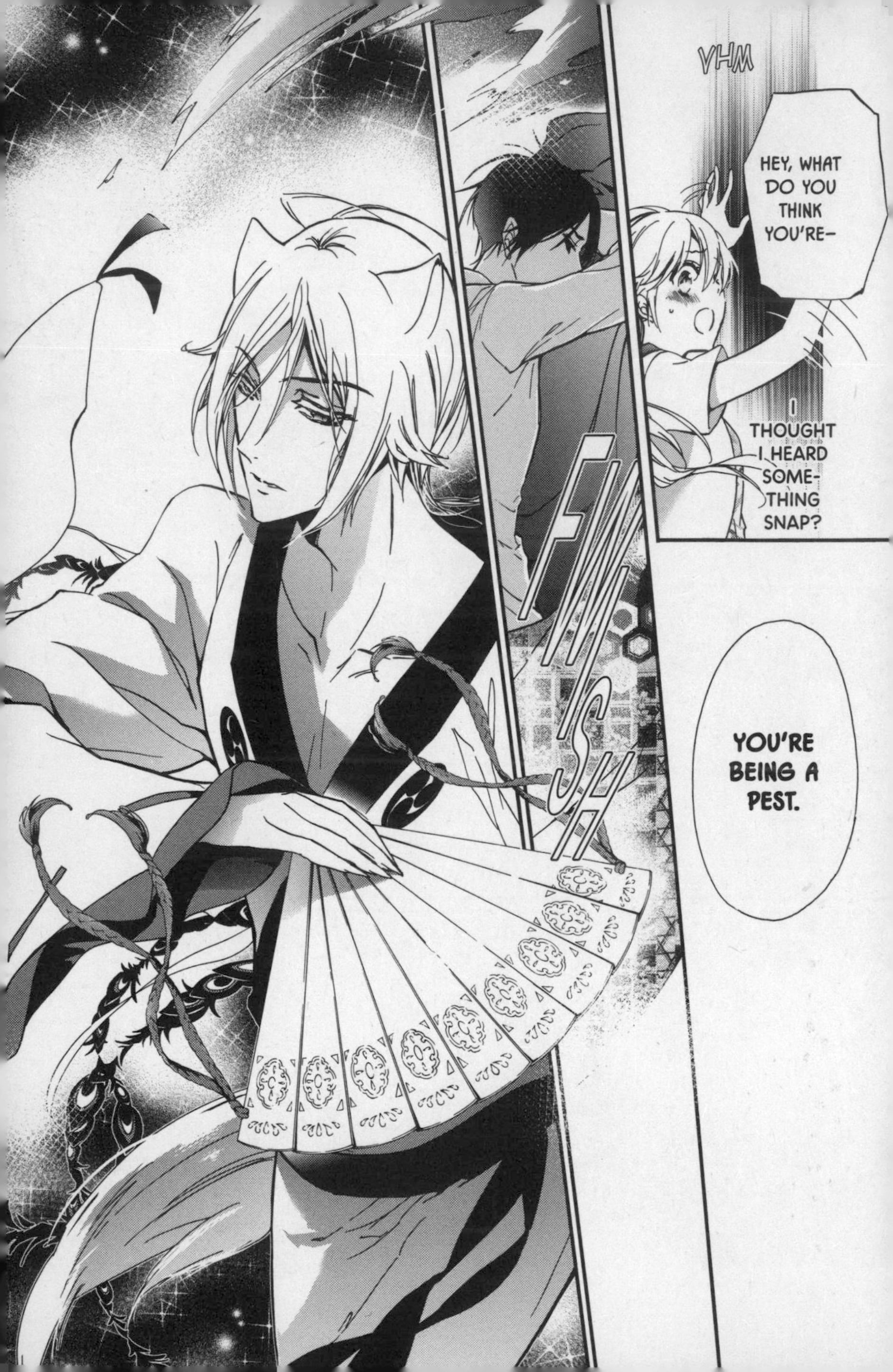
VHM
HEY, WHAT DO YOU THINK YOU'RE–
I THOUGHT I HEARD SOME-THING SNAP?
FWISH
YOU'RE BEING A PEST.

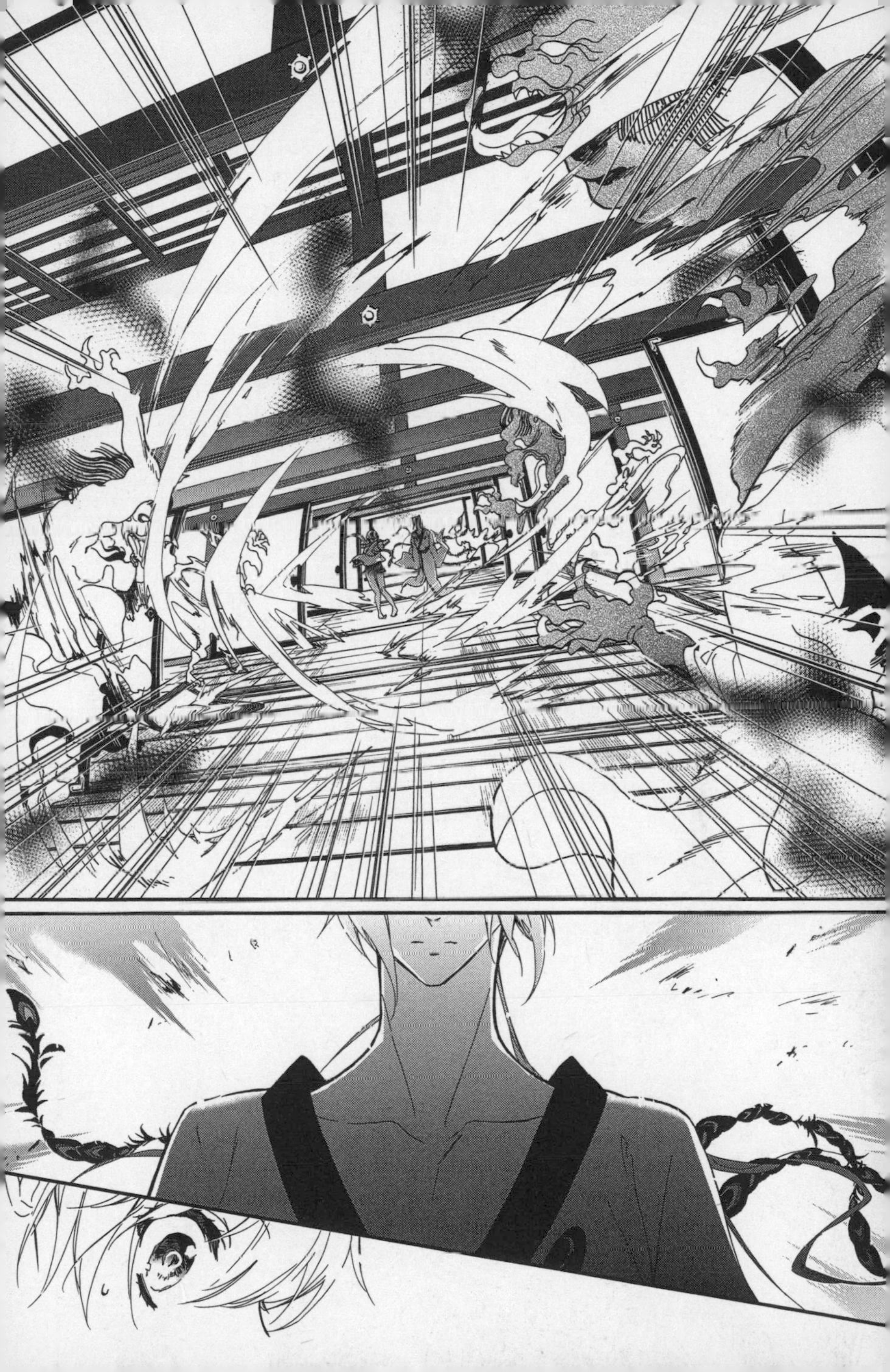

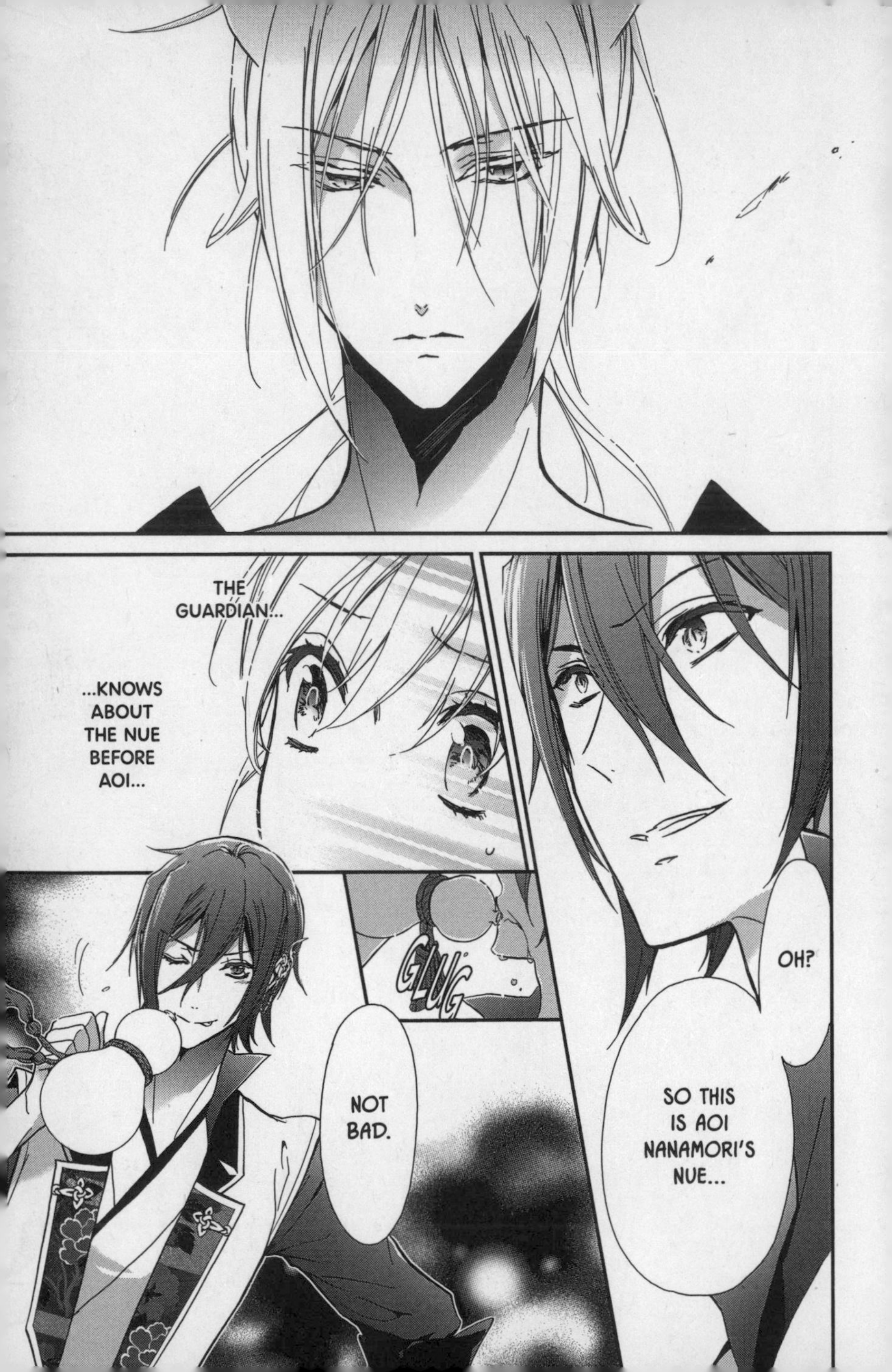
OH?
SO THIS IS AOI NANAMORI'S NUE...
THE GUARDIAN...
...KNOWS ABOUT THE NUE BEFORE AOI...
GLUG
NOT BAD.

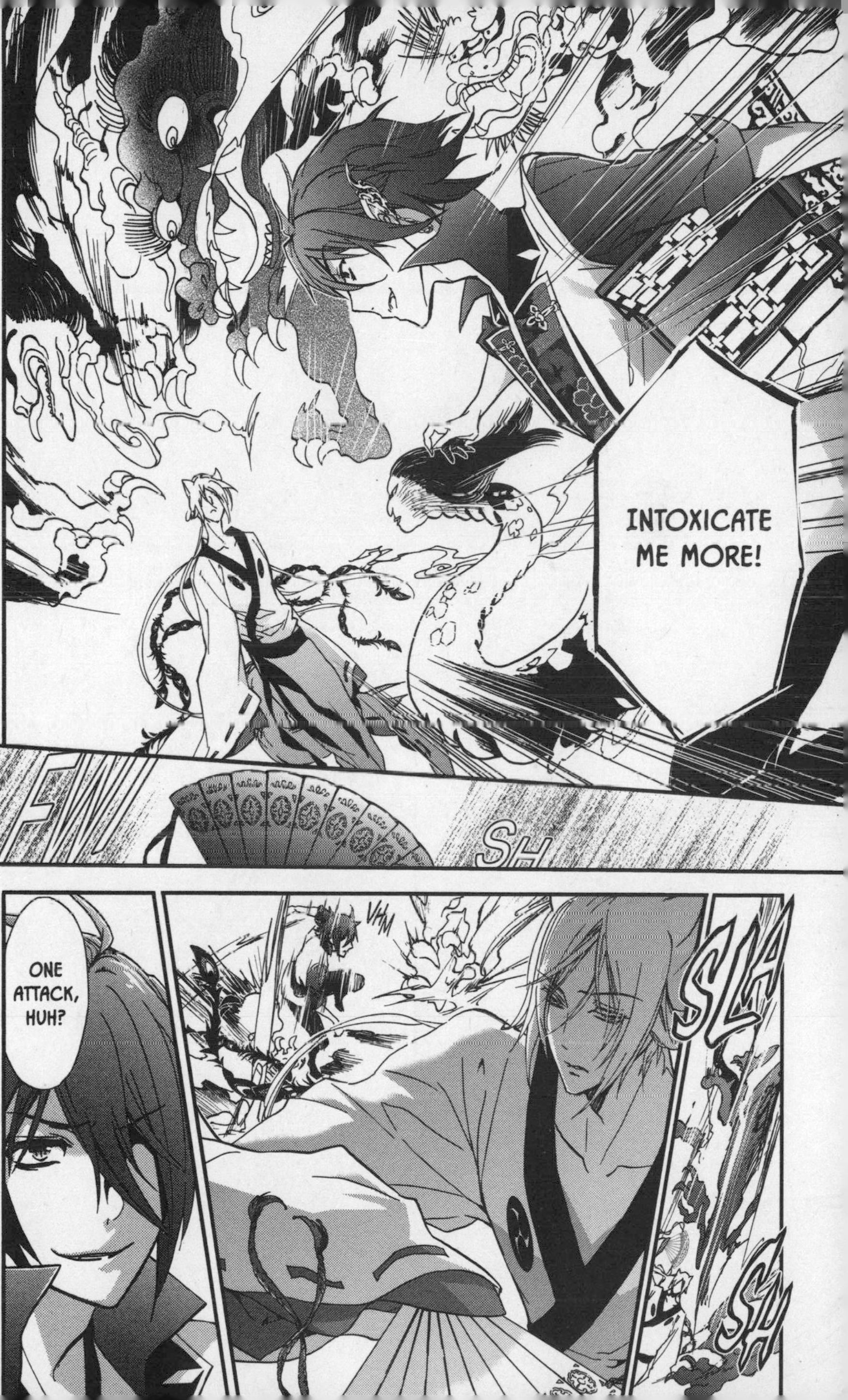
INTOXICATE ME MORE!
SH
FWI
SLA
VHM
SH
ONE ATTACK, HUH?

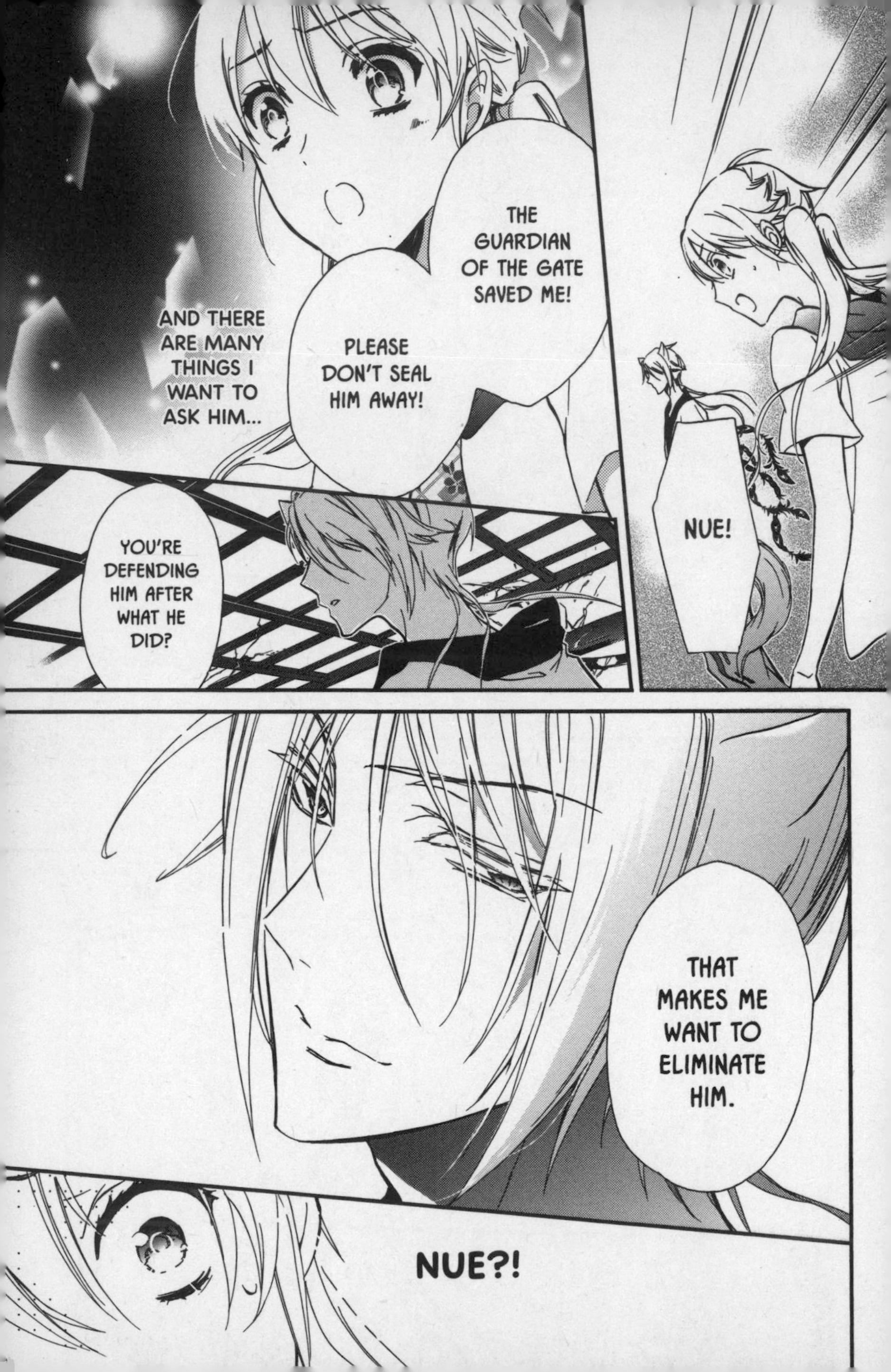
NUE!
THE GUARDIAN OF THE GATE SAVED ME!
PLEASE DON'T SEAL HIM AWAY!
AND THERE ARE MANY THINGS I WANT TO ASK HIM...
YOU'RE DEFENDING HIM AFTER WHAT HE DID?
THAT MAKES ME WANT TO ELIMINATE HIM.
NUE?!

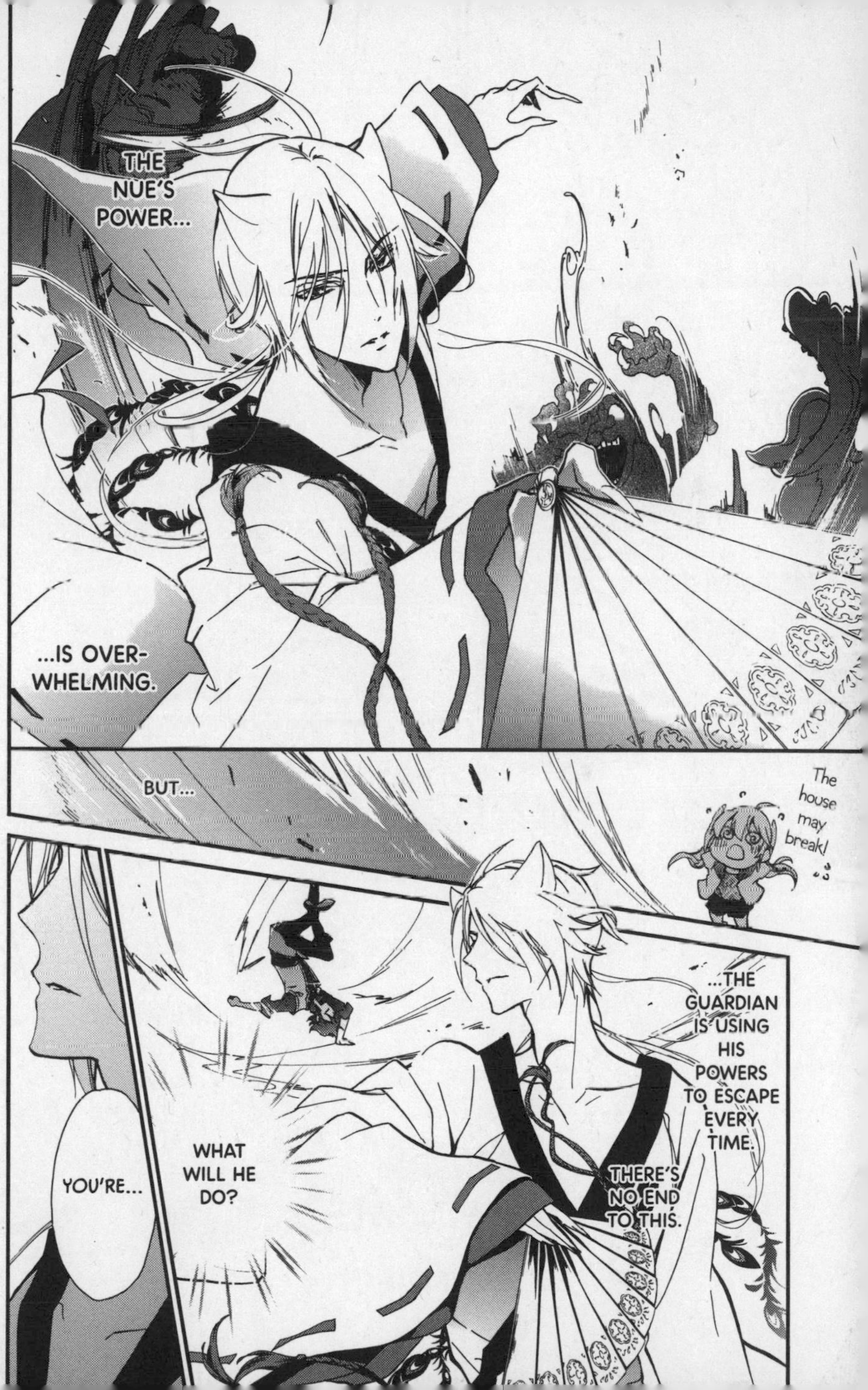

THE NUE'S POWER...
...IS OVER-WHELMING.
The house may break!
BUT...
...THE GUARDIAN IS USING HIS POWERS TO ESCAPE EVERY TIME.
THERE'S NO END TO THIS.
WHAT WILL HE DO?
YOU'RE...

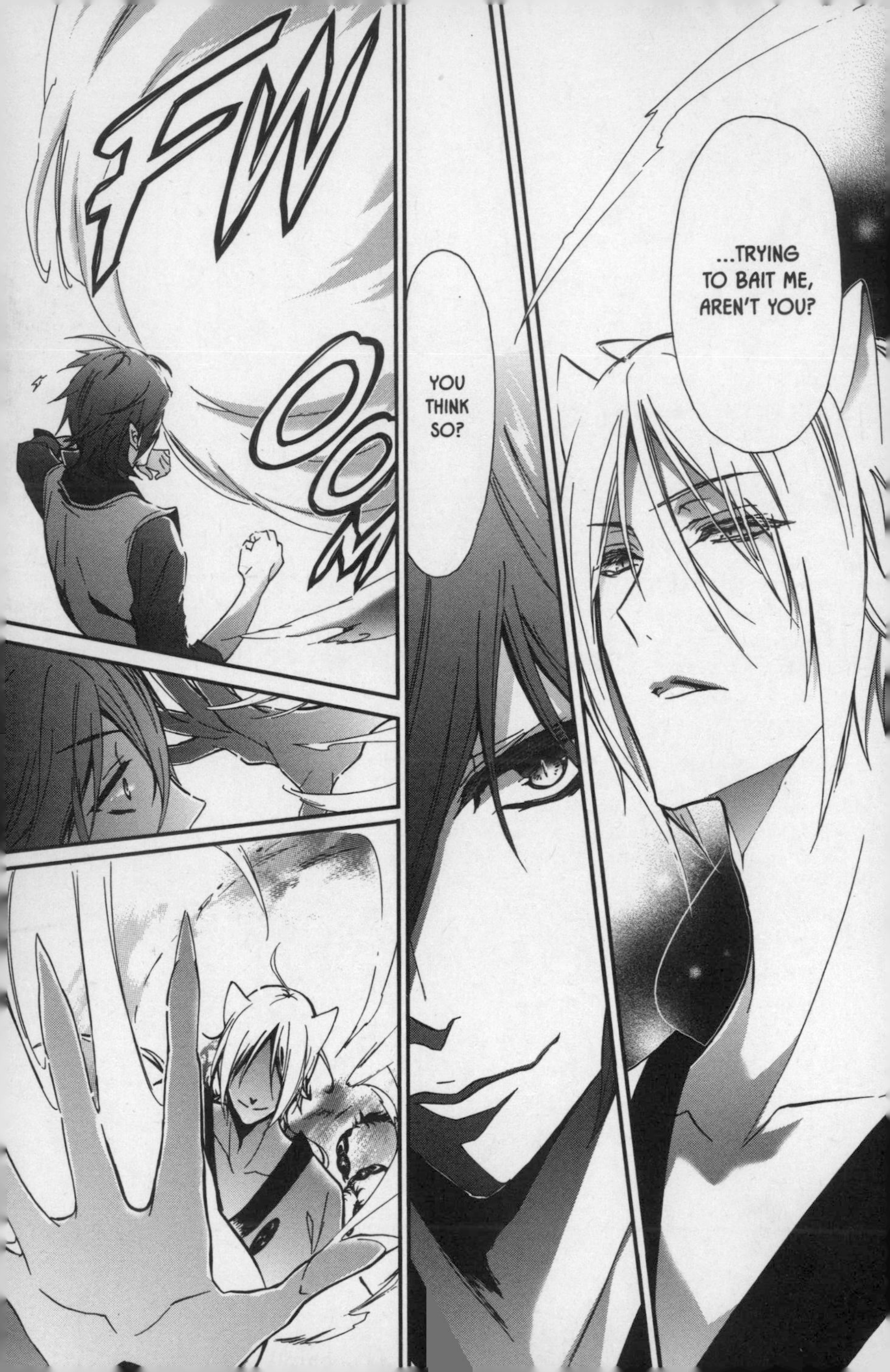
...TRYING TO BAIT ME, AREN'T YOU?
YOU THINK SO?
FWOOOM

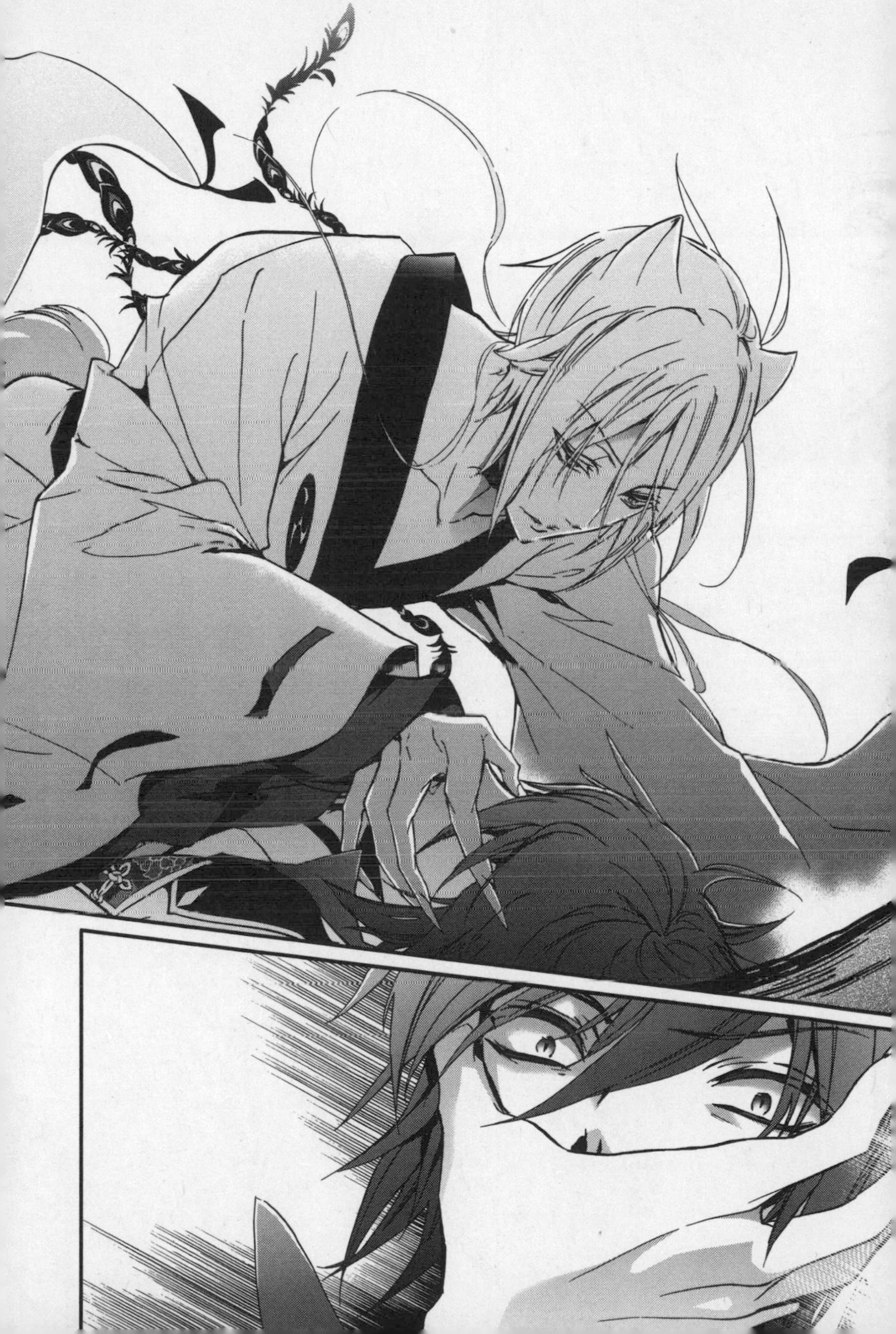

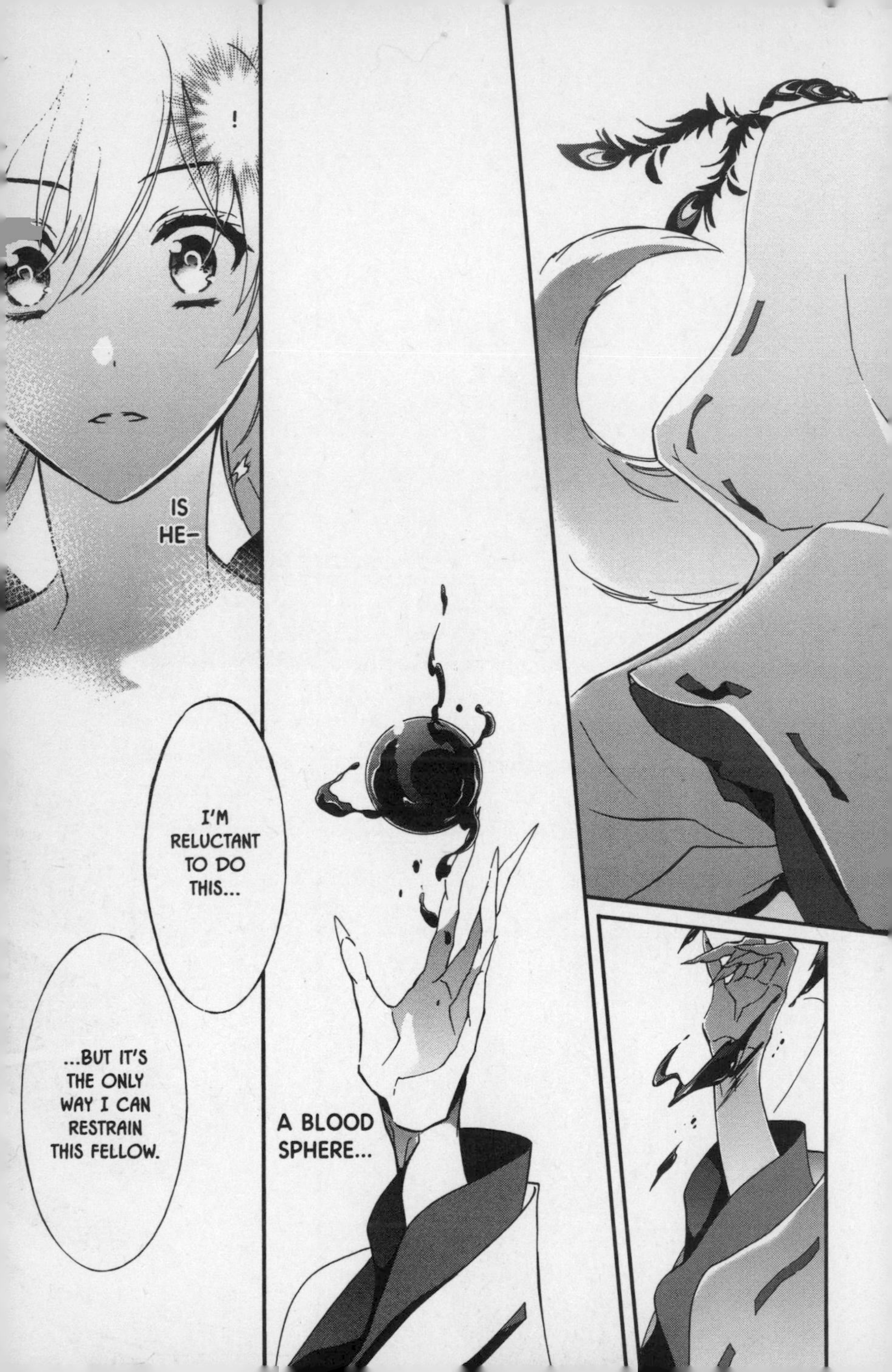
A BLOOD SPHERE...
!
IS HE–
I'M RELUCTANT TO DO THIS...
...BUT IT'S THE ONLY WAY I CAN RESTRAIN THIS FELLOW.

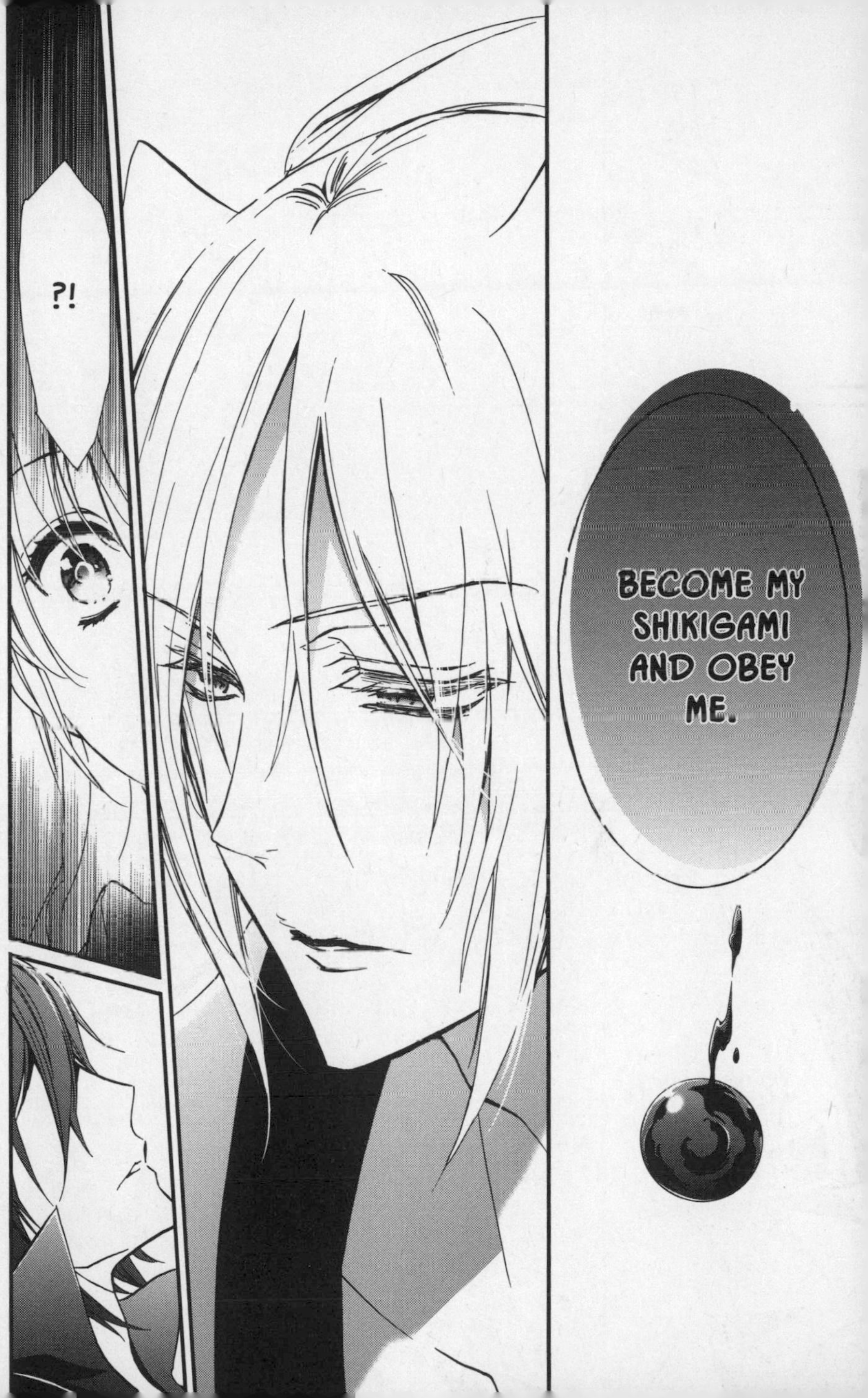
BECOME MY SHIKIGAMI AND OBEY ME.
?!

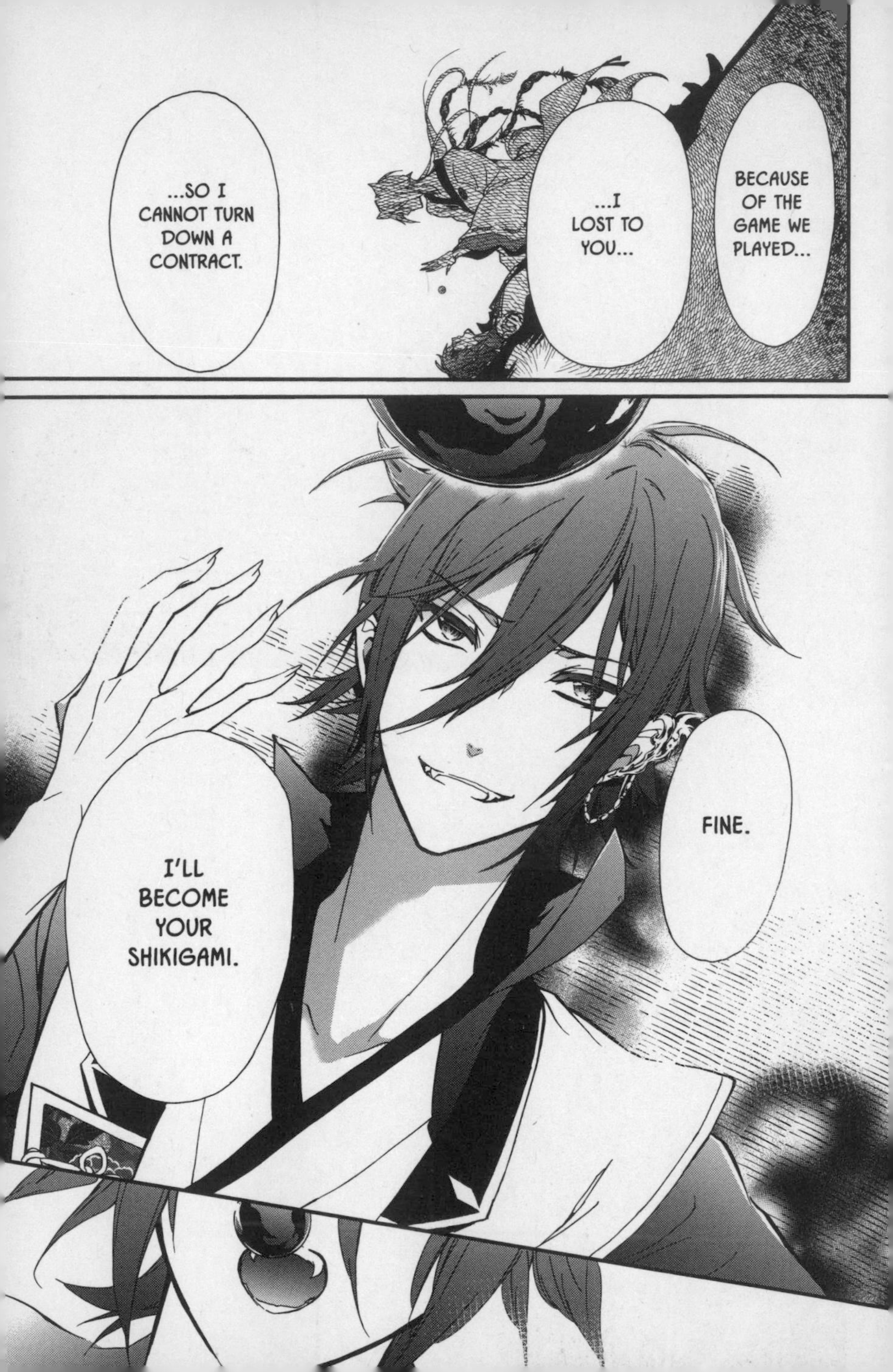
BECAUSE OF THE GAME WE PLAYED...
...I LOST TO YOU...
...SO I CANNOT TURN DOWN A CONTRACT.
FINE.
I'LL BECOME YOUR SHIKIGAMI.

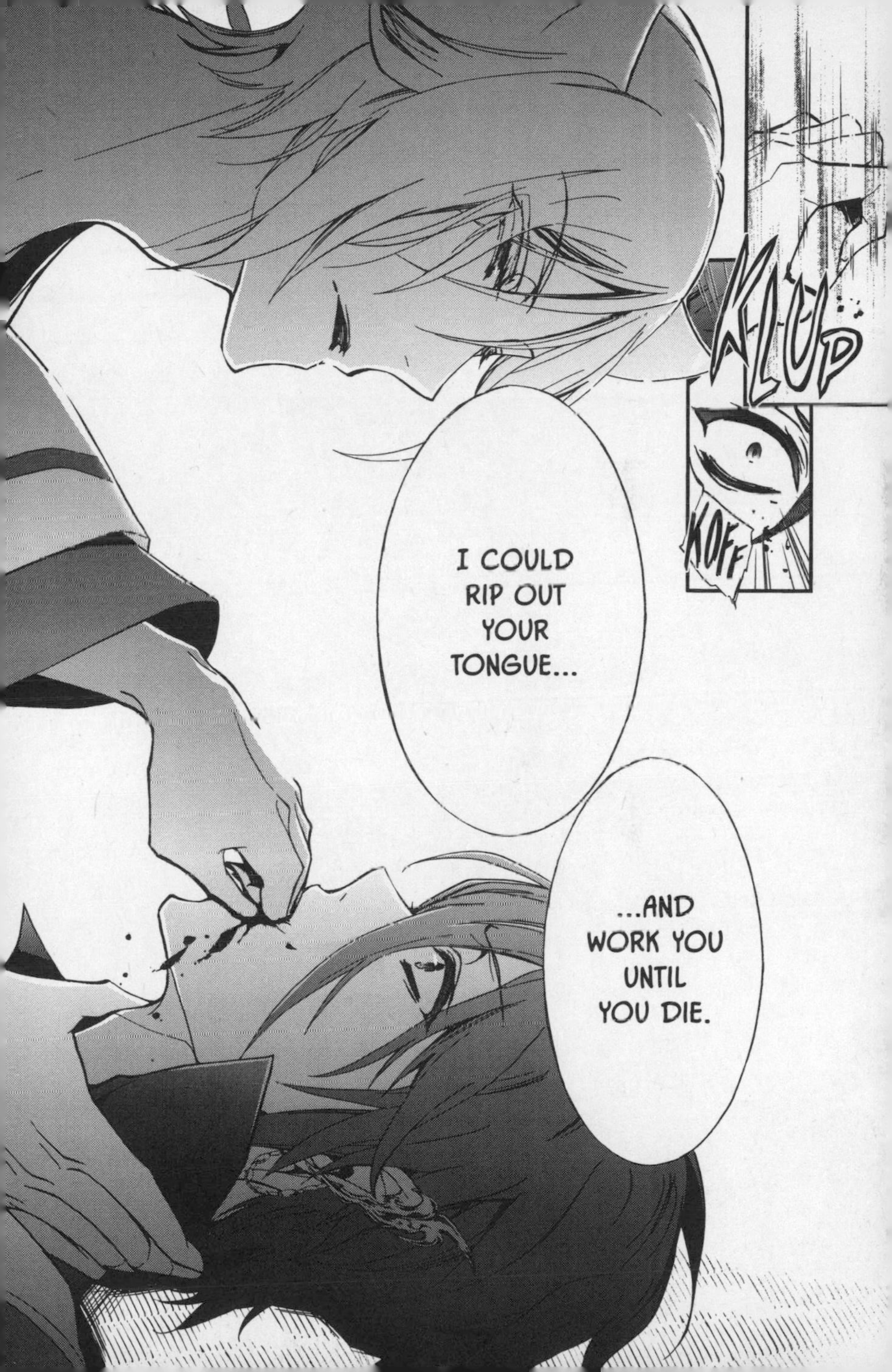
KLUD
KOFF
I COULD RIP OUT YOUR TONGUE...
...AND WORK YOU UNTIL YOU DIE.

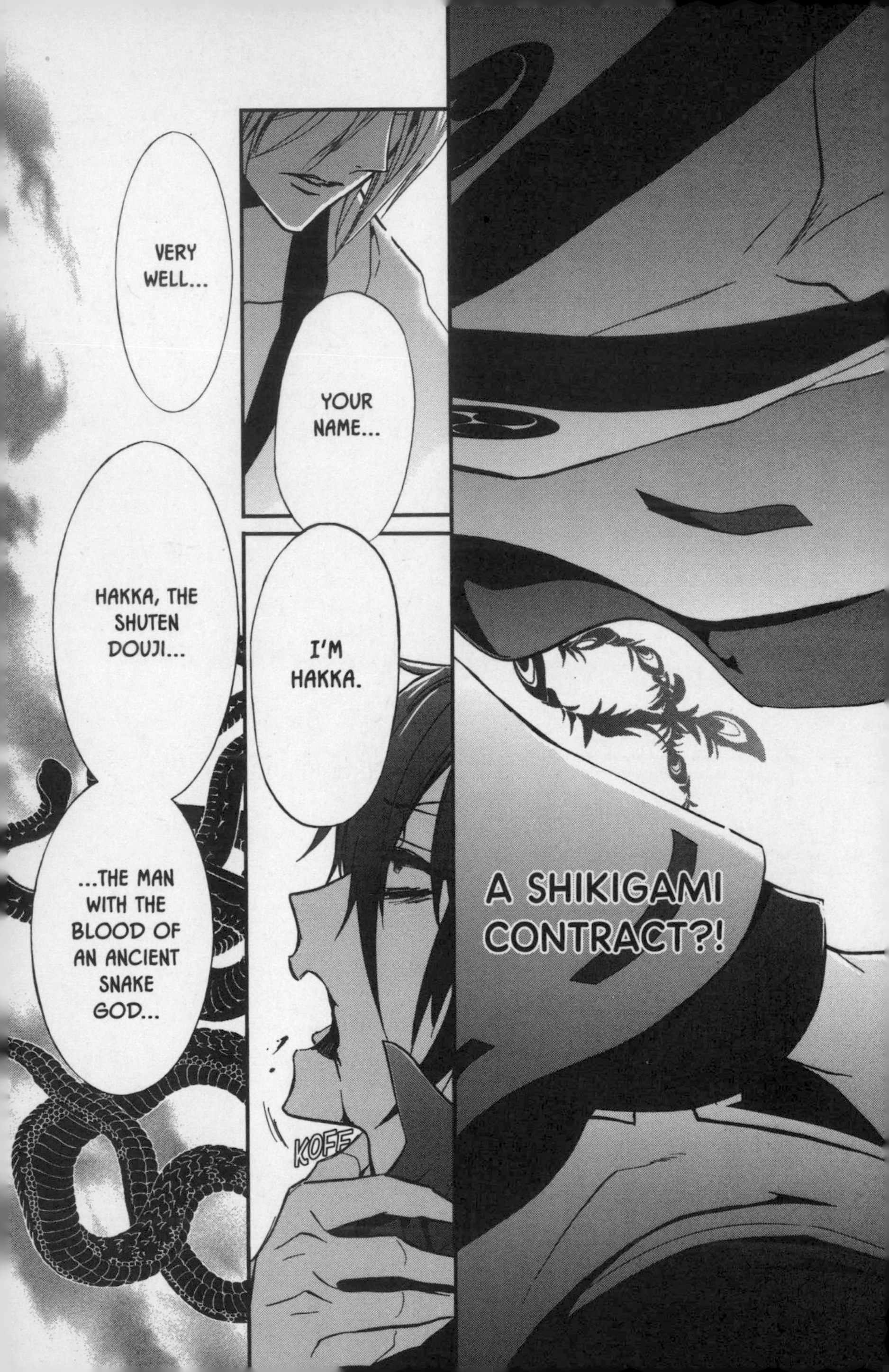
A SHIKIGAMI CONTRACT?!
YOUR NAME...
I'M HAKKA.
KOFF
VERY WELL...
HAKKA, THE SHUTEN DOUJI...
...THE MAN WITH THE BLOOD OF AN ANCIENT SNAKE GOD...

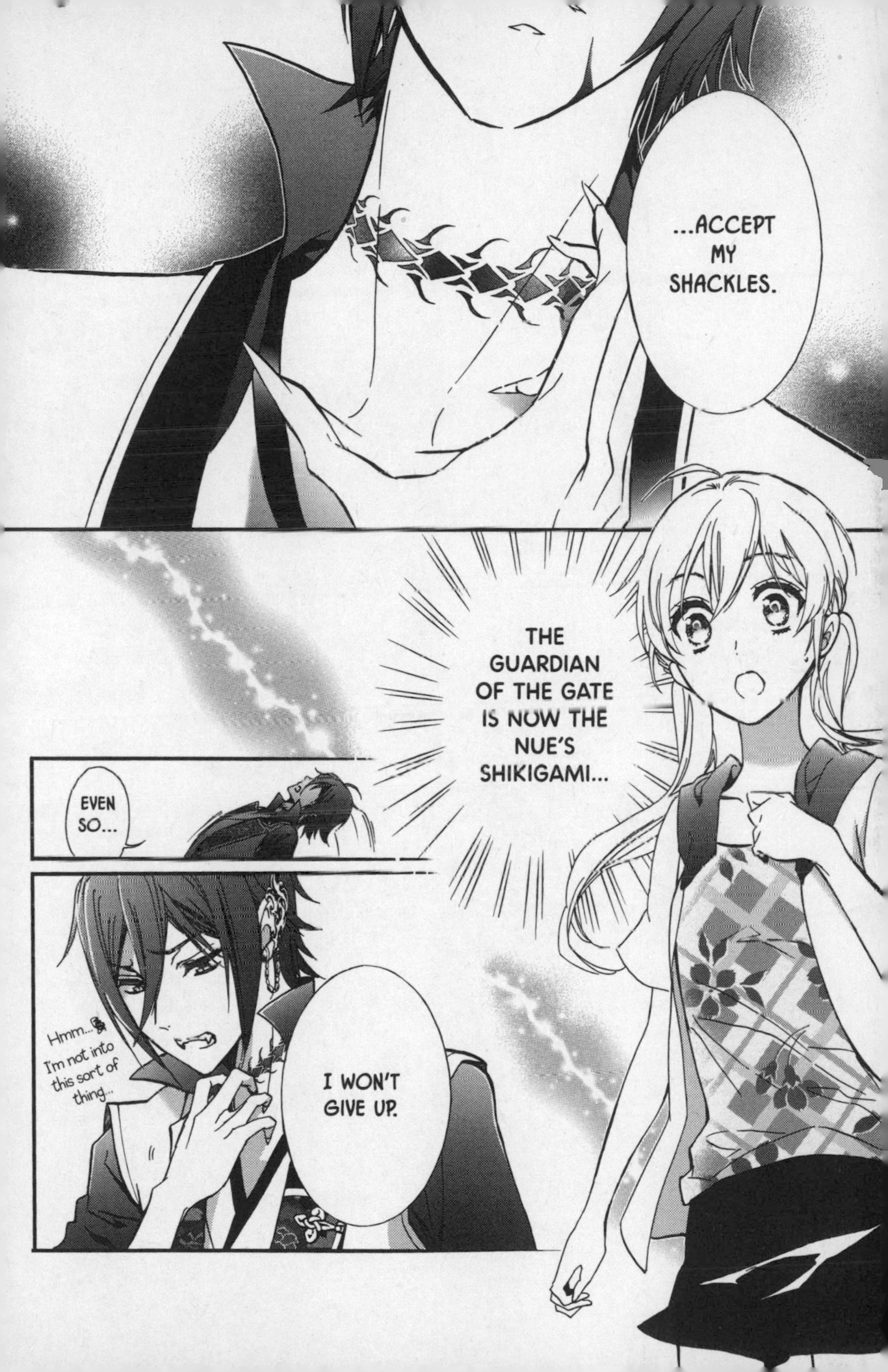
...ACCEPT MY SHACKLES.
THE GUARDIAN OF THE GATE IS NOW THE NUE'S SHIKIGAMI...
EVEN SO...
I WON'T GIVE UP.
Hmm... I'm not into this sort of thing...

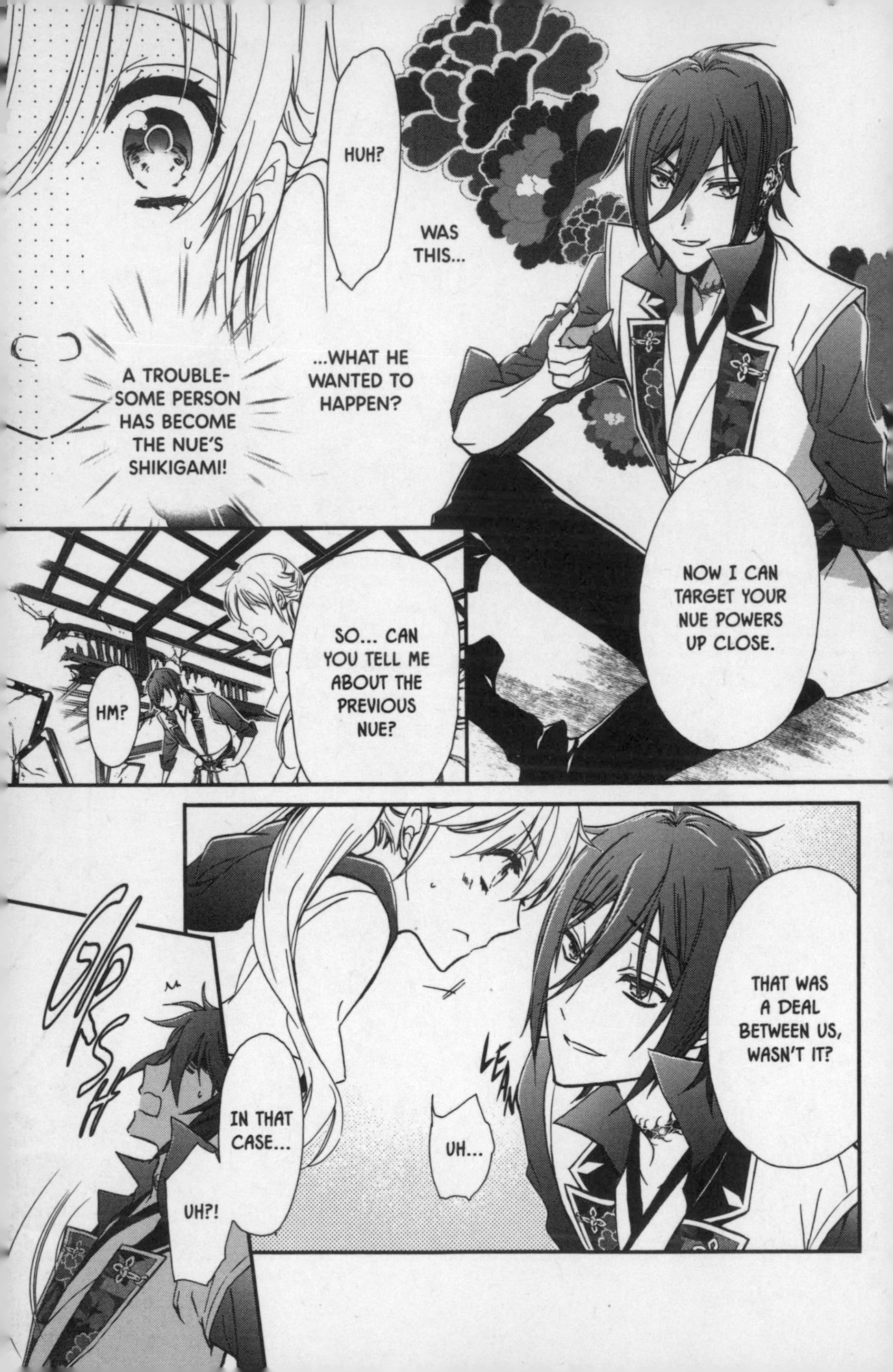
NOW I CAN TARGET YOUR NUE POWERS UP CLOSE.
HUH?
WAS THIS...
...WHAT HE WANTED TO HAPPEN?
A TROUBLE-SOME PERSON HAS BECOME THE NUE'S SHIKIGAMI!
SO... CAN YOU TELL ME ABOUT THE PREVIOUS NUE?
HM?
THAT WAS A DEAL BETWEEN US, WASN'T IT?
LEAN
UH...
IN THAT CASE...
UH?!

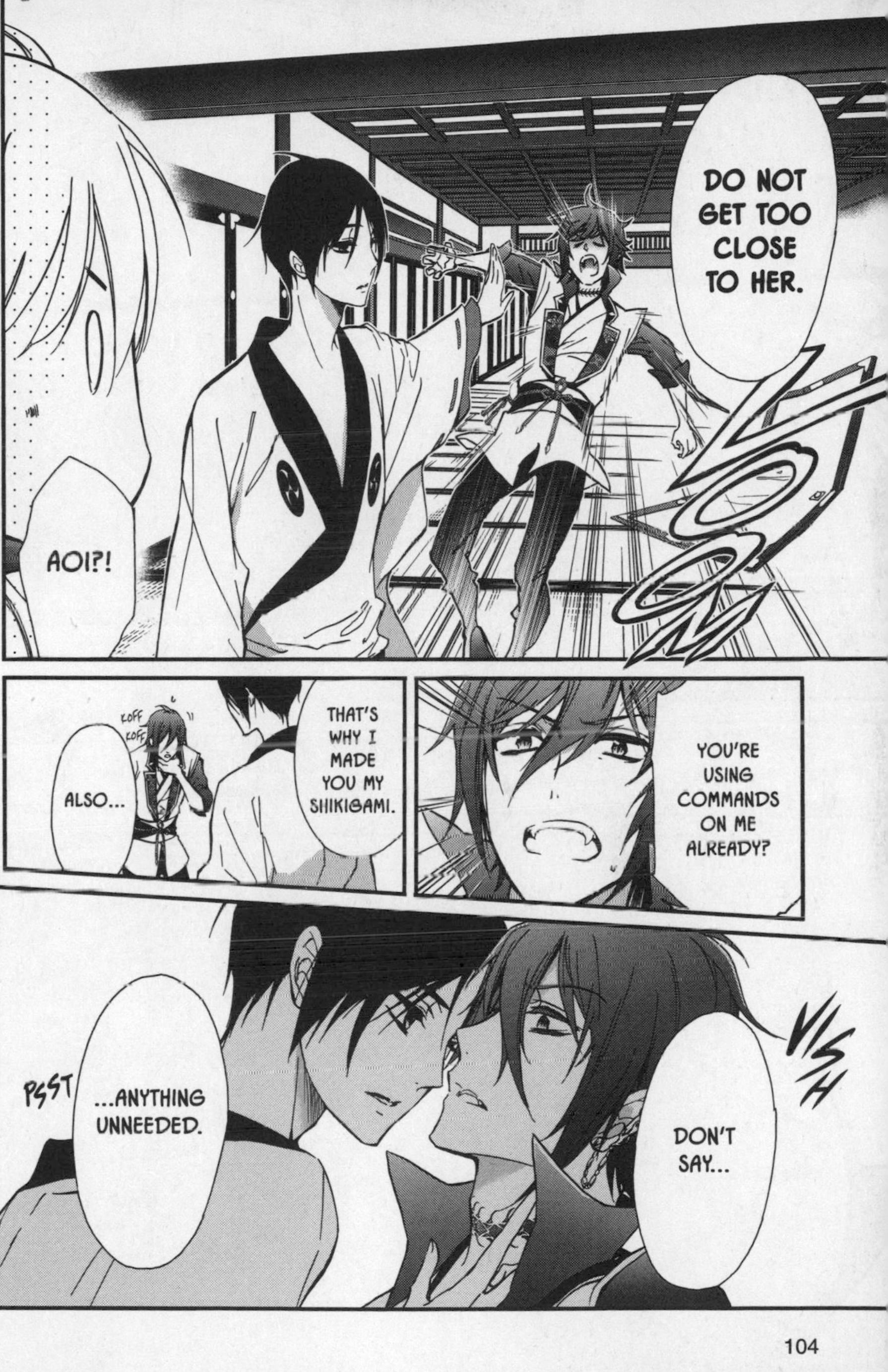

DO NOT GET TOO CLOSE TO HER.
AOI?!
YOU'RE USING COMMANDS ON ME ALREADY?
THAT'S WHY I MADE YOU MY SHIKIGAMI.
KOFF KOFF
ALSO...
VISH
DON'T SAY...
PSST
...ANYTHING UNNEEDED.

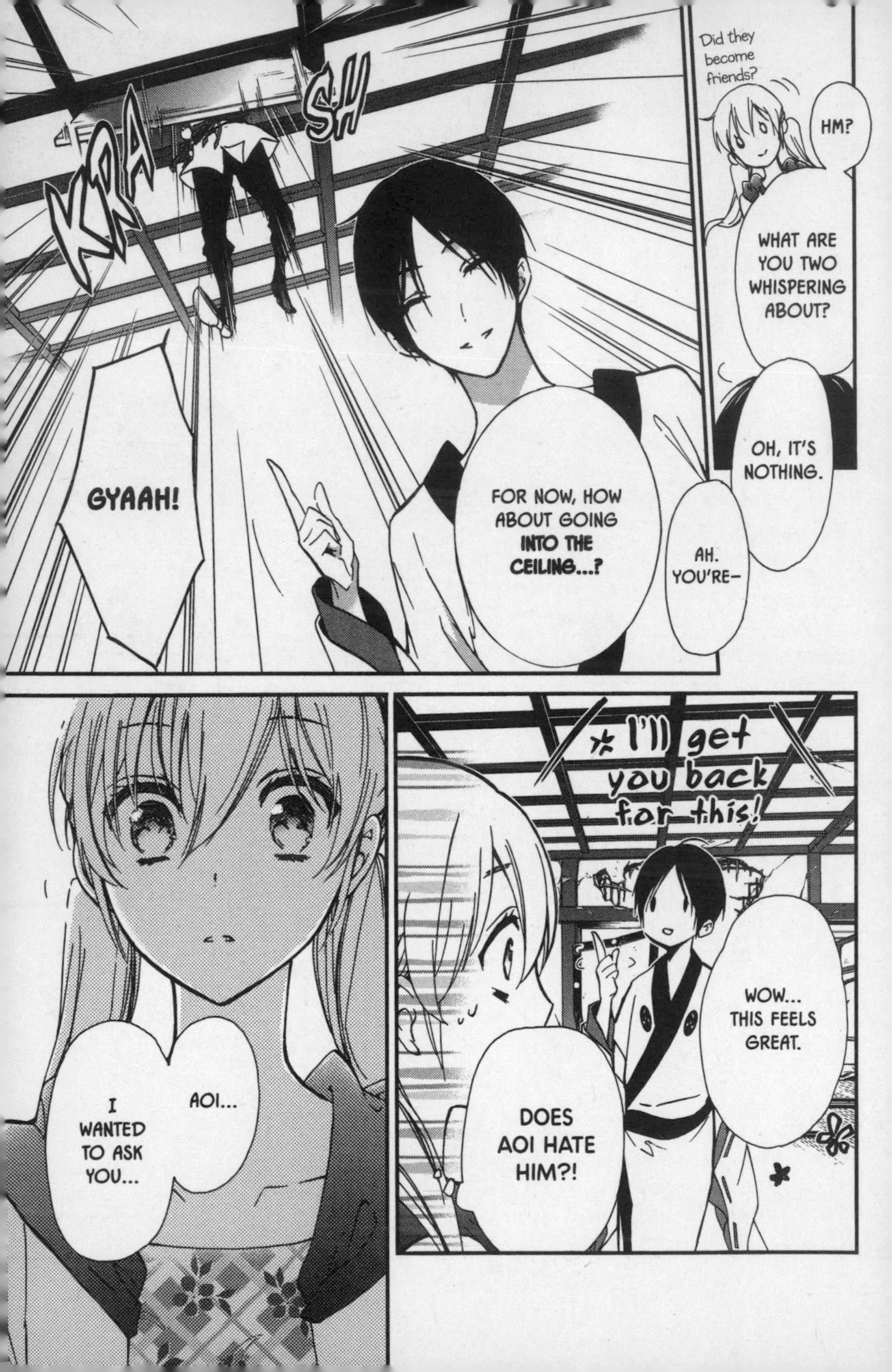
Did they become friends?
HM?
WHAT ARE YOU TWO WHISPERING ABOUT?
OH, IT'S NOTHING.
AH. YOU'RE—
FOR NOW, HOW ABOUT GOING INTO THE CEILING...?
KRASH
GYAAH!
I'll get you back for this!
WOW... THIS FEELS GREAT.
DOES AOI HATE HIM?!
AOI...
I WANTED TO ASK YOU...

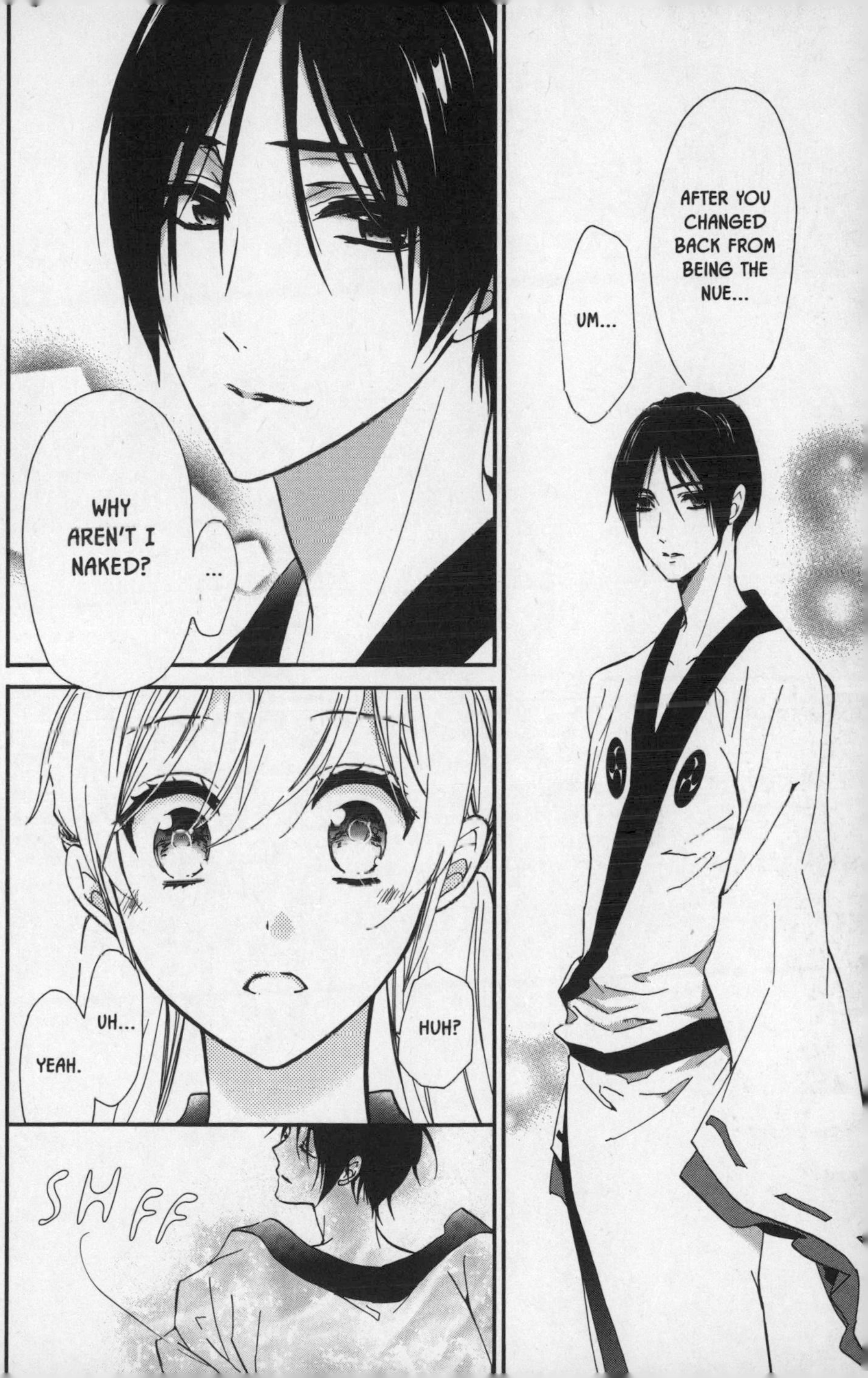
AFTER YOU CHANGED BACK FROM BEING THE NUE...
UM...
...
WHY AREN'T I NAKED?
HUH?
UH...
YEAH.
SHFF

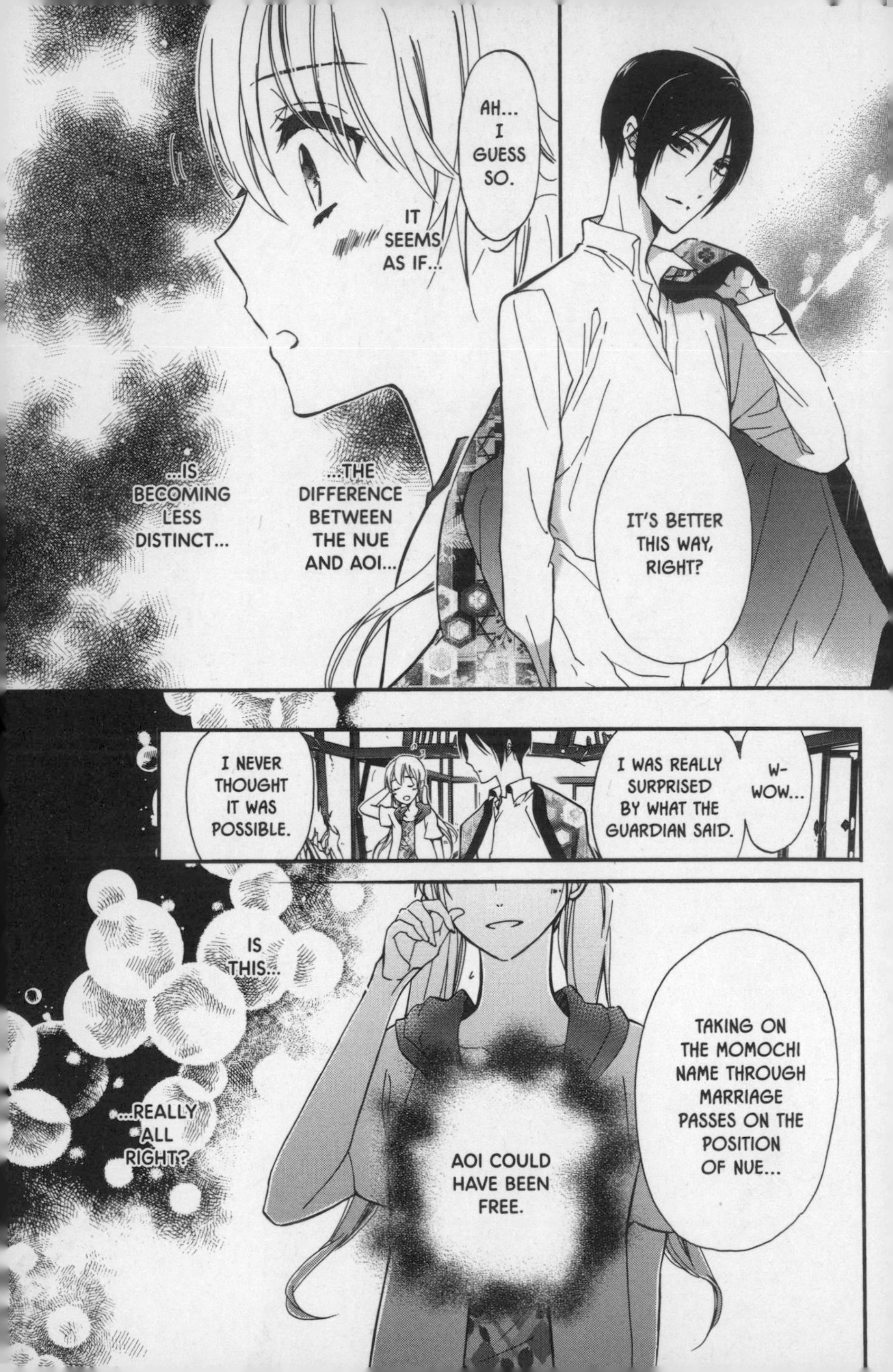
IT'S BETTER THIS WAY, RIGHT?
AH... I GUESS SO.
IT SEEMS AS IF...
...THE DIFFERENCE BETWEEN THE NUE AND AOI...
...IS BECOMING LESS DISTINCT...
W-WOW...
I WAS REALLY SURPRISED BY WHAT THE GUARDIAN SAID.
I NEVER THOUGHT IT WAS POSSIBLE.
TAKING ON THE MOMOCHI NAME THROUGH MARRIAGE PASSES ON THE POSITION OF NUE...
AOI COULD HAVE BEEN FREE.
IS THIS...
...REALLY ALL RIGHT?

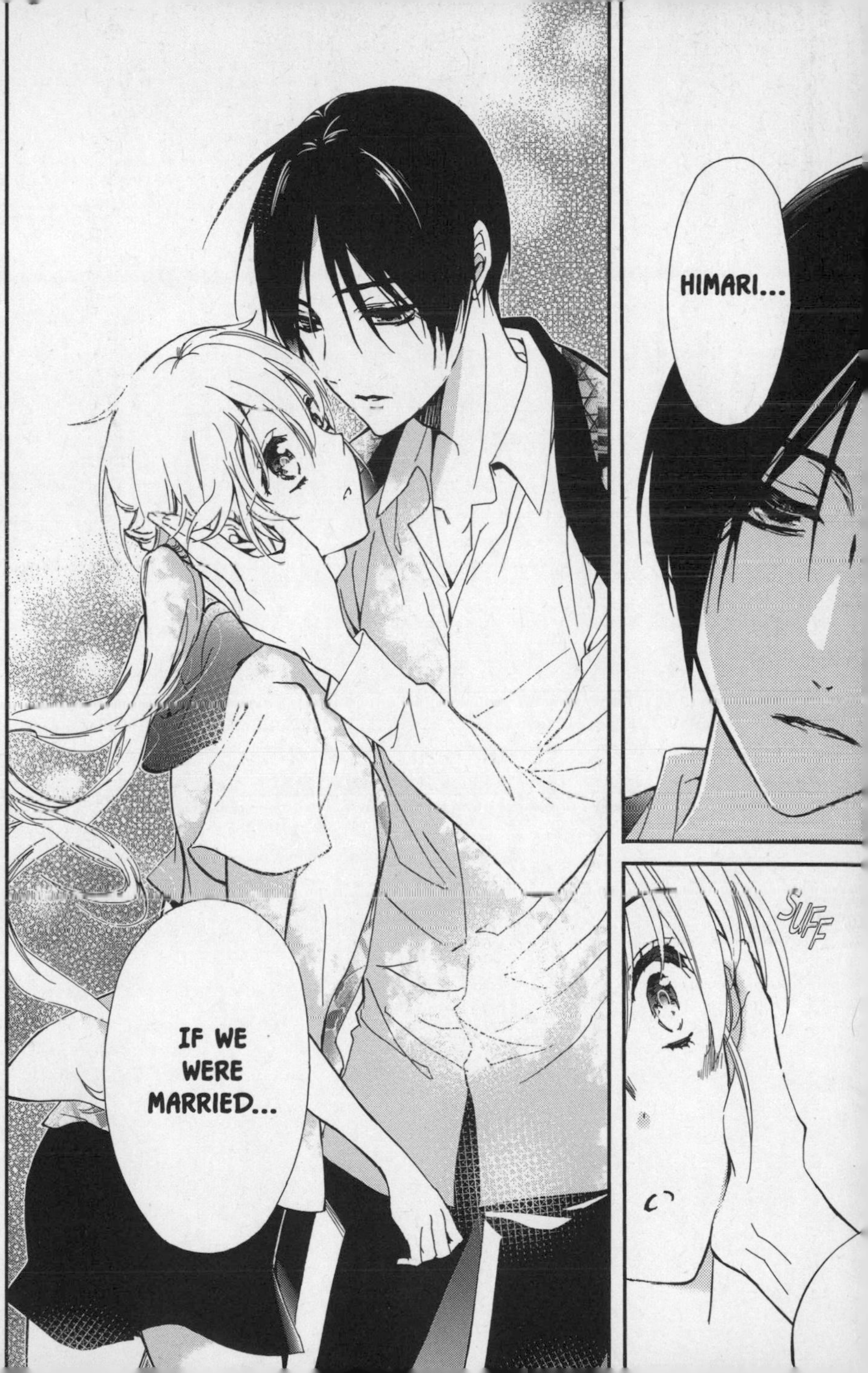
HIMARI...
SUFF
IF WE WERE MARRIED...

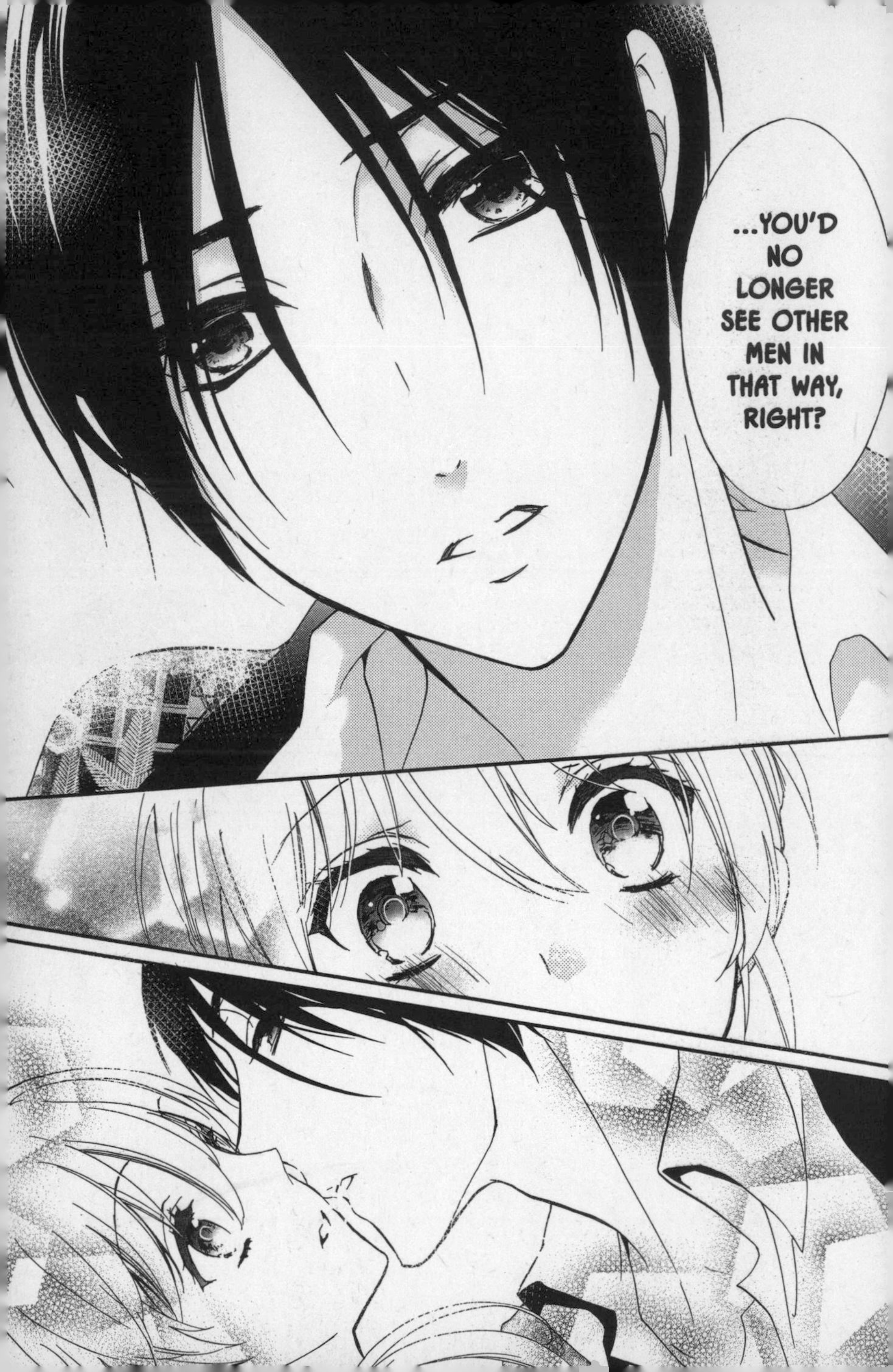
...YOU'D NO LONGER SEE OTHER MEN IN THAT WAY, RIGHT?

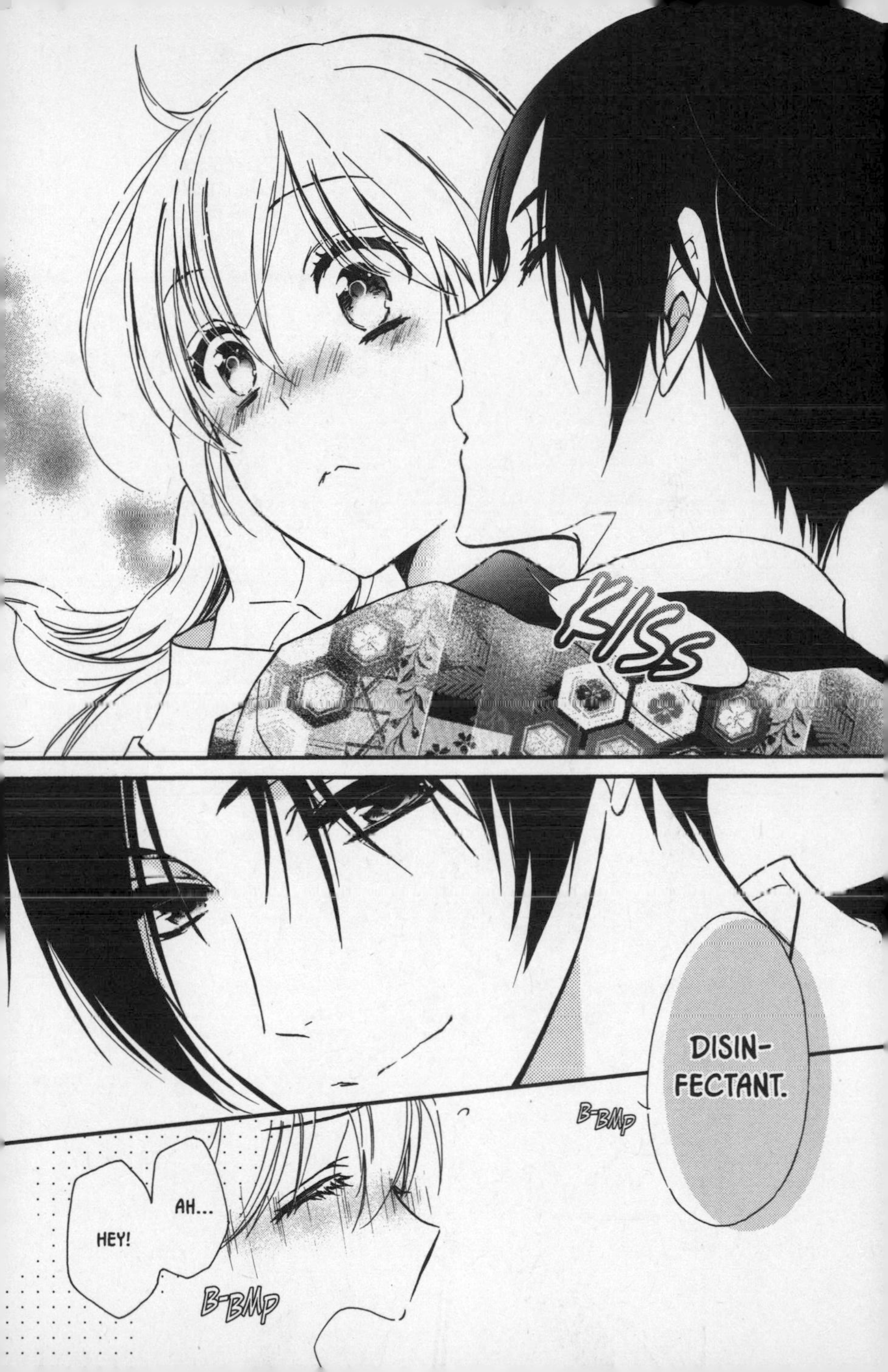
KISS
DISIN-FECTANT.
B-BMP
AH...
HEY!
B-BMP

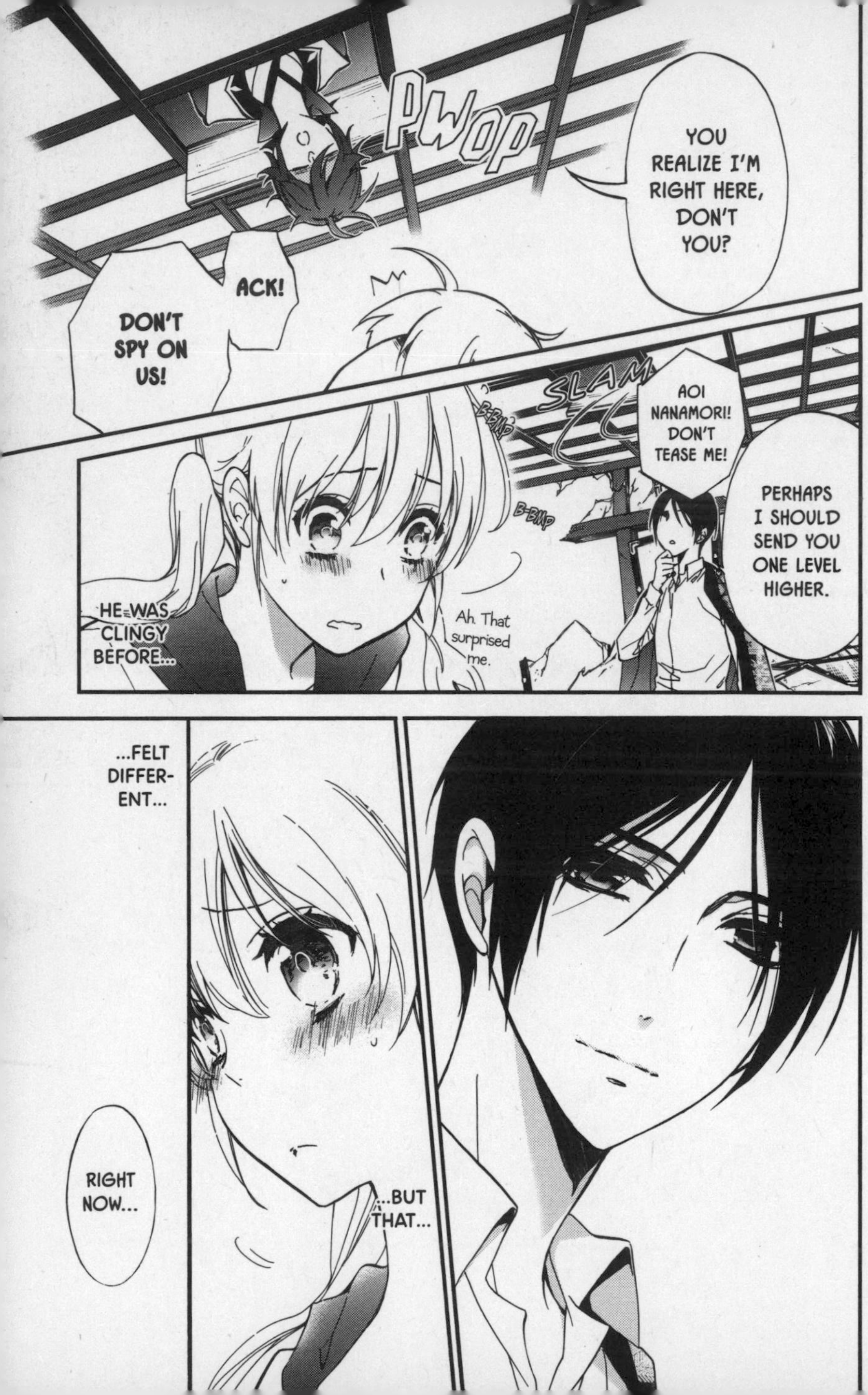
YOU REALIZE I'M RIGHT HERE, DON'T YOU?
PWOP
ACK!
DON'T SPY ON US!
SLAM
AOI NANAMORI! DON'T TEASE ME!
PERHAPS I SHOULD SEND YOU ONE LEVEL HIGHER.
B-BMP
B-BMP
Ah. That surprised me.
HE WAS CLINGY BEFORE...
...BUT THAT...
...FELT DIFFER-ENT...
RIGHT NOW...

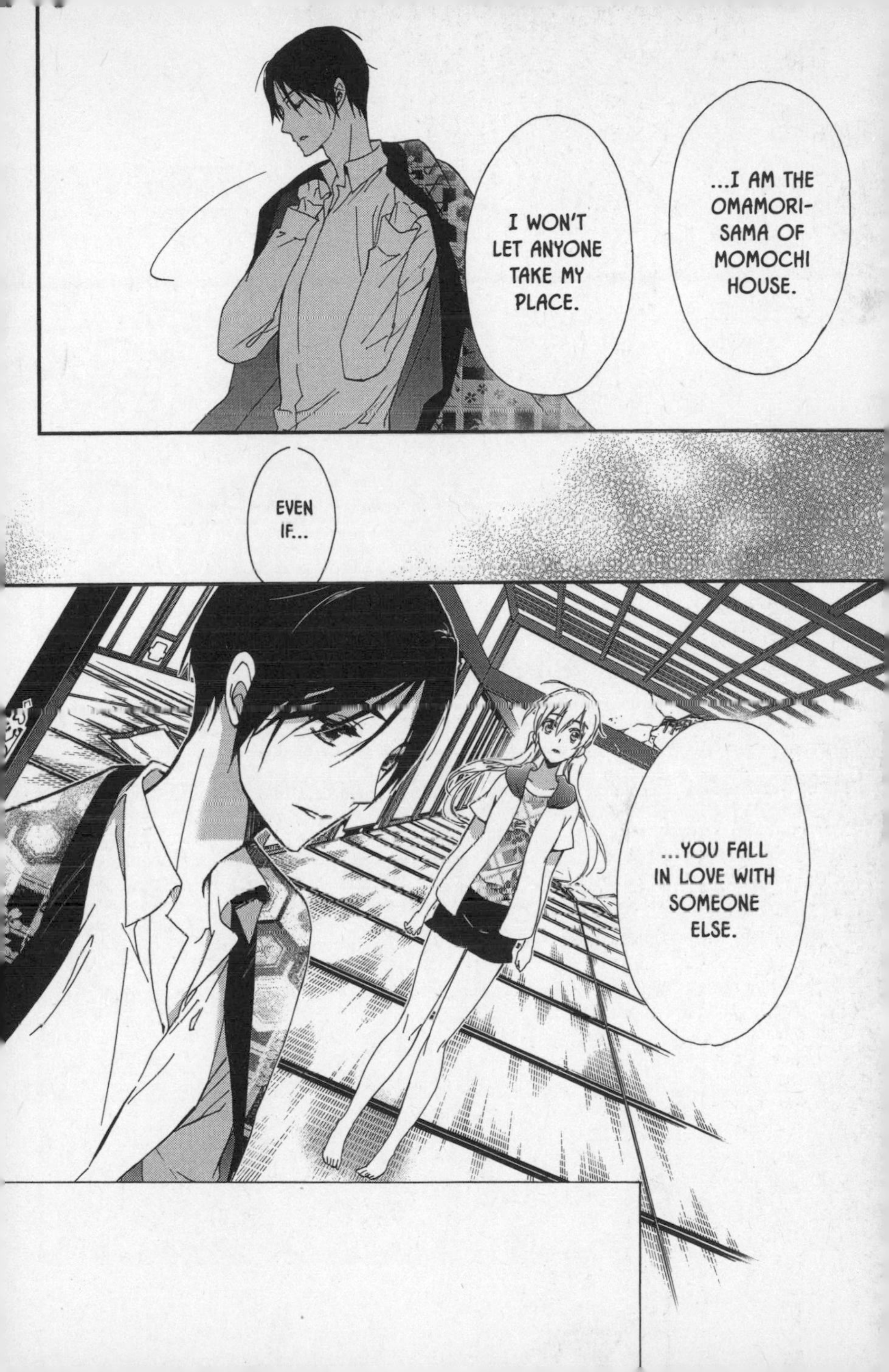
...I AM THE OMAMORI-SAMA OF MOMOCHI HOUSE.
I WON'T LET ANYONE TAKE MY PLACE.
EVEN IF...
...YOU FALL IN LOVE WITH SOMEONE ELSE.

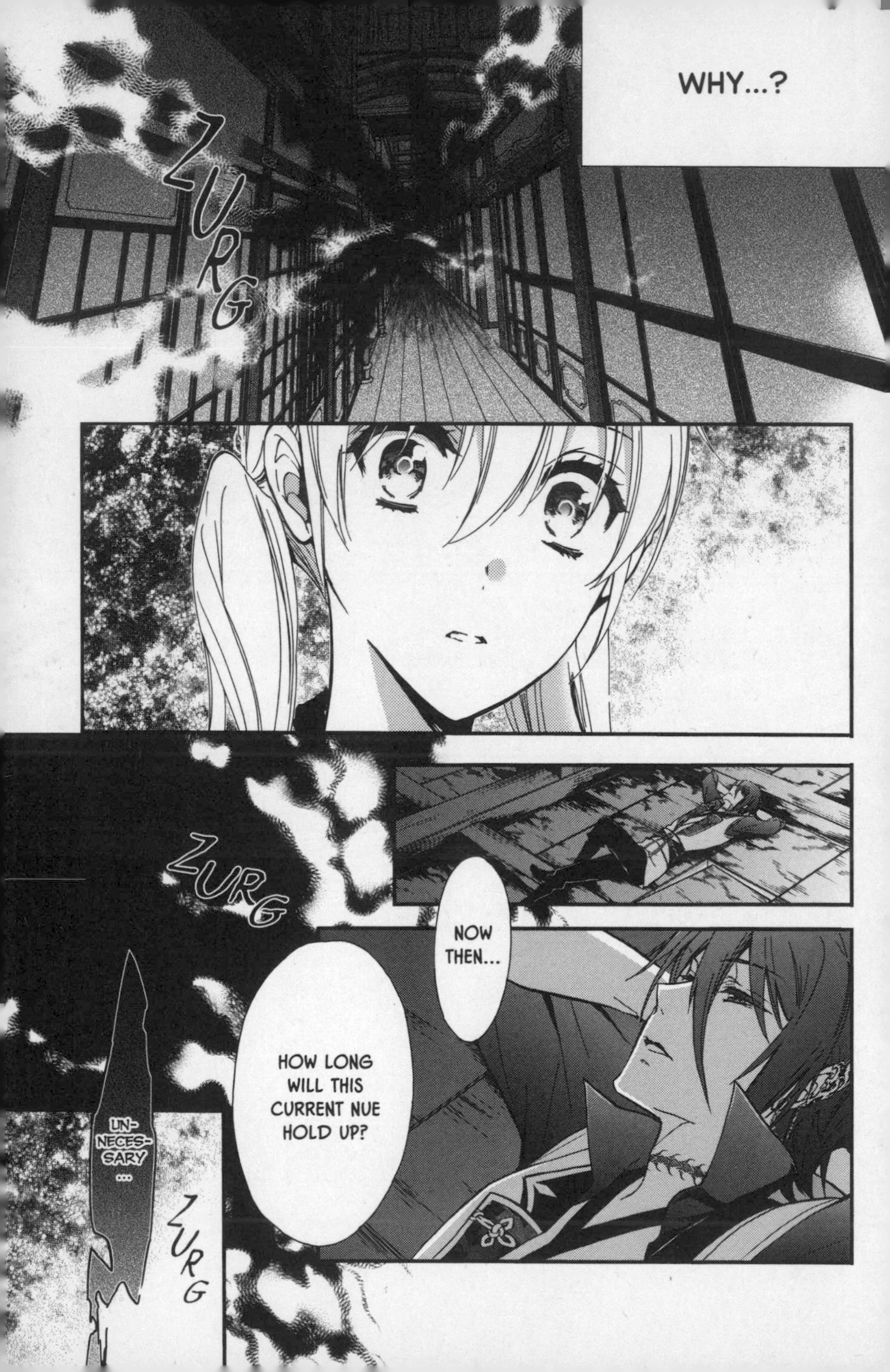
WHY...?
ZURG
NOW THEN...
HOW LONG WILL THIS CURRENT NUE HOLD UP?
ZURG
UN-NECES-SARY ...
ZURG

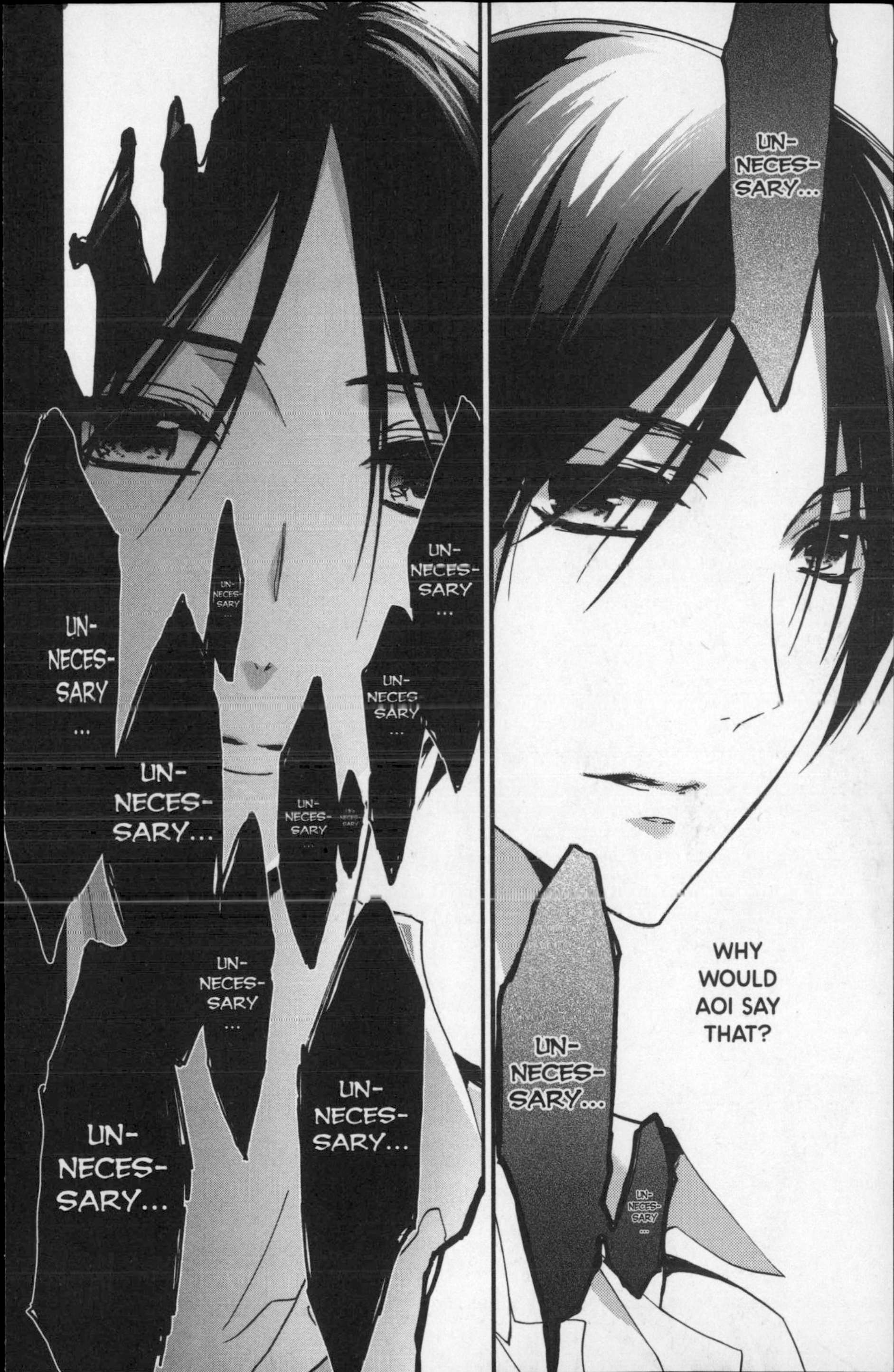
UN-NECES-SARY...
WHY WOULD AOI SAY THAT?
UN-NECES-SARY...
UN-NECES-SARY ...
UN-NECES-SARY ...
UN-NECES-SARY ...
UN-NECES-SARY ...
UN-NECES-SARY ...
UN-NECES-SARY ...
UN-NECES-SARY...
UN-NECES-SARY ...
UN-NECES-SARY...
UN-NECES-SARY...

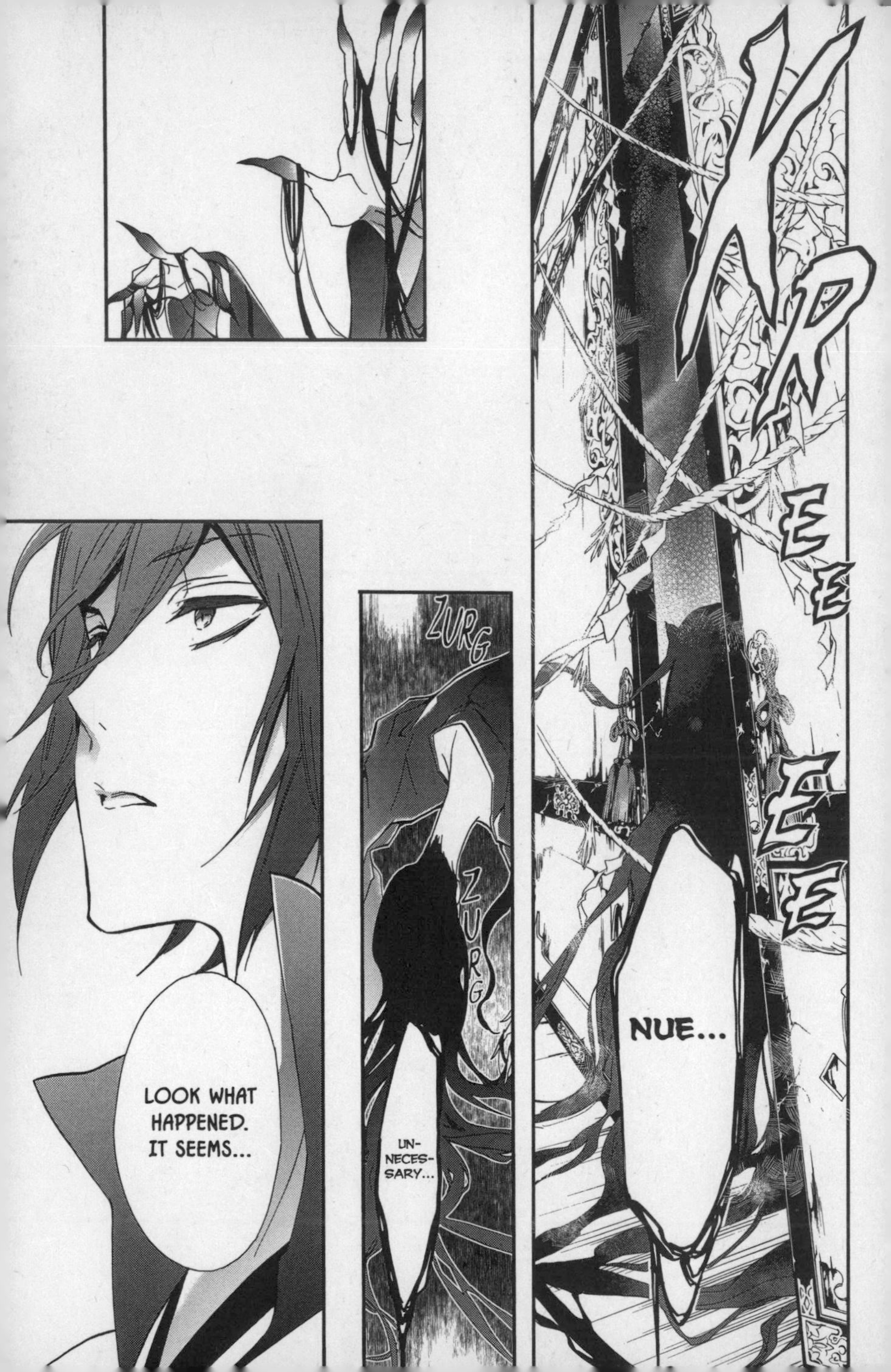
WREEEE
NUE...
ZURG
ZURG
ZURG
UN-
NECES-
SARY...
LOOK WHAT HAPPENED. IT SEEMS...

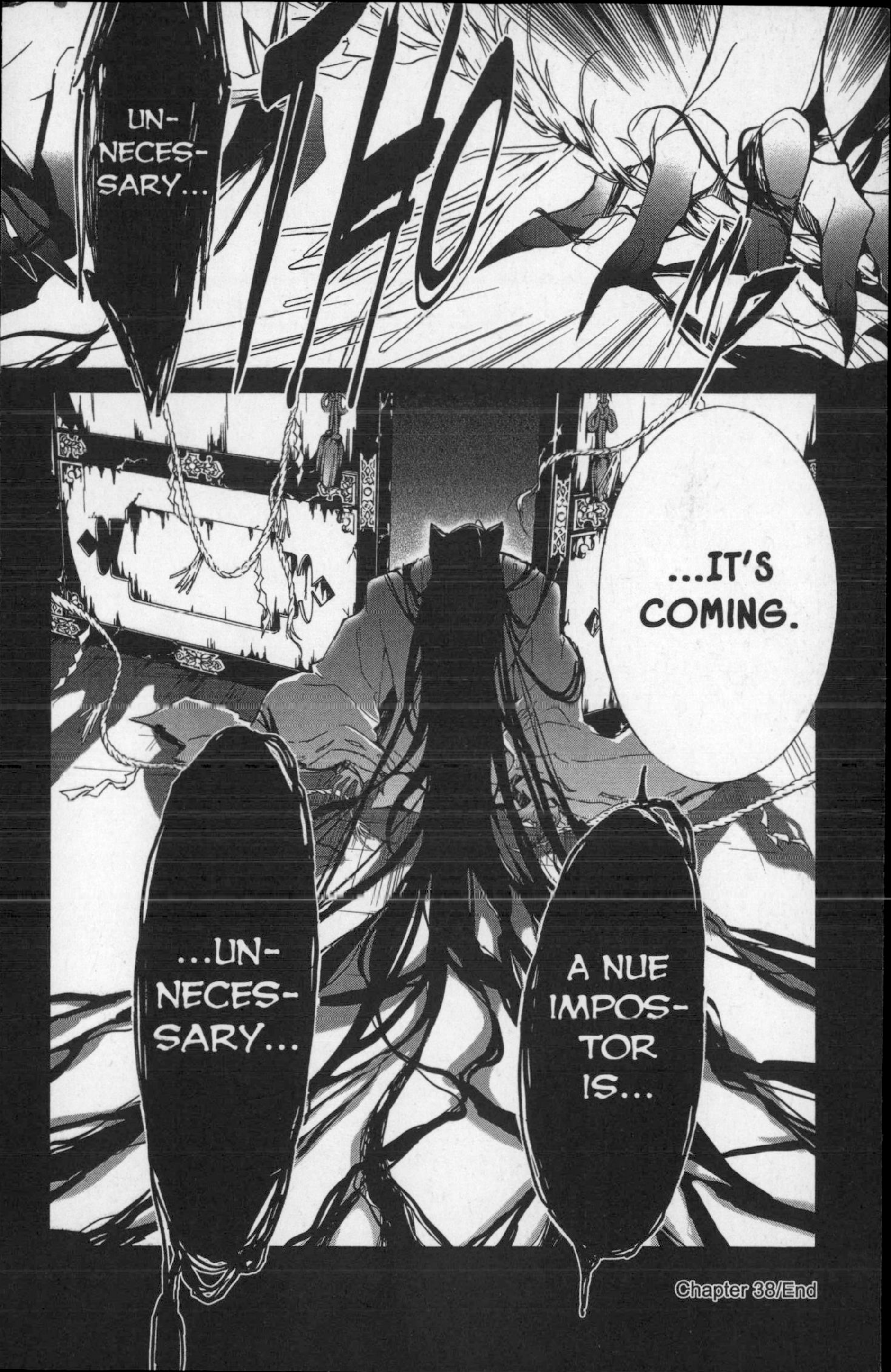
UN-NECES-SARY...
...IT'S COMING.
A NUE IMPOS-TOR IS...
...UN-NECES-SARY...

Chapter 38/End

The
DEMON
PRINCE
of MOMOCHI
HOUSE

The
DEMON
PRINCE
of MOMOCHI
HOUSE

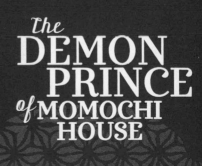

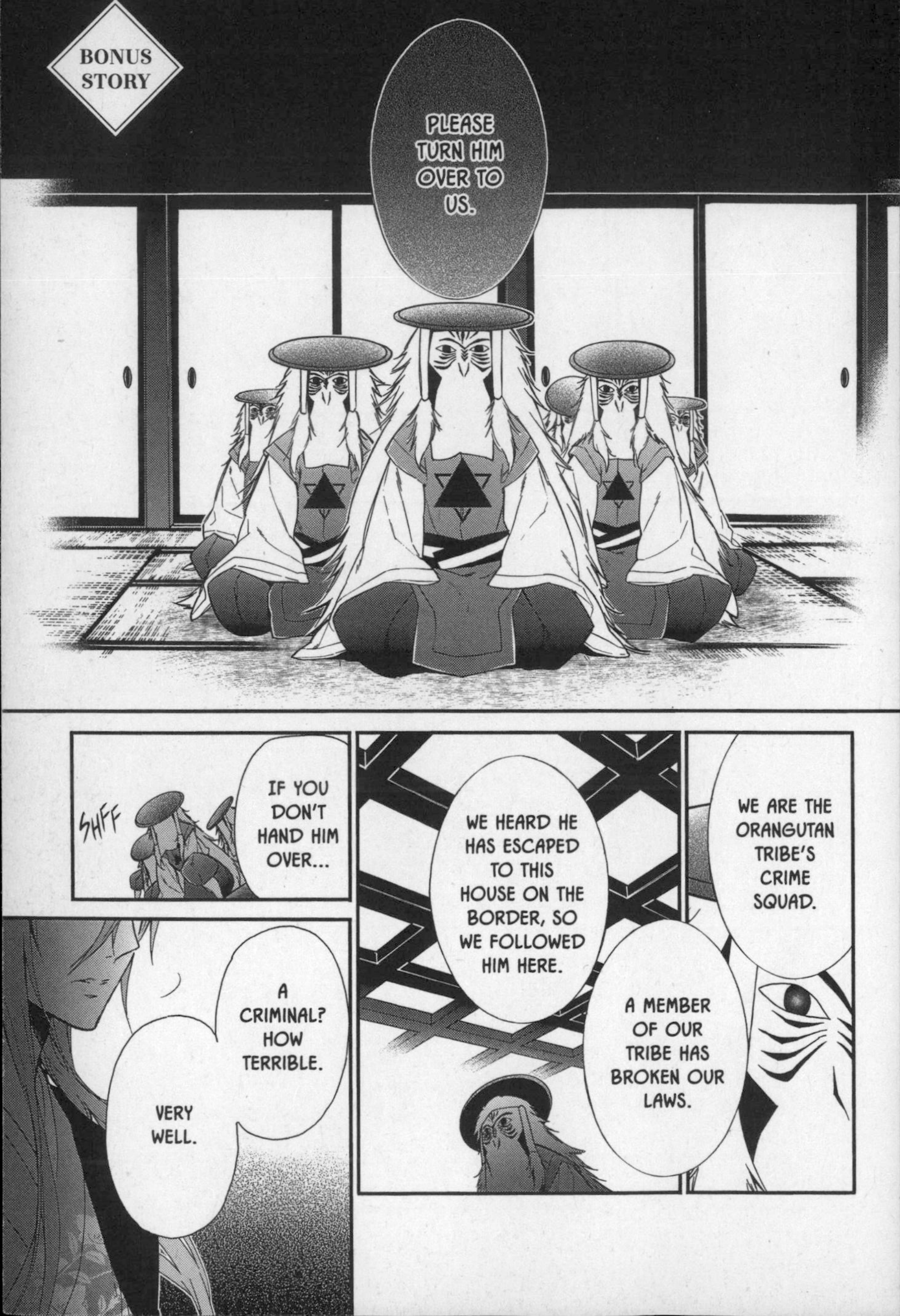
BONUS STORY
PLEASE TURN HIM OVER TO US.
WE ARE THE ORANGUTAN TRIBE'S CRIME SQUAD.
A MEMBER OF OUR TRIBE HAS BROKEN OUR LAWS.
WE HEARD HE HAS ESCAPED TO THIS HOUSE ON THE BORDER, SO WE FOLLOWED HIM HERE.
SHFF
IF YOU DON'T HAND HIM OVER...
A CRIMINAL? HOW TERRIBLE.
VERY WELL.

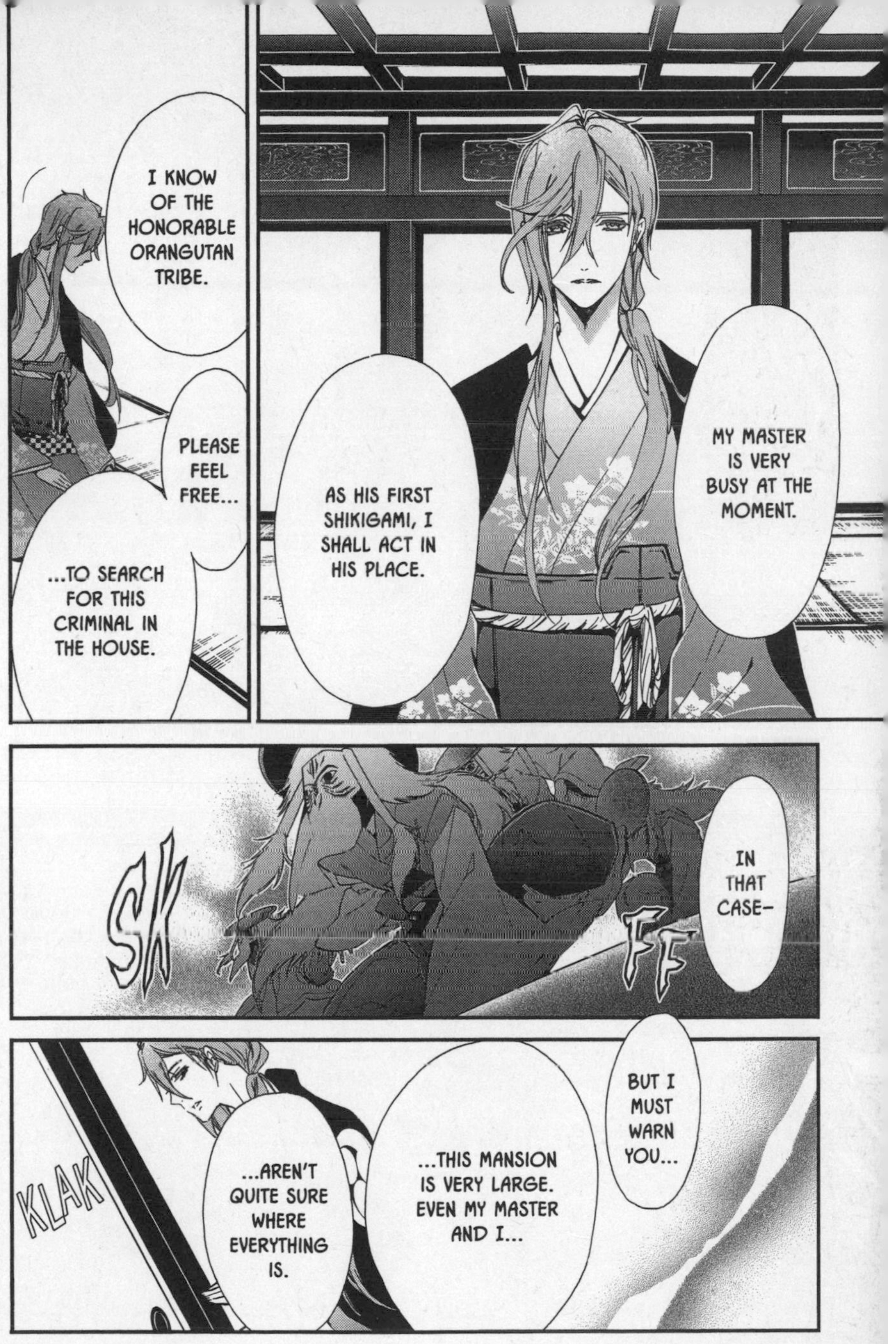
MY MASTER IS VERY BUSY AT THE MOMENT.
AS HIS FIRST SHIKIGAMI, I SHALL ACT IN HIS PLACE.
I KNOW OF THE HONORABLE ORANGUTAN TRIBE.
PLEASE FEEL FREE...
...TO SEARCH FOR THIS CRIMINAL IN THE HOUSE.
IN THAT CASE—
SK
FF
BUT I MUST WARN YOU...
...THIS MANSION IS VERY LARGE. EVEN MY MASTER AND I...
...AREN'T QUITE SURE WHERE EVERYTHING IS.
KLAK

BONUS STORY

To Capture an Orangutan: A Comedic Tale

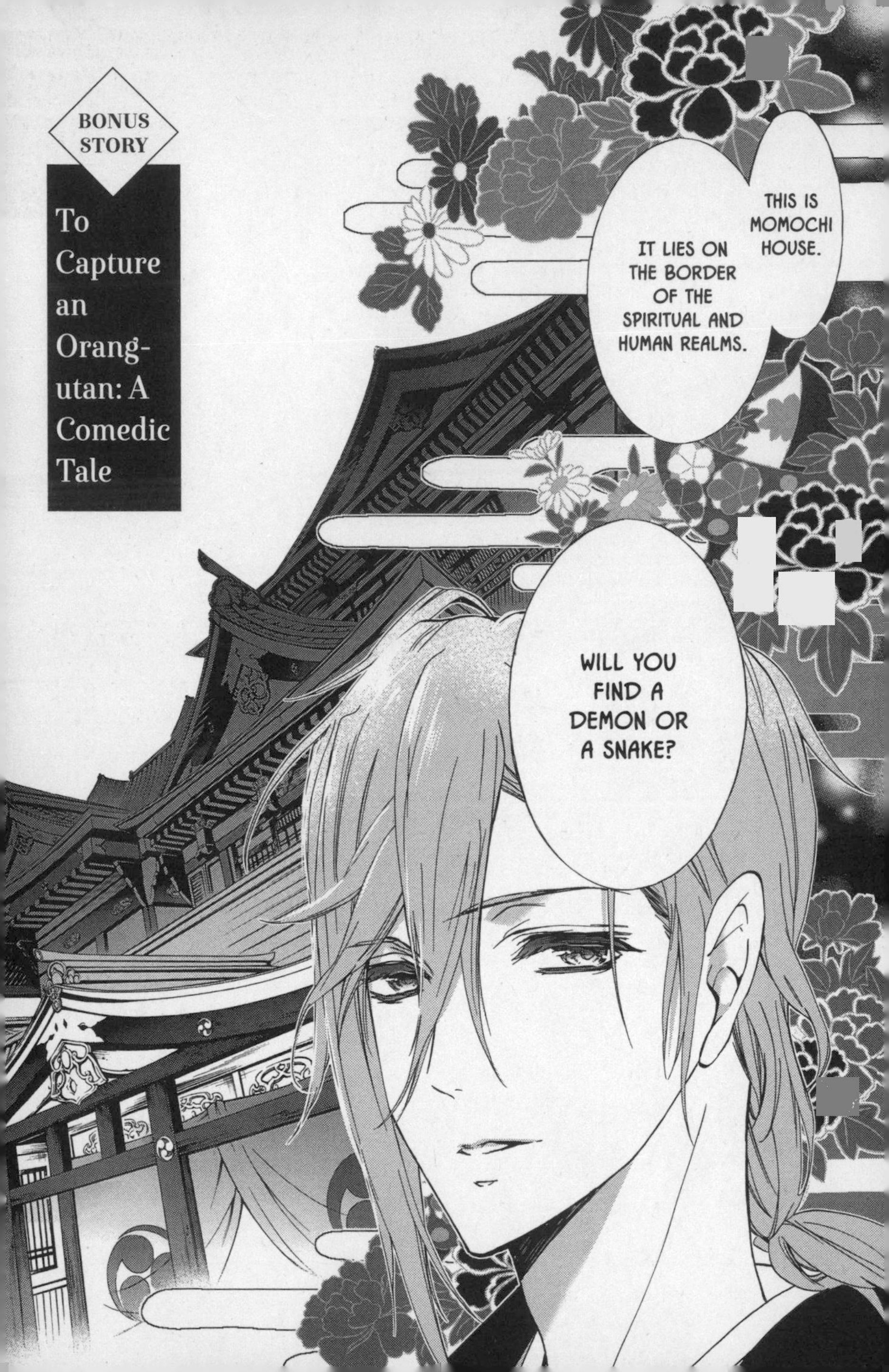
THIS IS MOMOCHI HOUSE.
IT LIES ON THE BORDER OF THE SPIRITUAL AND HUMAN REALMS.
WILL YOU FIND A DEMON OR A SNAKE?

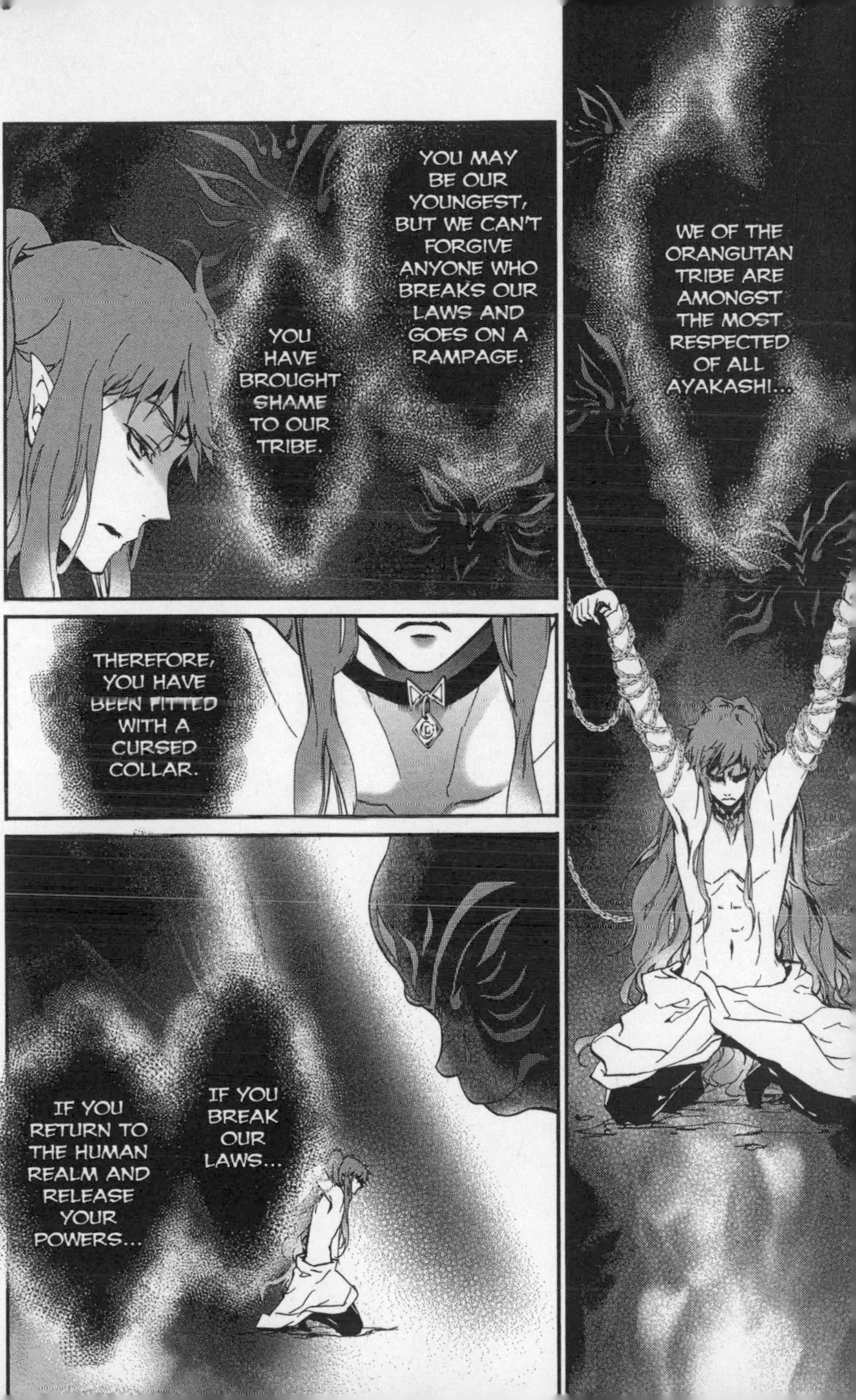
WE OF THE ORANGUTAN TRIBE ARE AMONGST THE MOST RESPECTED OF ALL AYAKASHI...
YOU MAY BE OUR YOUNGEST, BUT WE CAN'T FORGIVE ANYONE WHO BREAKS OUR LAWS AND GOES ON A RAMPAGE.
YOU HAVE BROUGHT SHAME TO OUR TRIBE.
THEREFORE, YOU HAVE BEEN FITTED WITH A CURSED COLLAR.
IF YOU BREAK OUR LAWS...
IF YOU RETURN TO THE HUMAN REALM AND RELEASE YOUR POWERS...

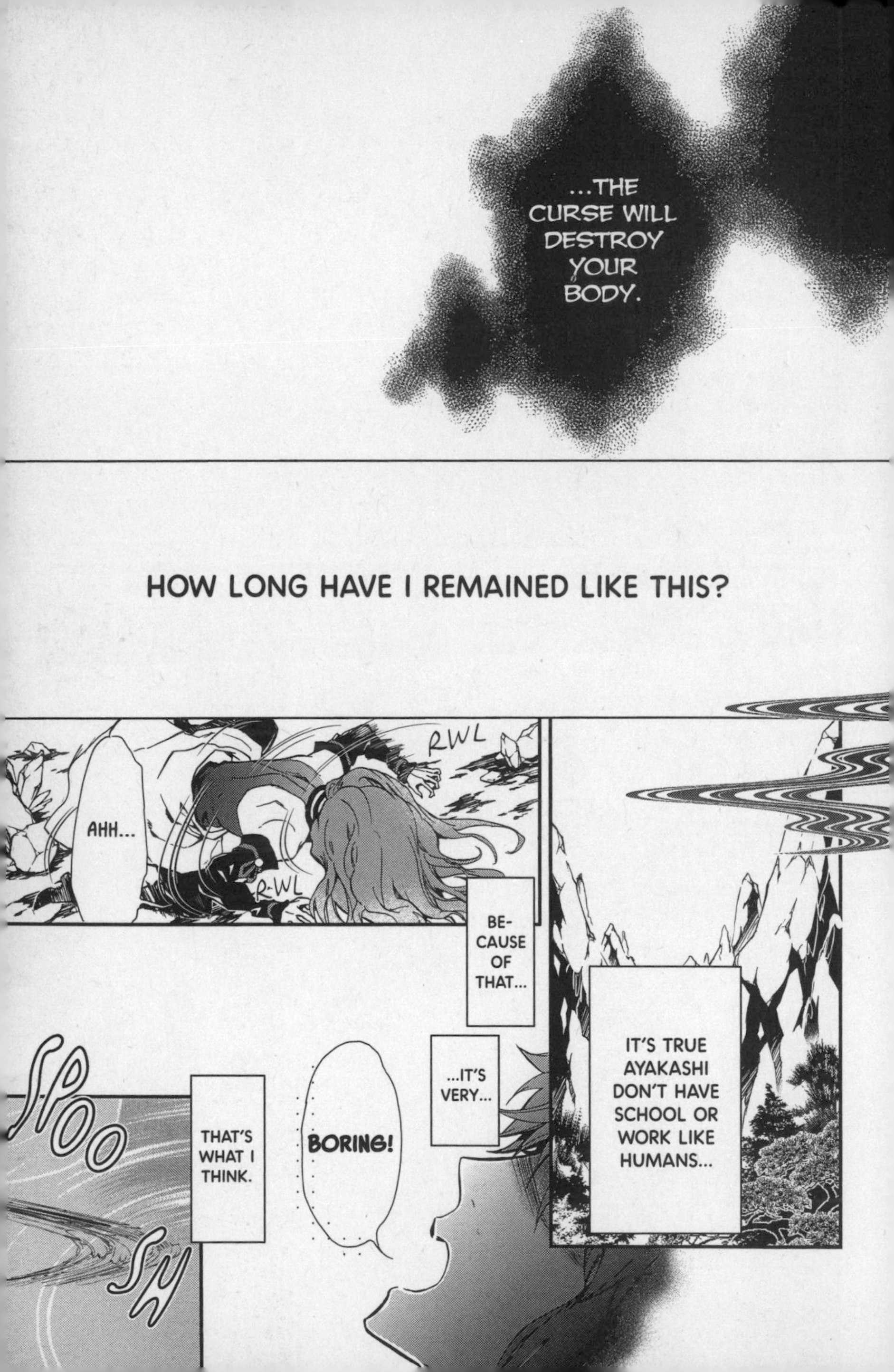
...THE CURSE WILL DESTROY YOUR BODY.
HOW LONG HAVE I REMAINED LIKE THIS?
IT'S TRUE AYAKASHI DON'T HAVE SCHOOL OR WORK LIKE HUMANS...
RWL
AHH...
R-WL
BE-CAUSE OF THAT...
...IT'S VERY...
BORING!
THAT'S WHAT I THINK.
SPLOOSH

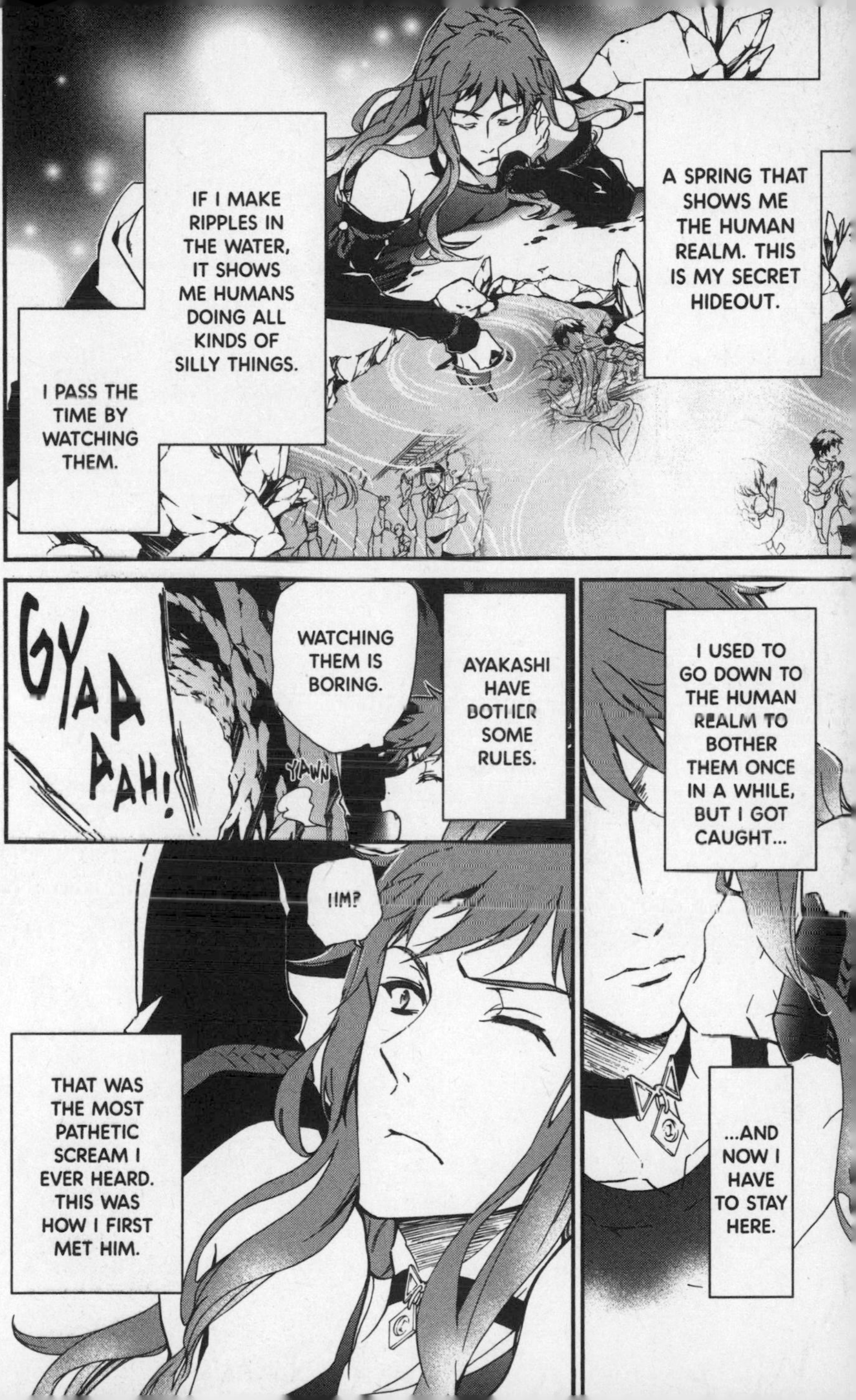
A SPRING THAT SHOWS ME THE HUMAN REALM. THIS IS MY SECRET HIDEOUT.
IF I MAKE RIPPLES IN THE WATER, IT SHOWS ME HUMANS DOING ALL KINDS OF SILLY THINGS.
I PASS THE TIME BY WATCHING THEM.
I USED TO GO DOWN TO THE HUMAN REALM TO BOTHER THEM ONCE IN A WHILE, BUT I GOT CAUGHT...
...AND NOW I HAVE TO STAY HERE.
AYAKASHI HAVE BOTHERSOME RULES.
WATCHING THEM IS BORING.
YAWN
GYAAPAH!
HM?
THAT WAS THE MOST PATHETIC SCREAM I EVER HEARD. THIS WAS HOW I FIRST MET HIM.

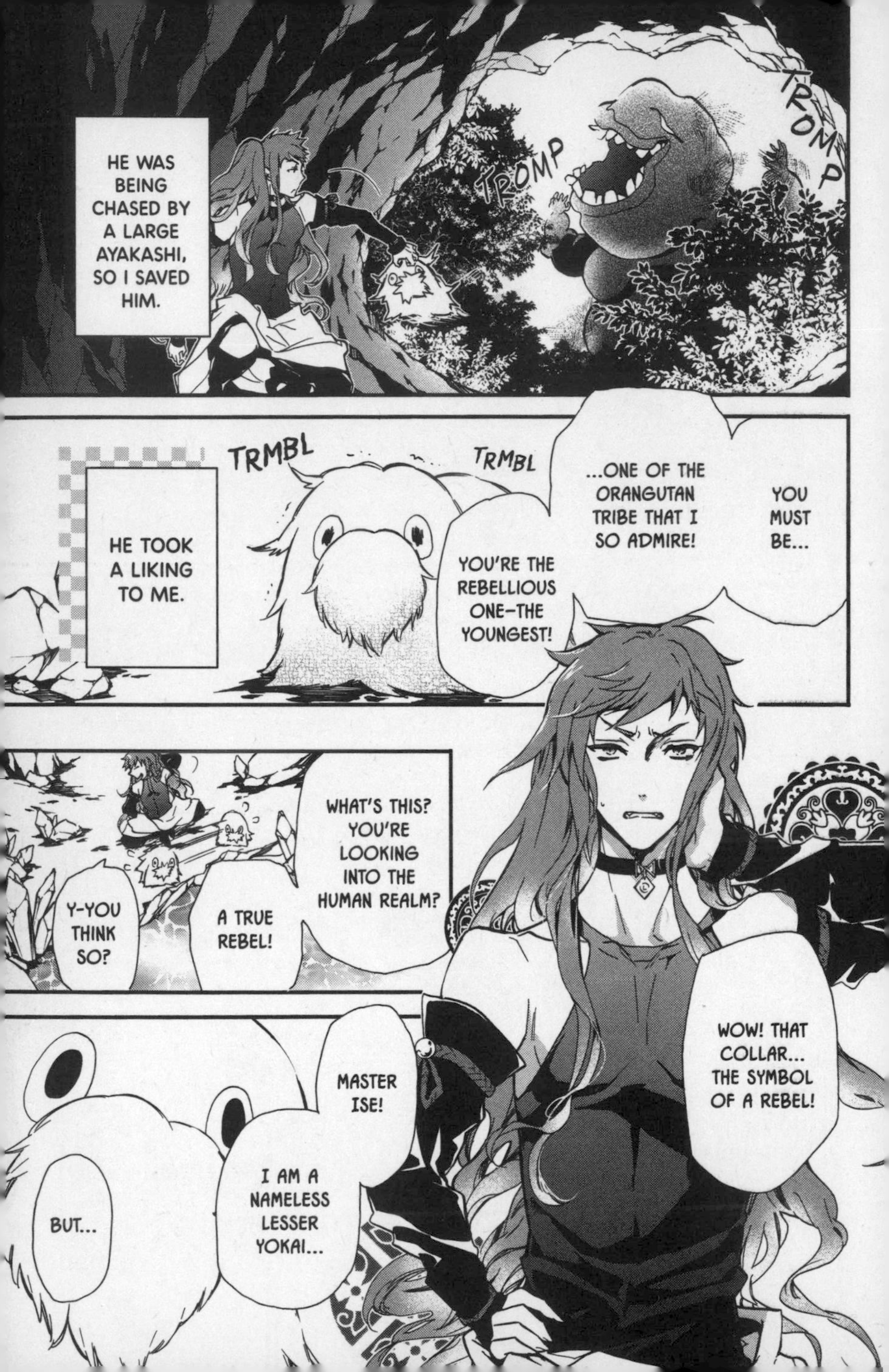

TROMP TROMP
TROMP
HE WAS BEING CHASED BY A LARGE AYAKASHI, SO I SAVED HIM.
YOU MUST BE...
...ONE OF THE ORANGUTAN TRIBE THAT I SO ADMIRE!
YOU'RE THE REBELLIOUS ONE—THE YOUNGEST!
TRMBL
TRMBL
HE TOOK A LIKING TO ME.
WOW! THAT COLLAR... THE SYMBOL OF A REBEL!
WHAT'S THIS? YOU'RE LOOKING INTO THE HUMAN REALM?
A TRUE REBEL!
Y-YOU THINK SO?
MASTER ISE!
I AM A NAMELESS LESSER YOKAI...
BUT...

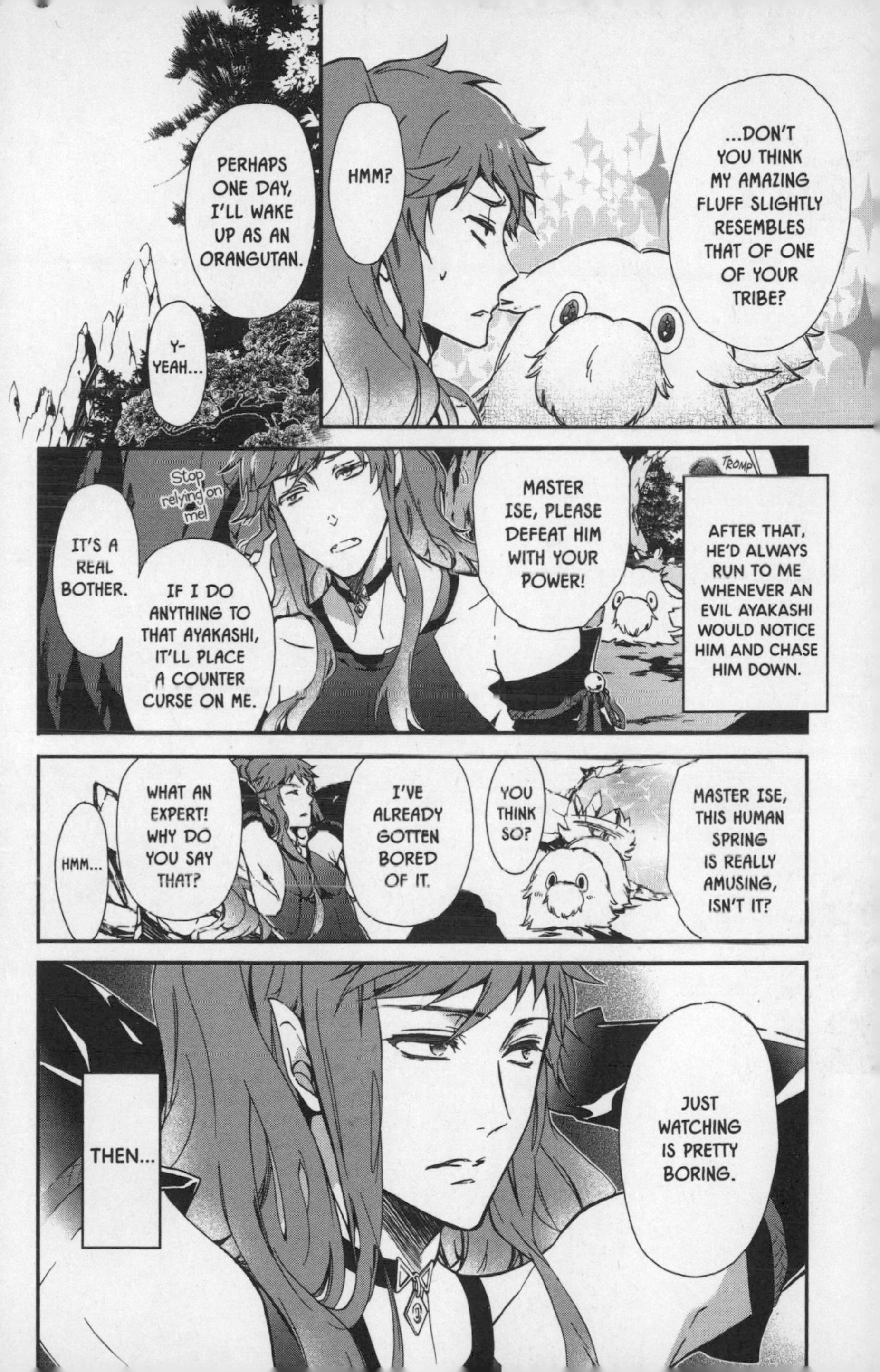
...DON'T YOU THINK MY AMAZING FLUFF SLIGHTLY RESEMBLES THAT OF ONE OF YOUR TRIBE?
HMM?
PERHAPS ONE DAY, I'LL WAKE UP AS AN ORANGUTAN.
Y-YEAH...
TROMP
AFTER THAT, HE'D ALWAYS RUN TO ME WHENEVER AN EVIL AYAKASHI WOULD NOTICE HIM AND CHASE HIM DOWN.
MASTER ISE, PLEASE DEFEAT HIM WITH YOUR POWER!
IF I DO ANYTHING TO THAT AYAKASHI, IT'LL PLACE A COUNTER CURSE ON ME.
Stop relying on me!
IT'S A REAL BOTHER.
MASTER ISE, THIS HUMAN SPRING IS REALLY AMUSING, ISN'T IT?
YOU THINK SO?
I'VE ALREADY GOTTEN BORED OF IT.
WHAT AN EXPERT! WHY DO YOU SAY THAT?
HMM...
JUST WATCHING IS PRETTY BORING.
THEN...

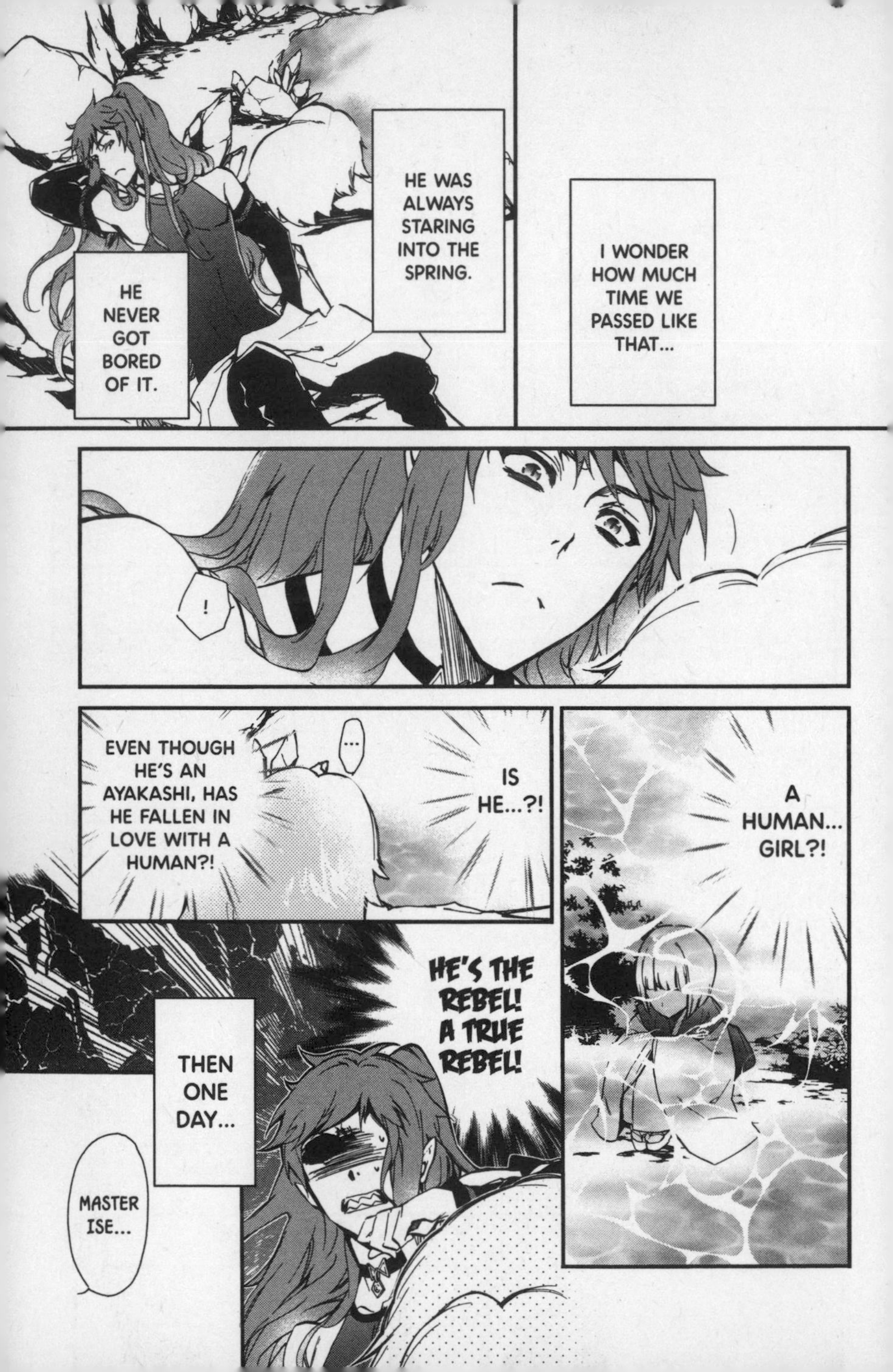
I WONDER HOW MUCH TIME WE PASSED LIKE THAT...
HE WAS ALWAYS STARING INTO THE SPRING.
HE NEVER GOT BORED OF IT.
!
A HUMAN... GIRL?!
IS HE...?!
...
EVEN THOUGH HE'S AN AYAKASHI, HAS HE FALLEN IN LOVE WITH A HUMAN?!
HE'S THE REBEL! A TRUE REBEL!
THEN ONE DAY...
MASTER ISE...

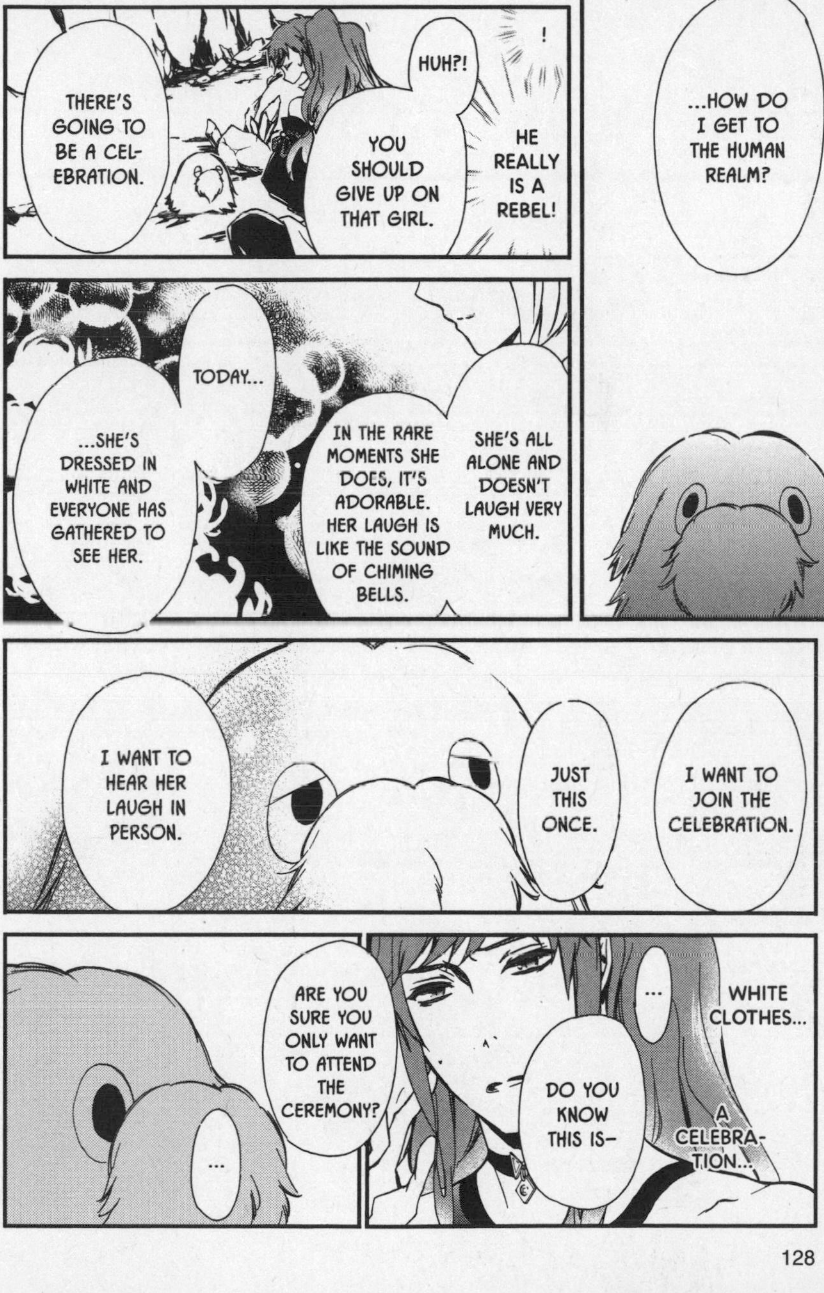
...HOW DO I GET TO THE HUMAN REALM?
!
HE REALLY IS A REBEL!
HUH?!
YOU SHOULD GIVE UP ON THAT GIRL.
THERE'S GOING TO BE A CEL-EBRATION.
SHE'S ALL ALONE AND DOESN'T LAUGH VERY MUCH.
IN THE RARE MOMENTS SHE DOES, IT'S ADORABLE. HER LAUGH IS LIKE THE SOUND OF CHIMING BELLS.
TODAY...
...SHE'S DRESSED IN WHITE AND EVERYONE HAS GATHERED TO SEE HER.
I WANT TO JOIN THE CELEBRATION.
JUST THIS ONCE.
I WANT TO HEAR HER LAUGH IN PERSON.
WHITE CLOTHES...
...
A CELEBRA-TION...
DO YOU KNOW THIS IS–
ARE YOU SURE YOU ONLY WANT TO ATTEND THE CEREMONY?
...

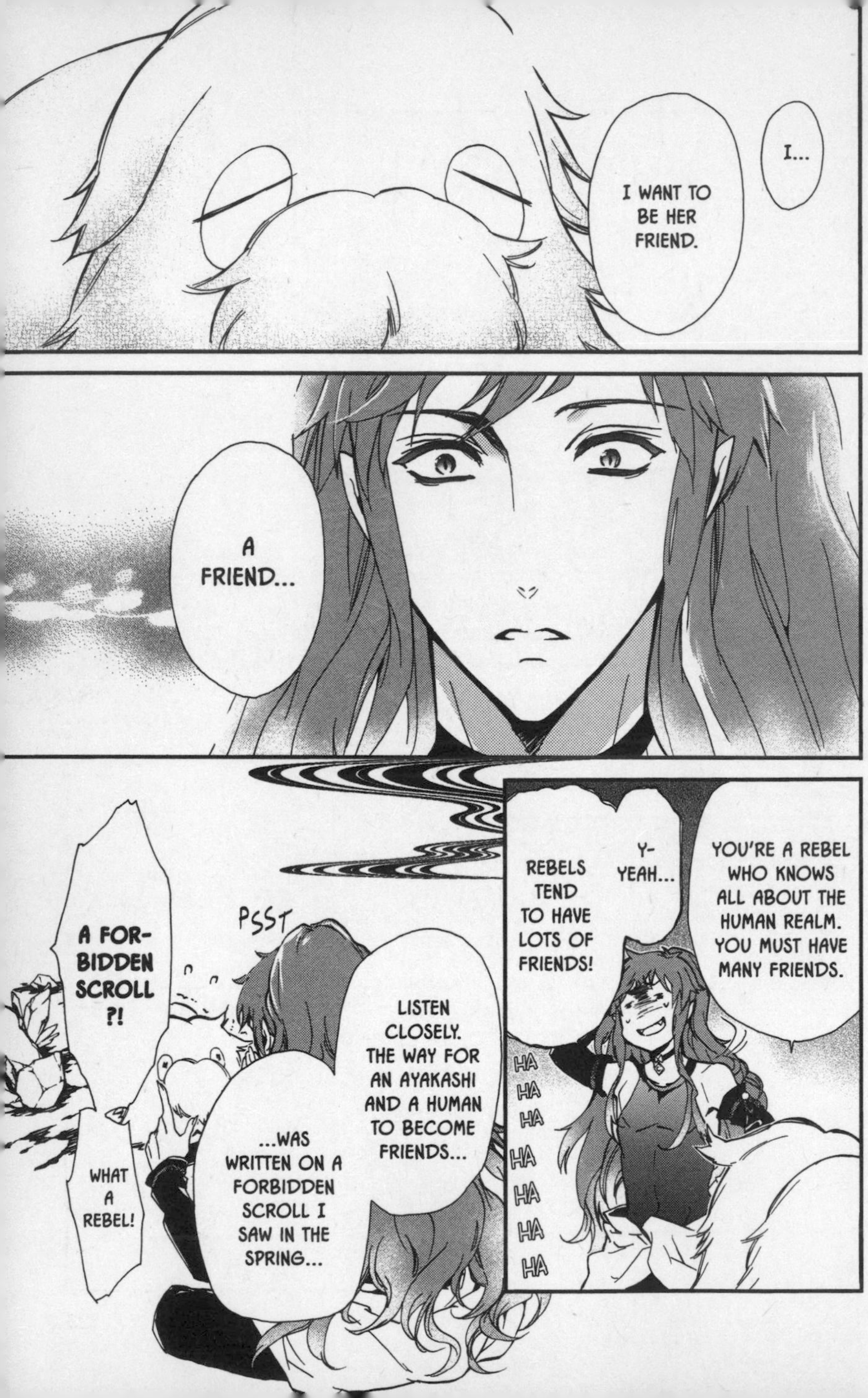
I...
I WANT TO BE HER FRIEND.
A FRIEND...
YOU'RE A REBEL WHO KNOWS ALL ABOUT THE HUMAN REALM. YOU MUST HAVE MANY FRIENDS.
Y-YEAH...
REBELS TEND TO HAVE LOTS OF FRIENDS!
HA HA HA HA HA HA HA
PSST
LISTEN CLOSELY. THE WAY FOR AN AYAKASHI AND A HUMAN TO BECOME FRIENDS...
...WAS WRITTEN ON A FORBIDDEN SCROLL I SAW IN THE SPRING...
A FOR-BIDDEN SCROLL?!
WHAT A REBEL!

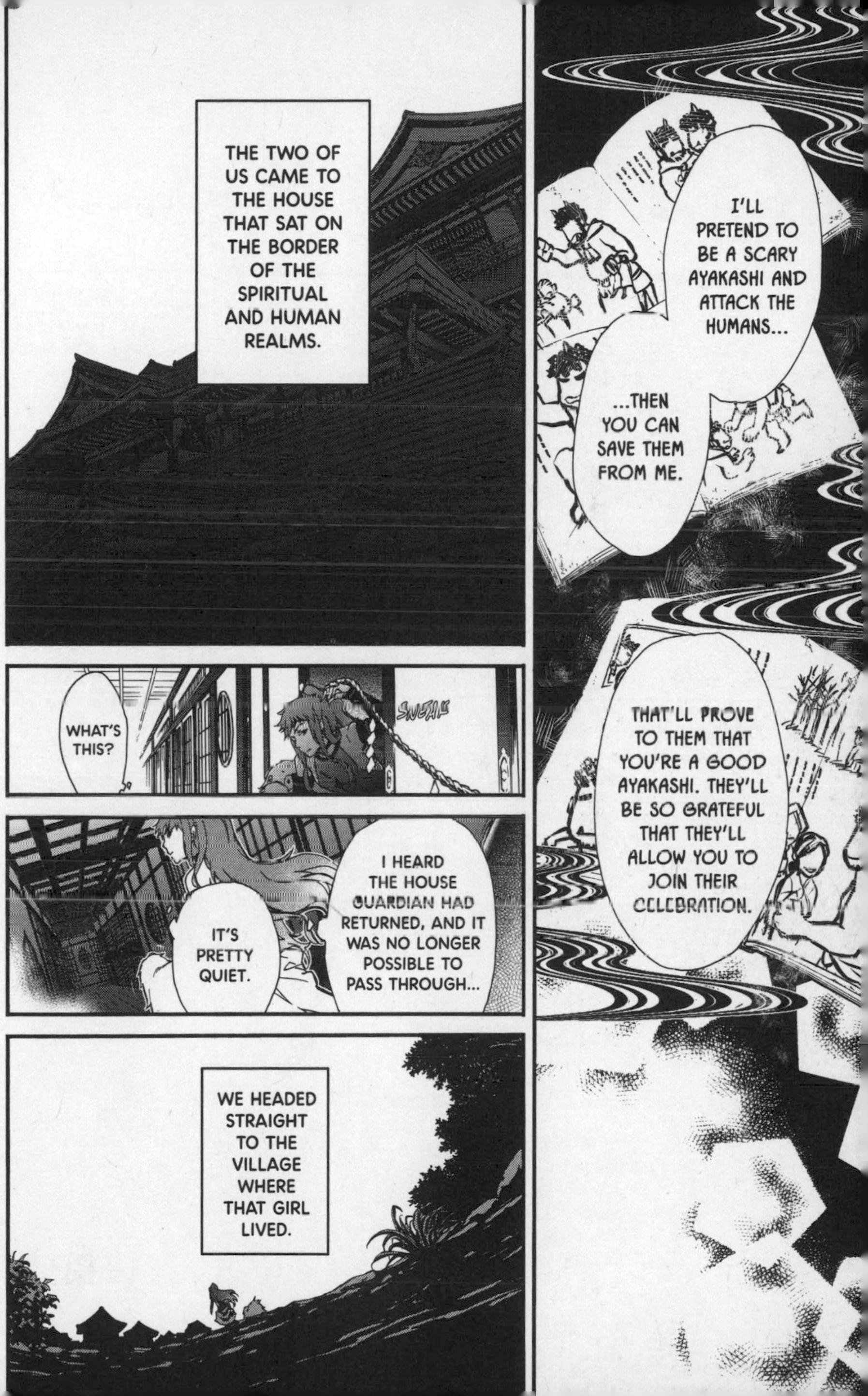
I'LL PRETEND TO BE A SCARY AYAKASHI AND ATTACK THE HUMANS...
...THEN YOU CAN SAVE THEM FROM ME.
THAT'LL PROVE TO THEM THAT YOU'RE A GOOD AYAKASHI. THEY'LL BE SO GRATEFUL THAT THEY'LL ALLOW YOU TO JOIN THEIR CELEBRATION.
THE TWO OF US CAME TO THE HOUSE THAT SAT ON THE BORDER OF THE SPIRITUAL AND HUMAN REALMS.
WHAT'S THIS?
I HEARD THE HOUSE GUARDIAN HAD RETURNED, AND IT WAS NO LONGER POSSIBLE TO PASS THROUGH...
IT'S PRETTY QUIET.
WE HEADED STRAIGHT TO THE VILLAGE WHERE THAT GIRL LIVED.

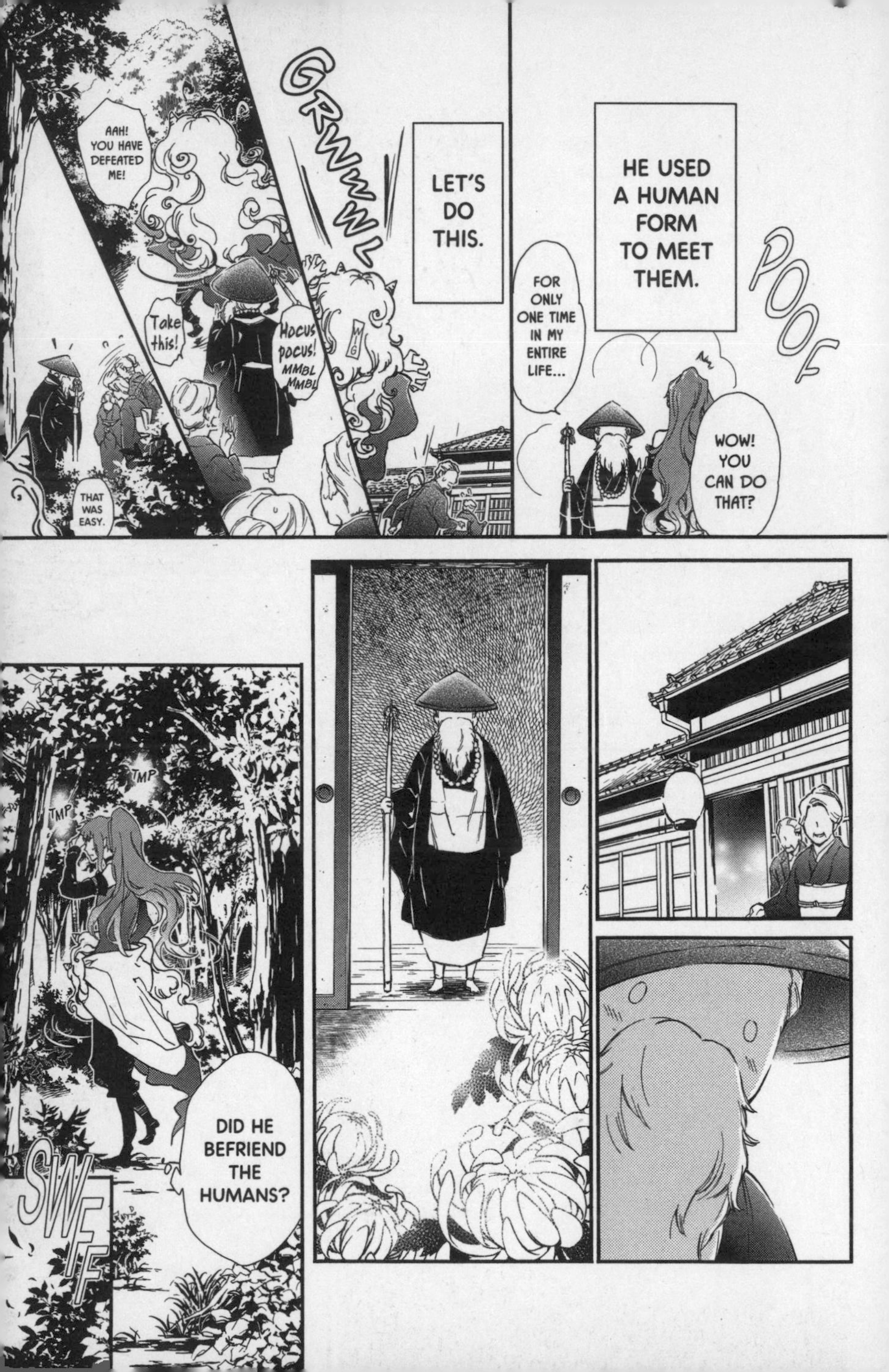
HE USED A HUMAN FORM TO MEET THEM.
FOR ONLY ONE TIME IN MY ENTIRE LIFE...
POOF
WOW! YOU CAN DO THAT?
LET'S DO THIS.
GRWWL
Hocus pocus! MMBL MMBL
AAH! YOU HAVE DEFEATED ME!
Take this!
THAT WAS EASY.
TMP
TMP
DID HE BEFRIEND THE HUMANS?
SWFF

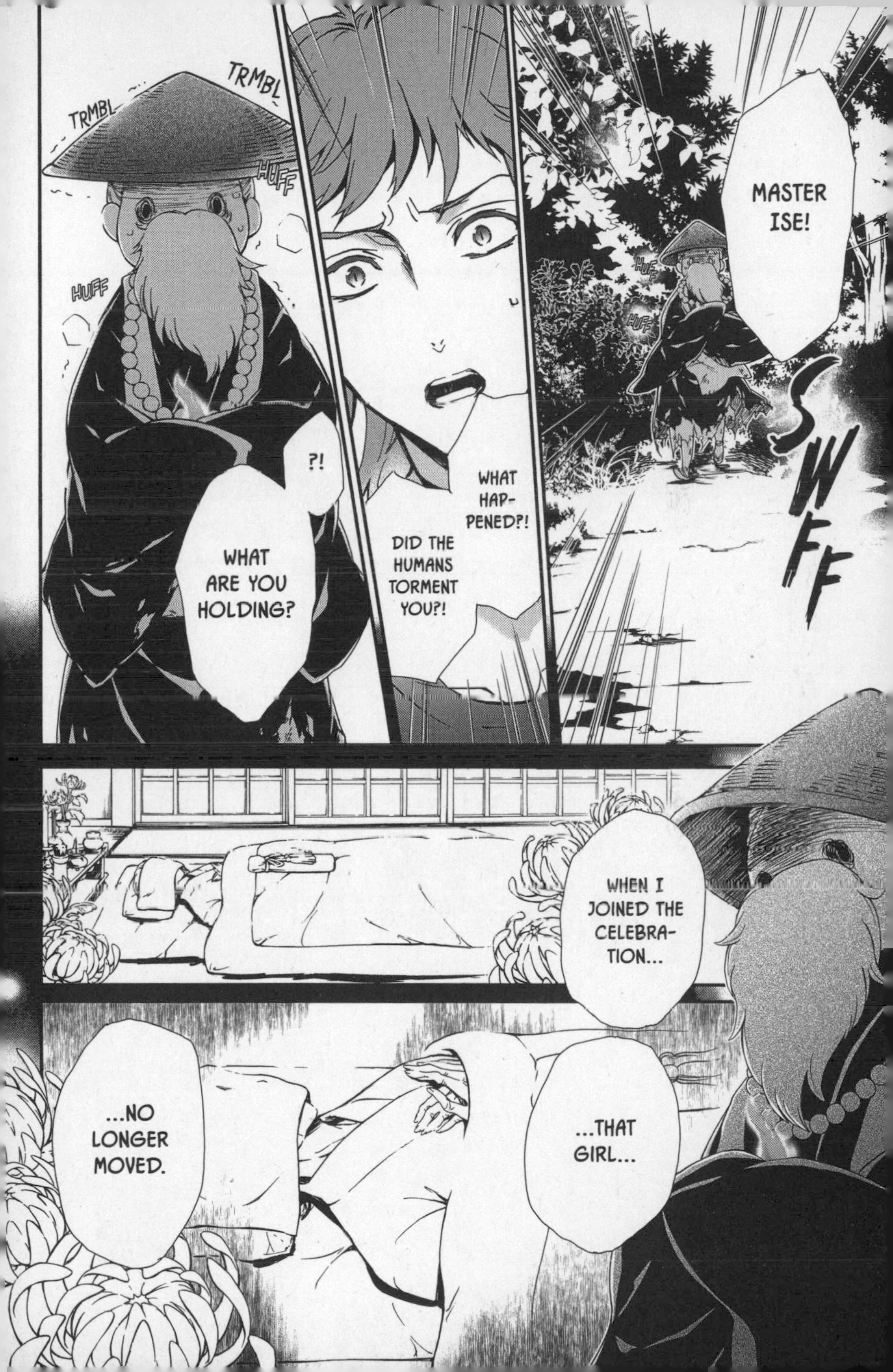
MASTER ISE!
HUFF
HUFF
SWFF
WHAT HAP-PENED?!
DID THE HUMANS TORMENT YOU?!
TRMBL
TRMBL
HUFF
HUFF
?!
WHAT ARE YOU HOLDING?
WHEN I JOINED THE CELEBRA-TION...
...THAT GIRL...
...NO LONGER MOVED.

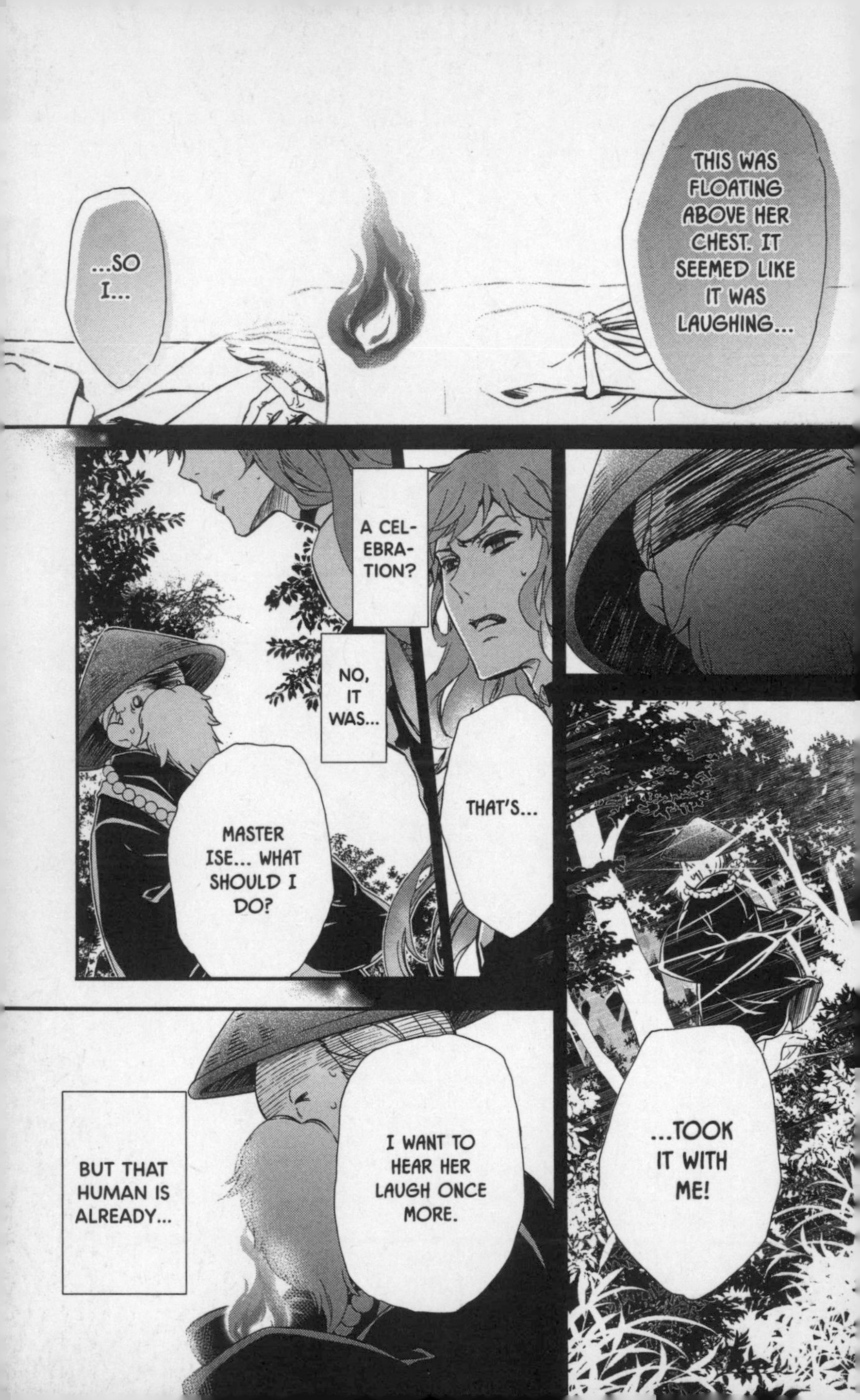
THIS WAS FLOATING ABOVE HER CHEST. IT SEEMED LIKE IT WAS LAUGHING...
...SO I...
...TOOK IT WITH ME!
A CEL-EBRA-TION?
NO, IT WAS...
THAT'S...
MASTER ISE... WHAT SHOULD I DO?
I WANT TO HEAR HER LAUGH ONCE MORE.
BUT THAT HUMAN IS ALREADY...

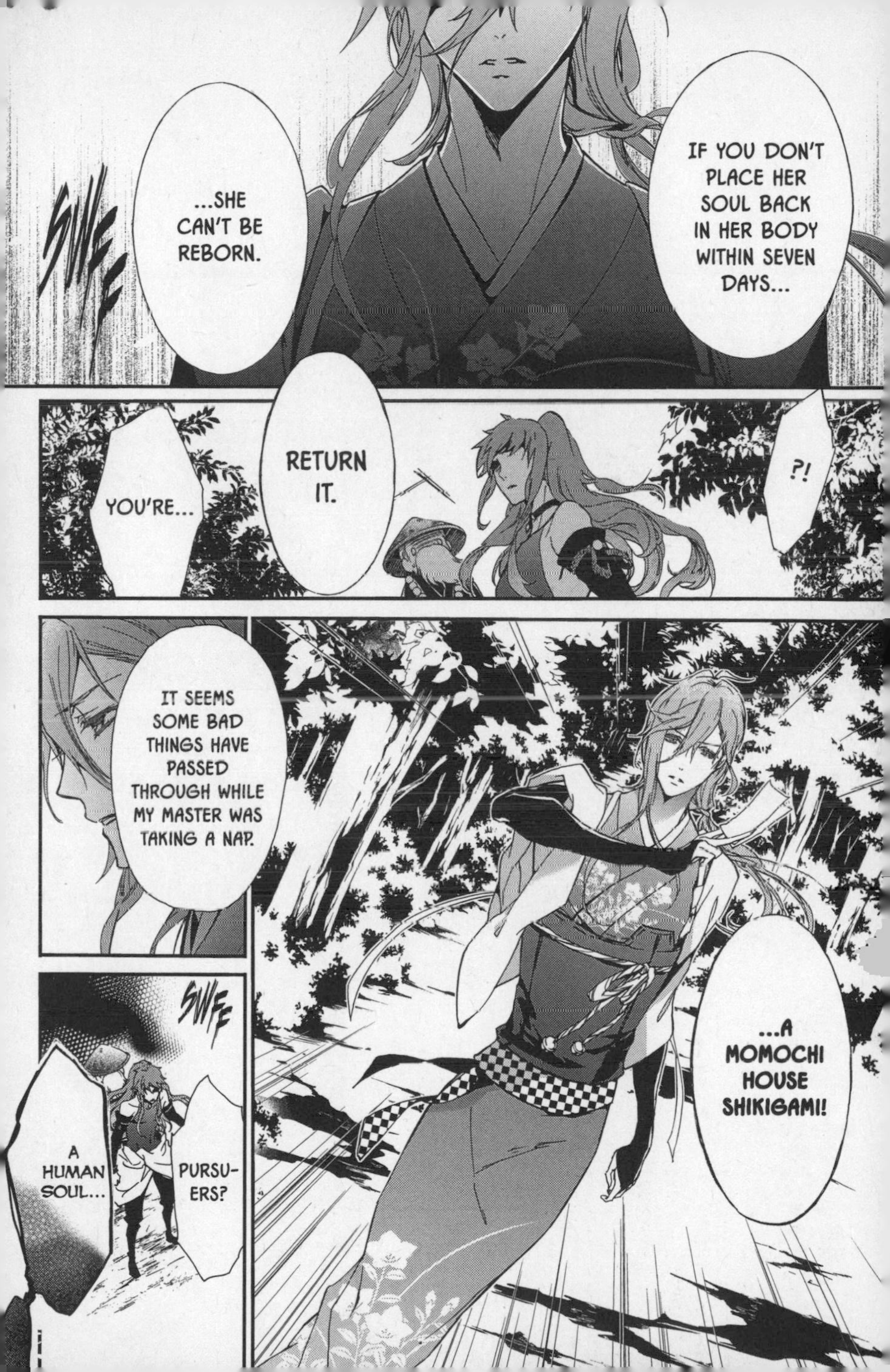
IF YOU DON'T PLACE HER SOUL BACK IN HER BODY WITHIN SEVEN DAYS...
...SHE CAN'T BE REBORN.
?!
RETURN IT.
YOU'RE...
...A MOMOCHI HOUSE SHIKIGAMI!
IT SEEMS SOME BAD THINGS HAVE PASSED THROUGH WHILE MY MASTER WAS TAKING A NAP.
PURSU-ERS?
A HUMAN SOUL...

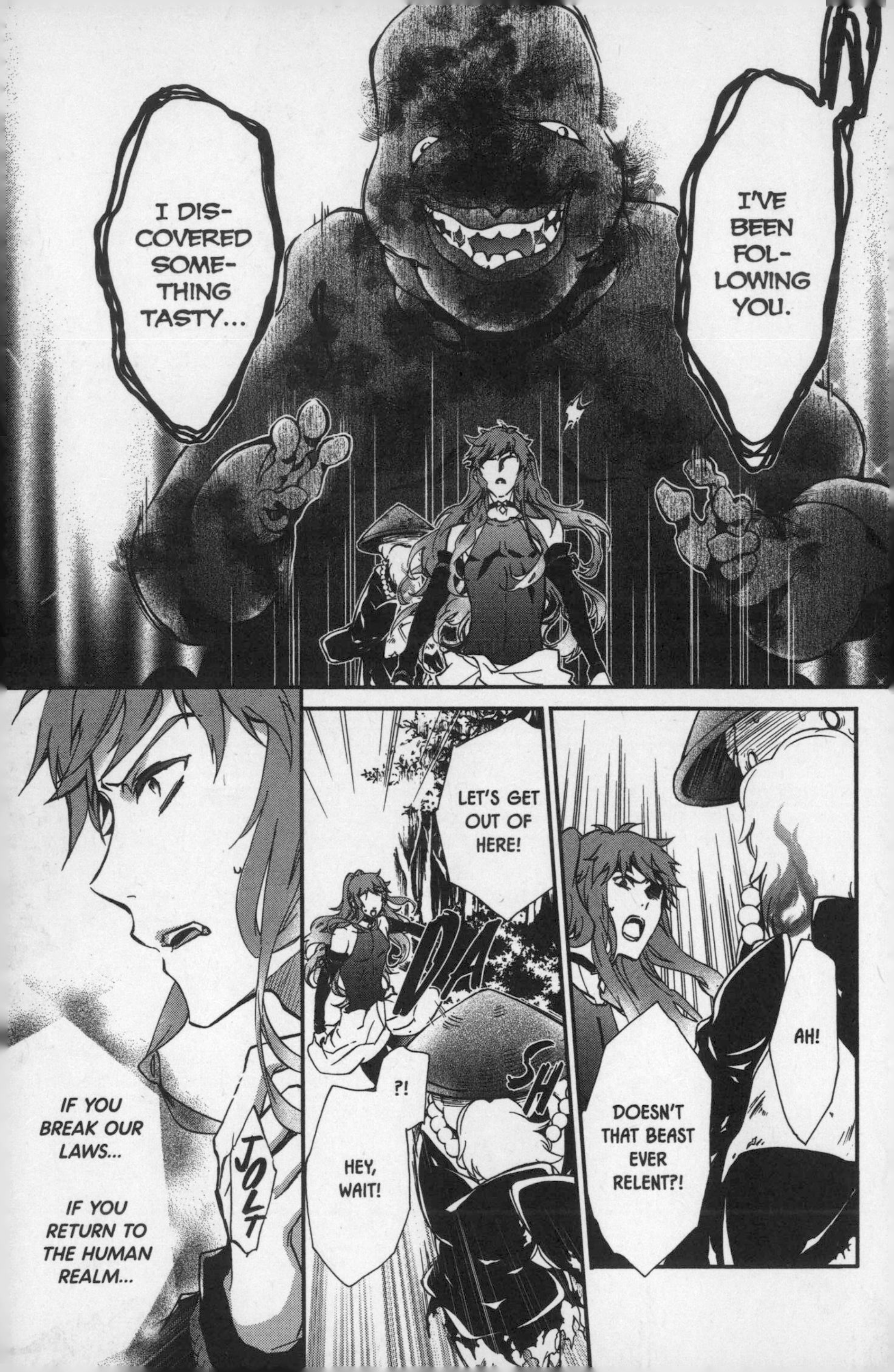
I'VE BEEN FOL-LOWING YOU.
I DIS-COVERED SOME-THING TASTY...
AH!
DOESN'T THAT BEAST EVER RELENT?!
LET'S GET OUT OF HERE!
DA
SH
?!
HEY, WAIT!
IF YOU BREAK OUR LAWS...
JOLT
IF YOU RETURN TO THE HUMAN REALM...

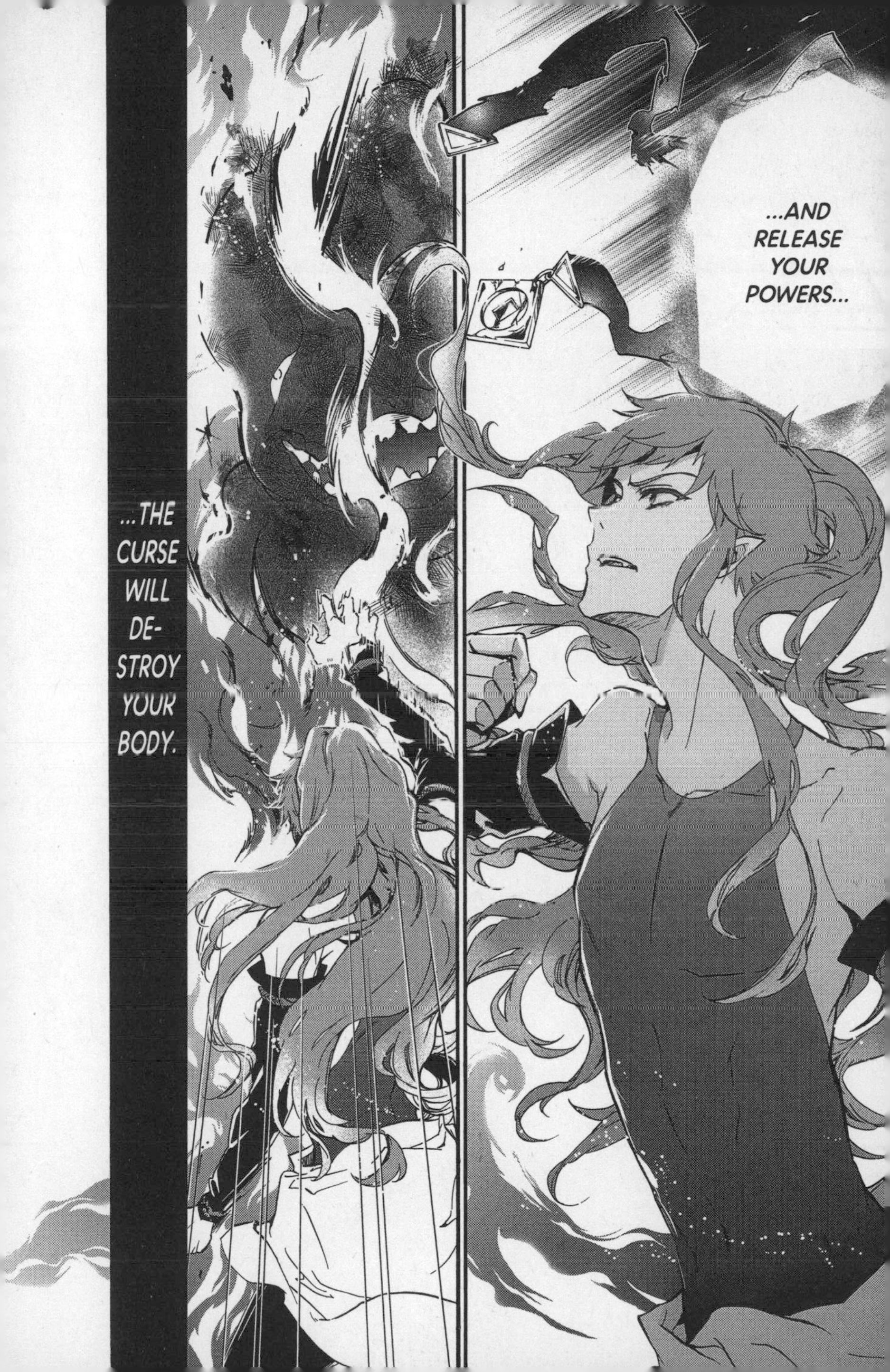
...AND RELEASE YOUR POWERS...
...THE CURSE WILL DE- STROY YOUR BODY.

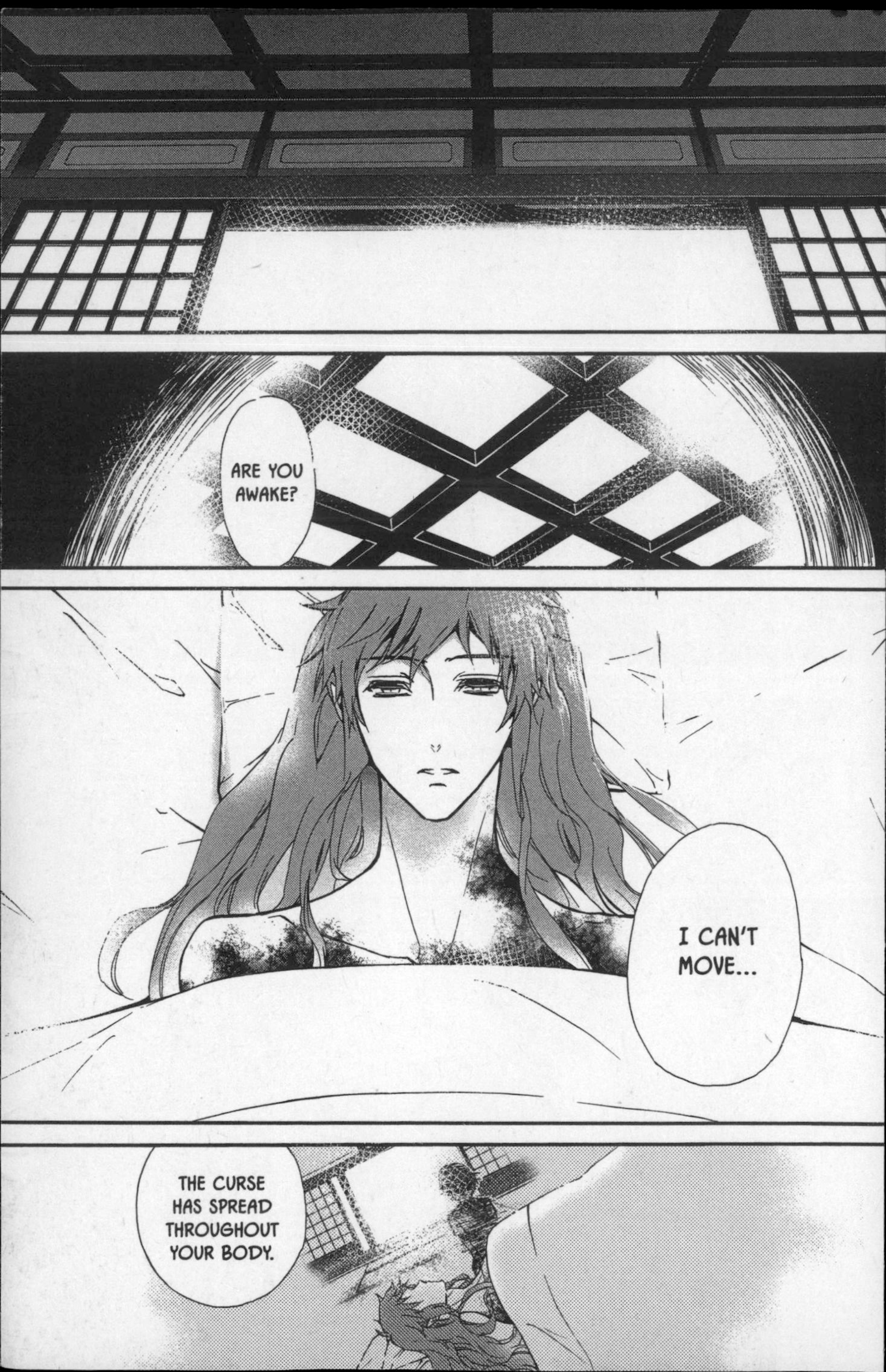
ARE YOU AWAKE?
I CAN'T MOVE...
THE CURSE HAS SPREAD THROUGHOUT YOUR BODY.

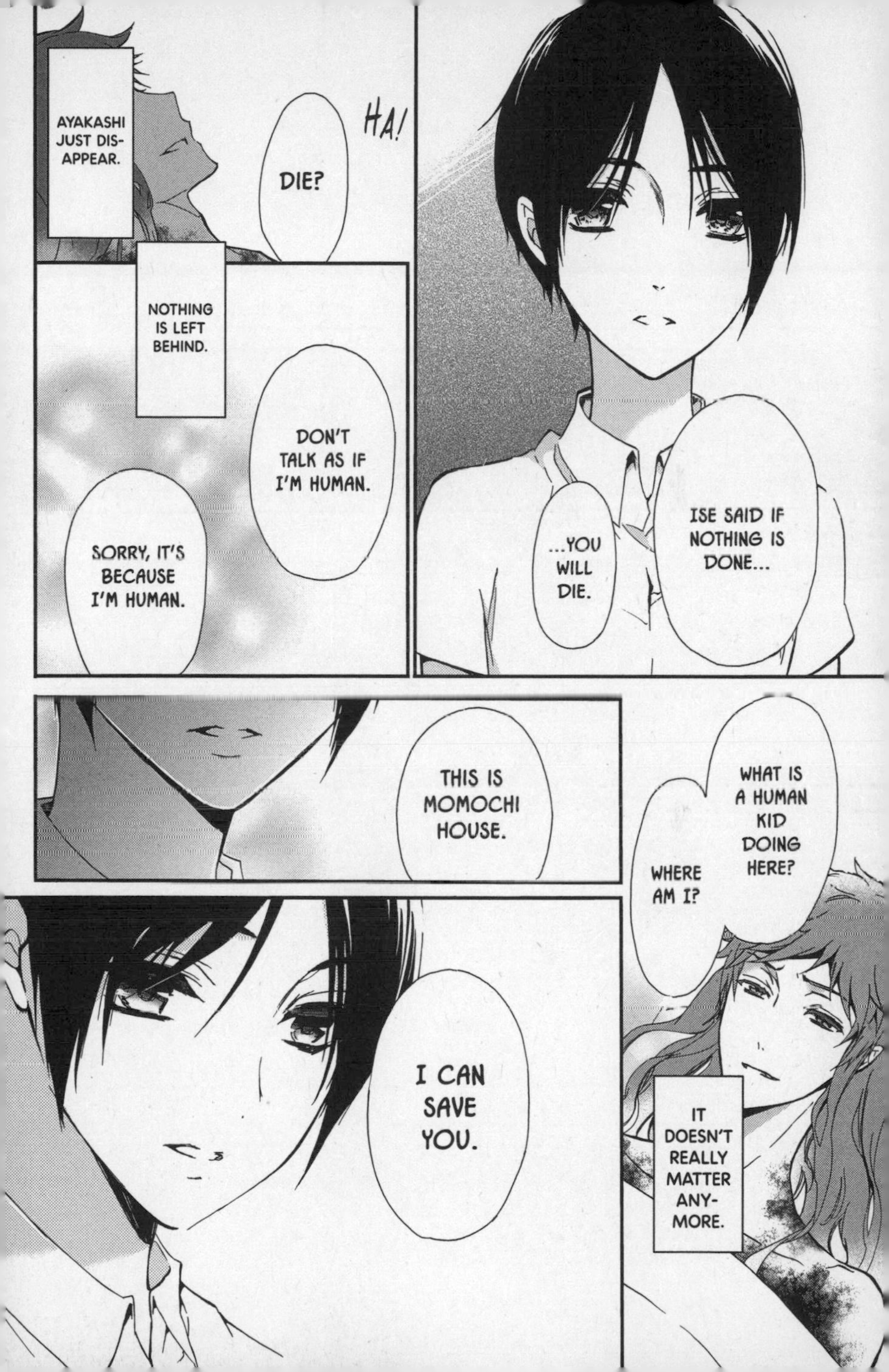
ISE SAID IF NOTHING IS DONE...
...YOU WILL DIE.
HA!
DIE?
AYAKASHI JUST DIS-APPEAR.
NOTHING IS LEFT BEHIND.
DON'T TALK AS IF I'M HUMAN.
SORRY, IT'S BECAUSE I'M HUMAN.
WHAT IS A HUMAN KID DOING HERE?
WHERE AM I?
IT DOESN'T REALLY MATTER ANY-MORE.
THIS IS MOMOCHI HOUSE.
I CAN SAVE YOU.

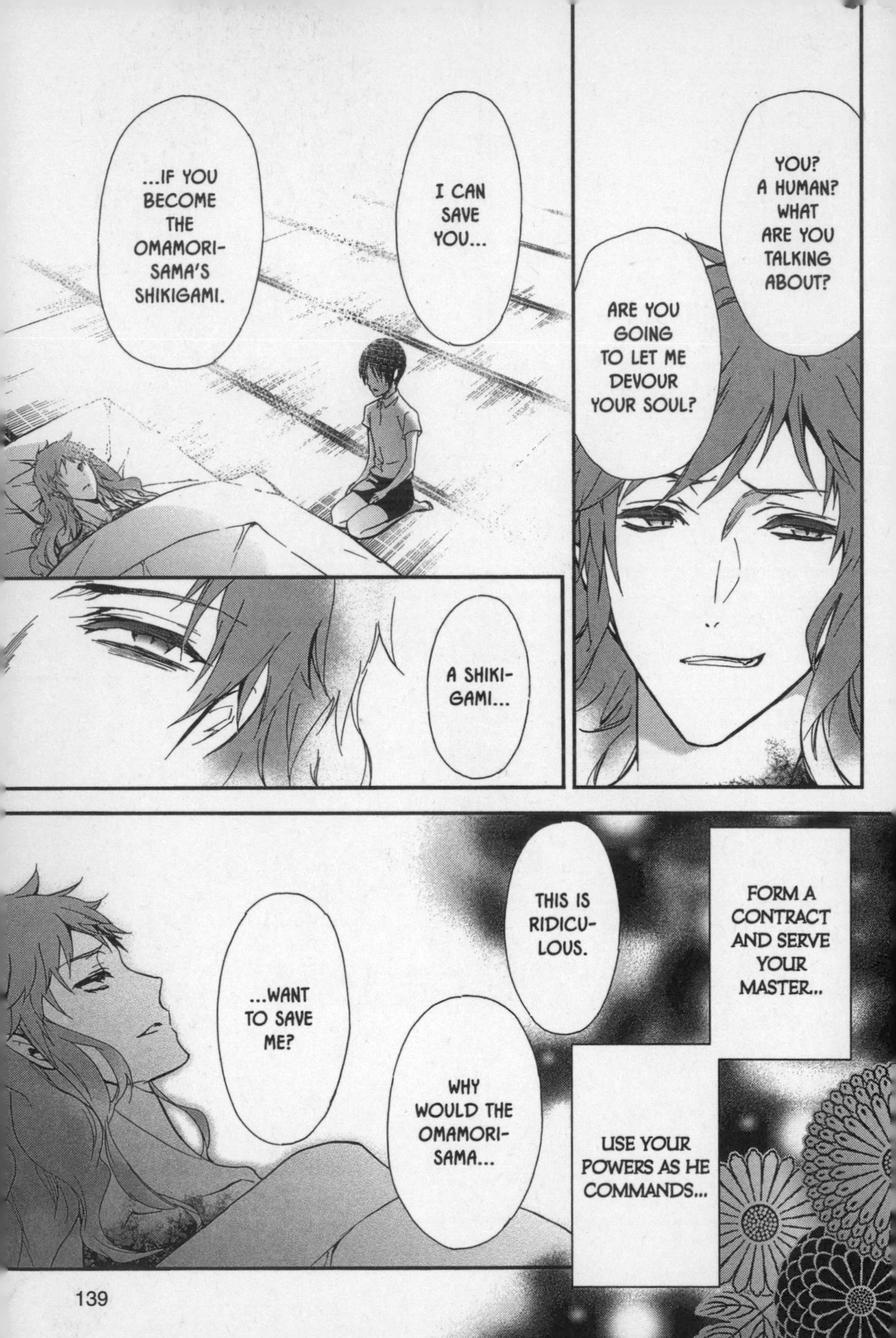
YOU? A HUMAN? WHAT ARE YOU TALKING ABOUT?
ARE YOU GOING TO LET ME DEVOUR YOUR SOUL?
I CAN SAVE YOU...
...IF YOU BECOME THE OMAMORI-SAMA'S SHIKIGAMI.
A SHIKI-GAMI...
FORM A CONTRACT AND SERVE YOUR MASTER...
USE YOUR POWERS AS HE COMMANDS...
THIS IS RIDICU-LOUS.
WHY WOULD THE OMAMORI-SAMA...
...WANT TO SAVE ME?

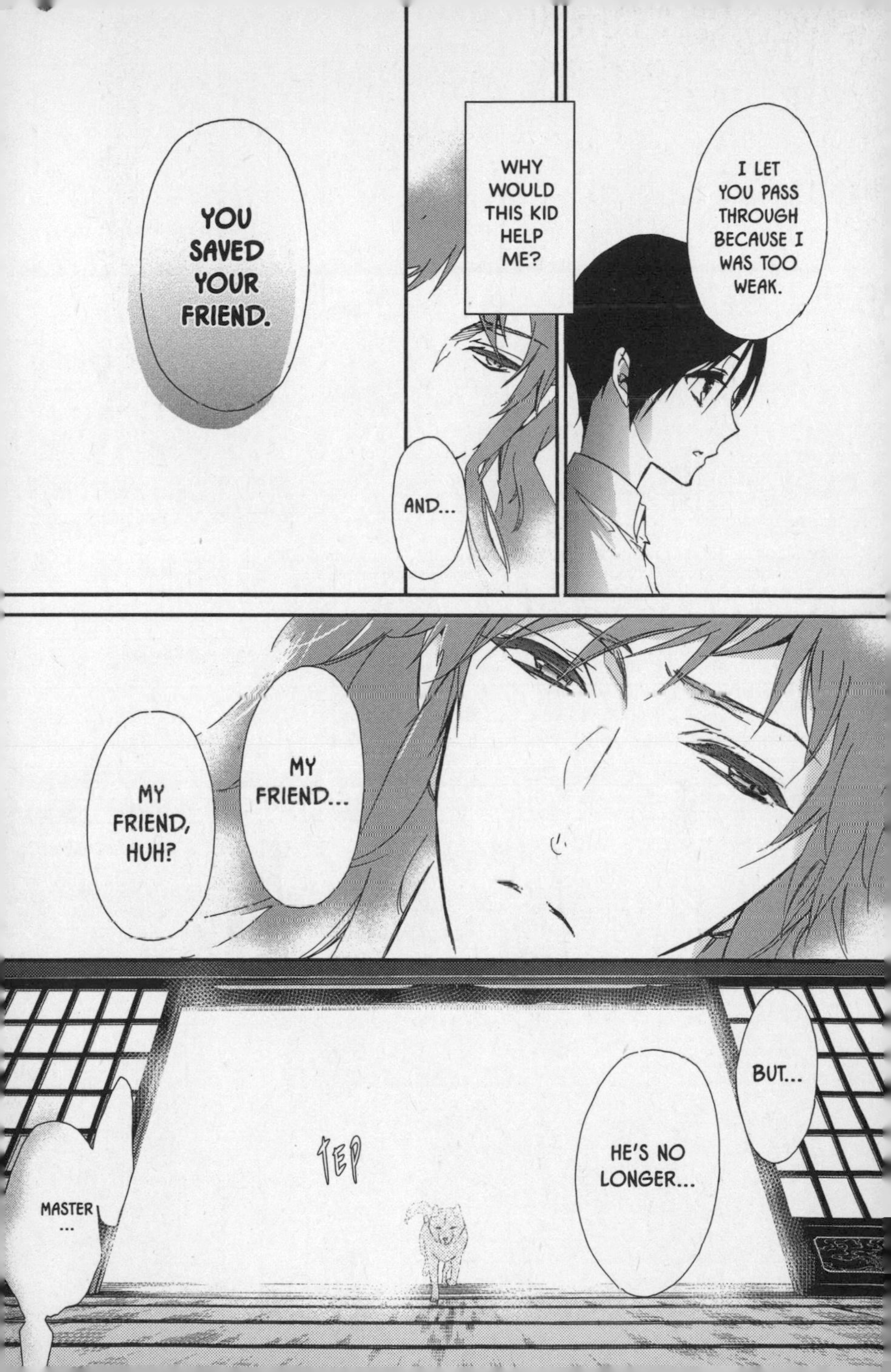
I LET YOU PASS THROUGH BECAUSE I WAS TOO WEAK.
WHY WOULD THIS KID HELP ME?
AND...
YOU SAVED YOUR FRIEND.
MY FRIEND...
MY FRIEND, HUH?
BUT...
HE'S NO LONGER...
TEP
MASTER ...

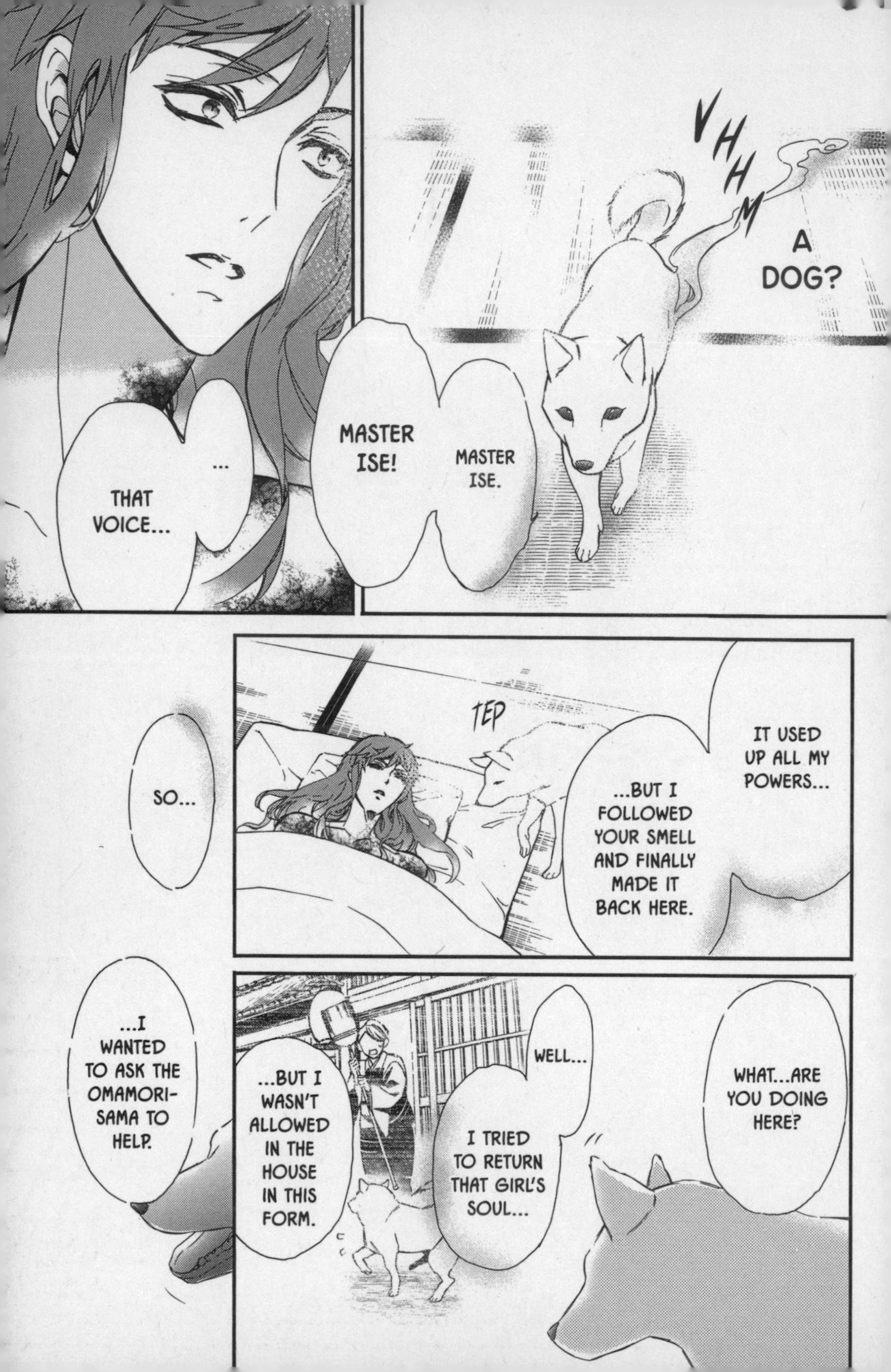
VHHM
A DOG?
MASTER ISE.
MASTER ISE!
...
THAT VOICE...
IT USED UP ALL MY POWERS...
TEP
...BUT I FOLLOWED YOUR SMELL AND FINALLY MADE IT BACK HERE.
SO...
WHAT...ARE YOU DOING HERE?
WELL...
I TRIED TO RETURN THAT GIRL'S SOUL...
...BUT I WASN'T ALLOWED IN THE HOUSE IN THIS FORM.
...I WANTED TO ASK THE OMAMORI-SAMA TO HELP.

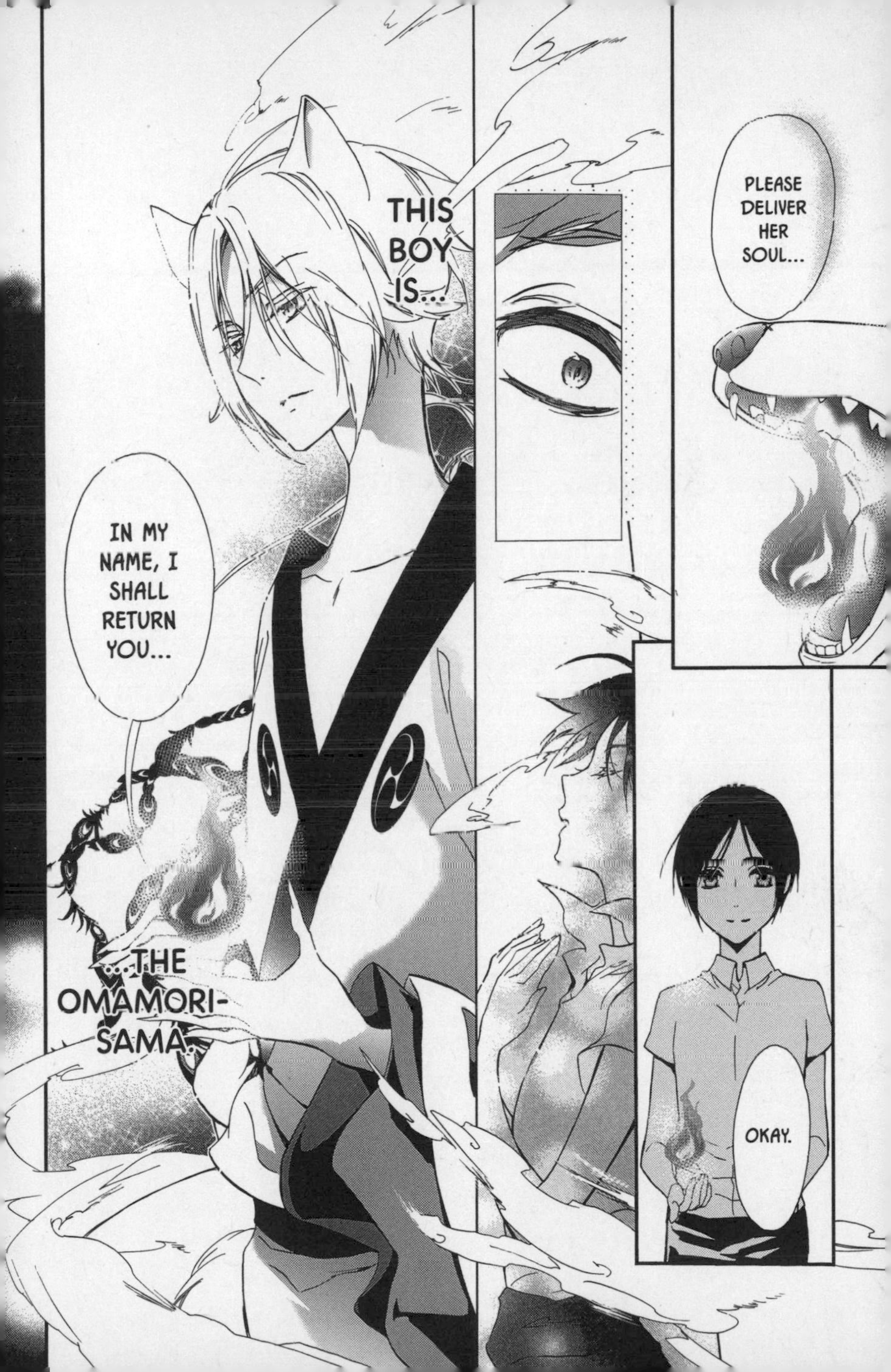
PLEASE DELIVER HER SOUL...
OKAY.
THIS BOY IS...
IN MY NAME, I SHALL RETURN YOU...
...THE OMAMORI-SAMA.

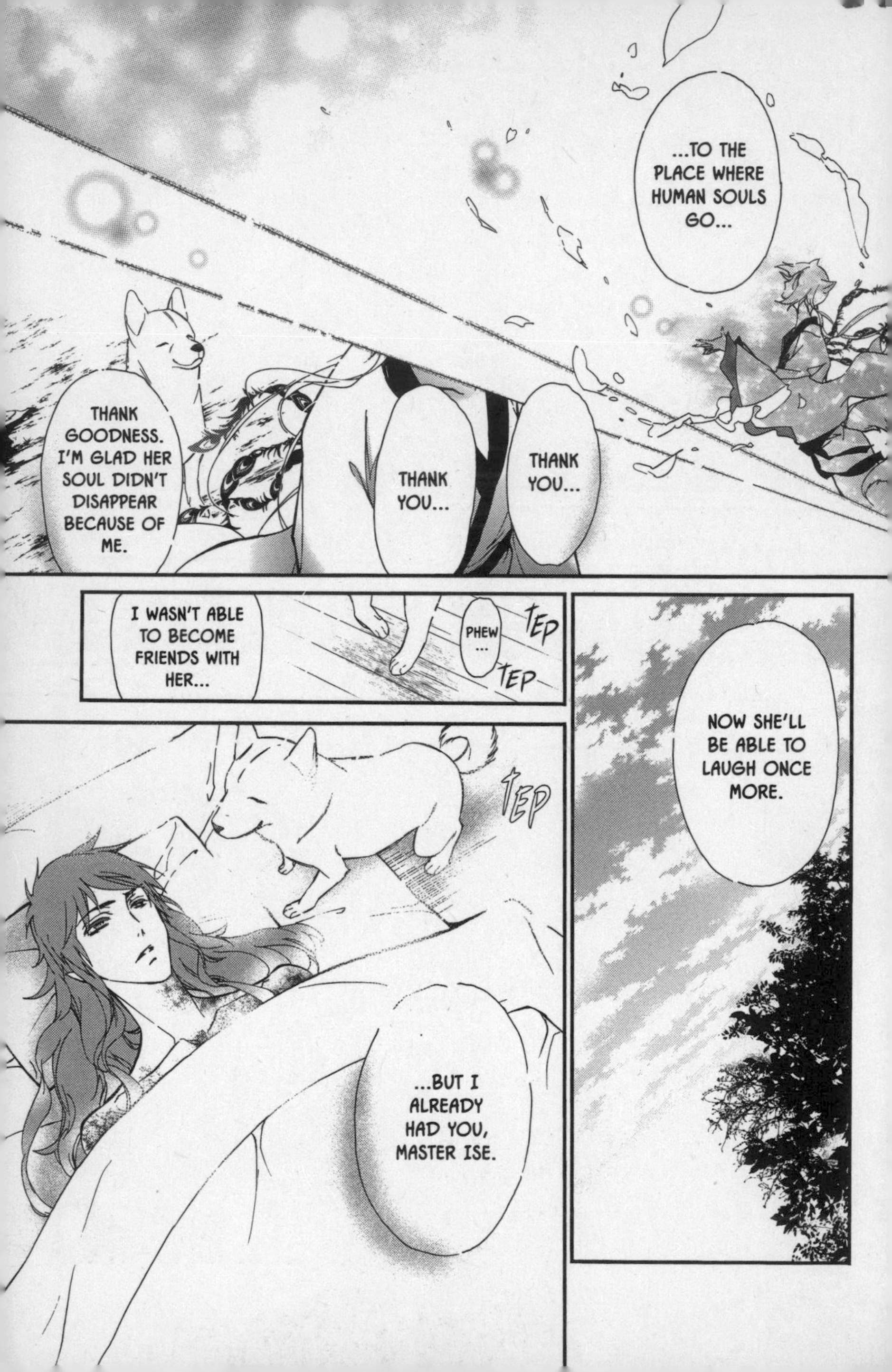
...TO THE PLACE WHERE HUMAN SOULS GO...
THANK YOU...
THANK YOU...
THANK GOODNESS. I'M GLAD HER SOUL DIDN'T DISAPPEAR BECAUSE OF ME.
NOW SHE'LL BE ABLE TO LAUGH ONCE MORE.
TEP
TEP
PHEW...
I WASN'T ABLE TO BECOME FRIENDS WITH HER...
TEP
...BUT I ALREADY HAD YOU, MASTER ISE.

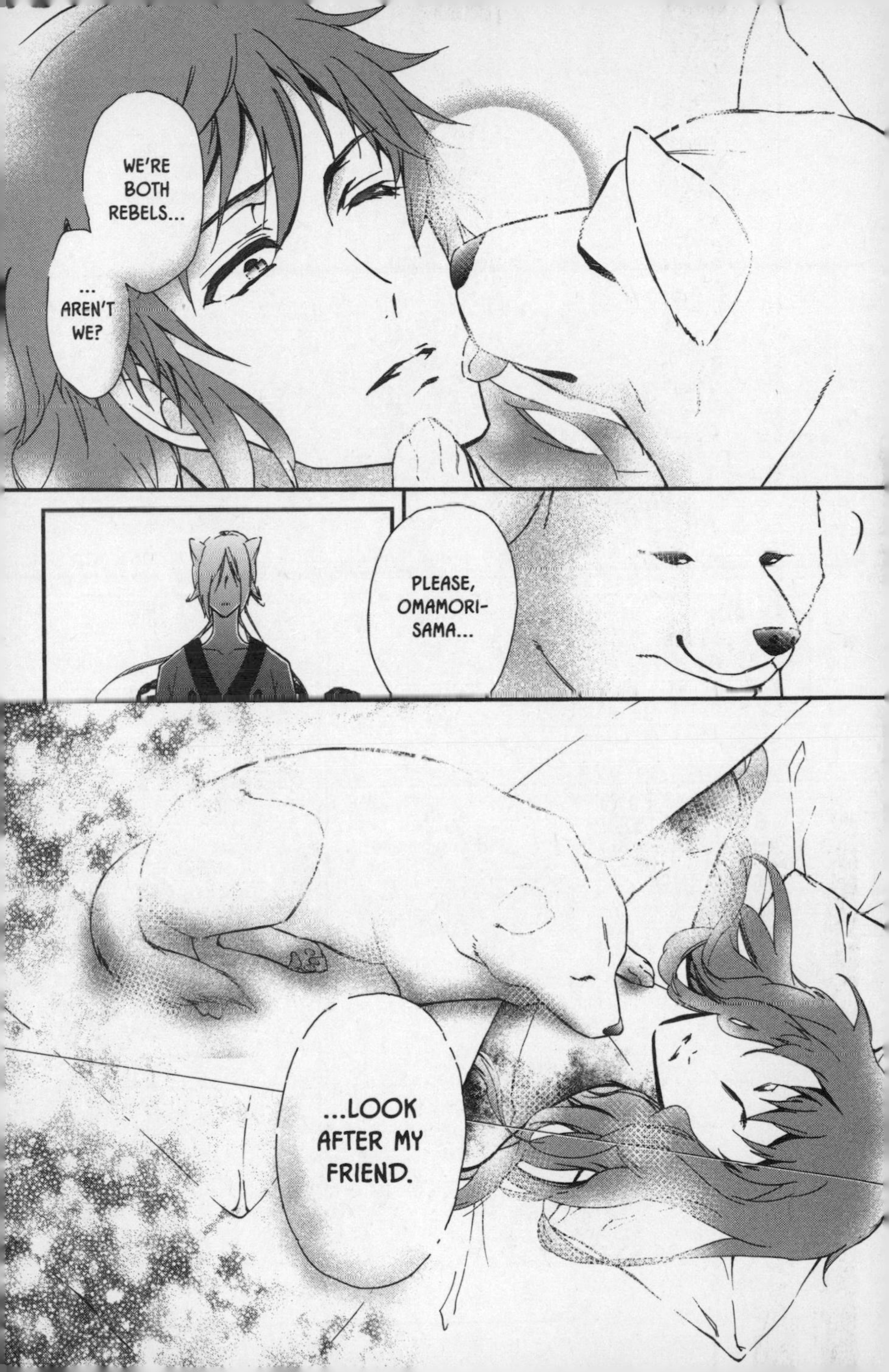
WE'RE BOTH REBELS...
...AREN'T WE?
PLEASE, OMAMORI-SAMA...
...LOOK AFTER MY FRIEND.

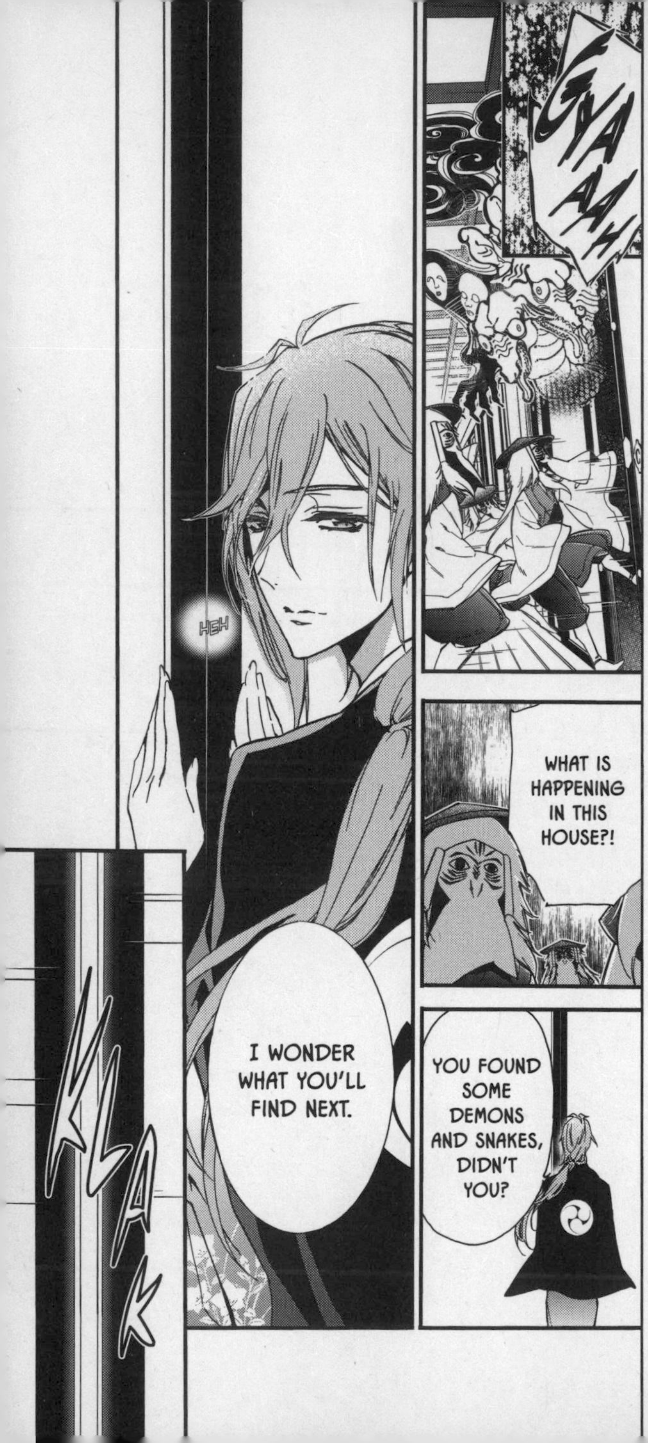
GYAAAAH
WHAT IS HAPPENING IN THIS HOUSE?!
YOU FOUND SOME DEMONS AND SNAKES, DIDN'T YOU?
HEH
I WONDER WHAT YOU'LL FIND NEXT.
KLAK

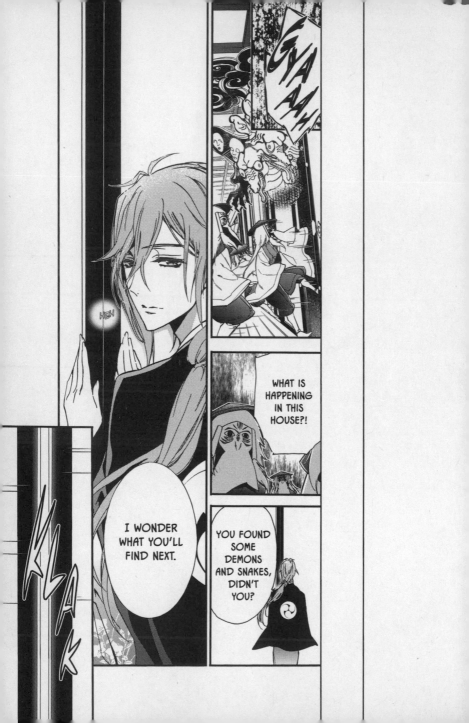

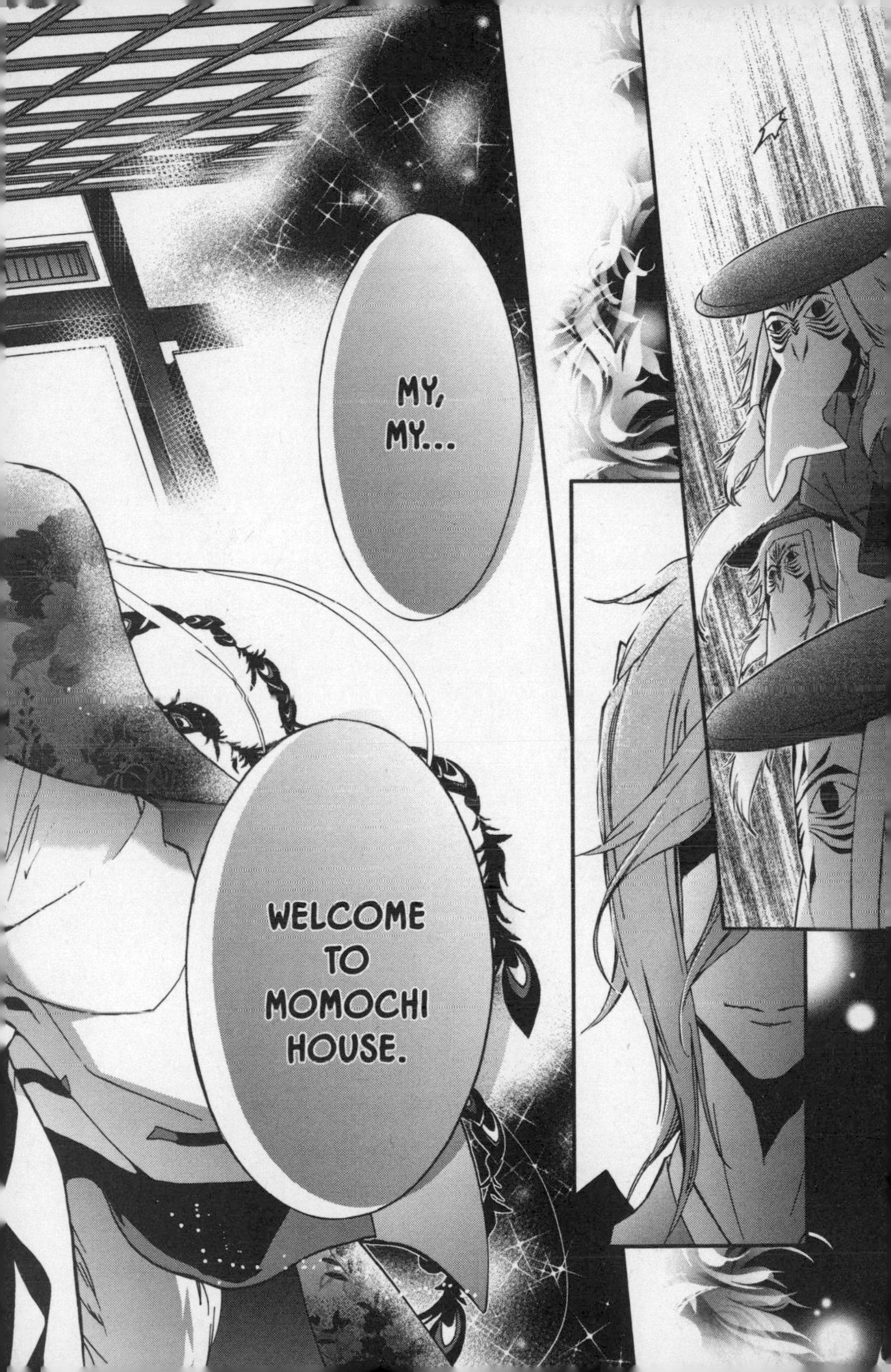
MY, MY...
WELCOME TO MOMOCHI HOUSE.

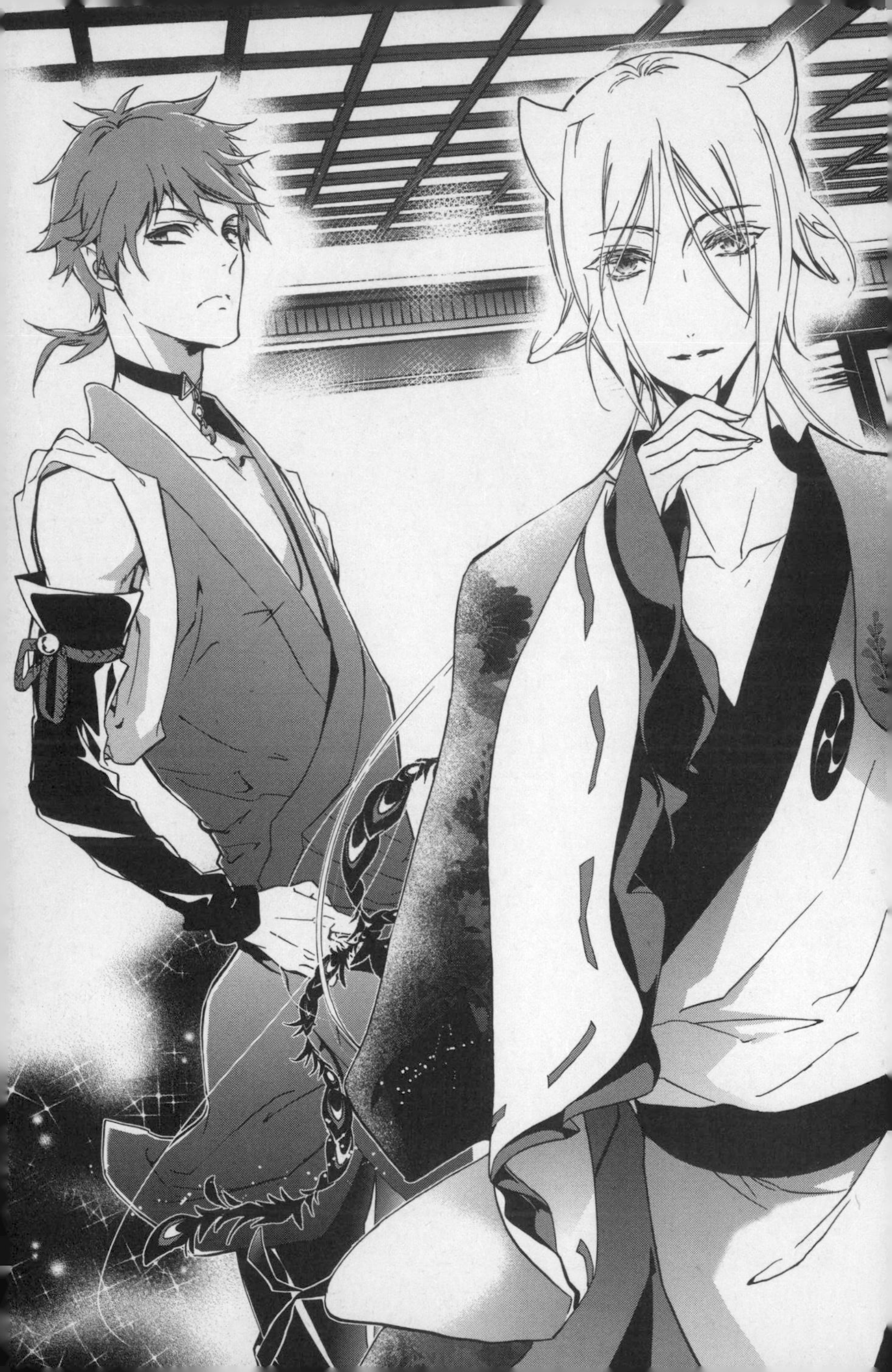

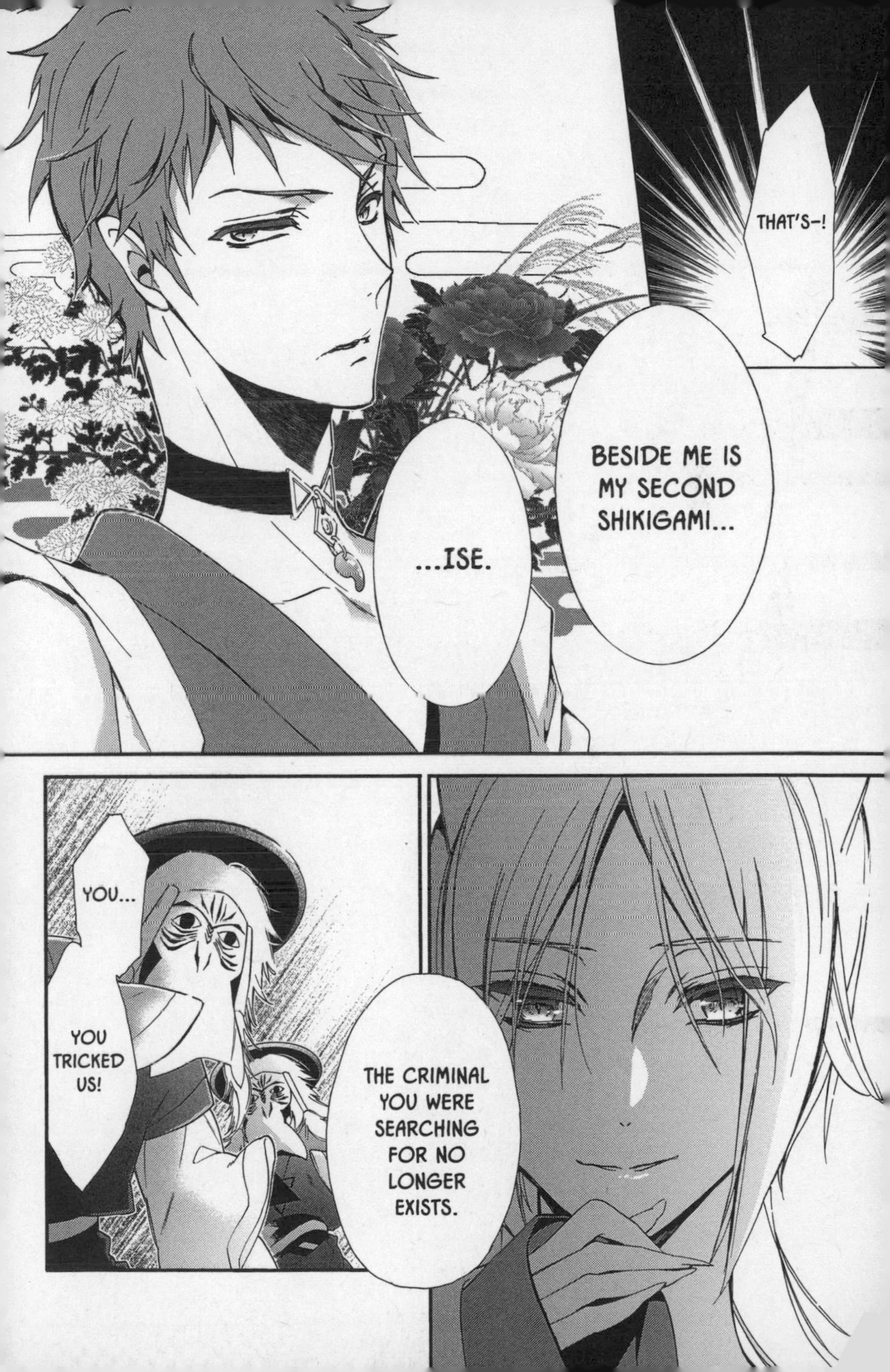
THAT'S-!
BESIDE ME IS MY SECOND SHIKIGAMI...
...ISE.
THE CRIMINAL YOU WERE SEARCHING FOR NO LONGER EXISTS.
YOU...
YOU TRICKED US!

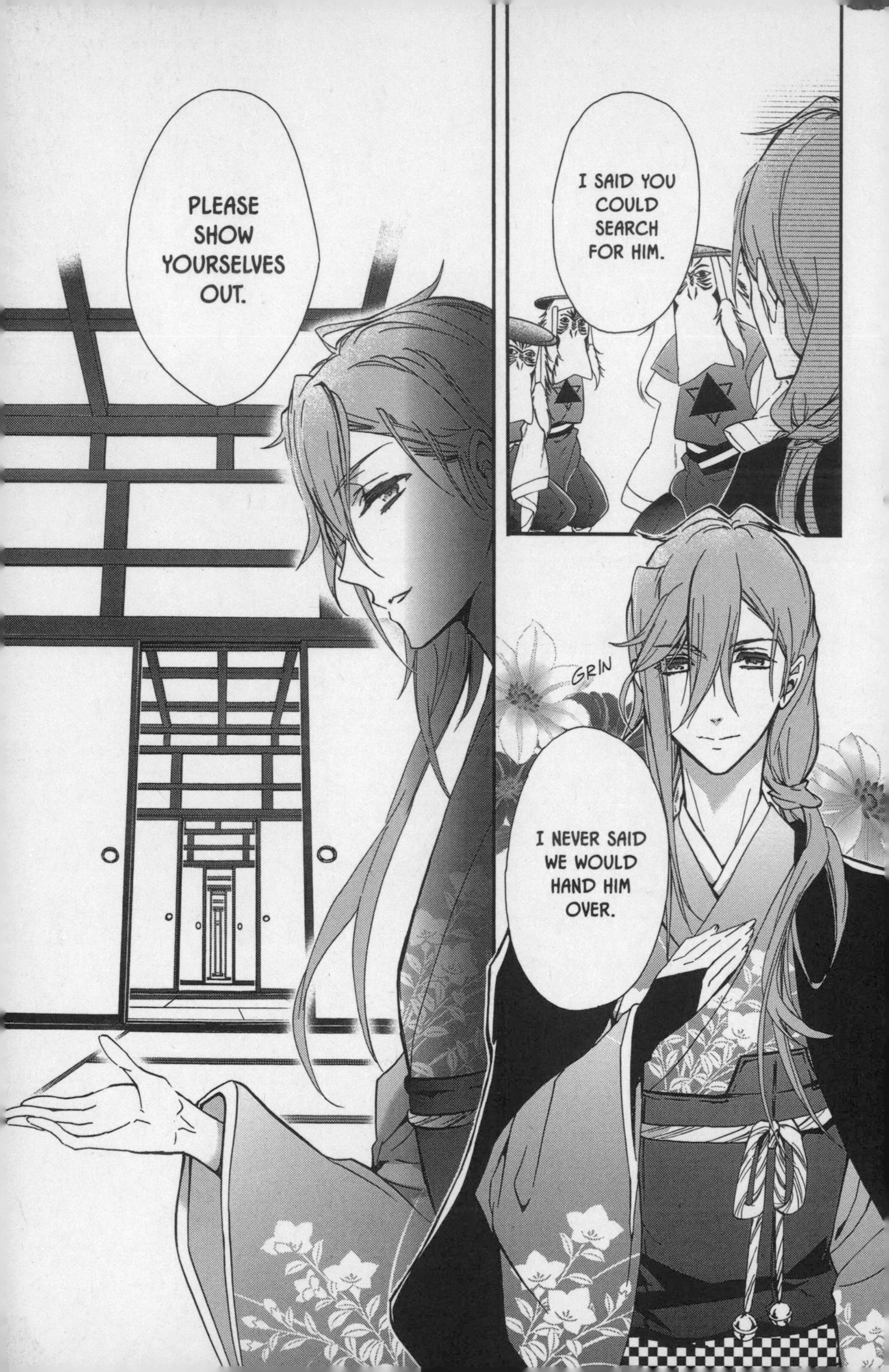
I SAID YOU COULD SEARCH FOR HIM.
GRIN
I NEVER SAID WE WOULD HAND HIM OVER.
PLEASE SHOW YOURSELVES OUT.

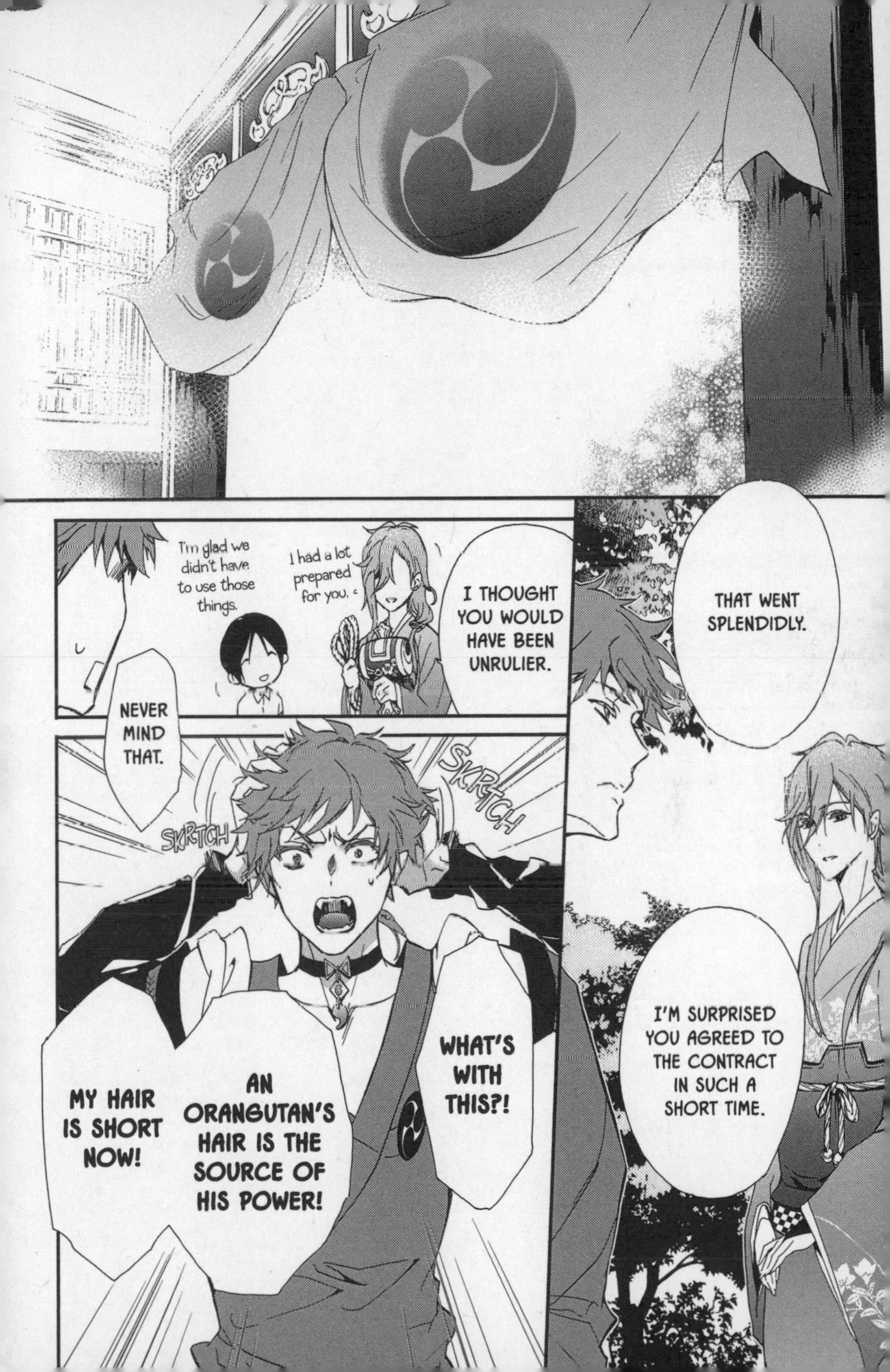
THAT WENT SPLENDIDLY.
I'M SURPRISED YOU AGREED TO THE CONTRACT IN SUCH A SHORT TIME.
I THOUGHT YOU WOULD HAVE BEEN UNRULIER.
I had a lot prepared for you.
I'm glad we didn't have to use those things.
NEVER MIND THAT.
SKRTCH
SKRTCH
WHAT'S WITH THIS?!
AN ORANGUTAN'S HAIR IS THE SOURCE OF HIS POWER!
MY HAIR IS SHORT NOW!

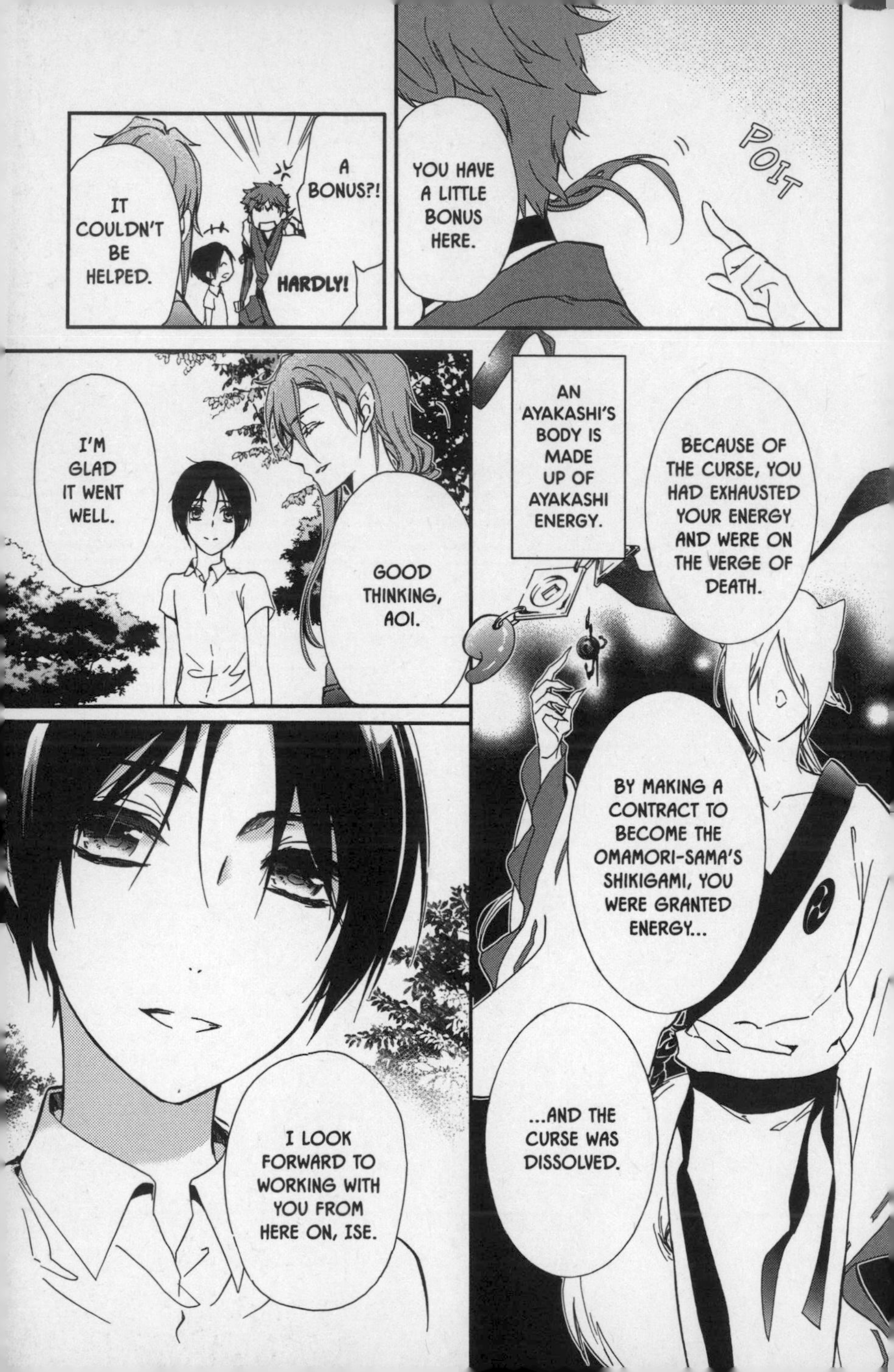
POIT
YOU HAVE A LITTLE BONUS HERE.
A BONUS?!
IT COULDN'T BE HELPED.
HARDLY!
AN AYAKASHI'S BODY IS MADE UP OF AYAKASHI ENERGY.
BECAUSE OF THE CURSE, YOU HAD EXHAUSTED YOUR ENERGY AND WERE ON THE VERGE OF DEATH.
BY MAKING A CONTRACT TO BECOME THE OMAMORI-SAMA'S SHIKIGAMI, YOU WERE GRANTED ENERGY...
...AND THE CURSE WAS DISSOLVED.
GOOD THINKING, AOI.
I'M GLAD IT WENT WELL.
I LOOK FORWARD TO WORKING WITH YOU FROM HERE ON, ISE.

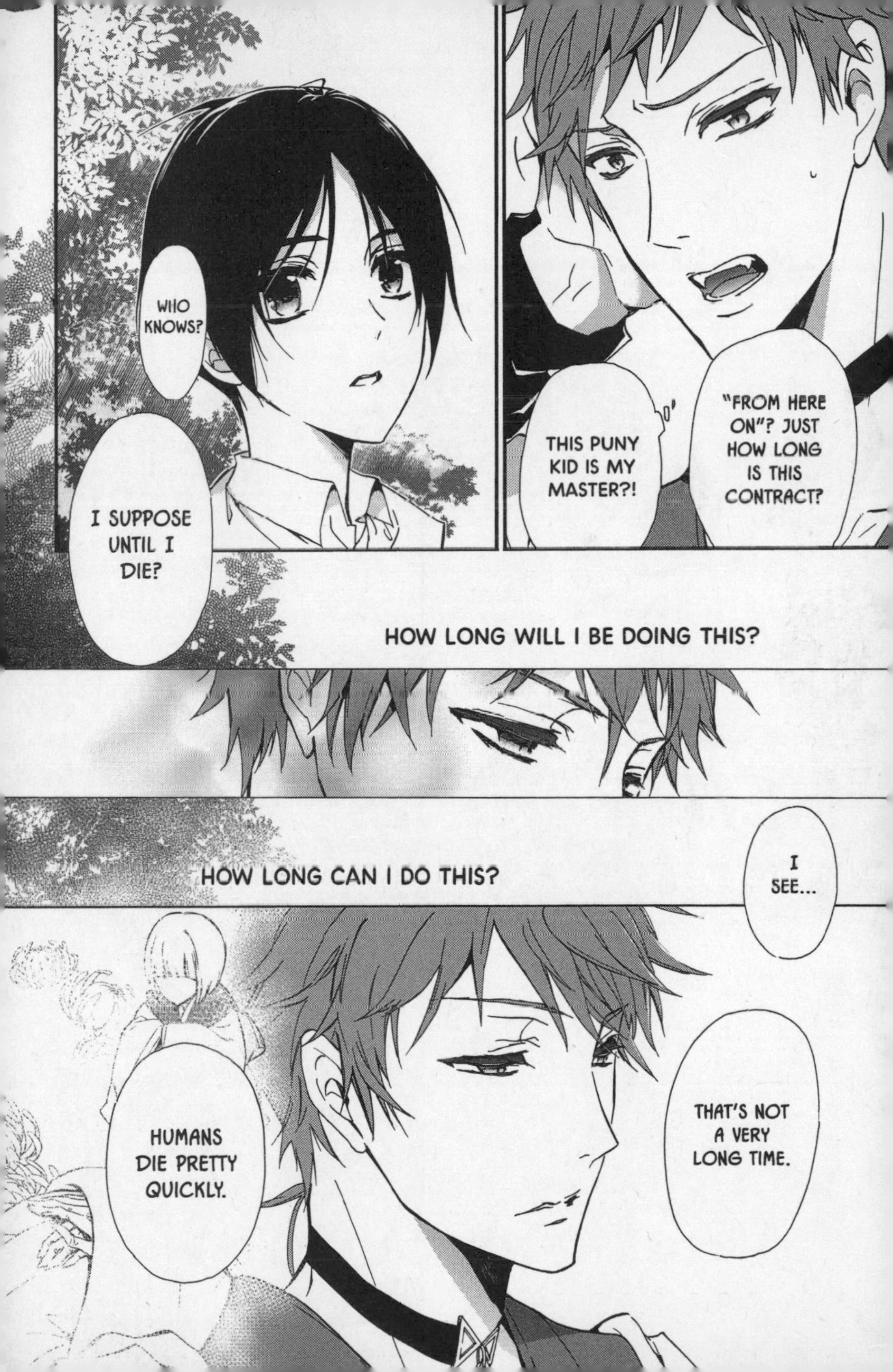
"FROM HERE ON"? JUST HOW LONG IS THIS CONTRACT?
THIS PUNY KID IS MY MASTER?!
WHO KNOWS?
I SUPPOSE UNTIL I DIE?
HOW LONG WILL I BE DOING THIS?
I SEE...
HOW LONG CAN I DO THIS?
THAT'S NOT A VERY LONG TIME.
HUMANS DIE PRETTY QUICKLY.

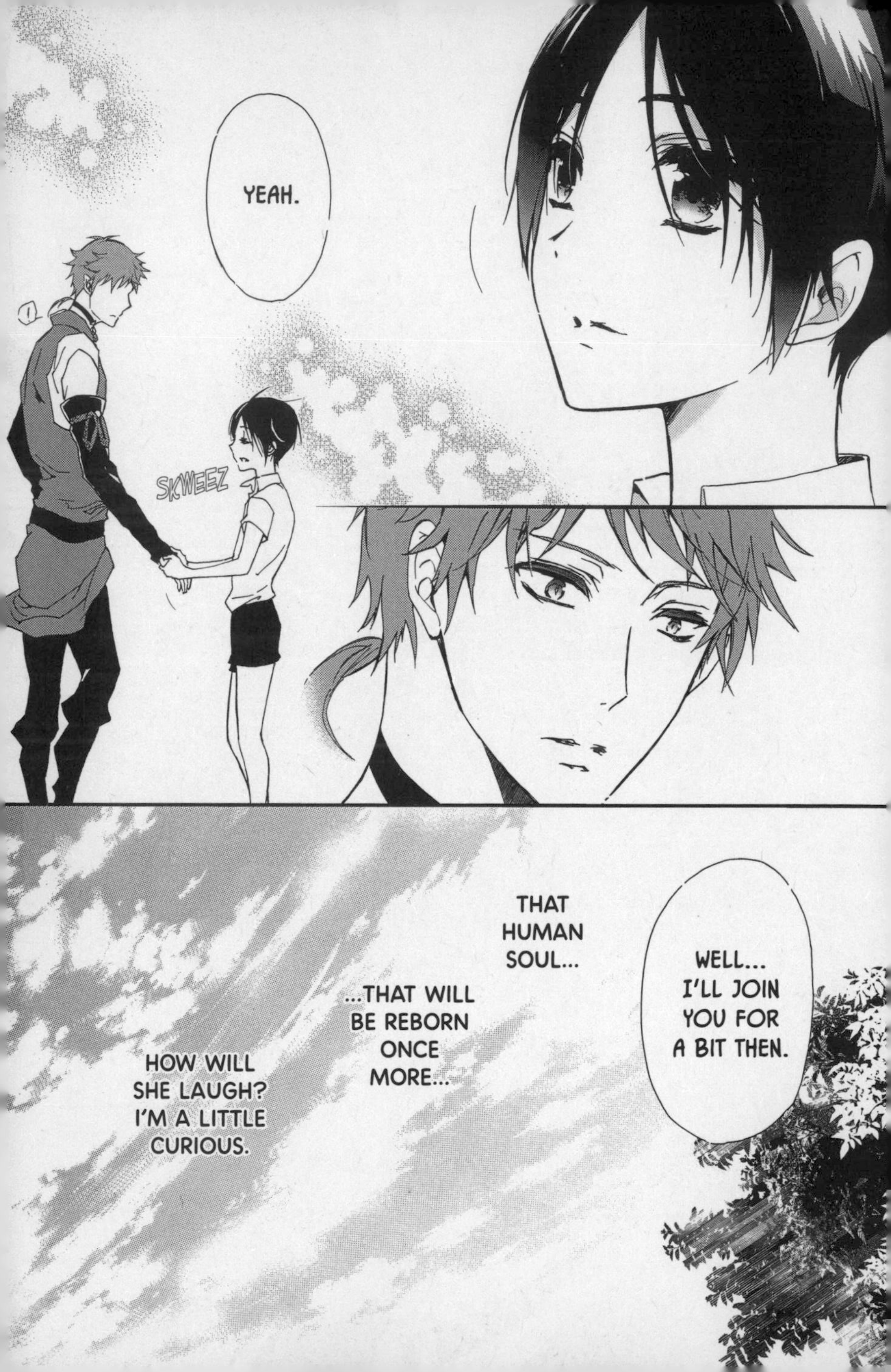
YEAH.
!
SKWEEZ
WELL... I'LL JOIN YOU FOR A BIT THEN.
THAT HUMAN SOUL...
...THAT WILL BE REBORN ONCE MORE...
HOW WILL SHE LAUGH? I'M A LITTLE CURIOUS.

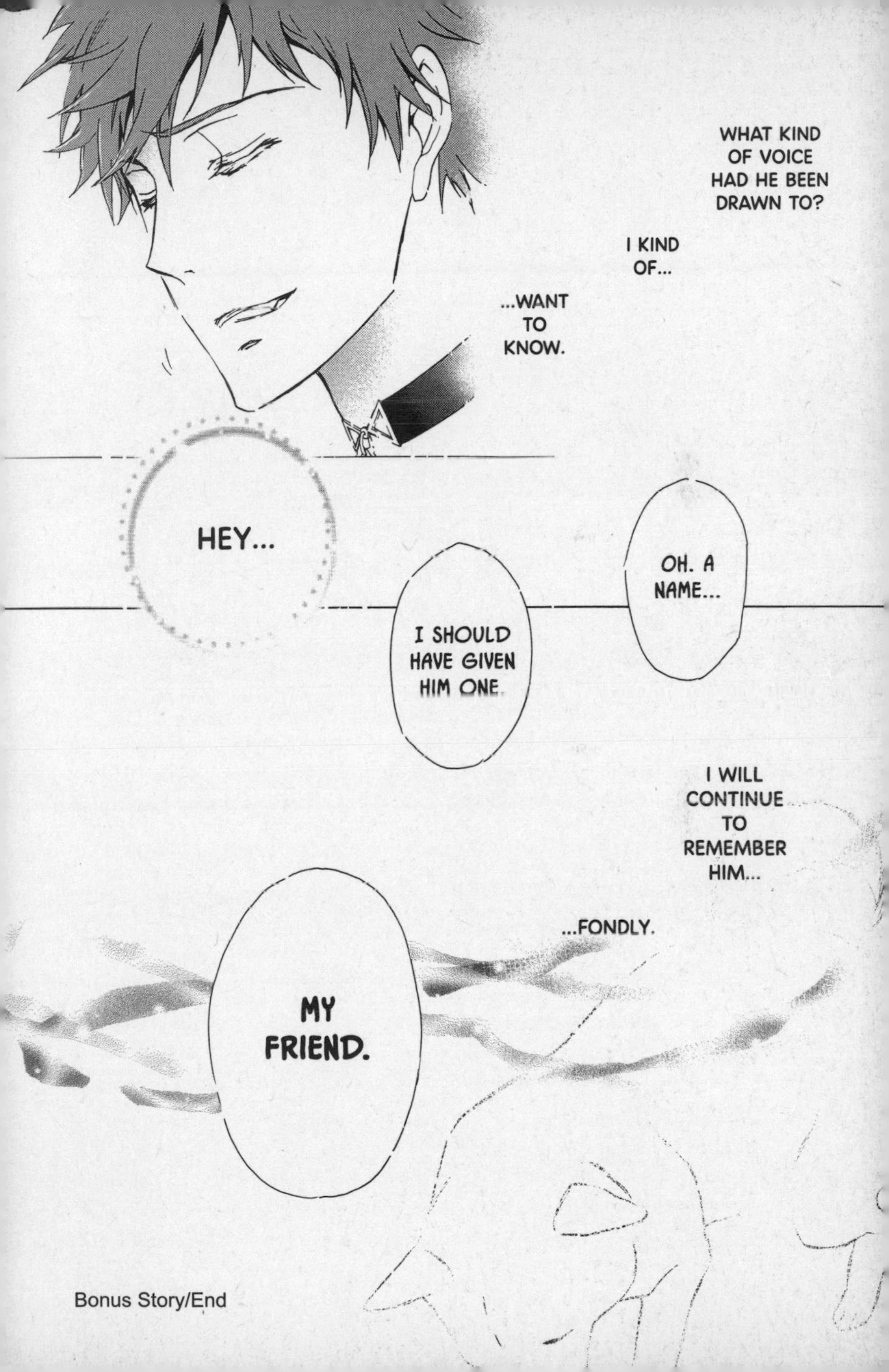
WHAT KIND OF VOICE HAD HE BEEN DRAWN TO?
I KIND OF...
...WANT TO KNOW.
OH. A NAME...
I SHOULD HAVE GIVEN HIM ONE.
HEY...
I WILL CONTINUE TO REMEMBER HIM...
...FONDLY.
MY FRIEND.

Bonus Story/End

the
DEMON
PRINCE
of MOMOCHI
HOUSE

This is volume 10 of *The Demon Prince of Momochi House.* Thankfully this series will continue beyond this volume. This time I had the opportunity to write a bonus story about Ise's past. It's a slightly long story. How was it? There's still more I want to write about. I hope I'll have your continued support.

And we finally have our first cover with Nue and Aoi. When *Momochi House* was about to be published in *Asuka* magazine, I was asked to draw the preview illustration. My editor told me to "draw them together even though they're the same person." It was a big revelation to me. Since then they've been my favorite subjects to draw. "Two sides of the same coin" is what I have in mind.

By the way, about the name Aoi. I was reading a book about Kyoto's Aoi Festival. Aoi ("hollyhock") is a play on words for *au hi* ("meeting day"). In other words, it's a day to meet the gods. That's where I got the inspiration. I'd like to go to the festival someday.

2016 x xx

Aya Shouoto

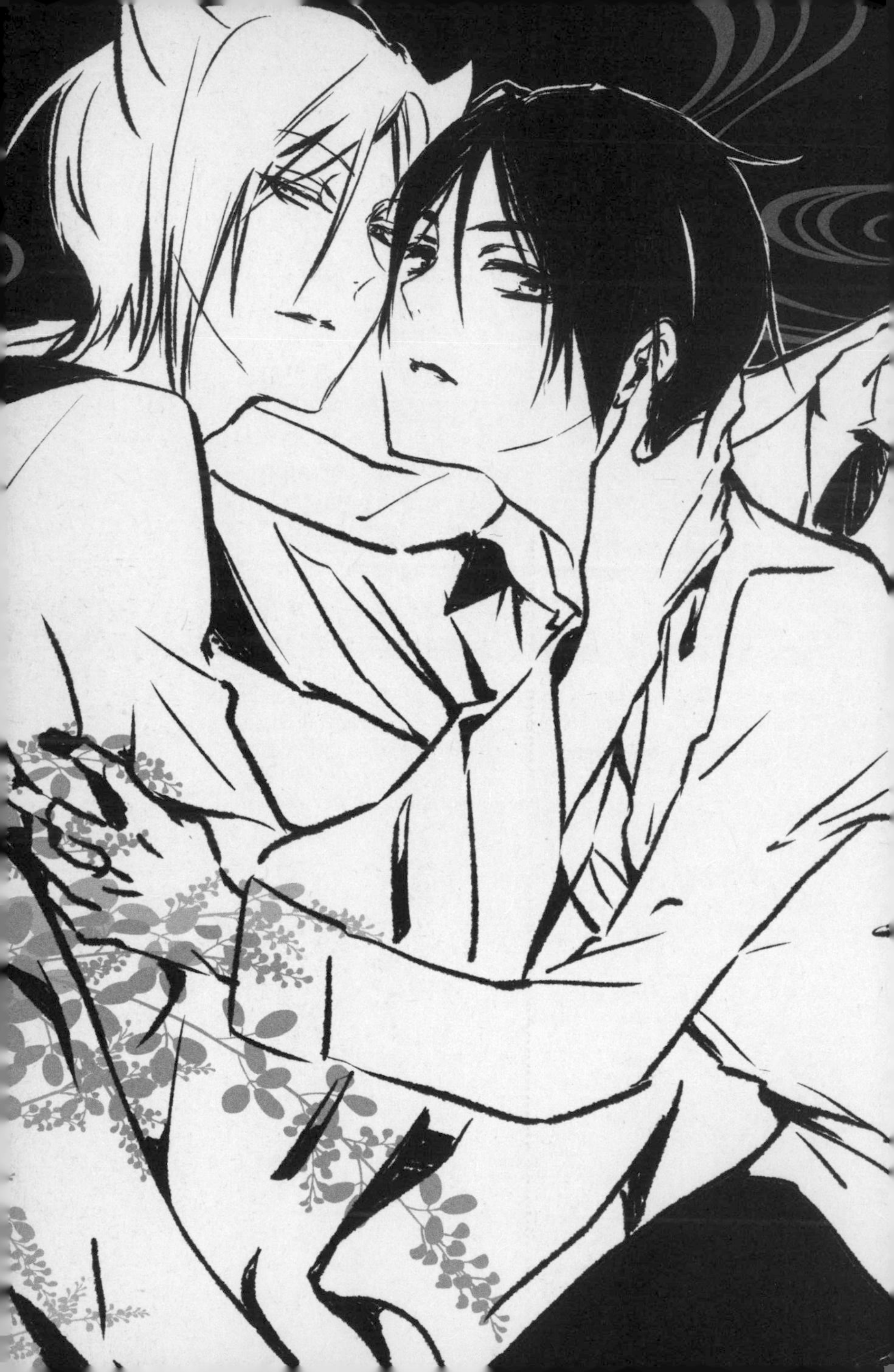

Let's celebrate volume 10!
I couldn't have spun the tale of
Momochi House without your
encouragement. Thank you very
much. The word *momochi* means
"multitude." It evokes the image of
things spread out as far as the eye
can see. That's what I had in mind
when I came up with this title. I
hope this story can expand in the
manner its name suggests.

> **-Aya Shouoto**

Aya Shouoto was born on December 25.
Her hobbies are traveling, staying at hotels,
sewing and daydreaming. She currently
lives in Tokyo and enjoys listening to J-pop
anime theme songs while she works.

The Demon Prince of Momochi House

Volume 10
Shojo Beat Edition

Story and Art by Aya Shouoto

Translation JN Productions
Touch-Up Art & Lettering Inori Fukuda Trant
Design Izumi Evers
Editor Nancy Thistlethwaite

MOMOCHISANCHI NO AYAKASHI OUJI Volume 10

First published in Japan in 2016 by KADOKAWA CORPORATION, Tokyo.
English translation rights arranged with KADOKAWA CORPORATION, Tokyo.

The stories, characters and incidents mentioned
in this publication are entirely fictional.

Printed in the U.S.A.

Published by VIZ Media, LLC
P.O. Box 77010
San Francisco, CA 94107

10 9 8 7 6 5 4 3 2 1
First printing, October 2017

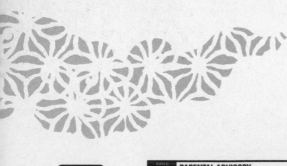

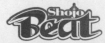

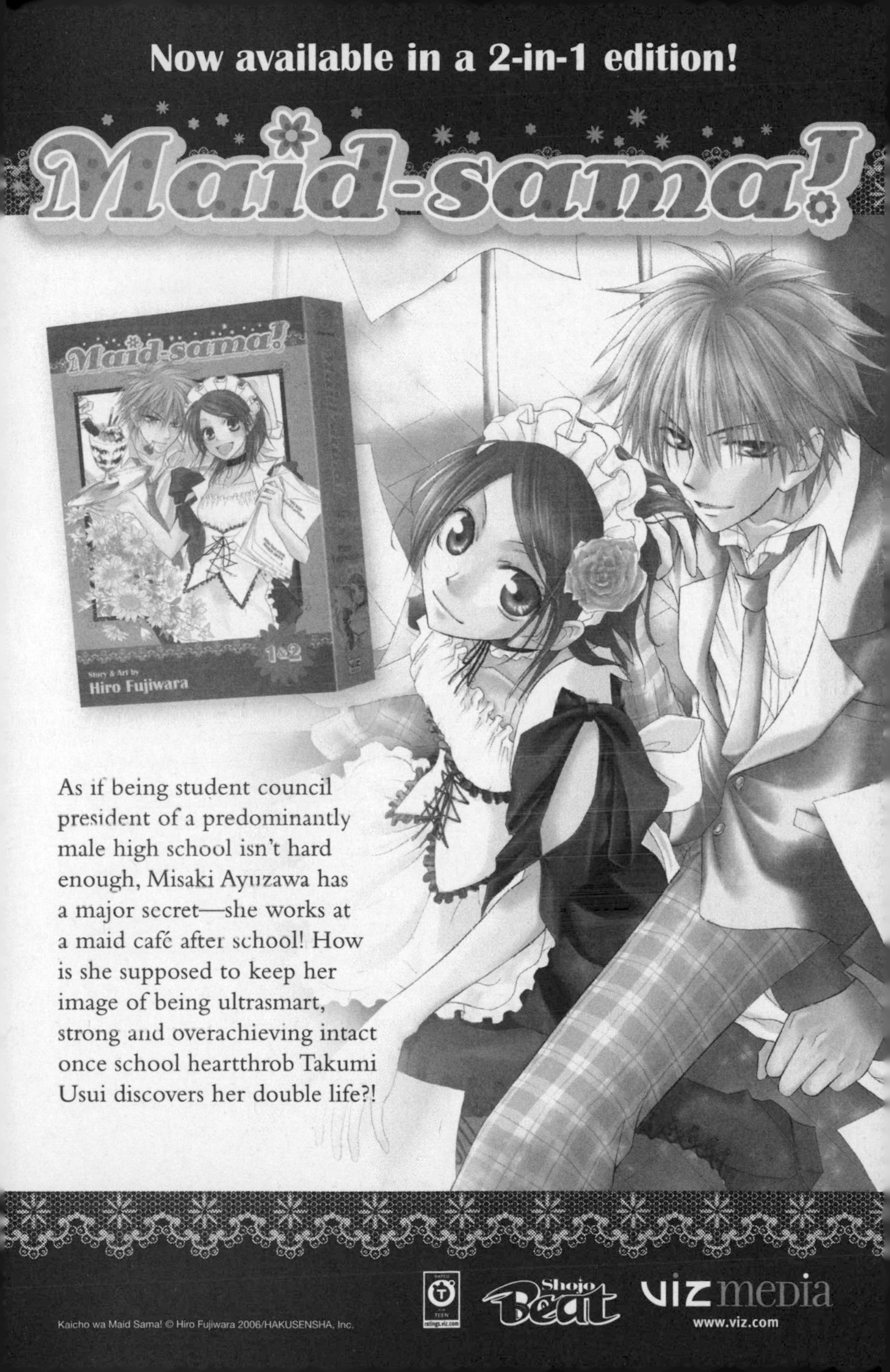
Now available in a 2-in-1 edition!
Maid-sama!
Maid-sama!
1&2
Story & Art by
Hiro Fujiwara
As if being student council president of a predominantly male high school isn't hard enough, Misaki Ayuzawa has a major secret—she works at a maid café after school! How is she supposed to keep her image of being ultrasmart, strong and overachieving intact once school heartthrob Takumi Usui discovers her double life?!
Kaicho wa Maid Sama! © Hiro Fujiwara 2006/HAKUSENSHA, Inc.
Shojo Beat
VIZ media
www.viz.com

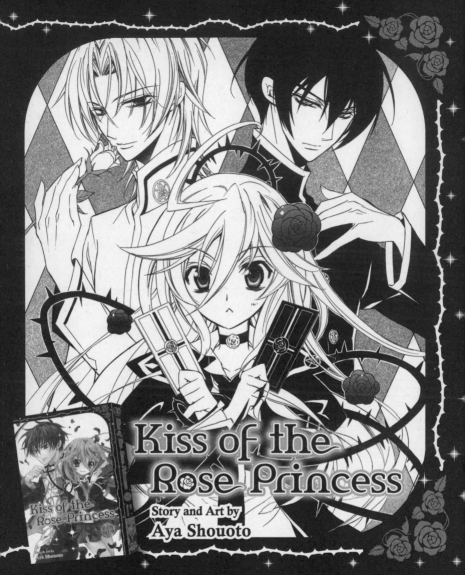

Kiss of the Rose Princess

Story and Art by Aya Shouoto

Anise Yamamoto has been told that if she ever removes the rose choker given to her by her father, a terrible punishment will befall her. Unfortunately she loses that choker when a bat-like being named Ninufa falls from the sky and hits her. Ninufa gives Anise four cards representing four knights whom she can summon with a kiss. But now that she has these gorgeous men at her beck and call, what exactly is her quest?!

$9⁹⁹ US / $12⁹⁹ CAN

www.viz.com

Honey So Sweet

Story and Art by Amu Meguro

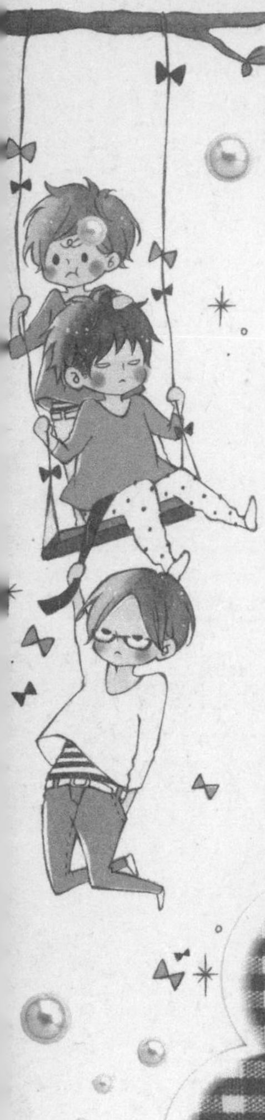

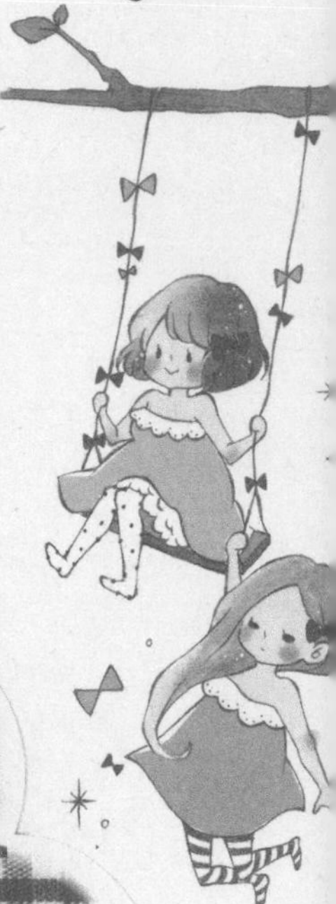

Little did Nao Kogure realize back in middle school that when she left an umbrella and a box of bandages in the rain for injured delinquent Taiga Onise that she would meet him again in high school. Nao wants nothing to do with the gruff and frightening Taiga, but he suddenly presents her with a huge bouquet of flowers and asks her to date him—with marriage in mind! Is Taiga really so scary, or is he a sweetheart in disguise?

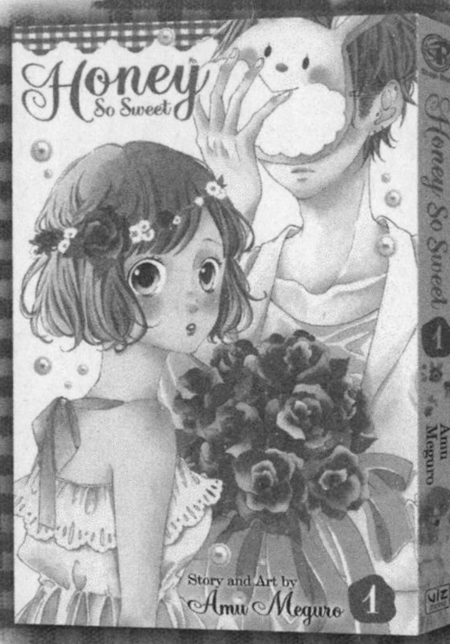
Honey So Sweet
Honey So Sweet 1
Amu Meguro
Story and Art by
Amu Meguro 1

Can she clean up her act...

...and STILL kick some butt?!

ORESAMA TEACHER

ORESAMA TEACHER

Izumi Tsubaki

Story & art by Izumi Tsubaki

Determined to make the best of the situation and make her mother proud, Mafuyu decides to turn over a new, feminine, well-behaved leaf. But her fighting spirit can't be kept down, and the night before school starts she finds herself defending some guy who's getting beaten up. One slip wouldn't have been a problem, except the guy is *...her teacher?!* How can Mafuyu learn to be a good girl if her teacher won't let her forget her wicked past?

Oresama Teacher, Vol. 1
ISBN: 978-1-4215-3863-1 • $9.99 US / $12.99 CAN

IN STORES NOW!

RATED
T
TEEN
ratings.viz.com

Shojo Beat

viz MEDIA

www.viz.com

"**Bloody**" **Mary**, a vampire with a death wish, has spent the past 400 years chasing down a modern-day exorcist named Maria who is thought to have inherited "The Blood of Maria" and is the only one who can kill Mary. To Mary's dismay, Maria doesn't know how to kill vampires. Desperate to die, Mary agrees to become Maria's bodyguard until Maria can find a way to kill him.

Bloody † Mary

Story and Art by
akaza samamiya